UQ HOLDER!

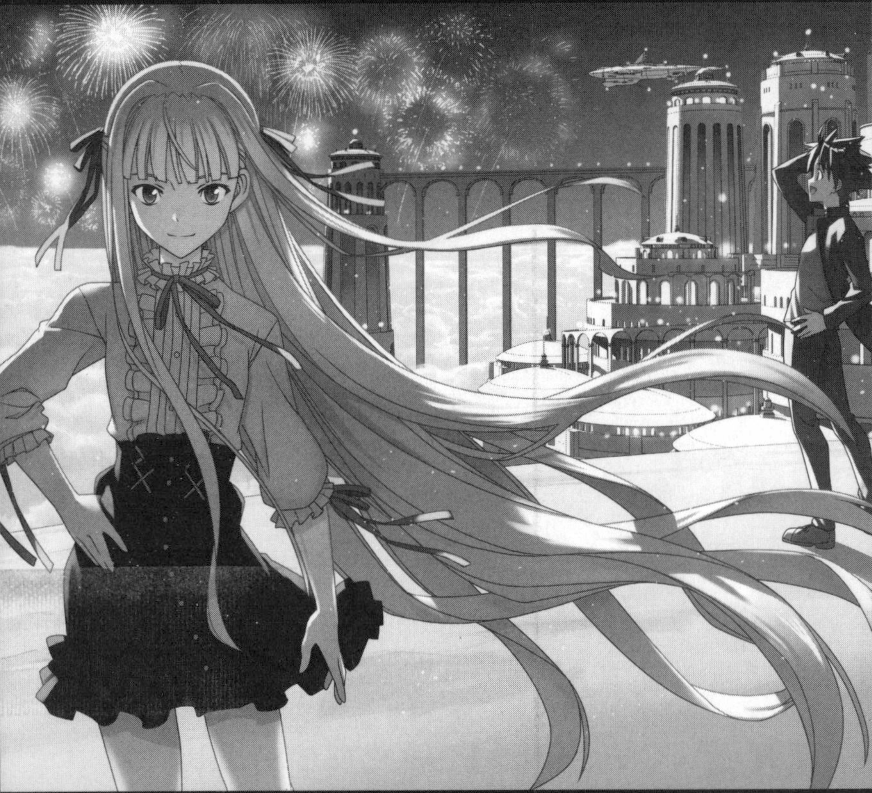

KEN AKAMATSU

vol.22

CHARACTERS

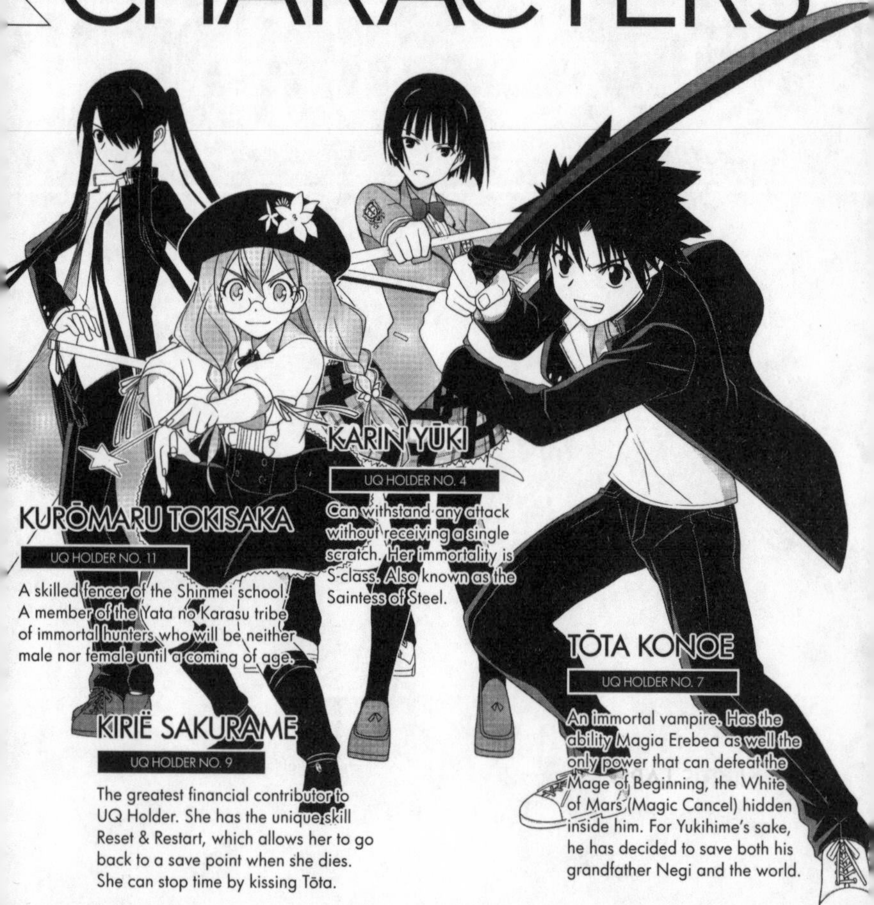

KURŌMARU TOKISAKA

UQ HOLDER NO. 11

A skilled fencer of the Shinmei school. A member of the Yata no Karasu tribe of immortal hunters who will be neither male nor female until a coming of age.

KARIN YŪKI

UQ HOLDER NO. 4

Can withstand any attack without receiving a single scratch. Her immortality is S-class. Also known as the Saintess of Steel.

KIRIË SAKURAME

UQ HOLDER NO. 9

The greatest financial contributor to UQ Holder. She has the unique skill Reset & Restart, which allows her to go back to a save point when she dies. She can stop time by kissing Tōta.

TŌTA KONOE

UQ HOLDER NO. 7

An immortal vampire. Has the ability Magia Erebea as well the only power that can defeat the Mage of Beginning, the White of Mars (Magic Cancel) hidden inside him. For Yukihime's sake, he has decided to save both his grandfather Negi and the world.

UQ HOLDER IMMORTAL NUMBERS

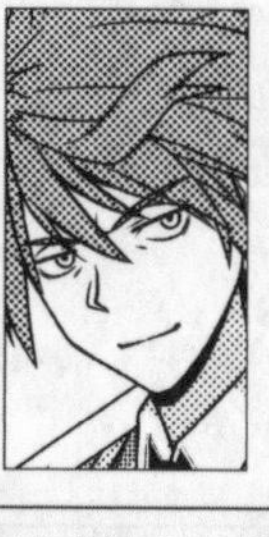

JINBEI SHISHIDO

UQ HOLDER NO. 2

UQ Holder's oldest member. Became an immortal in the middle ages, when he ate mermaid flesh in the Muromachi Period. Has the "Switcheroo" skill that switches the locations of physical objects.

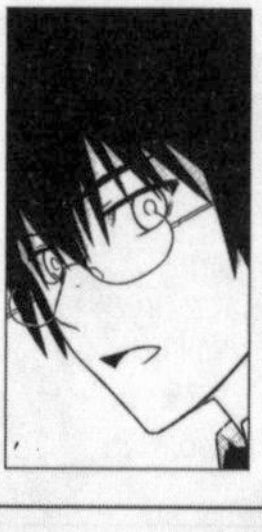

GENGORŌ MAKABE

UQ HOLDER NO. 6

Manages the business side of UQ Holder's hideout and inn. He has a skill known as Multiple Lives, so when he dies, another Gengorō appears.

UQ HOLDER!

Ken Akamatsu Presents

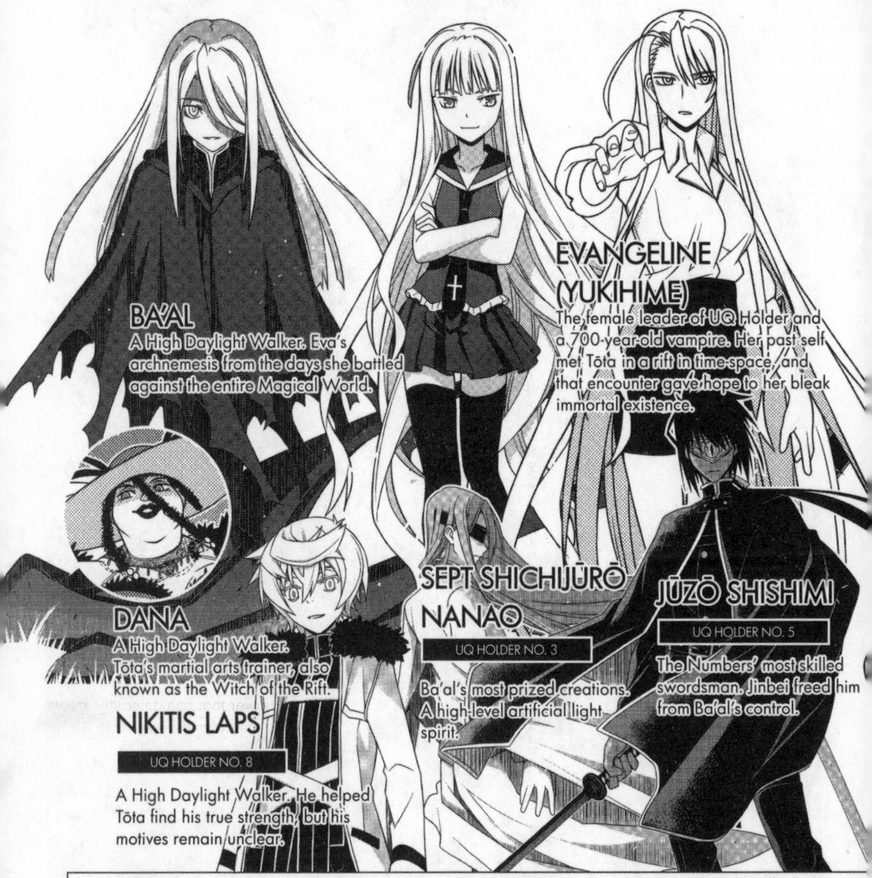

EVANGELINE (YUKIHIME)

The female leader of UQ Holder and a 700-year-old vampire. Her past self met Tōta in a rift in time-space, and that encounter gave hope to her bleak immortal existence.

BA'AL

A High Daylight Walker. Eva's archnemesis from the days she battled against the entire Magical World.

DANA

A High Daylight Walker. Tōta's martial arts trainer, also known as the Witch of the Rift.

SEPT SHICHIJŪRŌ NANAO

UQ HOLDER NO. 3

Ba'al's most prized creations. A high-level artificial light spirit.

JŪZŌ SHISHIMI

UQ HOLDER NO. 5

The Numbers' most skilled swordsman. Jinbei freed him from Ba'al's control.

NIKITIS LAPS

UQ HOLDER NO. 8

A High Daylight Walker. He helped Tōta find his true strength, but his motives remain unclear.

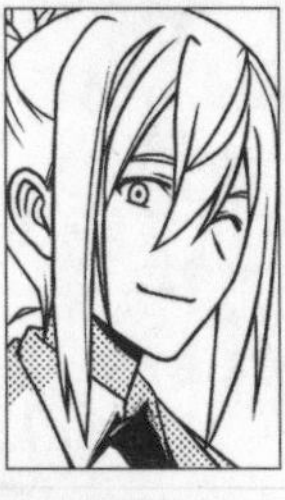

IKKŪ AMEYA

UQ HOLDER NO. 10

After falling into a coma at age 13 and lying in a hospital bed for 72 years, he became a full-body cyborg at age 85. He's very good with his hands. ♡

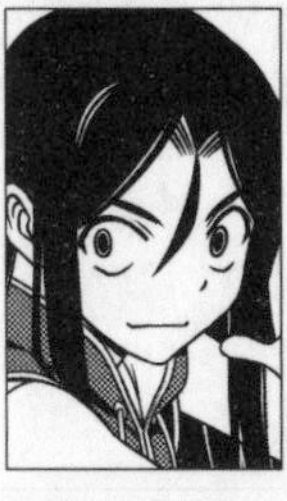

SANTA SASAKI

UQ HOLDER NO. 12

A revenant brought back to life through necromancy. He has multiple abilities, including flight, intangibility, possession, telekinesis, etc.

THE STORY SO FAR

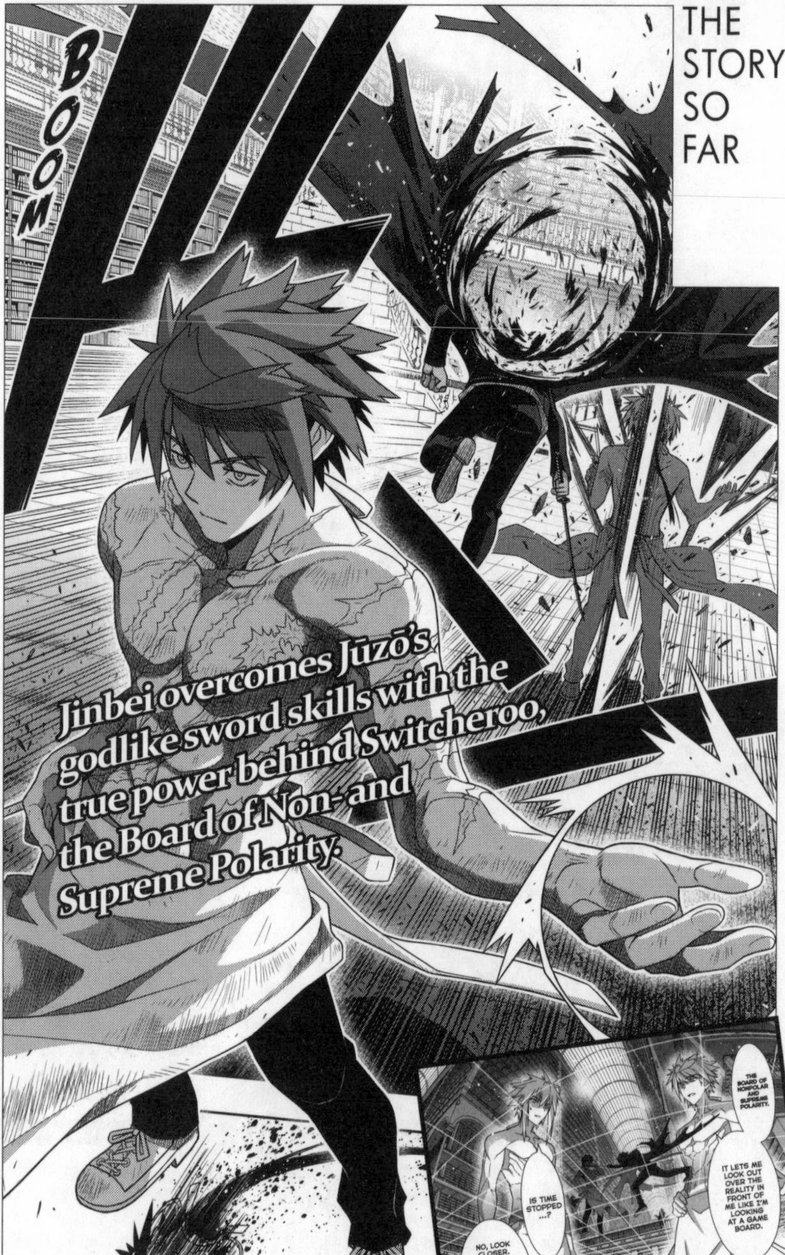
BOOM
Jinbei overcomes Jūzō's godlike sword skills with the true power behind Switcheroo, the Board of Non- and Supreme Polarity.
THE BOARD OF NONPOLAR AND SUPREME POLARITY.
IT LETS ME LOOK OUT OVER THE REALITY IN FRONT OF ME LIKE I'M LOOKING AT A GAME BOARD.
IS TIME STOPPED ...?
NO, LOOK CLOSER, THEY'RE STILL MOVING AROUND LIKE CRAZY. IT DOESN'T GIVE ME THAT BIG OF AN ADVANTAGE.

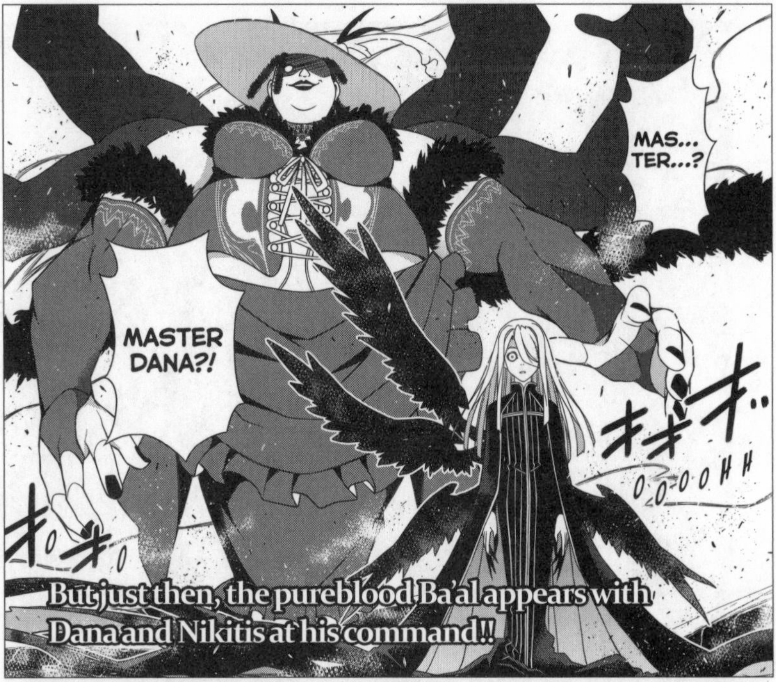
MAS... TER...?
OOOOHH
MASTER DANA?!
But just then, the pureblood Ba'al appears with Dana and Nikitis at his command!!

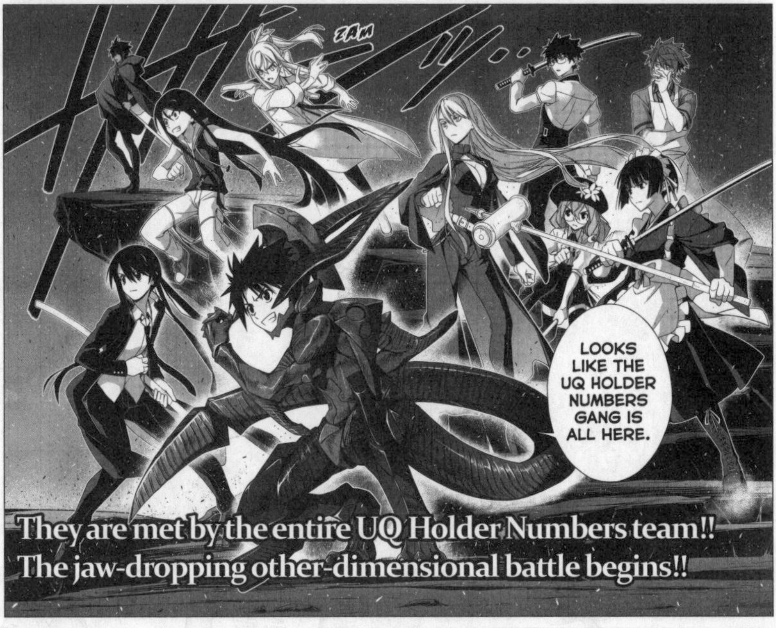
ZAM
LOOKS LIKE THE UQ HOLDER NUMBERS GANG IS ALL HERE.
They are met by the entire UQ Holder Numbers team!!
The jaw-dropping other-dimensional battle begins!!

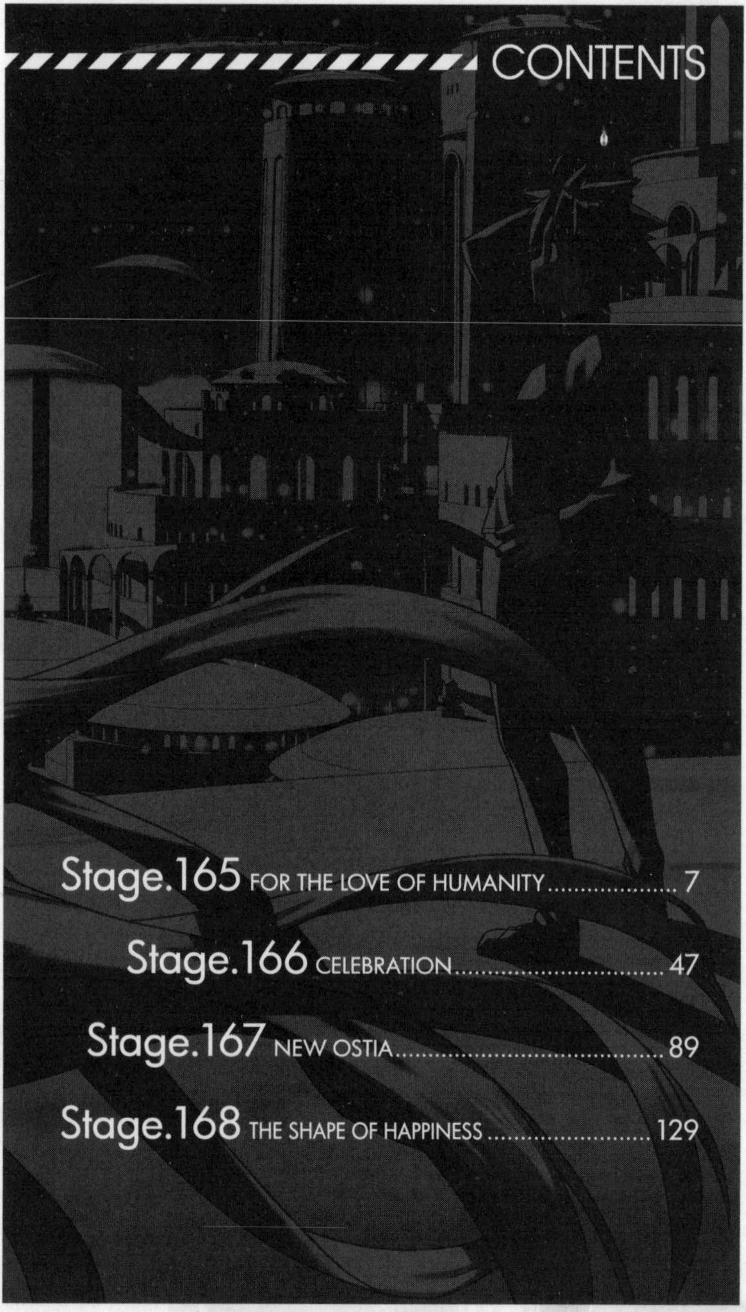

CONTENTS

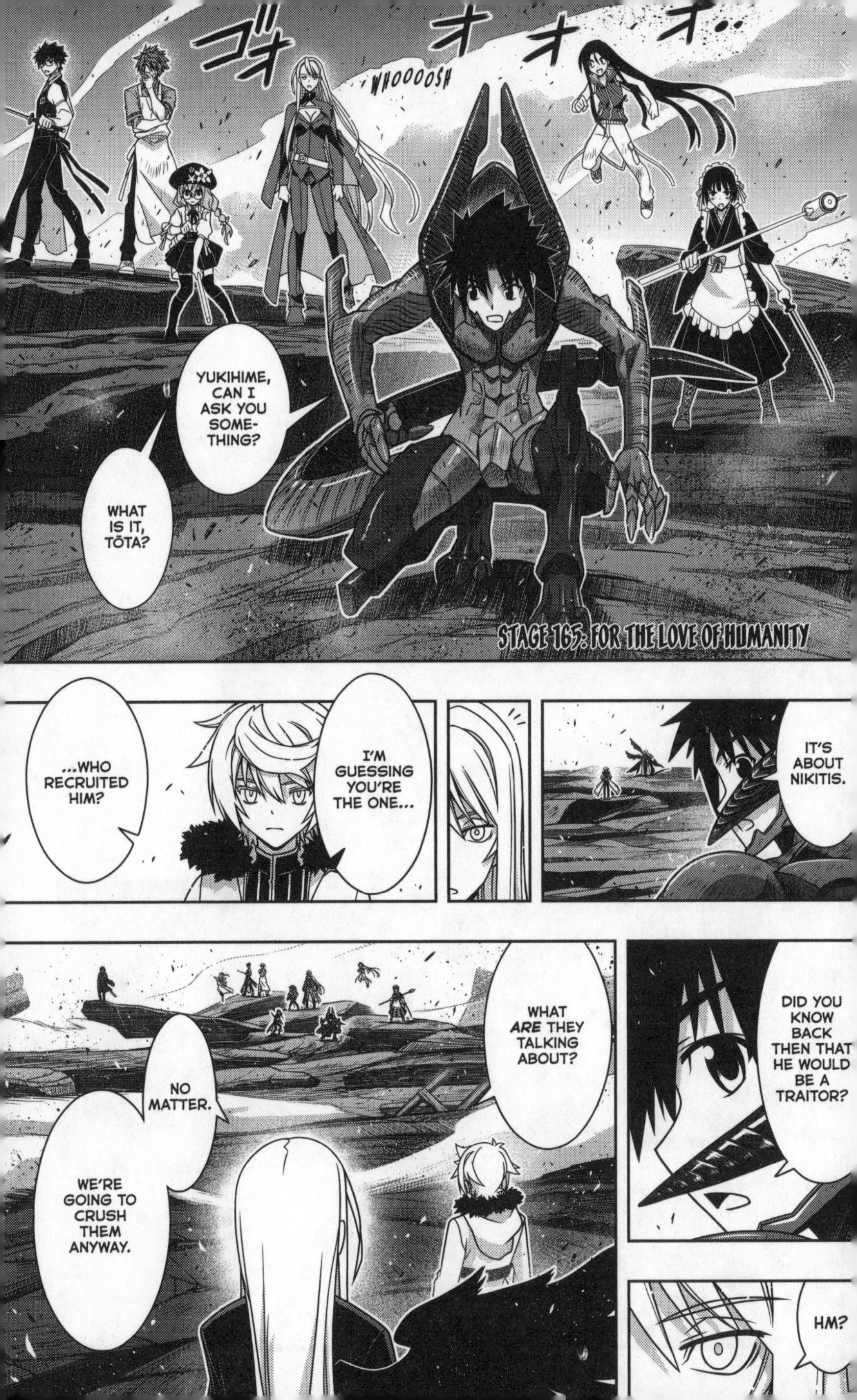
ゴオ オ オ オ・・
WHOOOOSH
YUKIHIME, CAN I ASK YOU SOME-THING?
WHAT IS IT, TŌTA?
STAGE 165: FOR THE LOVE OF HUMANITY
IT'S ABOUT NIKITIS.
I'M GUESSING YOU'RE THE ONE...
...WHO RECRUITED HIM?
DID YOU KNOW BACK THEN THAT HE WOULD BE A TRAITOR?
HM?
WHAT *ARE* THEY TALKING ABOUT?
NO MATTER.
WE'RE GOING TO CRUSH THEM ANYWAY.

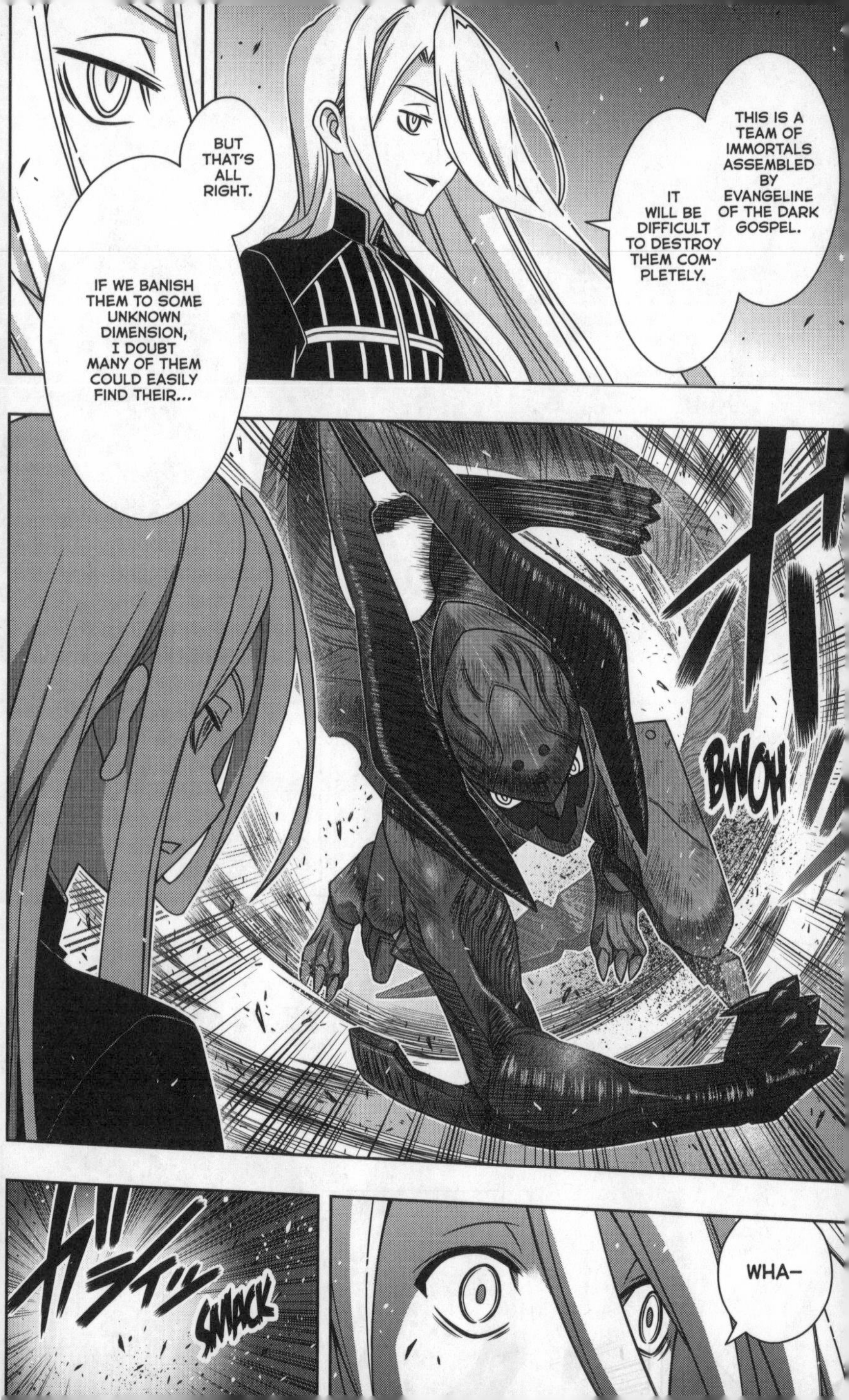
THIS IS A TEAM OF IMMORTALS ASSEMBLED BY EVANGELINE OF THE DARK GOSPEL.
IT WILL BE DIFFICULT TO DESTROY THEM COMPLETELY.
BUT THAT'S ALL RIGHT.
IF WE BANISH THEM TO SOME UNKNOWN DIMENSION, I DOUBT MANY OF THEM COULD EASILY FIND THEIR...
BWOH
WHA–
SMACK

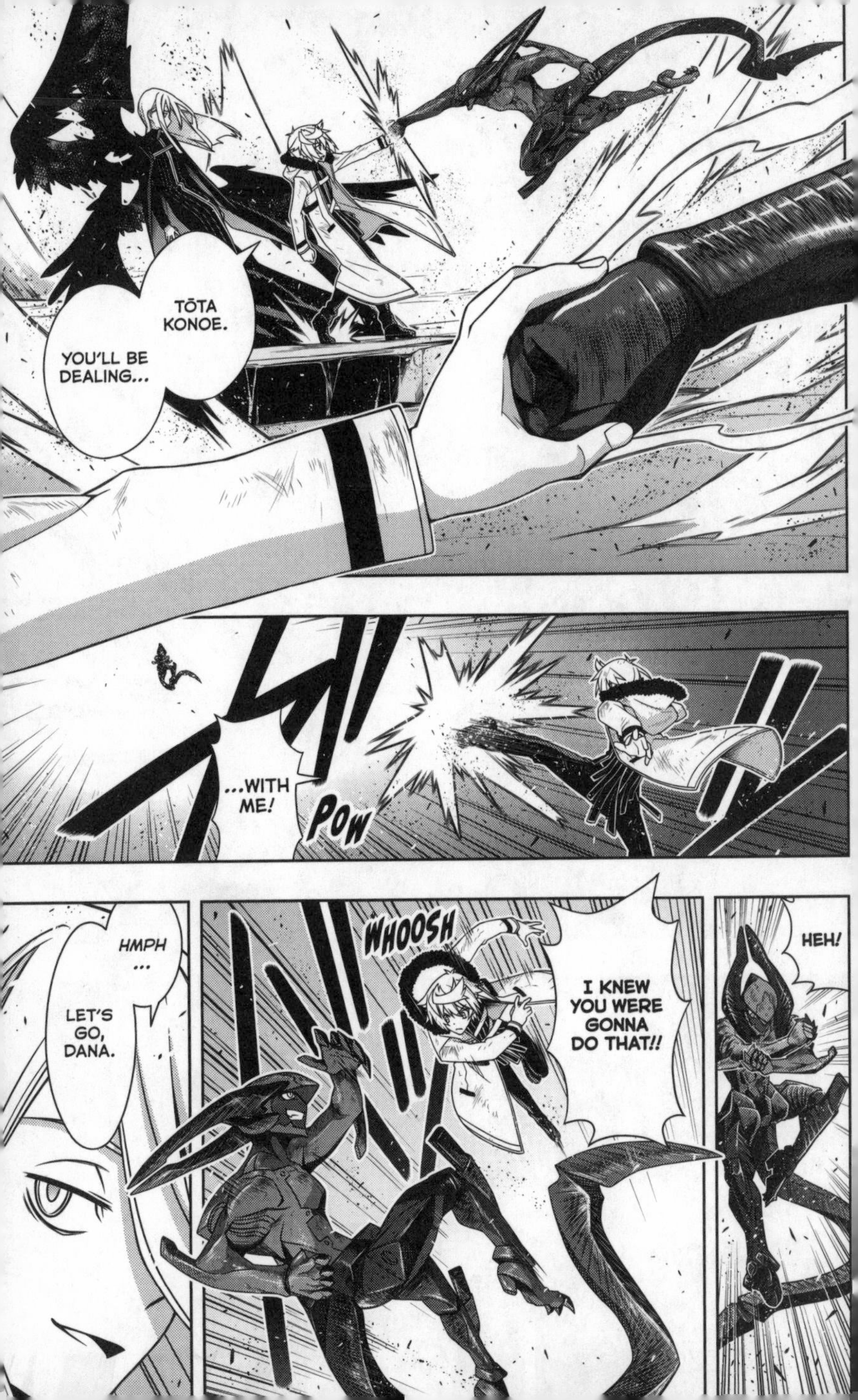
TŌTA KONOE.
YOU'LL BE DEALING...
...WITH ME!
POW
HEH!
I KNEW YOU WERE GONNA DO THAT!!
WHOOSH
HMPH ...
LET'S GO, DANA.

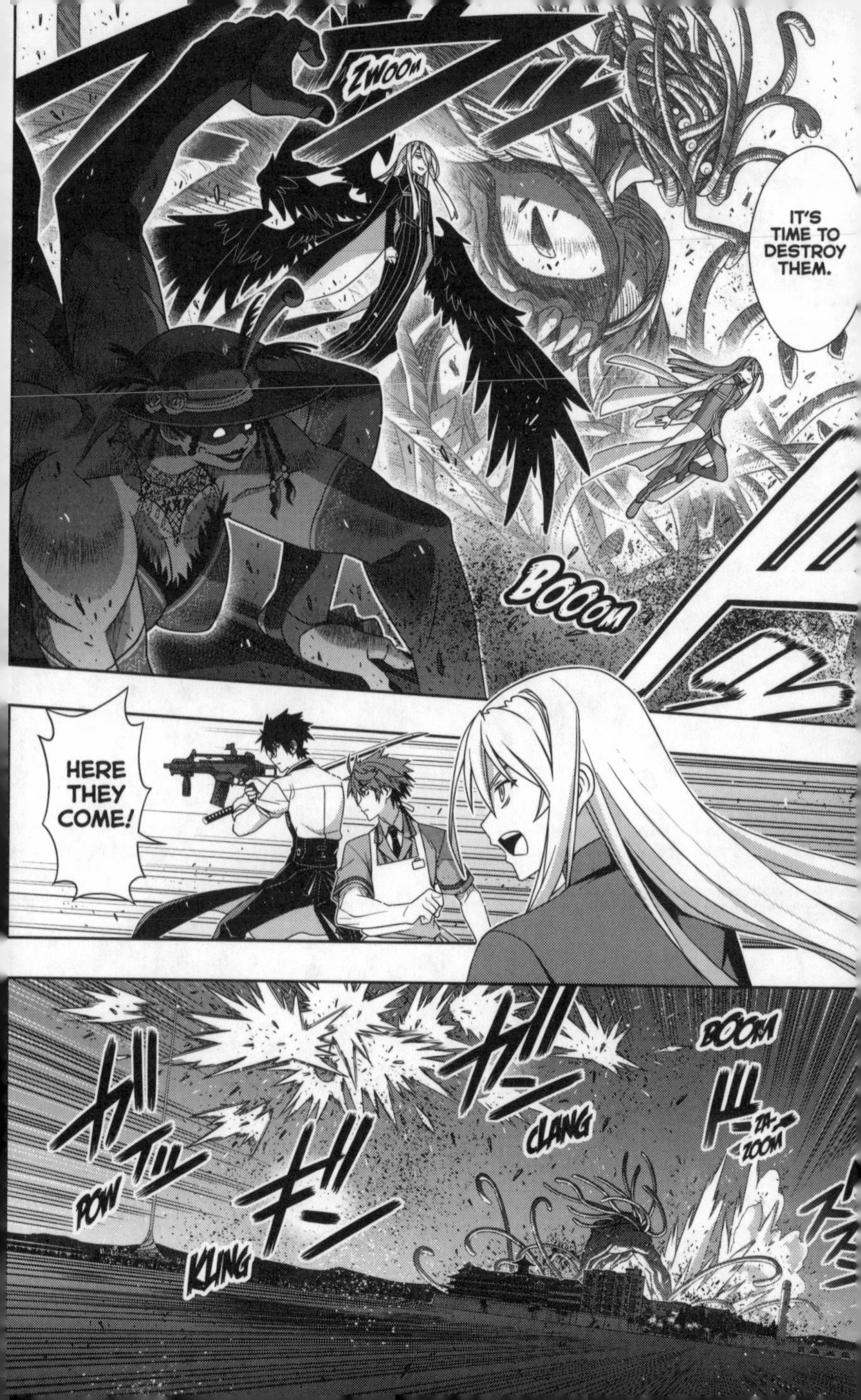
IT'S TIME TO DESTROY THEM.
ZWOOM
BOOOM
HERE THEY COME!
BOOM
ZA-ZOOM
CLANG
POW
KLING

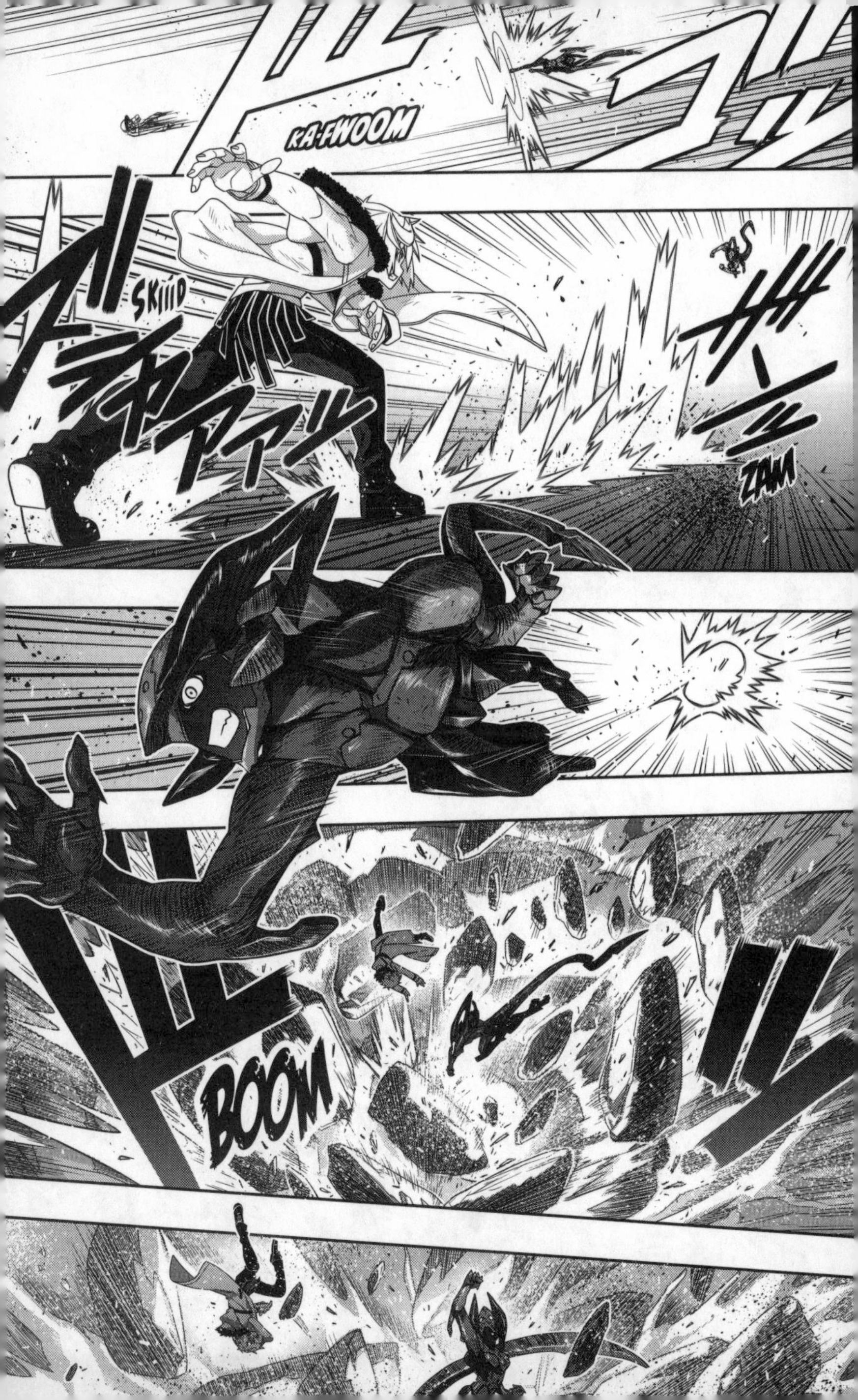
KA-FWOOM
ZAM
SKIIID
BOOM

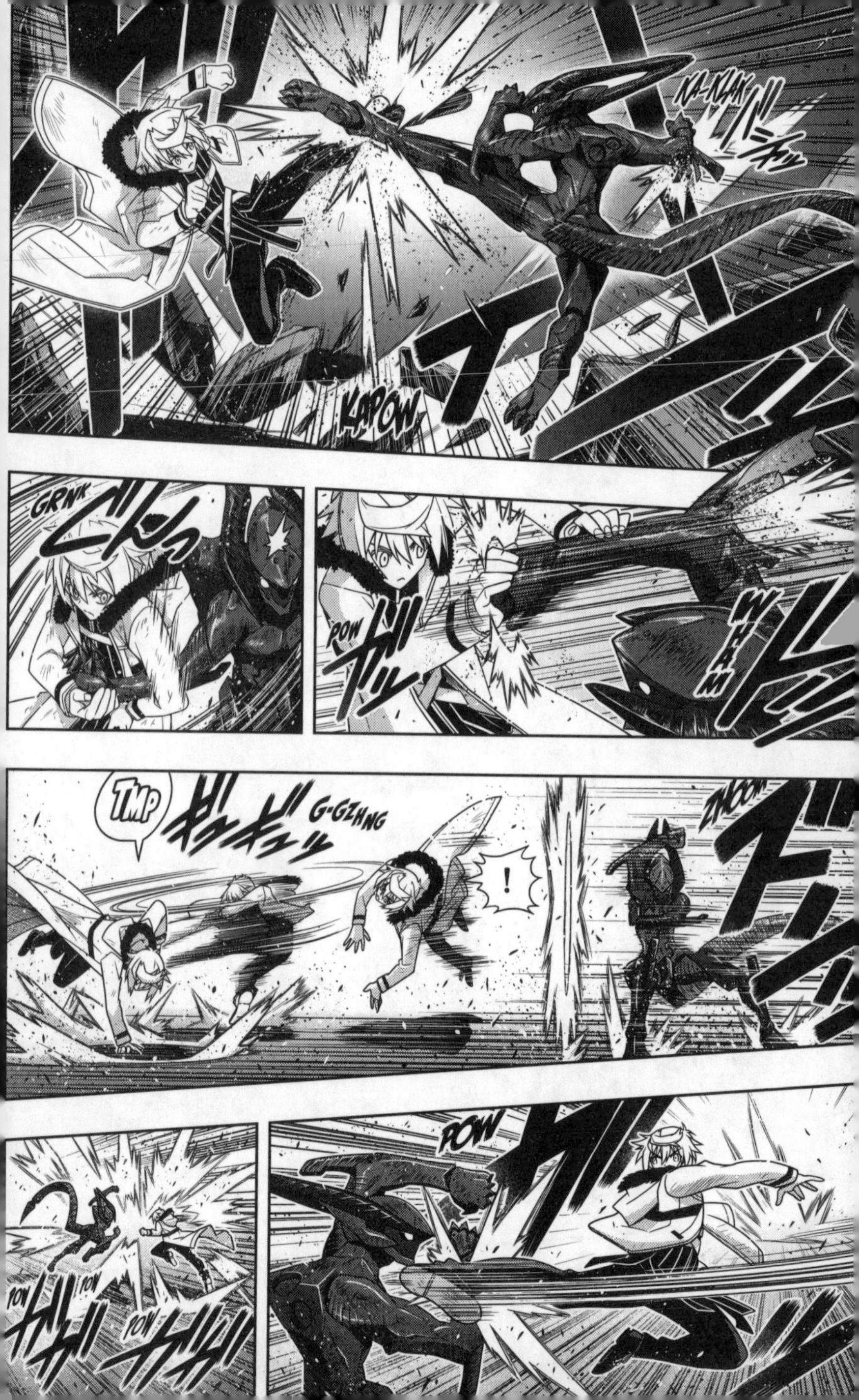
KA-KLAK
KAPOW
WHAM
POW
GRNK
ZHOOM
!
G-GZHNG
TMP
POW
POW
POW
POW

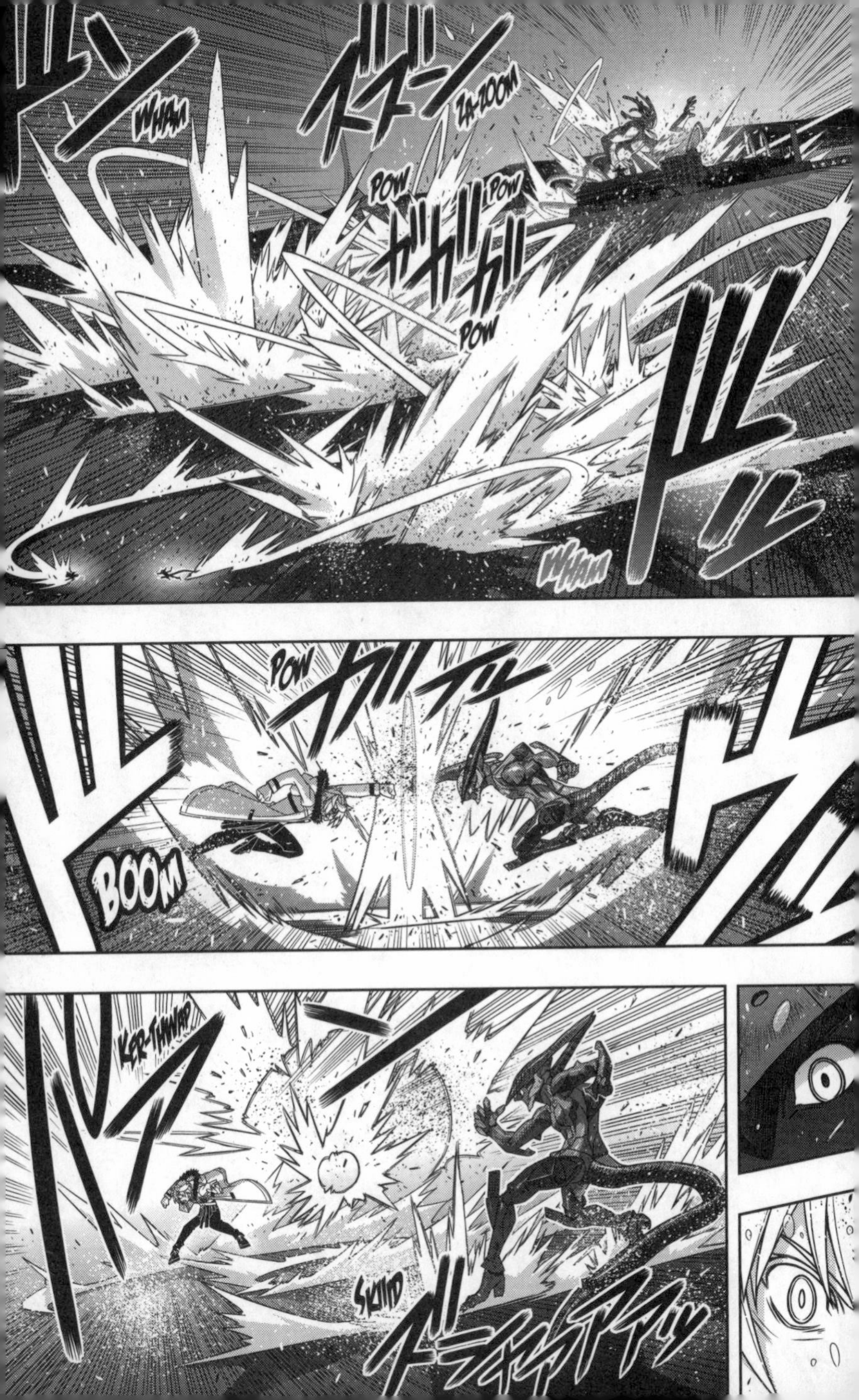
ZA-ZOOM
POW
POW
WHAM
POW
WHAM
POW
BOOM
KER-THWAP
SKIIID

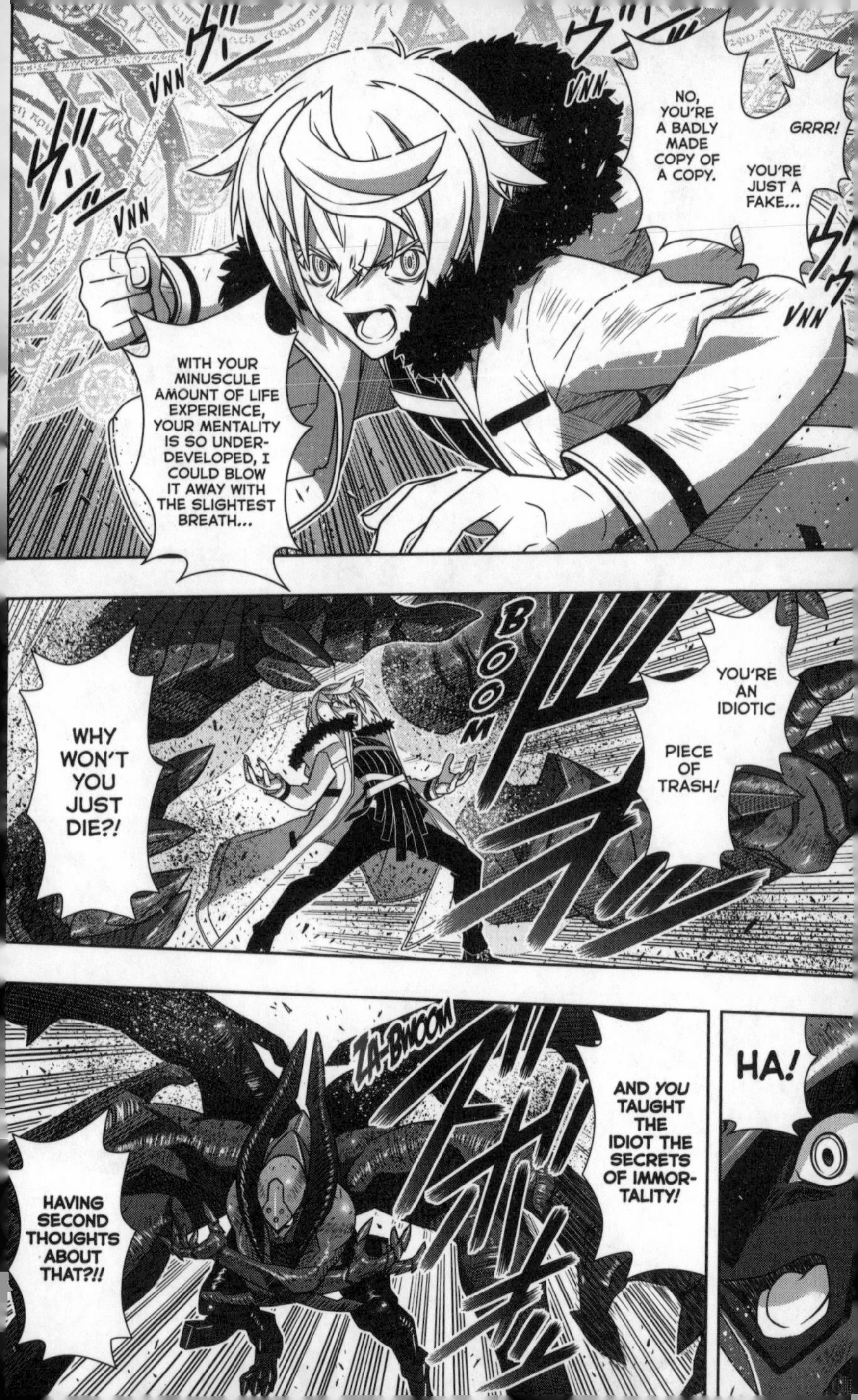
VNN
GRRR!
YOU'RE JUST A FAKE...
VNN
NO, YOU'RE A BADLY MADE COPY OF A COPY.
VNN
VNN
WITH YOUR MINUSCULE AMOUNT OF LIFE EXPERIENCE, YOUR MENTALITY IS SO UNDER-DEVELOPED, I COULD BLOW IT AWAY WITH THE SLIGHTEST BREATH...
YOU'RE AN IDIOTIC
PIECE OF TRASH!
BOOOOM
WHY WON'T YOU JUST DIE?!
HA!
AND *YOU* TAUGHT THE IDIOT THE SECRETS OF IMMOR-TALITY!
ZA-BWOOM
HAVING SECOND THOUGHTS ABOUT THAT?!!

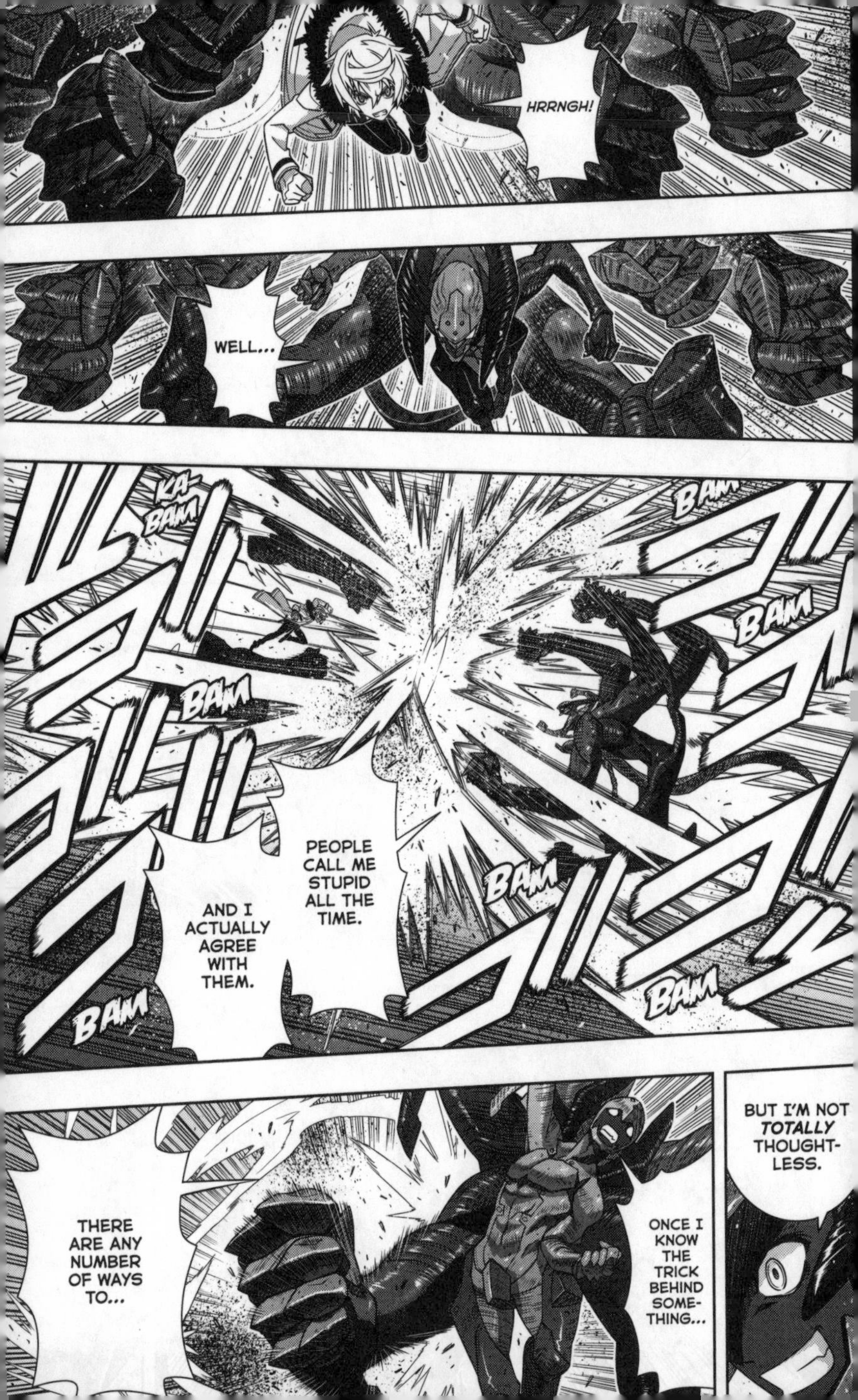
HRRNGH!
WELL...
BAM
KA-BAM
BAM
BAM
PEOPLE CALL ME STUPID ALL THE TIME.
AND I ACTUALLY AGREE WITH THEM.
BAM
BAM
BAM
BUT I'M NOT *TOTALLY* THOUGHT-LESS.
ONCE I KNOW THE TRICK BEHIND SOME-THING...
THERE ARE ANY NUMBER OF WAYS TO...

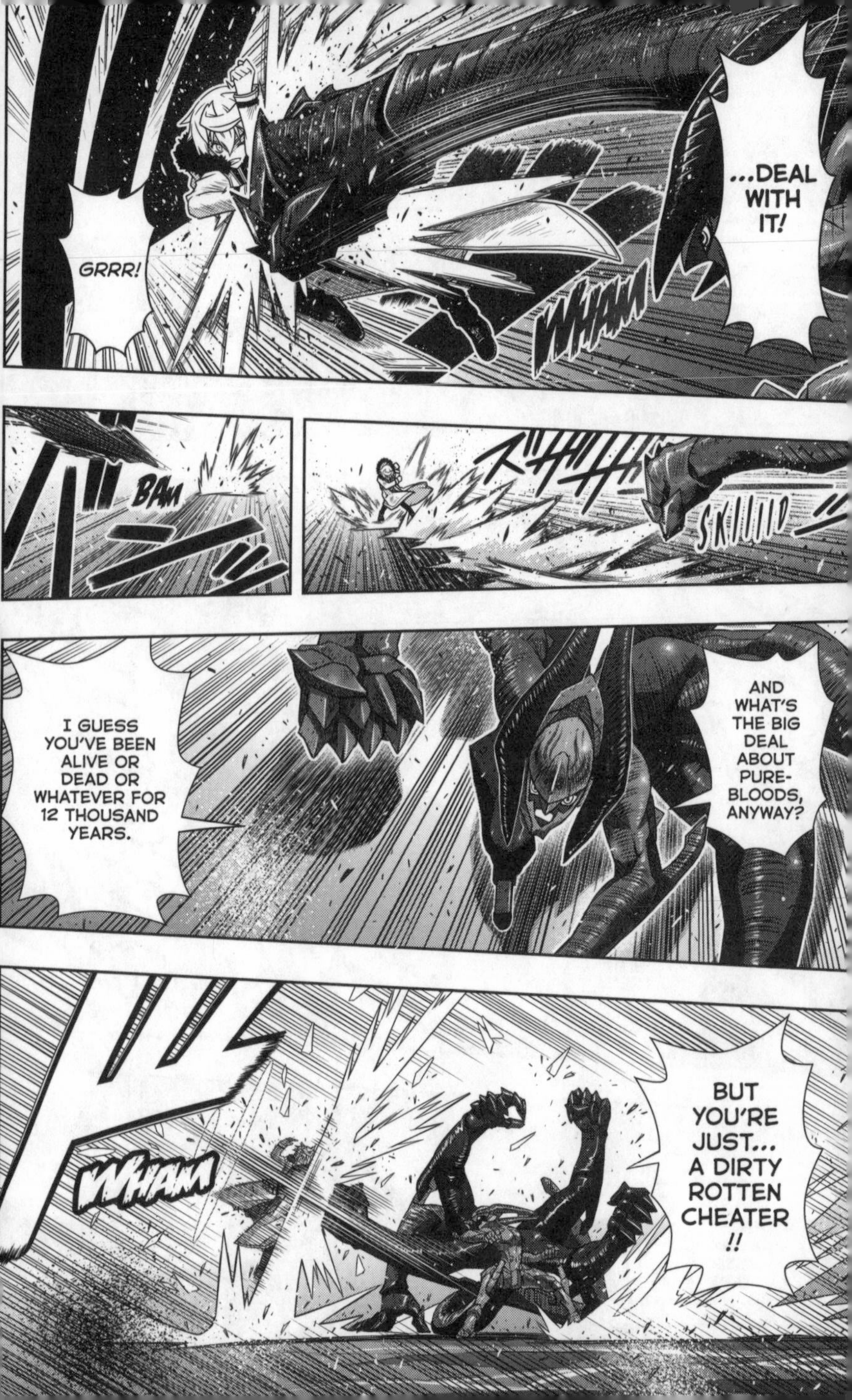
...DEAL WITH IT!
WHAM
GRRR!
SKIIIID
BAM
AND WHAT'S THE BIG DEAL ABOUT PURE-BLOODS, ANYWAY?
I GUESS YOU'VE BEEN ALIVE OR DEAD OR WHATEVER FOR 12 THOUSAND YEARS.
BUT YOU'RE JUST... A DIRTY ROTTEN CHEATER !!
WHAM

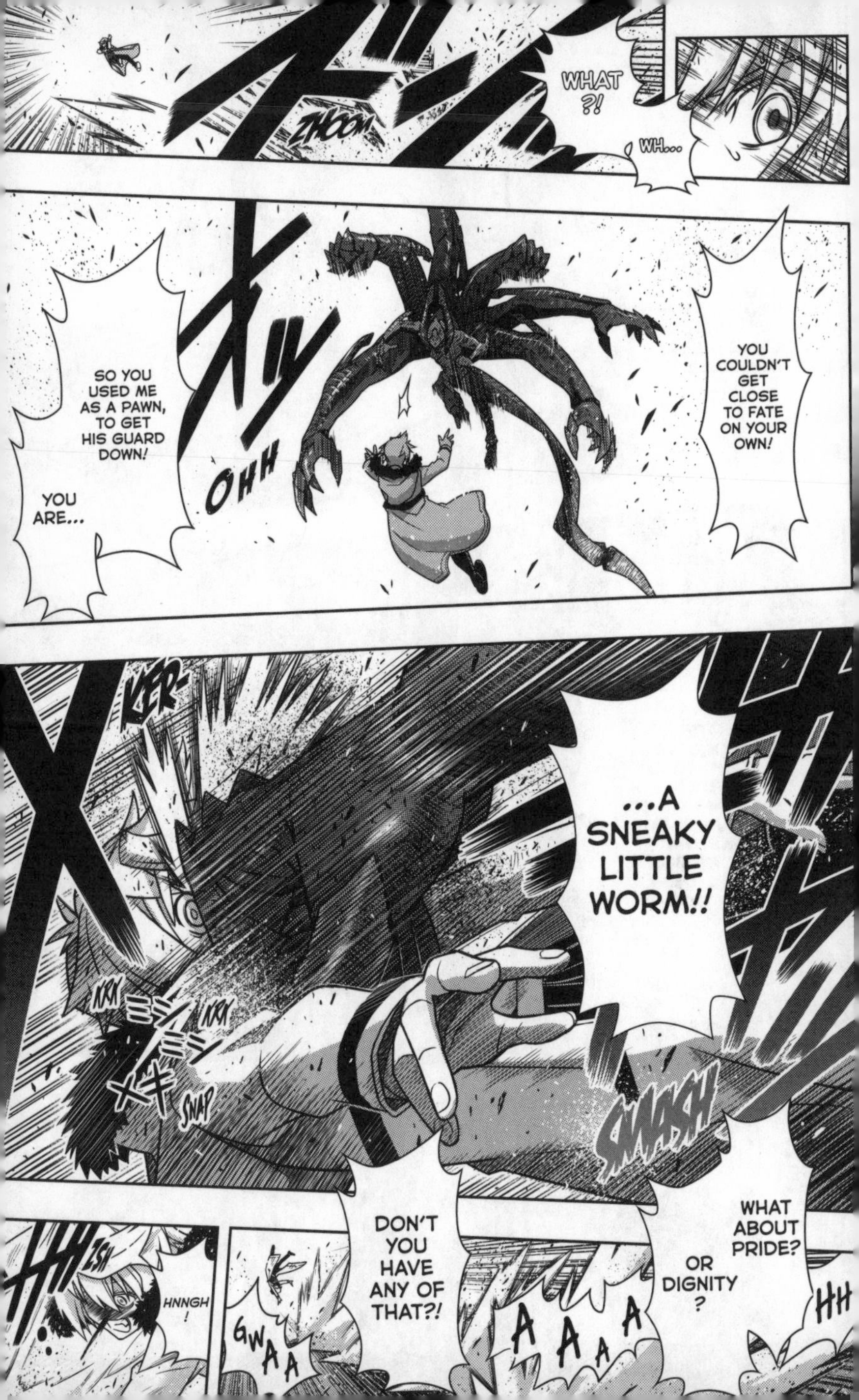

WH...
WHAT ?!
ZHOOM
YOU COULDN'T GET CLOSE TO FATE ON YOUR OWN!
SO YOU USED ME AS A PAWN, TO GET HIS GUARD DOWN!
YOU ARE...
OHH
...A SNEAKY LITTLE WORM!!
KER-
SMASH
KRK
KRK
SNAP
WHAT ABOUT PRIDE?
OR DIGNITY ?
DON'T YOU HAVE ANY OF THAT?!
AAAA
GWAA
HNNGH !
ZSH

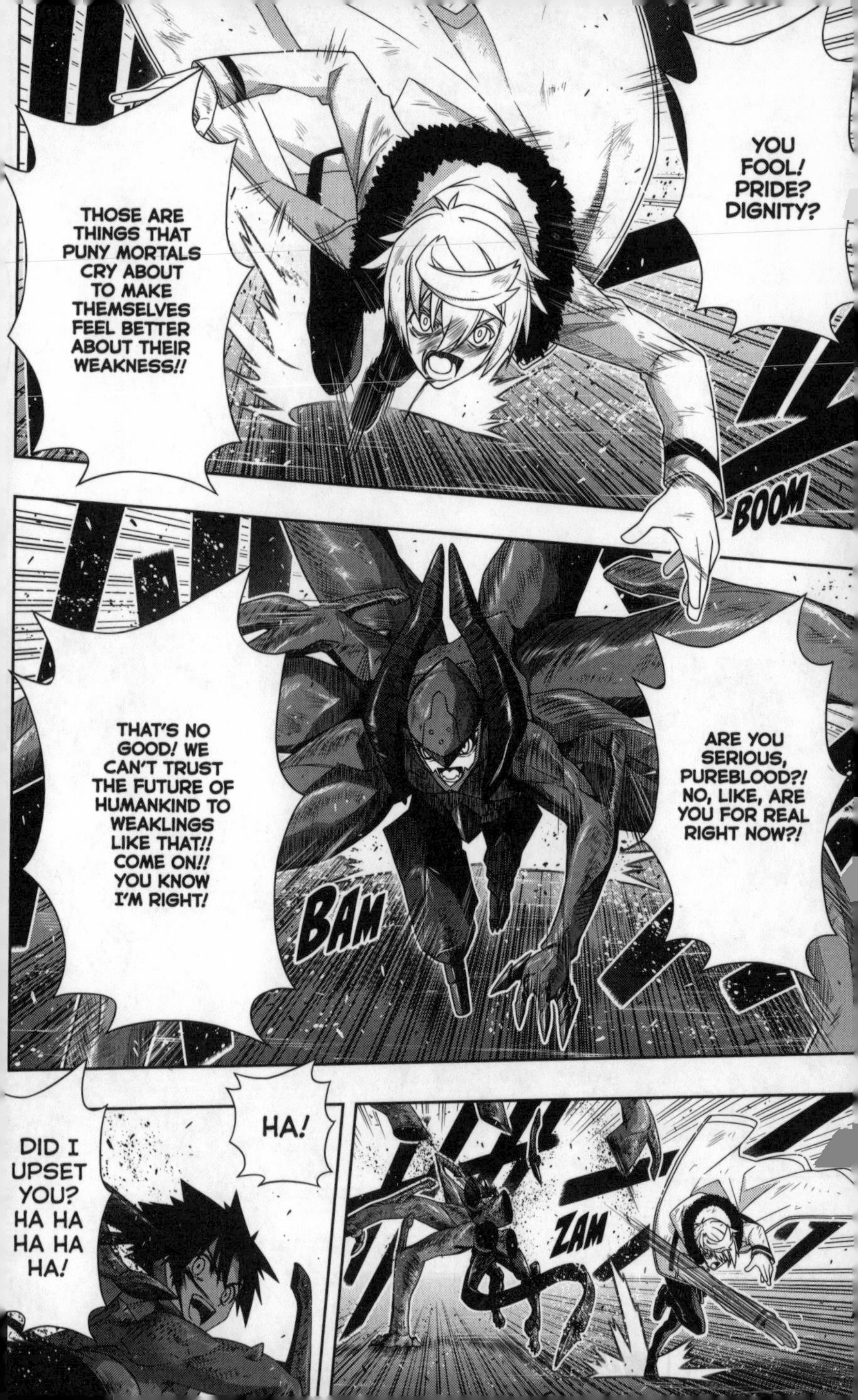
YOU FOOL! PRIDE? DIGNITY?
THOSE ARE THINGS THAT PUNY MORTALS CRY ABOUT TO MAKE THEMSELVES FEEL BETTER ABOUT THEIR WEAKNESS!!
BOOM
ARE YOU SERIOUS, PUREBLOOD?! NO, LIKE, ARE YOU FOR REAL RIGHT NOW?!
BAM
THAT'S NO GOOD! WE CAN'T TRUST THE FUTURE OF HUMANKIND TO WEAKLINGS LIKE THAT!! COME ON!! YOU KNOW I'M RIGHT!
ZAM
HA!
DID I UPSET YOU? HA HA HA HA HA!

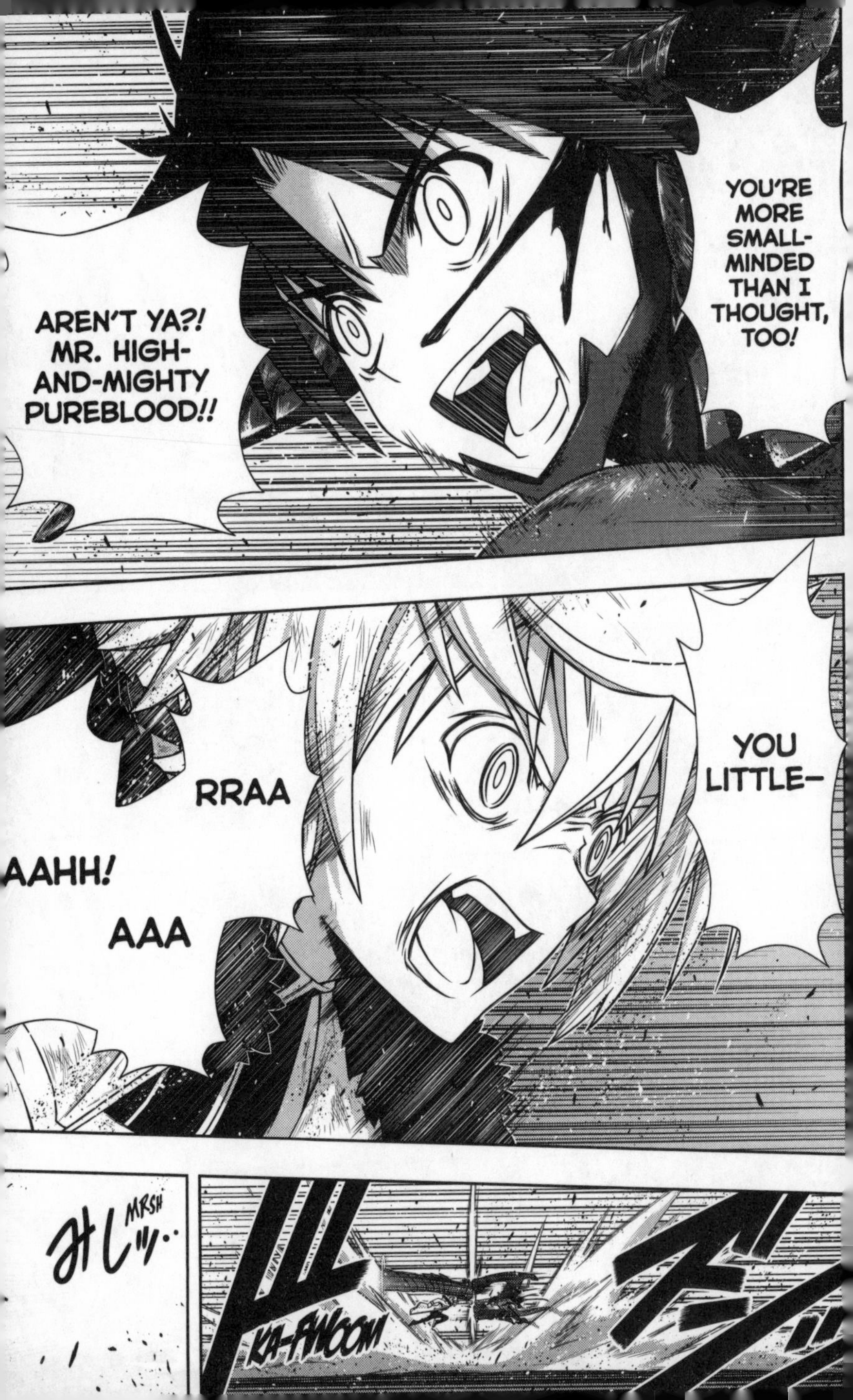
YOU'RE MORE SMALL-MINDED THAN I THOUGHT, TOO!
AREN'T YA?! MR. HIGH-AND-MIGHTY PUREBLOOD!!
YOU LITTLE–
RRAA
AAHH!
AAA
KA-FWOOM
みしッ‥
MRSH

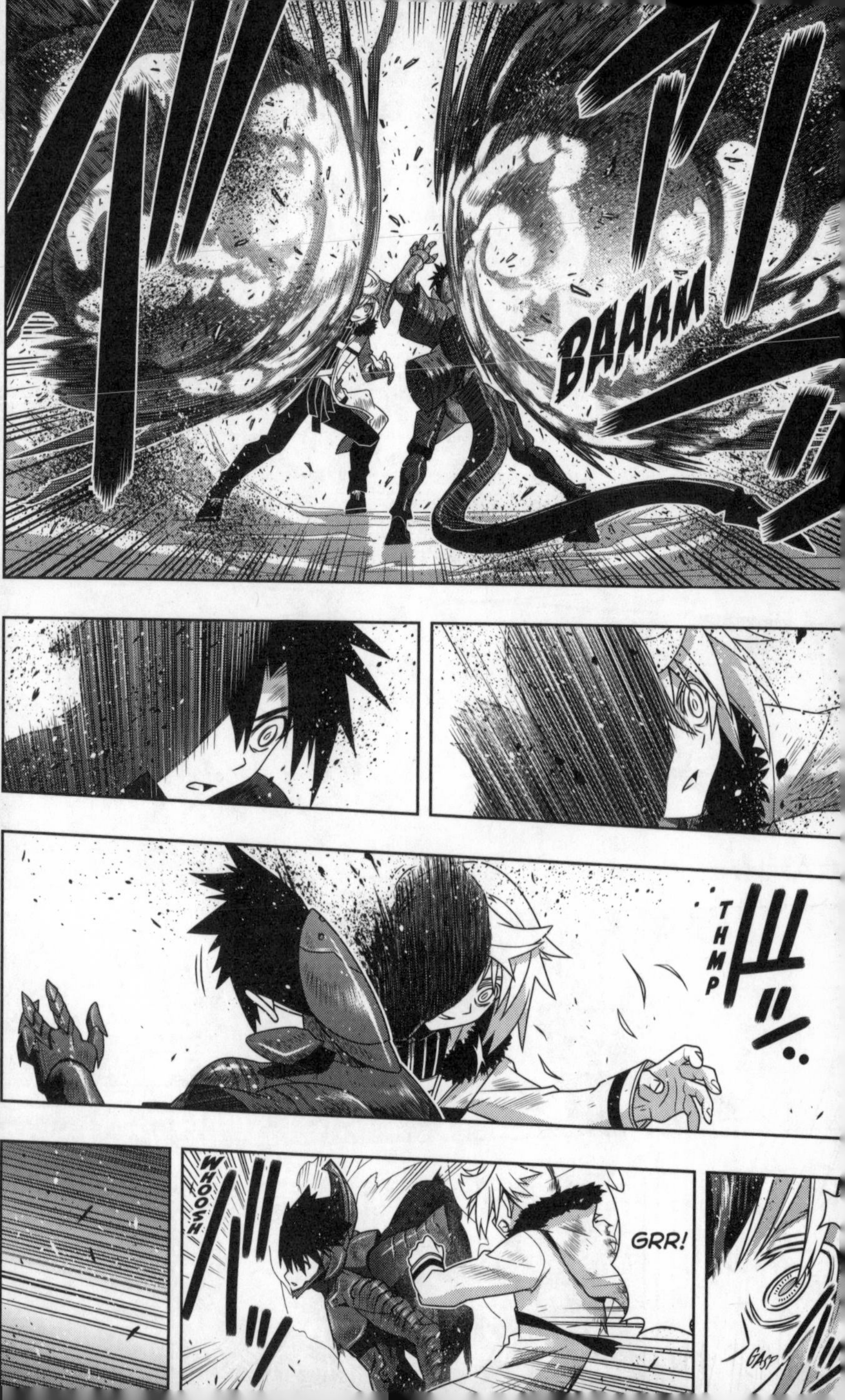
BAAAM
THMP
GASP
GRR!
WHOOSH

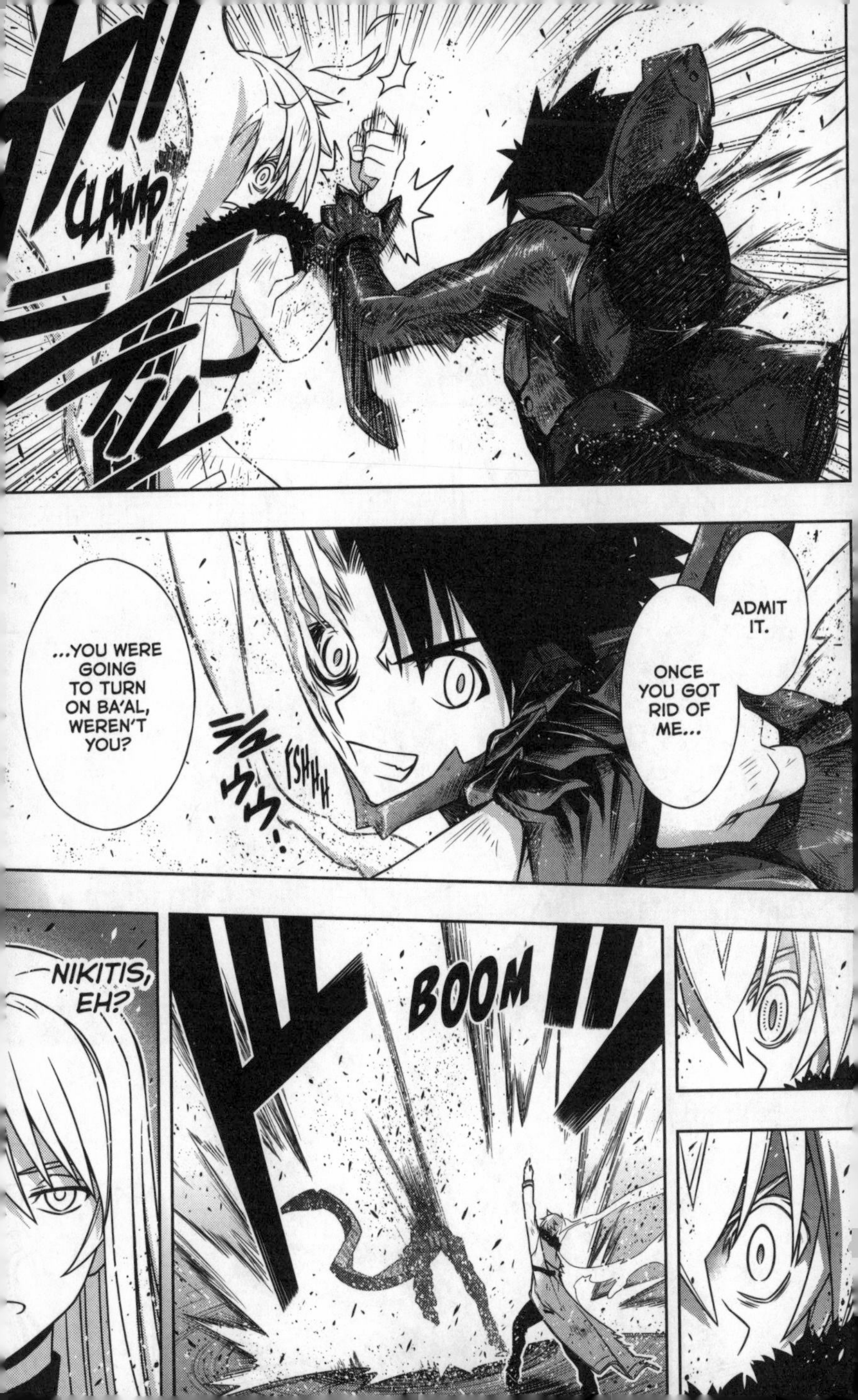
CLAMP
ADMIT IT.
ONCE YOU GOT RID OF ME...
...YOU WERE GOING TO TURN ON BA'AL, WEREN'T YOU?
YSHHH
BOOM
NIKITIS, EH?

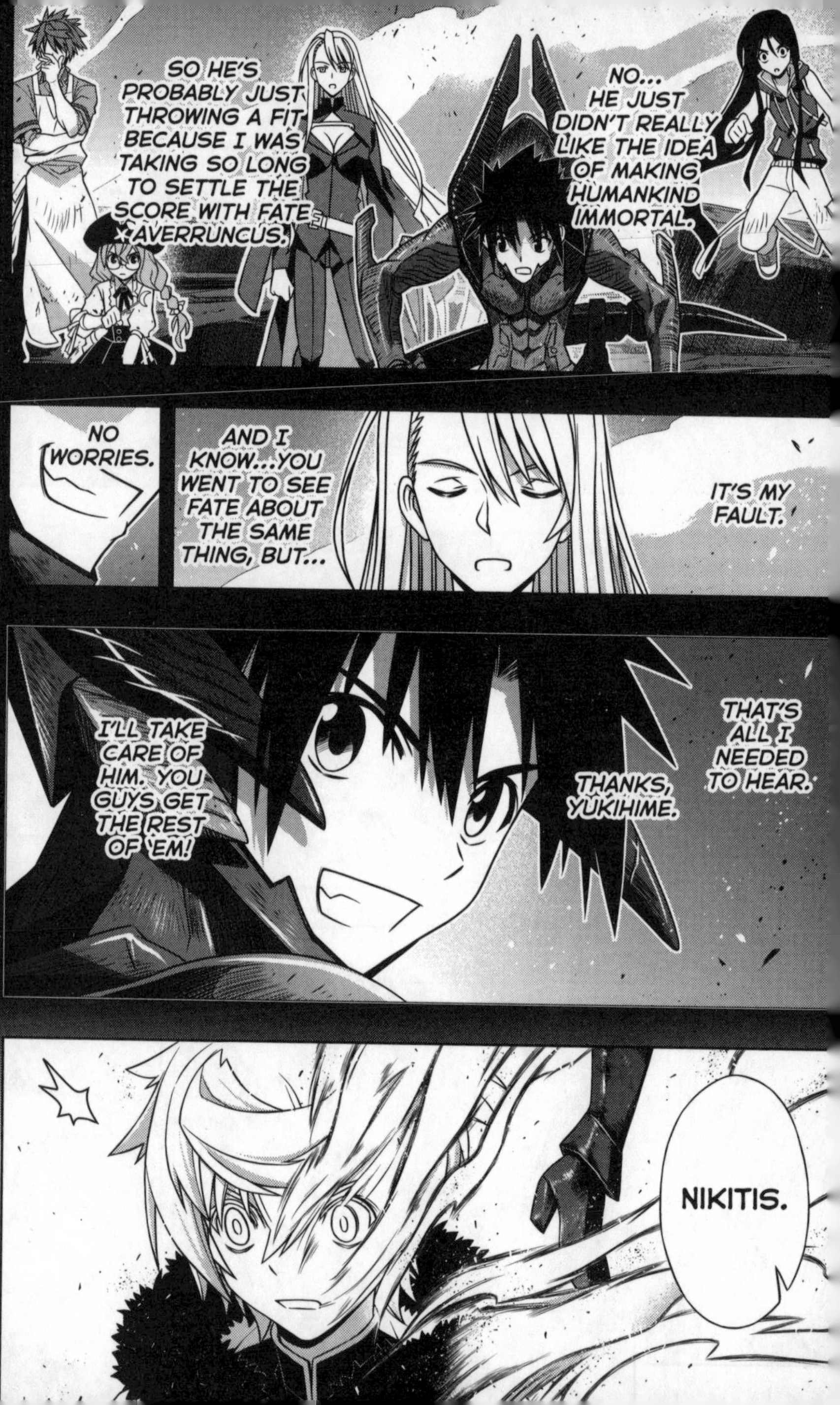
NO... HE JUST DIDN'T REALLY LIKE THE IDEA OF MAKING HUMANKIND IMMORTAL.
SO HE'S PROBABLY JUST THROWING A FIT BECAUSE I WAS TAKING SO LONG TO SETTLE THE SCORE WITH FATE AVERRUNCUS.
IT'S MY FAULT.
AND I KNOW...YOU WENT TO SEE FATE ABOUT THE SAME THING, BUT...
NO WORRIES.
THAT'S ALL I NEEDED TO HEAR.
THANKS, YUKIHIME.
I'LL TAKE CARE OF HIM. YOU GUYS GET THE REST OF 'EM!
NIKITIS.

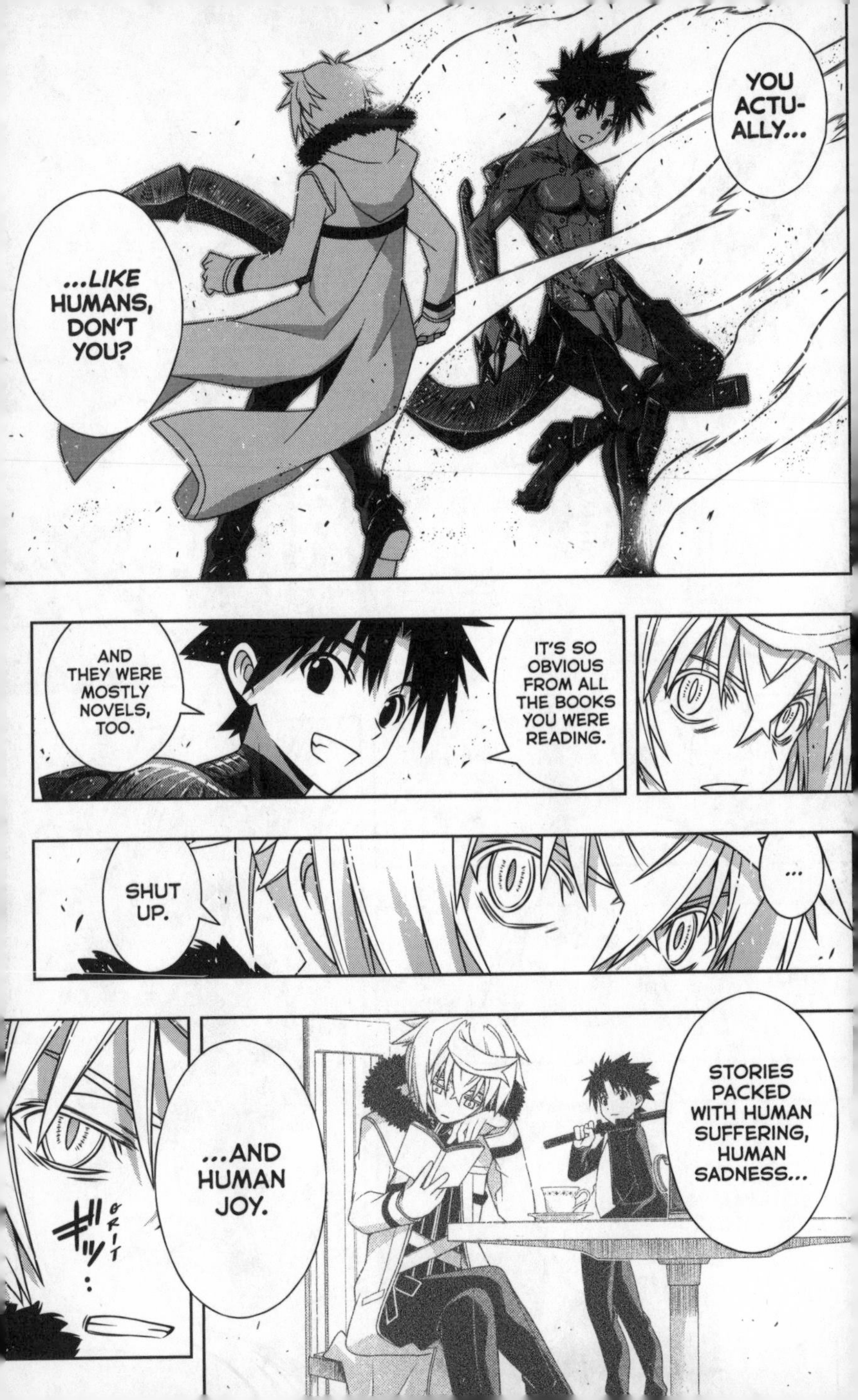
YOU ACTUALLY...
...LIKE HUMANS, DON'T YOU?
IT'S SO OBVIOUS FROM ALL THE BOOKS YOU WERE READING.
AND THEY WERE MOSTLY NOVELS, TOO.
...
SHUT UP.
STORIES PACKED WITH HUMAN SUFFERING, HUMAN SADNESS...
...AND HUMAN JOY.
GRIT

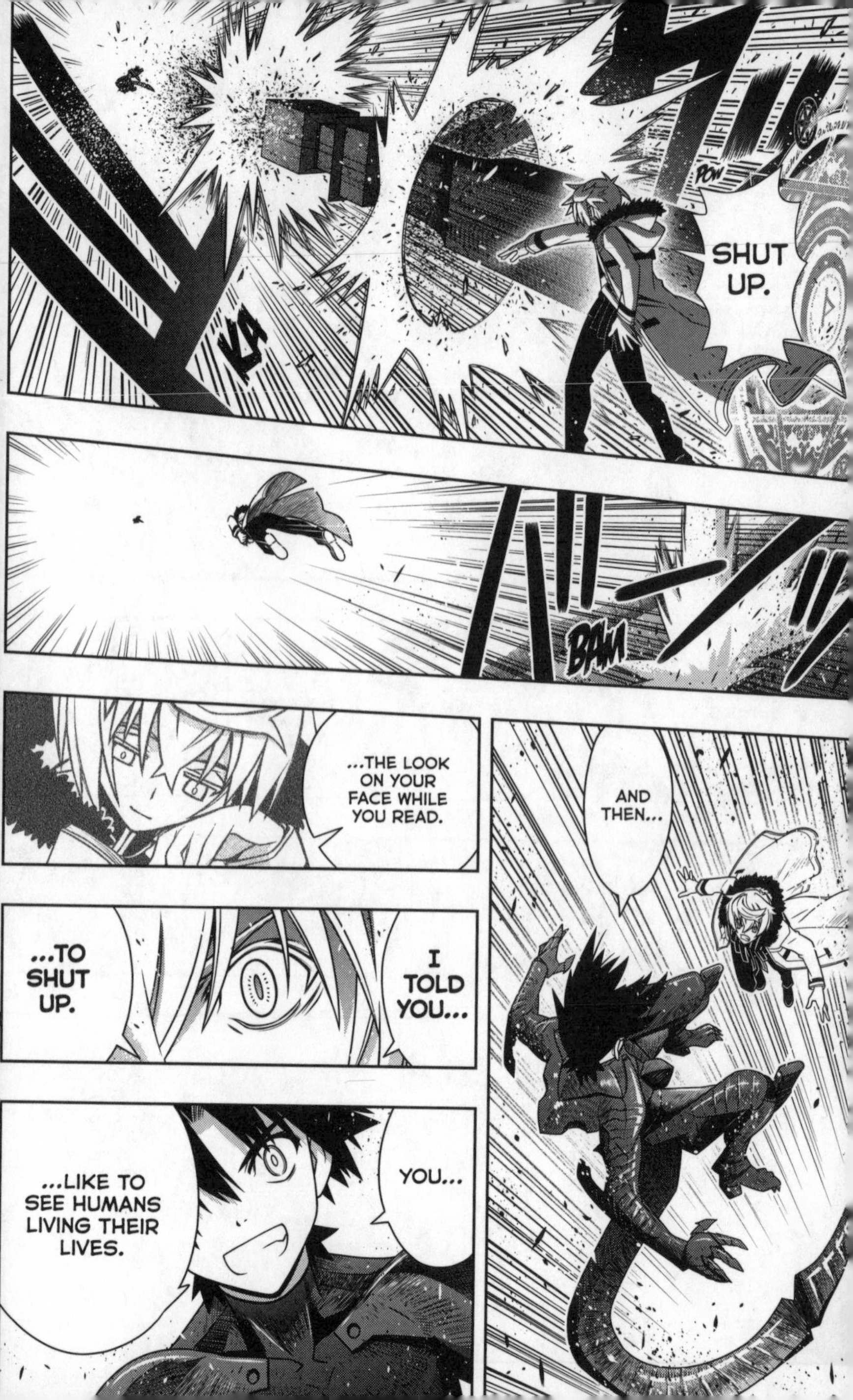
POW
SHUT UP.
KA
BAM
AND THEN...
...THE LOOK ON YOUR FACE WHILE YOU READ.
I TOLD YOU...
...TO SHUT UP.
YOU...
...LIKE TO SEE HUMANS LIVING THEIR LIVES.

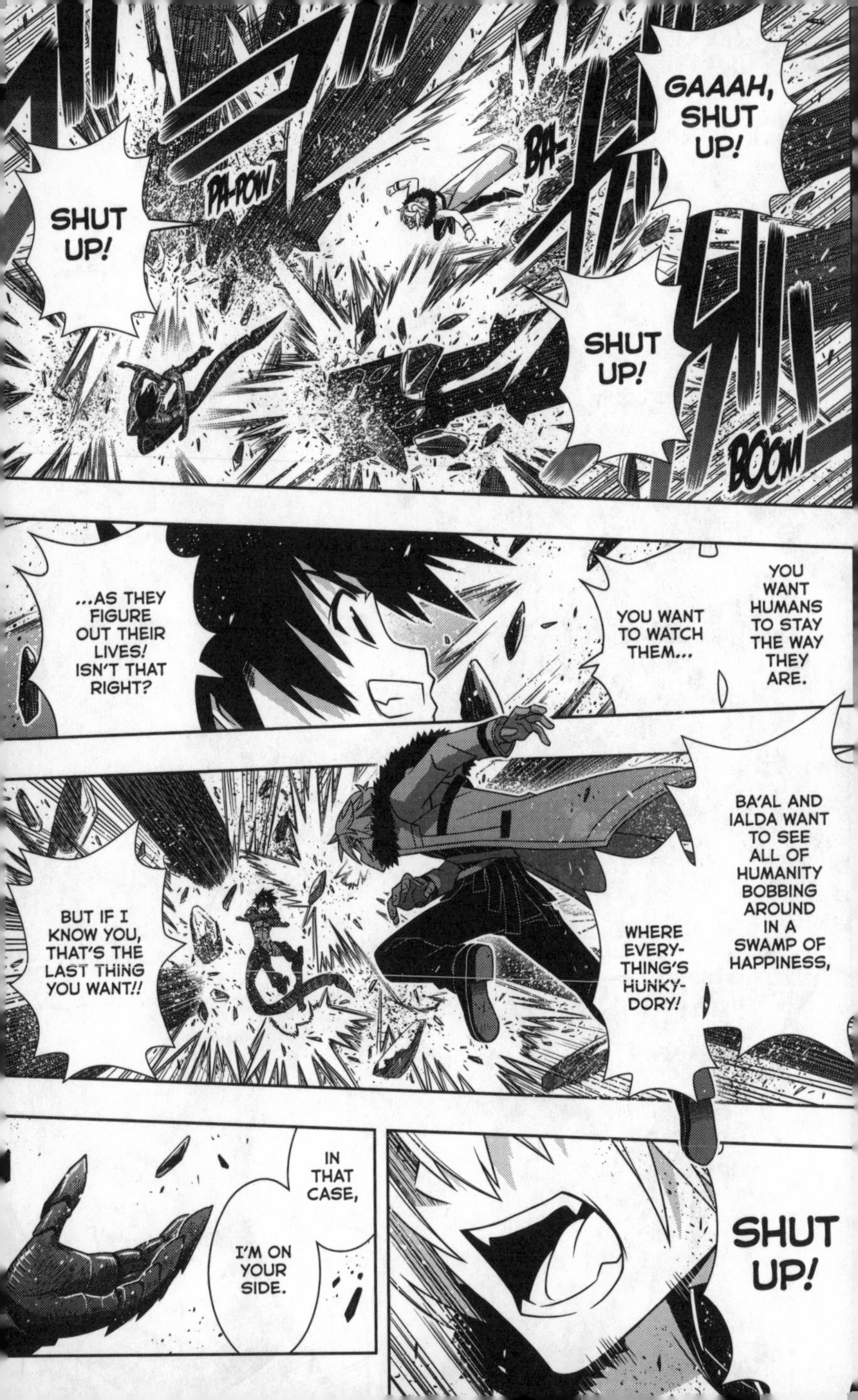
GAAAH, SHUT UP!
BA-
SHUT UP!
BOOM
PA-POW
SHUT UP!
YOU WANT HUMANS TO STAY THE WAY THEY ARE.
YOU WANT TO WATCH THEM...
...AS THEY FIGURE OUT THEIR LIVES! ISN'T THAT RIGHT?
BA'AL AND IALDA WANT TO SEE ALL OF HUMANITY BOBBING AROUND IN A SWAMP OF HAPPINESS,
WHERE EVERY-THING'S HUNKY-DORY!
BUT IF I KNOW YOU, THAT'S THE LAST THING YOU WANT!!
SHUT UP!
IN THAT CASE,
I'M ON YOUR SIDE.

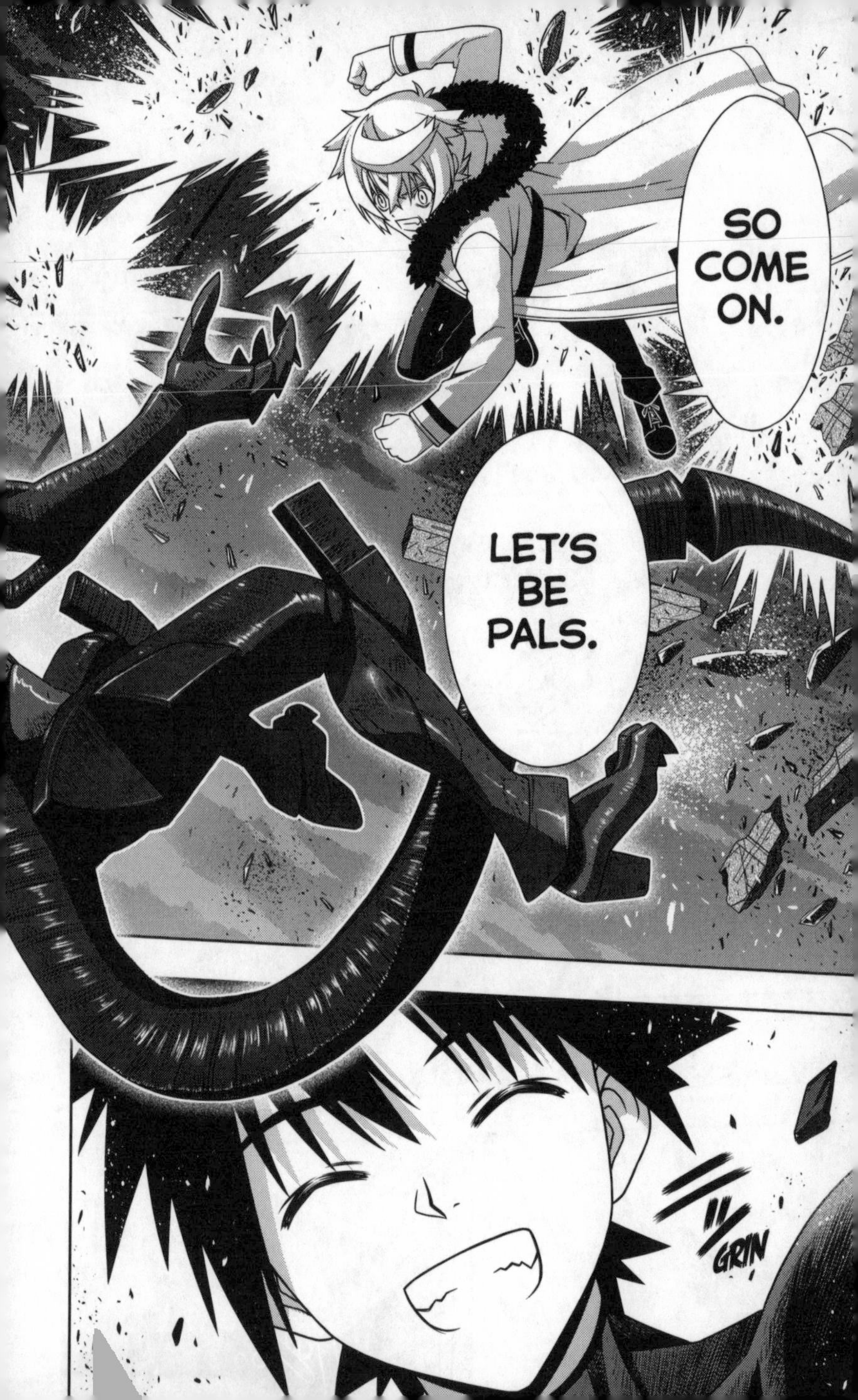
SO COME ON.
LET'S BE PALS.
GRIN

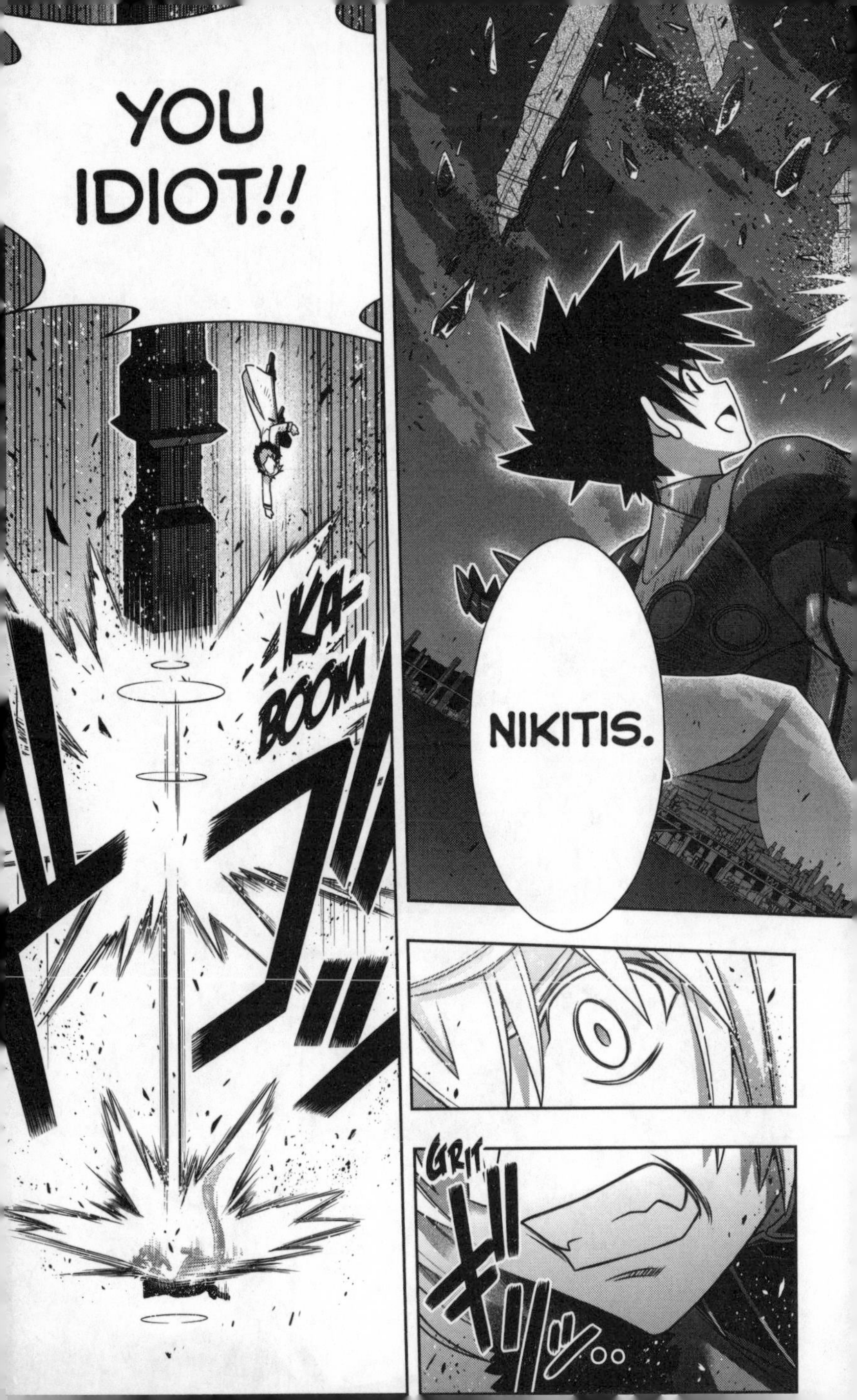
NIKITIS.
GRIT
YOU IDIOT!!
KA-BOOM

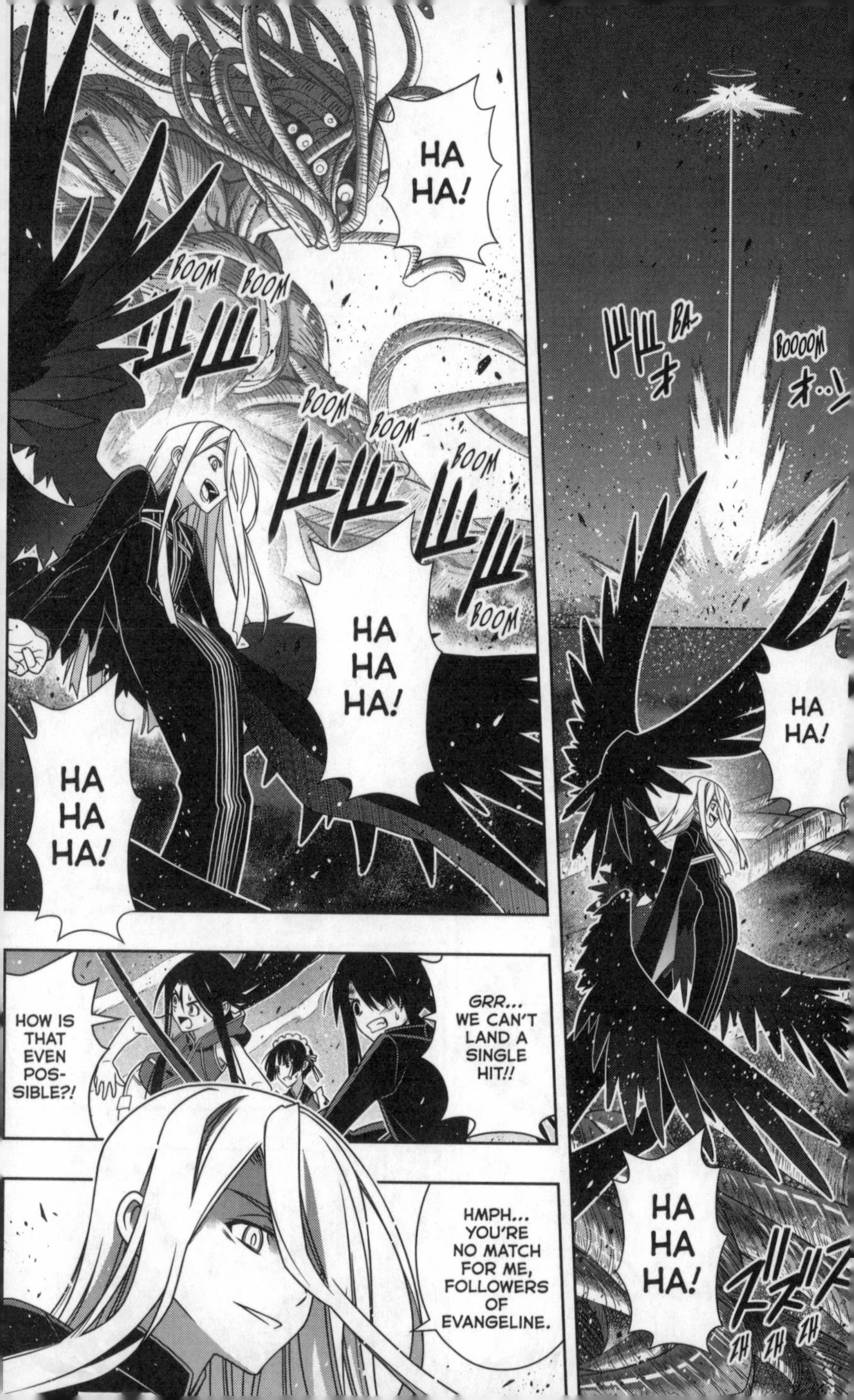
BA-
BOOOOM
HA HA!
HA HA HA!
ZH ZH ZH
HA HA!
BOOM BOOM
BOOM BOOM BOOM
BOOM
HA HA HA!
HA HA HA!
GRR... WE CAN'T LAND A SINGLE HIT!!
HOW IS THAT EVEN POS-SIBLE?!
HMPH... YOU'RE NO MATCH FOR ME, FOLLOWERS OF EVANGELINE.

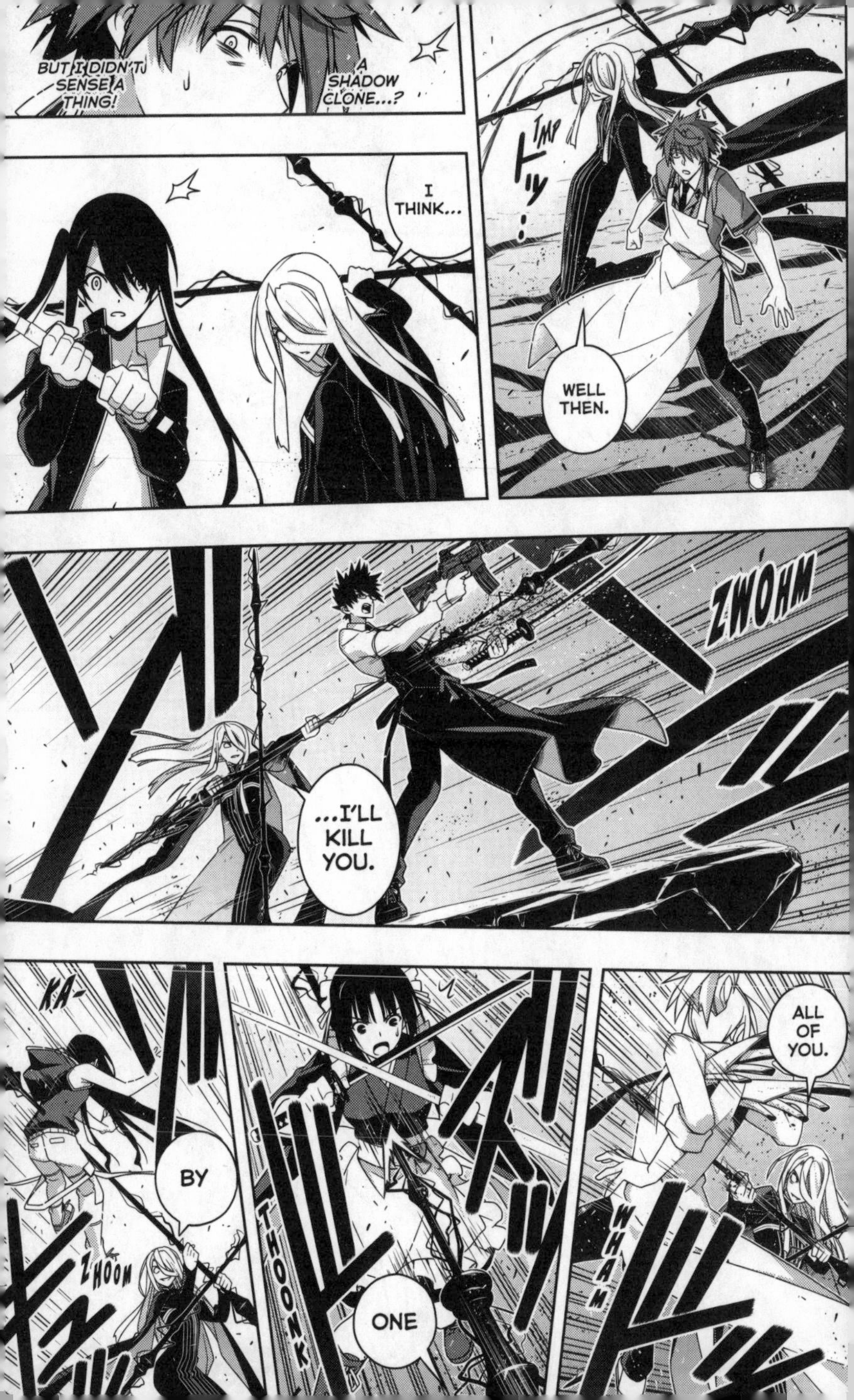
TMP
WELL THEN.
A SHADOW CLONE...?
BUT I DIDN'T SENSE A THING!
I THINK...
ZWOHM
...I'LL KILL YOU.
ALL OF YOU.
WHAM
ONE
THOONK
KA-
BY
ZHOOM

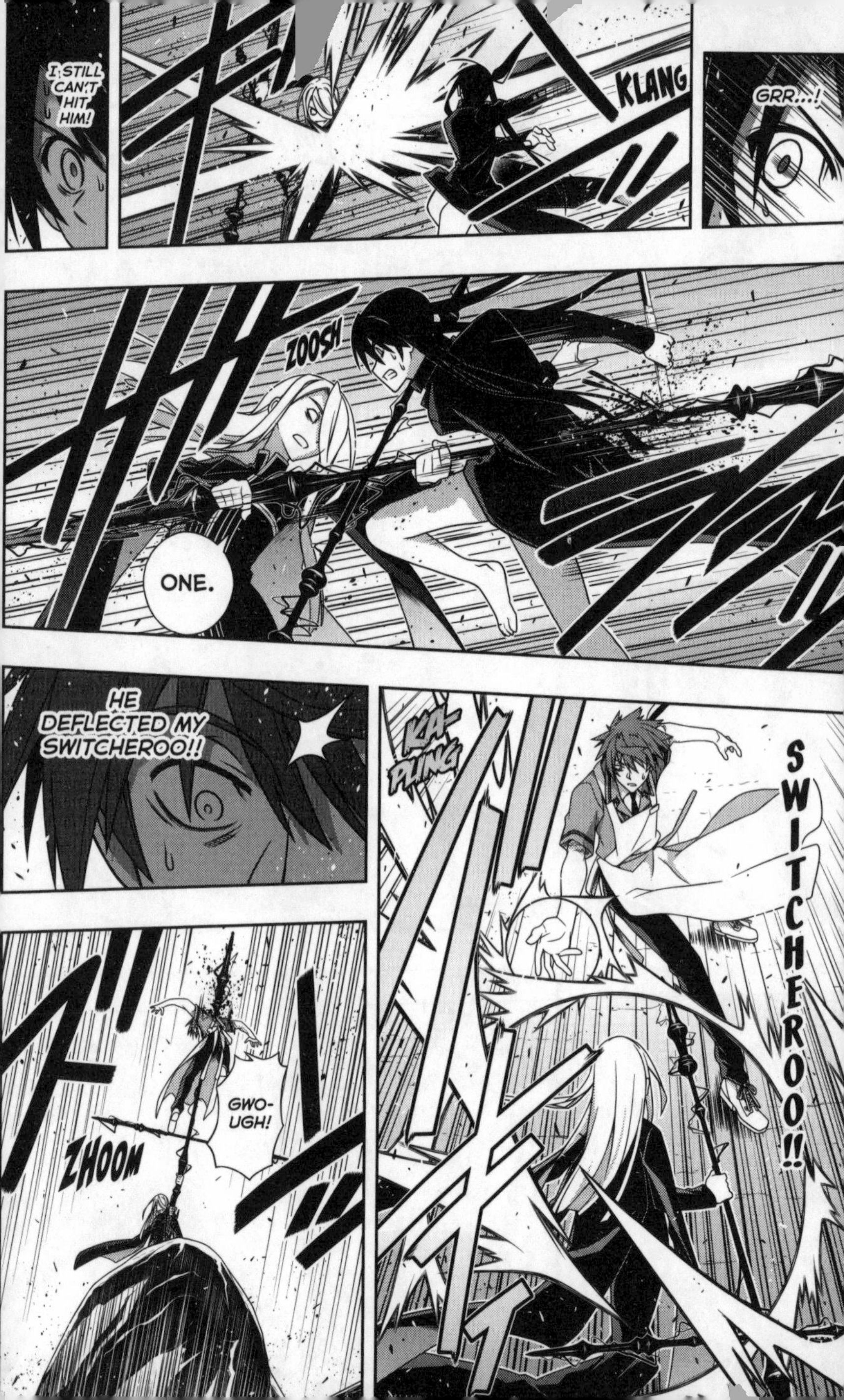
GRR...!
KLANG
I STILL CAN'T HIT HIM!
ZOOSH
ONE.
KA-PLING
SWITCHEROO!!
HE DEFLECTED MY SWITCHEROO!!
GWO-UGH!
ZHOOM

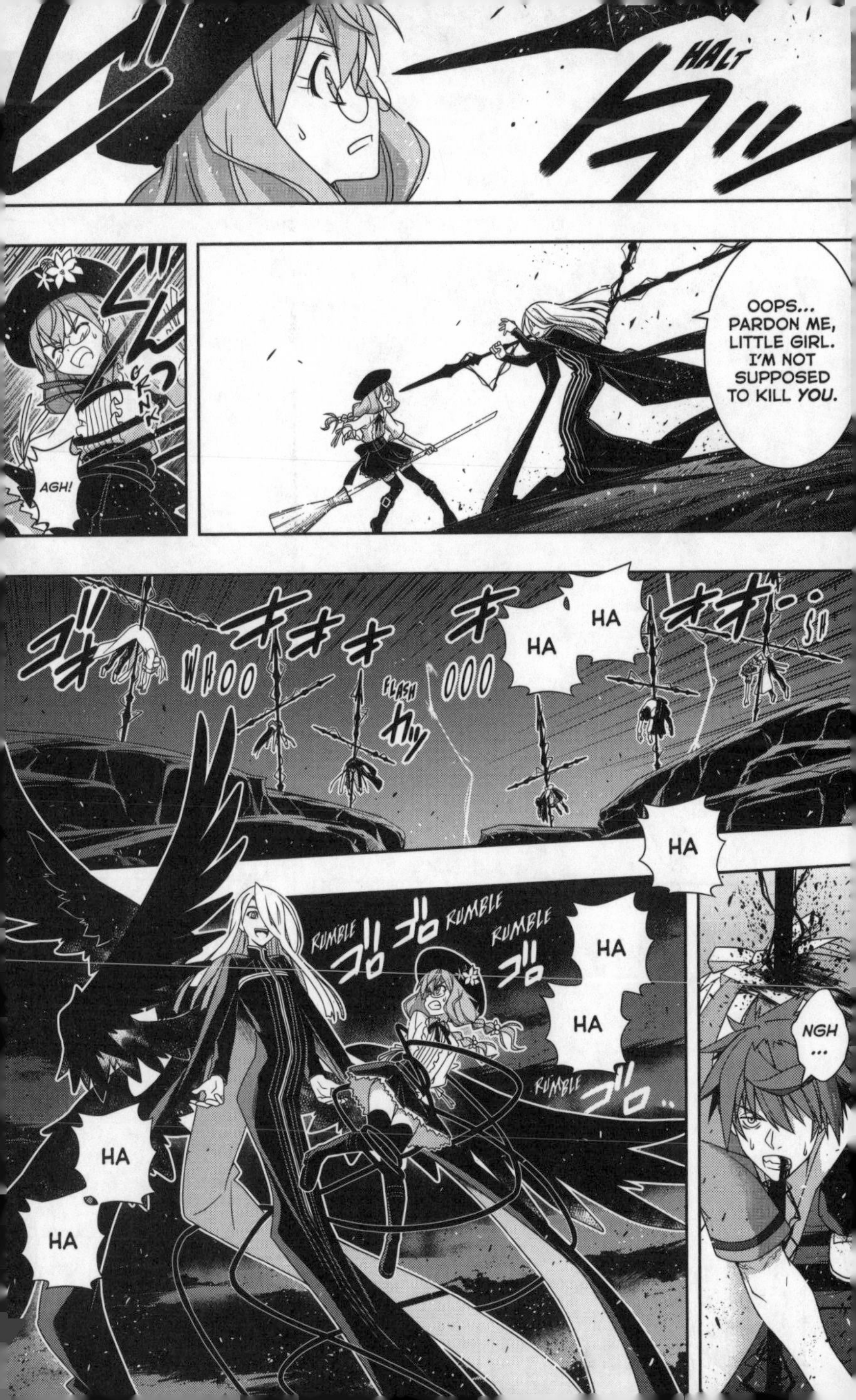
HALT
OOPS... PARDON ME, LITTLE GIRL. I'M NOT SUPPOSED TO KILL *YOU*.
GRNK
AGH!
SU
HA
HA
OOO
FLASH
WHOO
HA
NGH ...
HA
HA
RUMBLE
RUMBLE
RUMBLE
RUMBLE
HA
HA

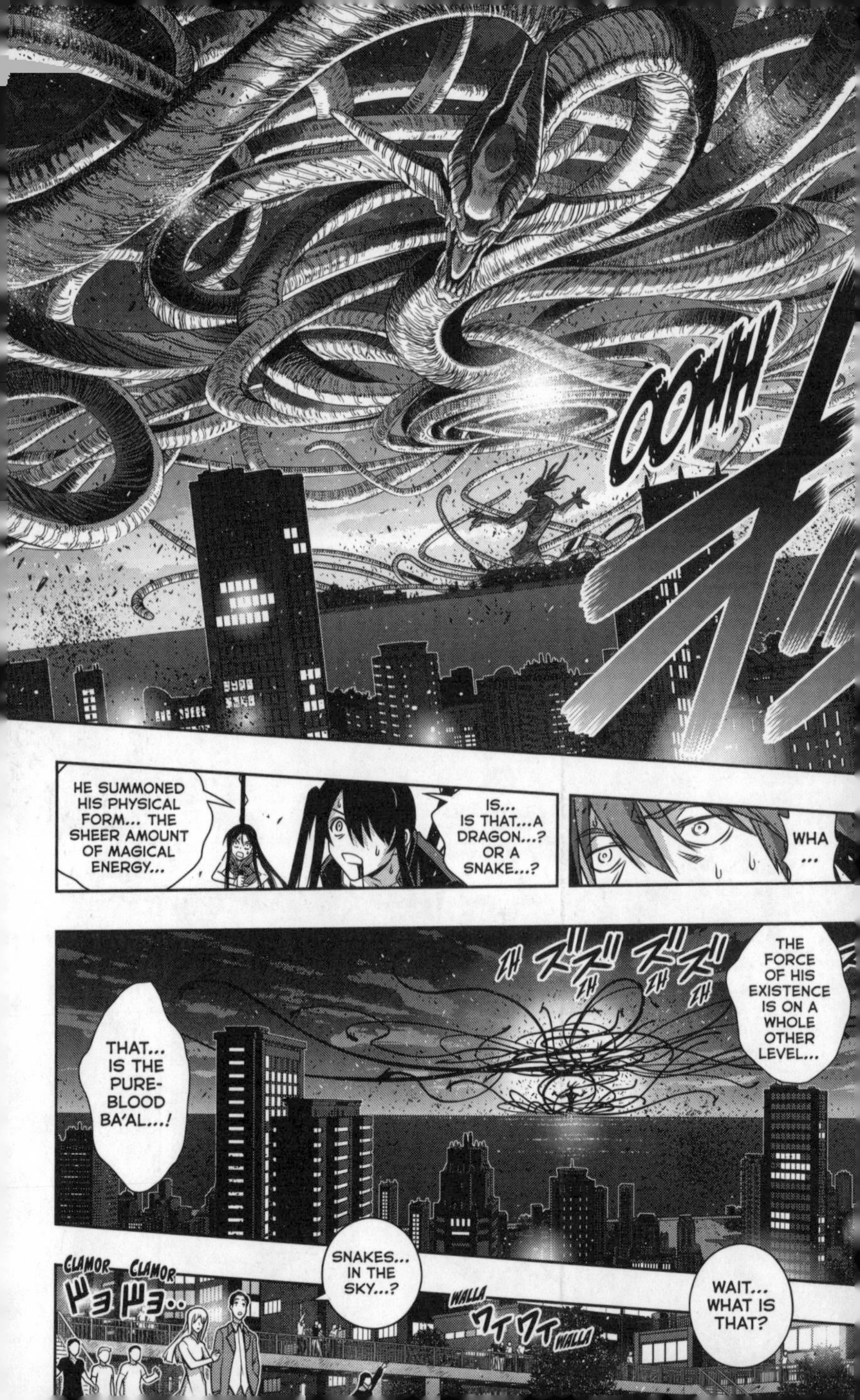
OOHH
WHA ...
IS... IS THAT...A DRAGON...? OR A SNAKE...?
HE SUMMONED HIS PHYSICAL FORM... THE SHEER AMOUNT OF MAGICAL ENERGY...
ZH ZH ZH ZH
THE FORCE OF HIS EXISTENCE IS ON A WHOLE OTHER LEVEL...
THAT... IS THE PURE-BLOOD BA'AL...!
WAIT... WHAT IS THAT?
WALLA ワイワイ WALLA
SNAKES... IN THE SKY...?
CLAMOR CLAMOR

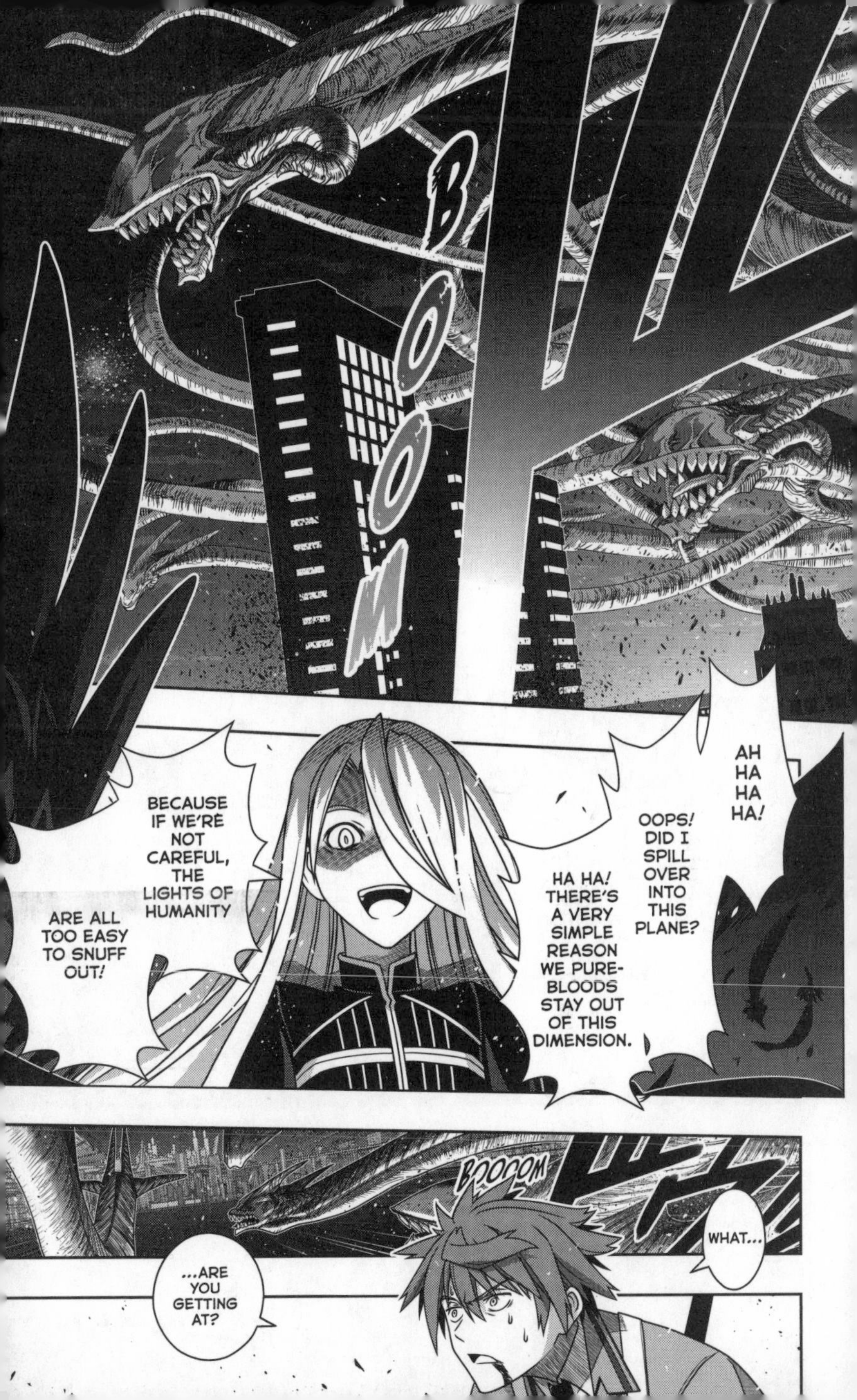
BOOOM
AH HA HA HA!
OOPS! DID I SPILL OVER INTO THIS PLANE?
HA HA! THERE'S A VERY SIMPLE REASON WE PURE-BLOODS STAY OUT OF THIS DIMENSION.
BECAUSE IF WE'RE NOT CAREFUL, THE LIGHTS OF HUMANITY
ARE ALL TOO EASY TO SNUFF OUT!
BOOOOM
WHAT...
...ARE YOU GETTING AT?

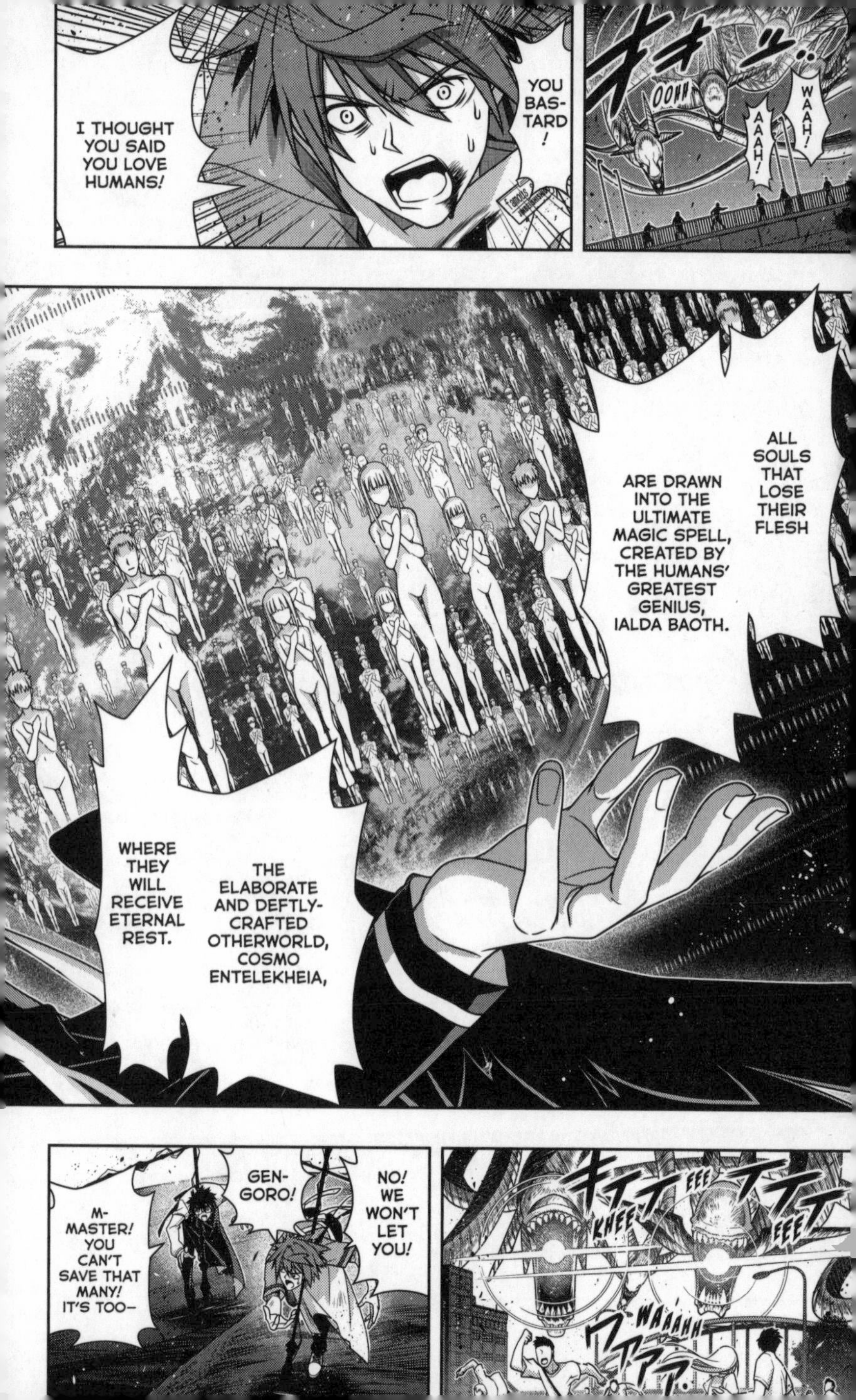
WAAAH!
AAAH!
OOHH
YOU BAS-TARD!
I THOUGHT YOU SAID YOU LOVE HUMANS!
ALL SOULS THAT LOSE THEIR FLESH
ARE DRAWN INTO THE ULTIMATE MAGIC SPELL, CREATED BY THE HUMANS' GREATEST GENIUS, IALDA BAOTH.
THE ELABORATE AND DEFTLY-CRAFTED OTHERWORLD, COSMO ENTELEKHEIA,
WHERE THEY WILL RECEIVE ETERNAL REST.
EEE
KHEE
EEE
WAAAHH
NO! WE WON'T LET YOU!
GEN-GORO!
M-MASTER! YOU CAN'T SAVE THAT MANY! IT'S TOO—

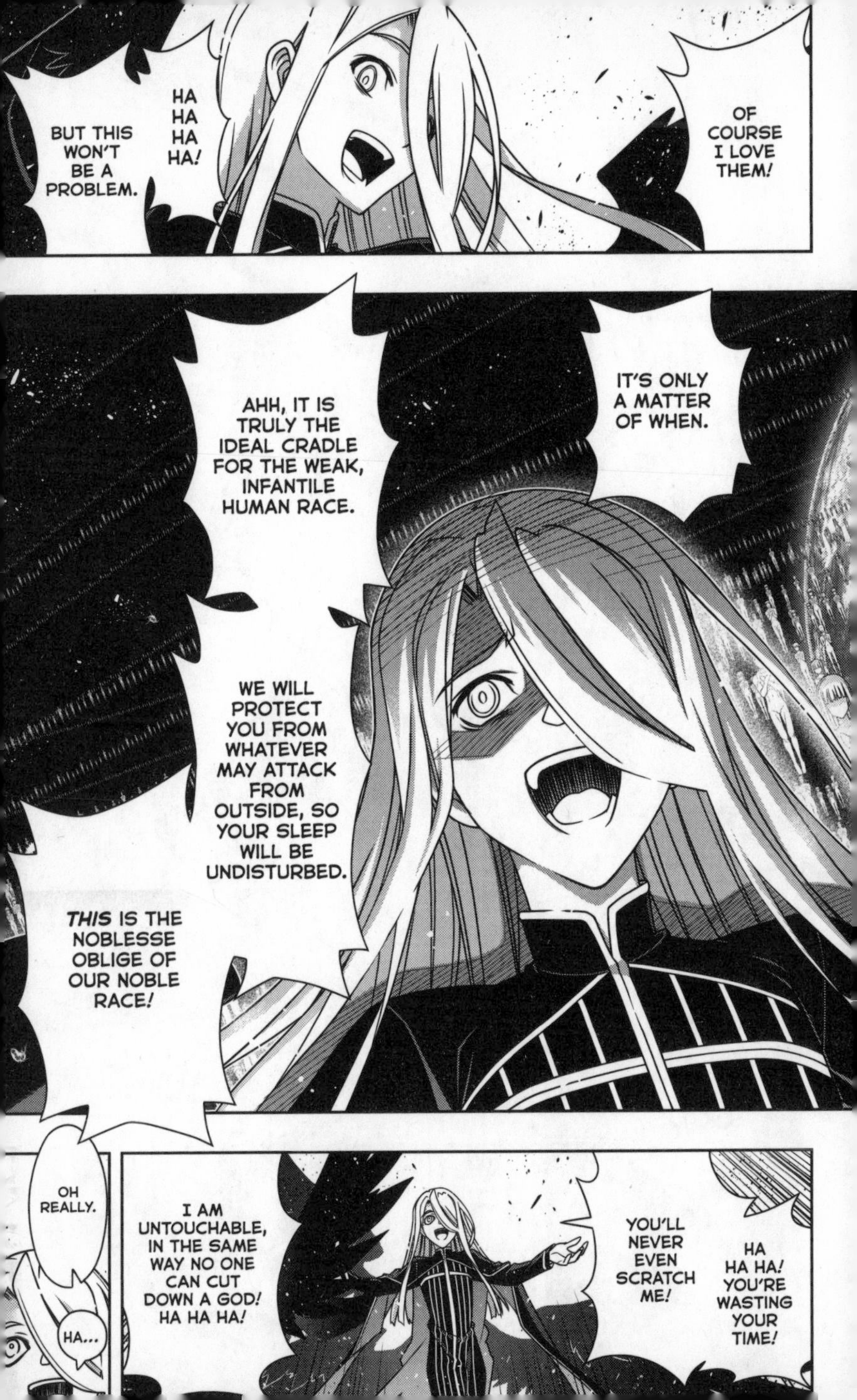
OF COURSE I LOVE THEM!
HA HA HA HA!
BUT THIS WON'T BE A PROBLEM.
IT'S ONLY A MATTER OF WHEN.
AHH, IT IS TRULY THE IDEAL CRADLE FOR THE WEAK, INFANTILE HUMAN RACE.
WE WILL PROTECT YOU FROM WHATEVER MAY ATTACK FROM OUTSIDE, SO YOUR SLEEP WILL BE UNDISTURBED.
THIS IS THE NOBLESSE OBLIGE OF OUR NOBLE RACE!
HA HA HA! YOU'RE WASTING YOUR TIME!
YOU'LL NEVER EVEN SCRATCH ME!
I AM UNTOUCHABLE, IN THE SAME WAY NO ONE CAN CUT DOWN A GOD! HA HA HA!
OH REALLY.
HA...

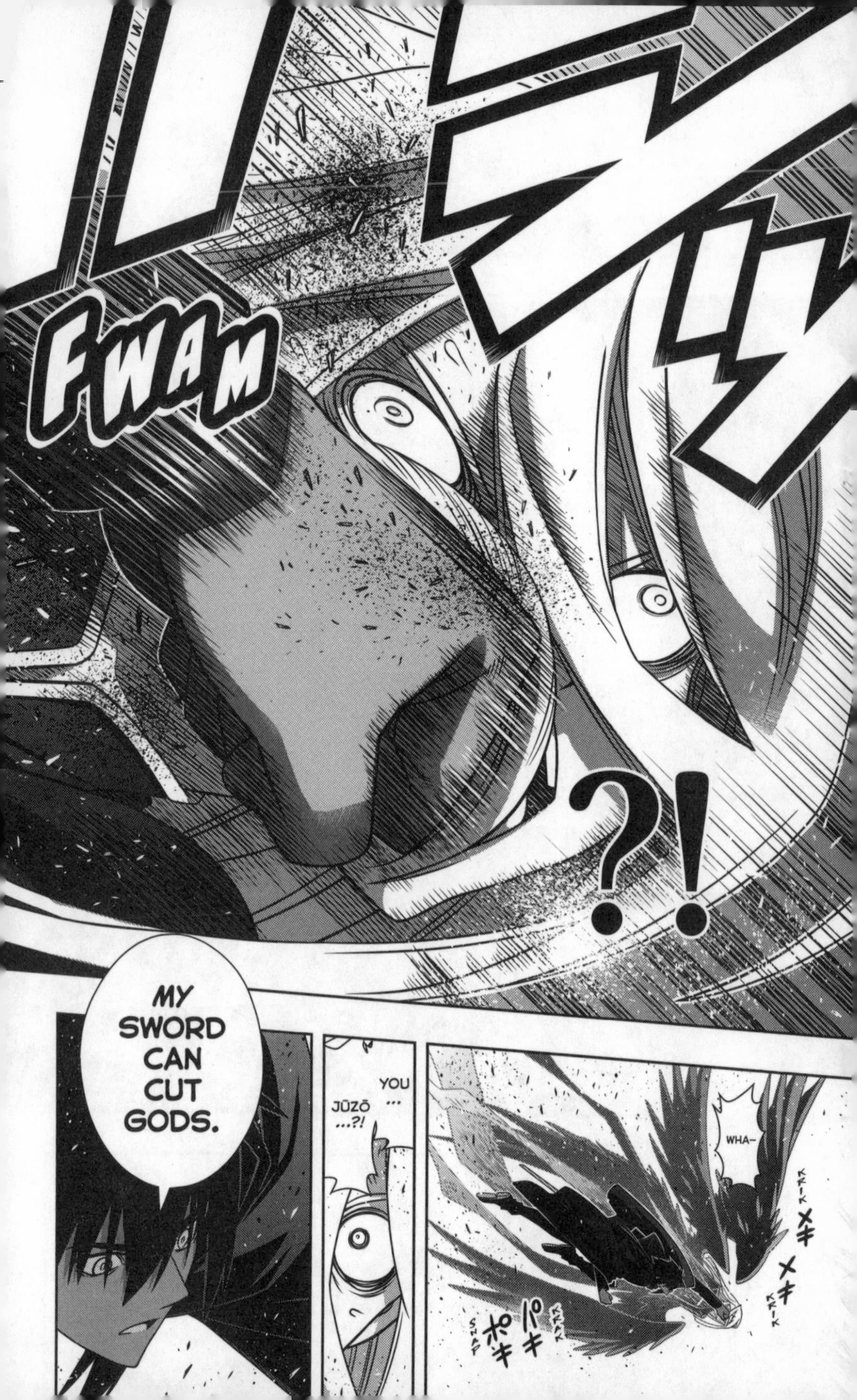
FWAM
?!
WHA—
KRIK
メキ
メキ
KRIK
KRAK
パキ
SNAP
ポキ
YOU ...
JŪZŌ ...?!
MY SWORD CAN CUT GODS.

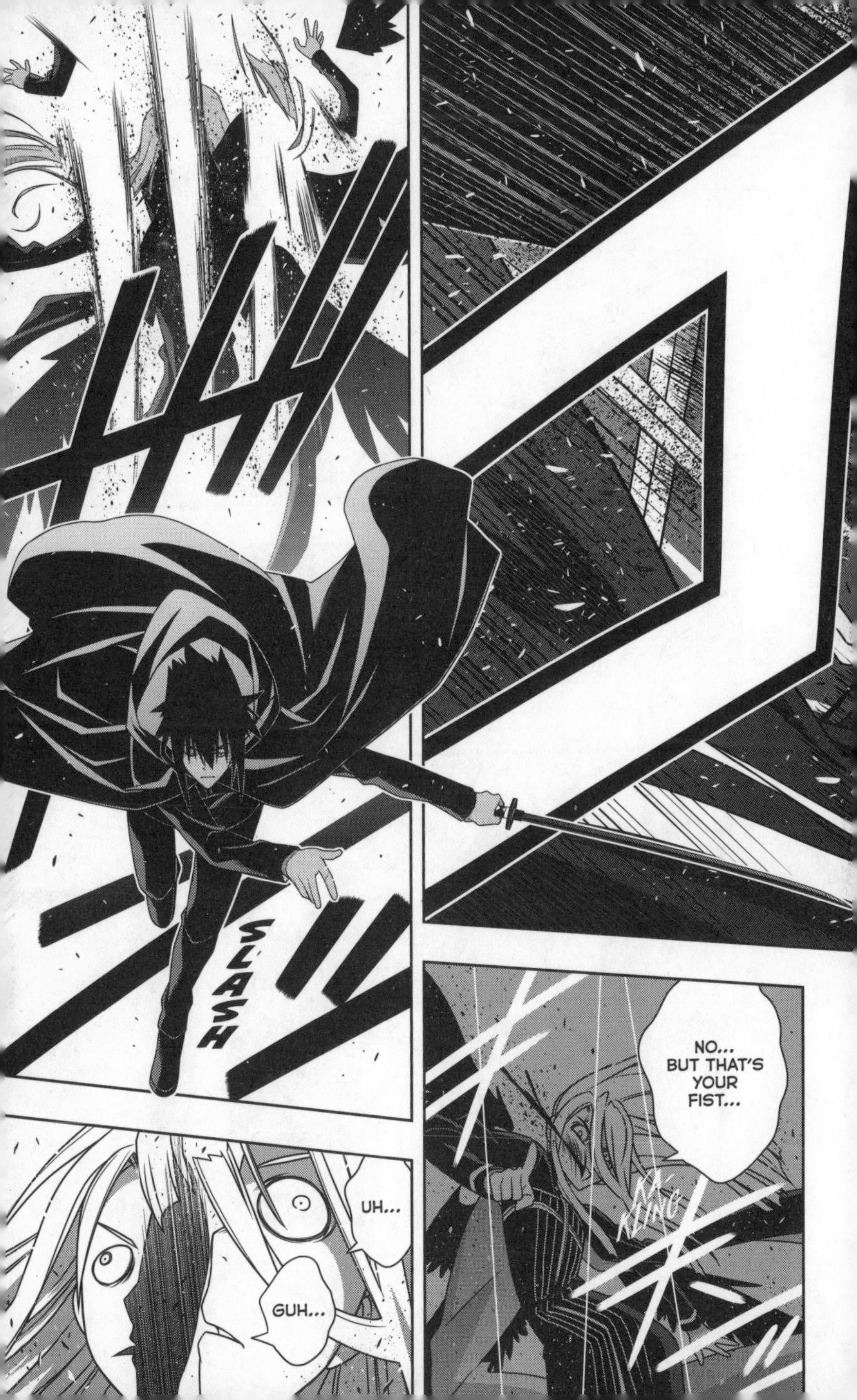
SLASH
NO... BUT THAT'S YOUR FIST...
KA-KLING
UH...
GUH...

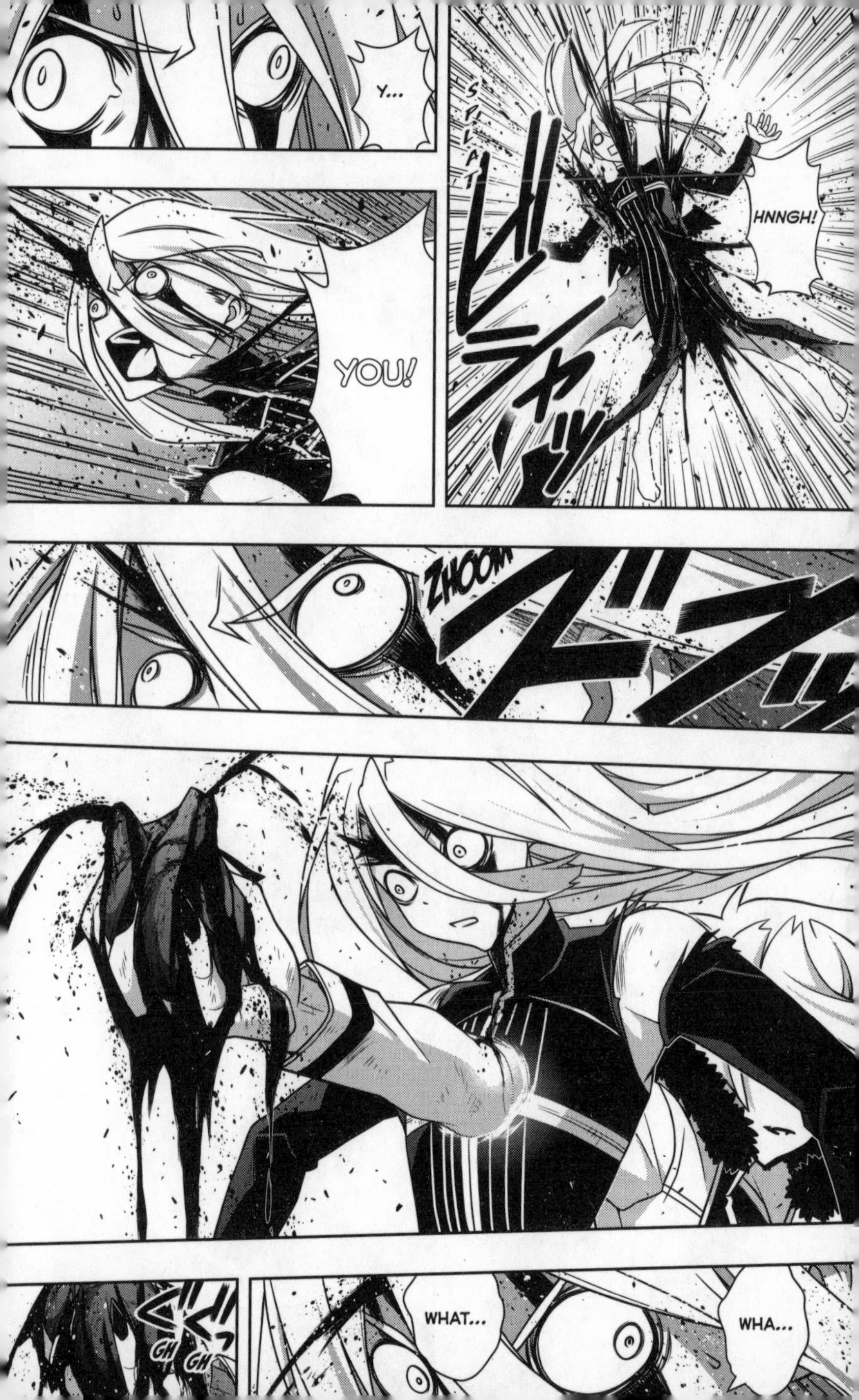
SPLAT
HNNGH!
Y...
YOU!
ZHOOM
WHA...
WHAT...
GH
GH

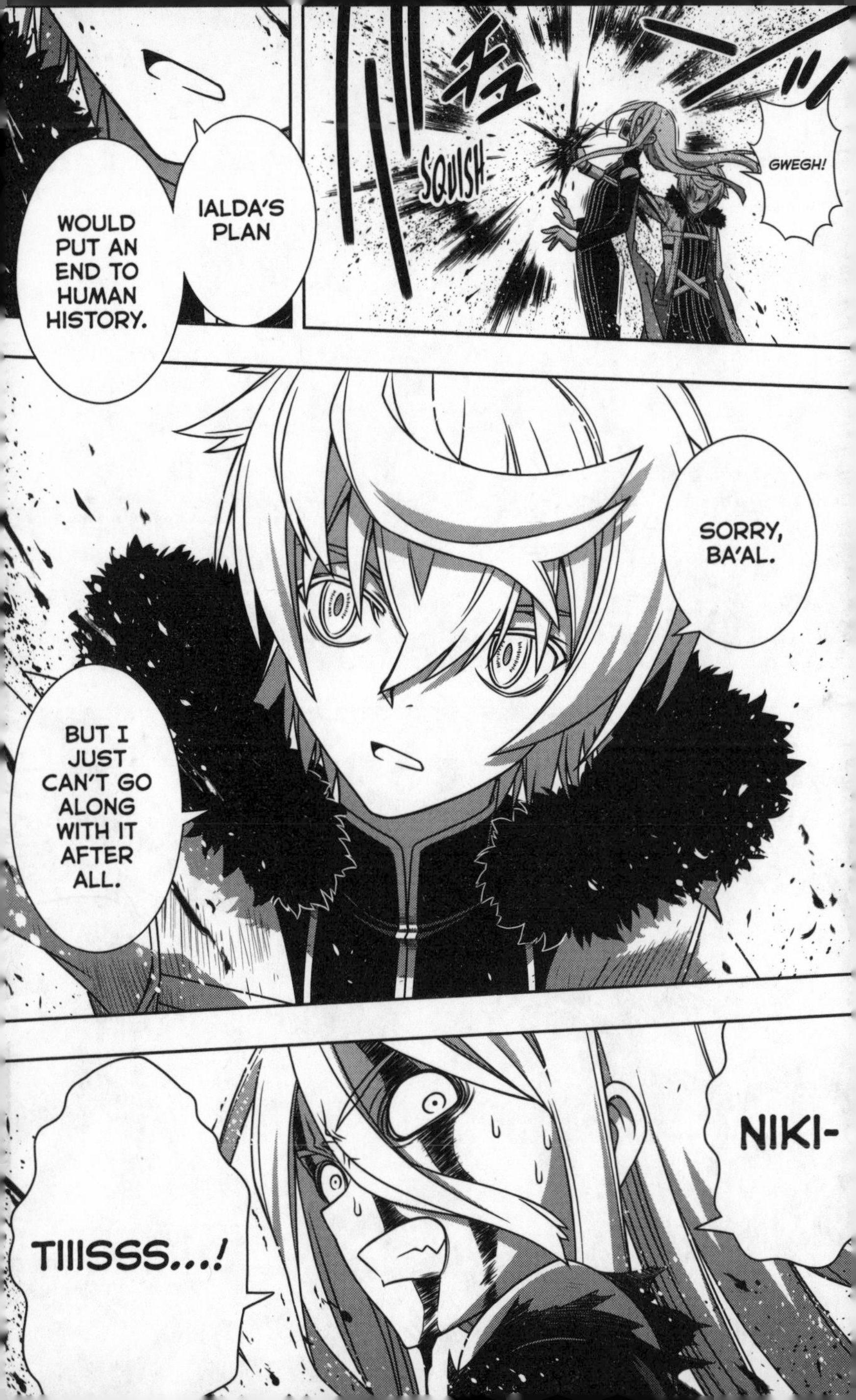
GWEGH!
SQUISH
IALDA'S PLAN
WOULD PUT AN END TO HUMAN HISTORY.
SORRY, BA'AL.
BUT I JUST CAN'T GO ALONG WITH IT AFTER ALL.
NIKI-
TIIISSS...!

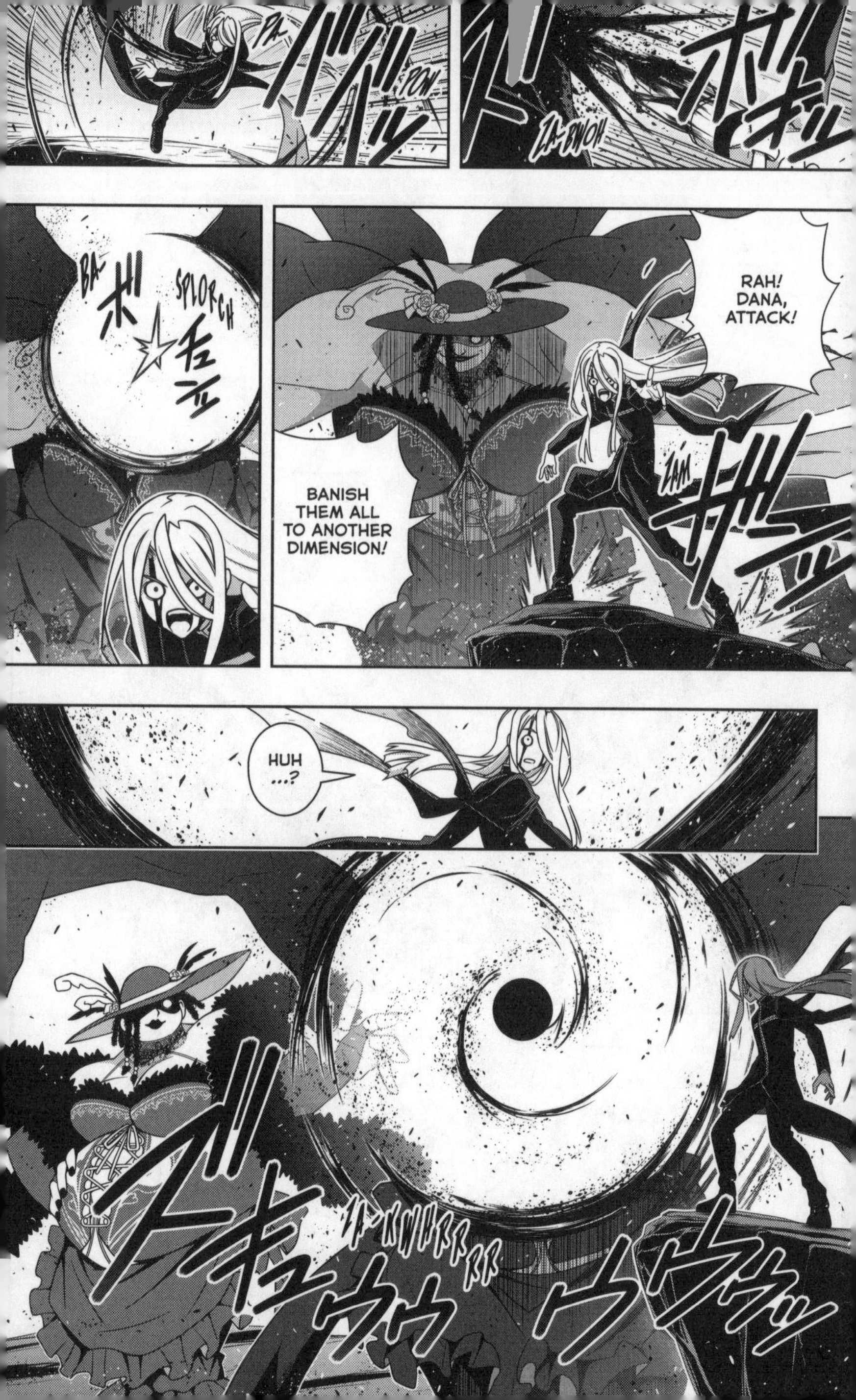
ZA-BWOH
PA
POW
RAH! DANA, ATTACK!
BANISH THEM ALL TO ANOTHER DIMENSION!
ZAM
BA
SPLORCH
HUH ...?
ZA-KWHRRRR

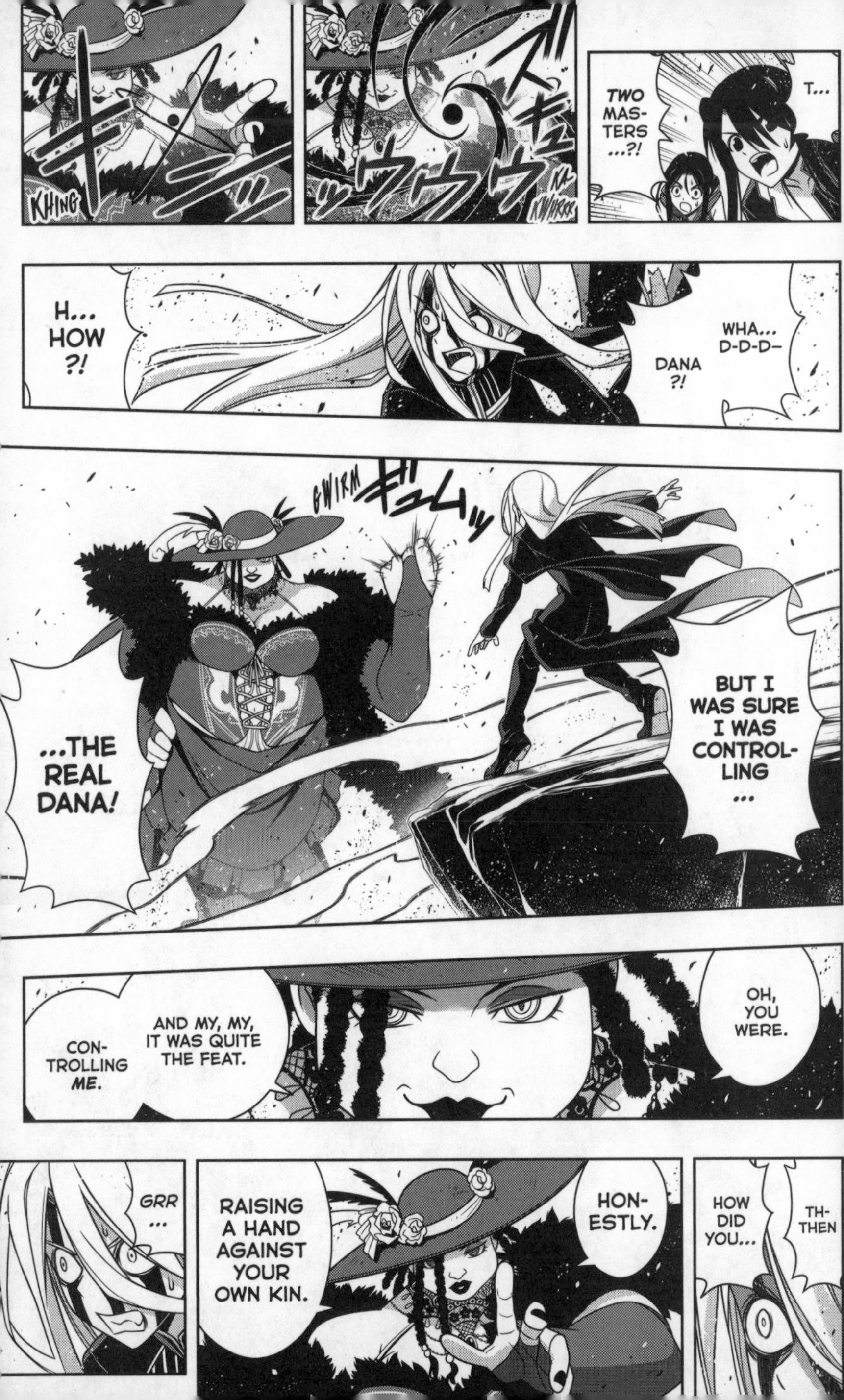
T...
TWO MASTERS...?!
KA KWHIRRR
KHING
WHA... D-D-D-
DANA ?!
H... HOW ?!
GWIRM
BUT I WAS SURE I WAS CONTROLLING ...
...THE REAL DANA!
OH, YOU WERE.
AND MY, MY, IT WAS QUITE THE FEAT.
CONTROLLING *ME*.
TH-THEN
HOW DID YOU...
HONESTLY.
RAISING A HAND AGAINST YOUR OWN KIN.
GRR ...

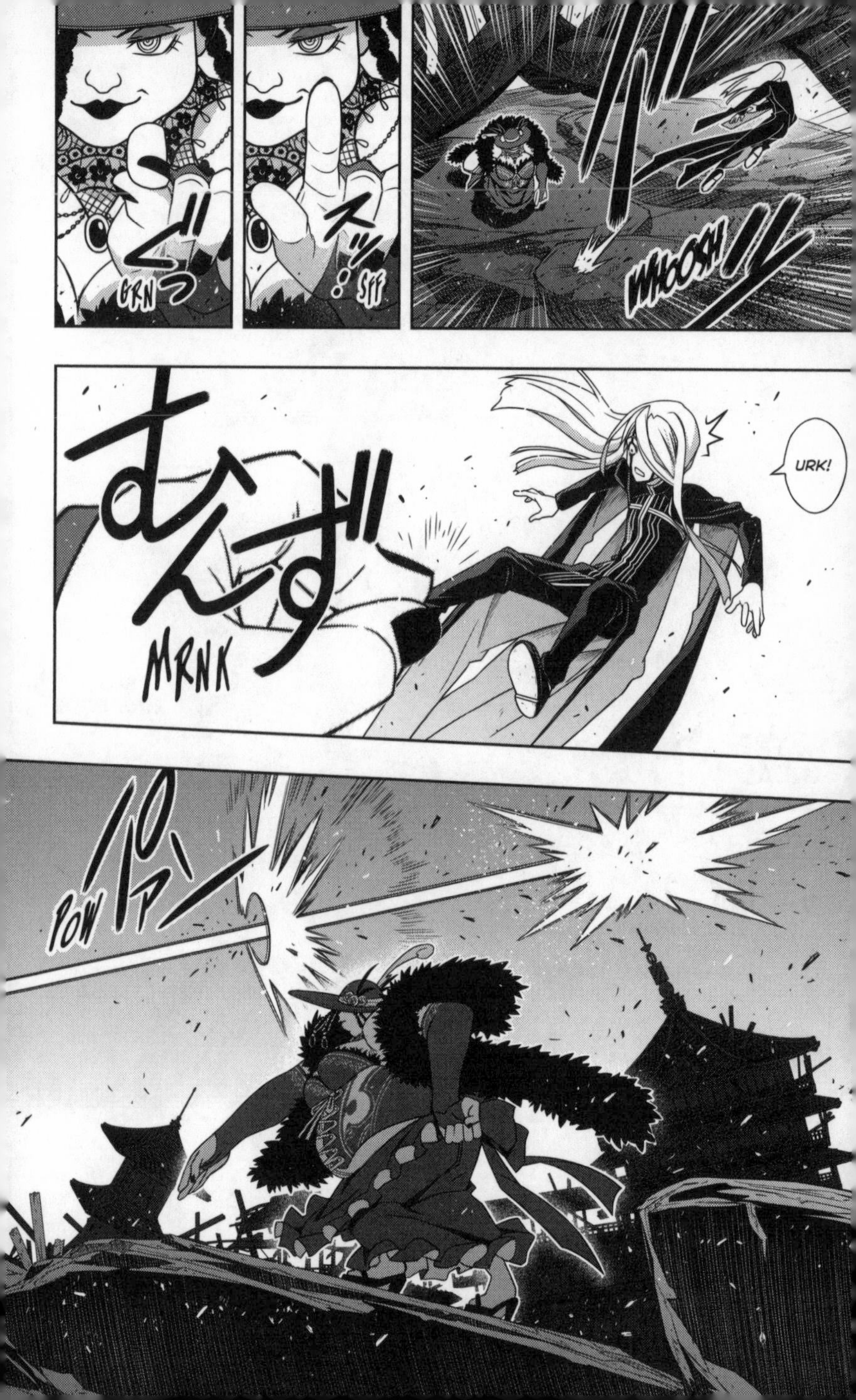
WHOOSH
スッ!
SFF
ぐっ
GRN
URK!
むんず
MRNK
POW

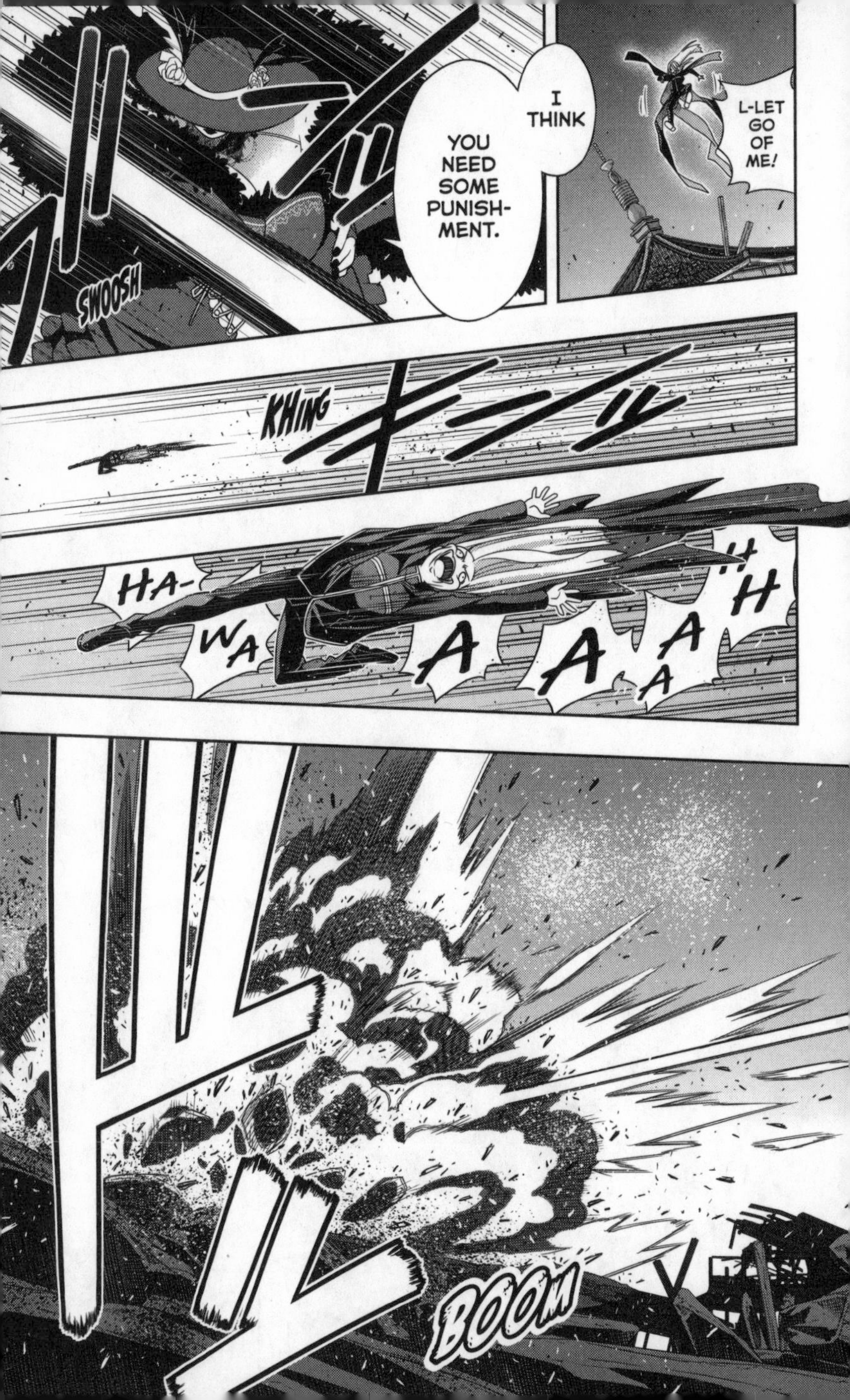

L-LET GO OF ME!
I THINK YOU NEED SOME PUNISHMENT.
SWOOSH
KHING
HA-WAAAAAAHH
BOOM

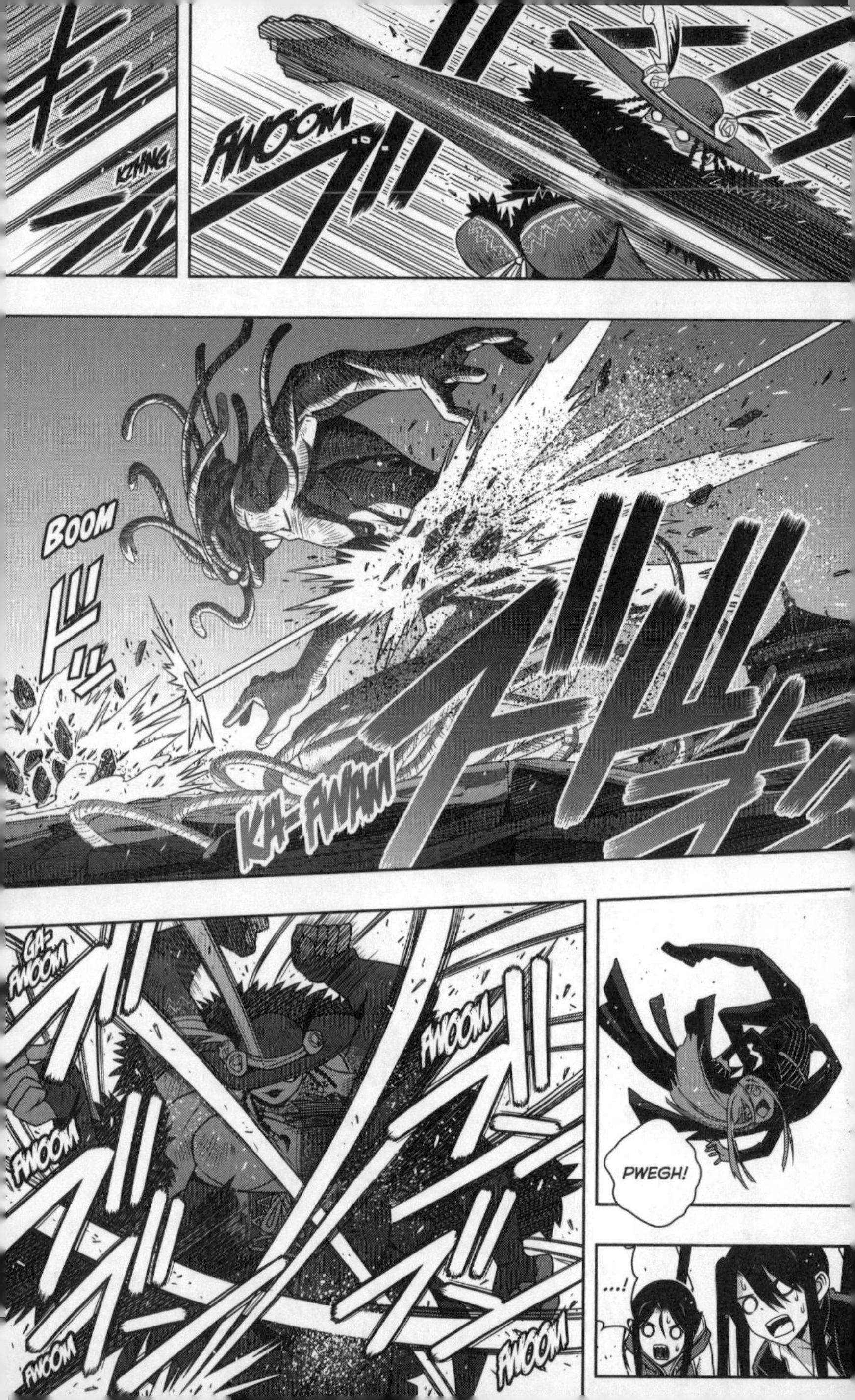
FWOOM
KZHNG
BOOM
KA-FWAM
PWEGH!
...!
FWOOM
GA-FWOOM
FWOOM
FWOOM
FWOOM

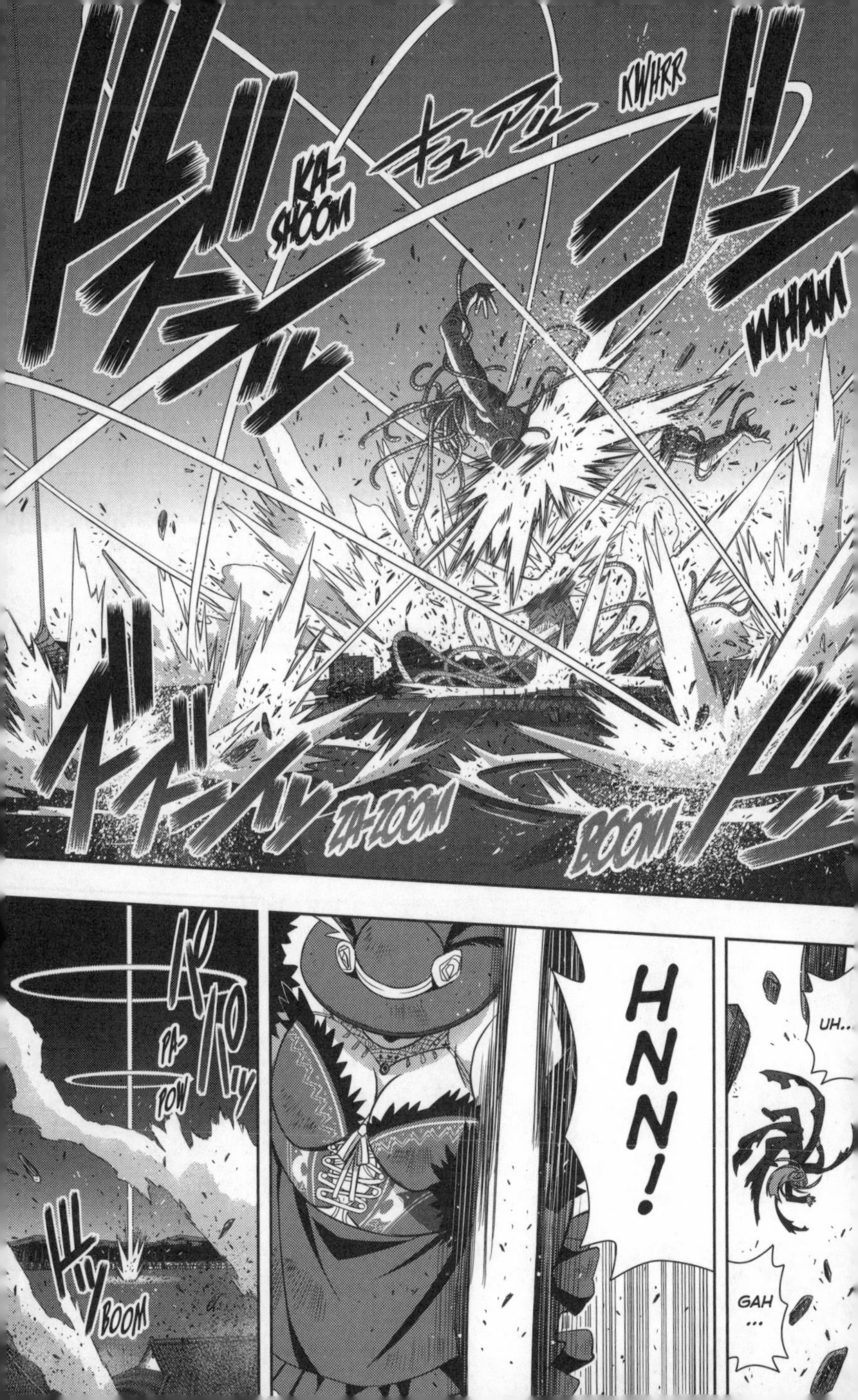
KWHRR
WHAM
KA-SHOOM
BOOM
ZA-ZOOM
UH...
GAH ...
HNN!
PA-POW
BOOM

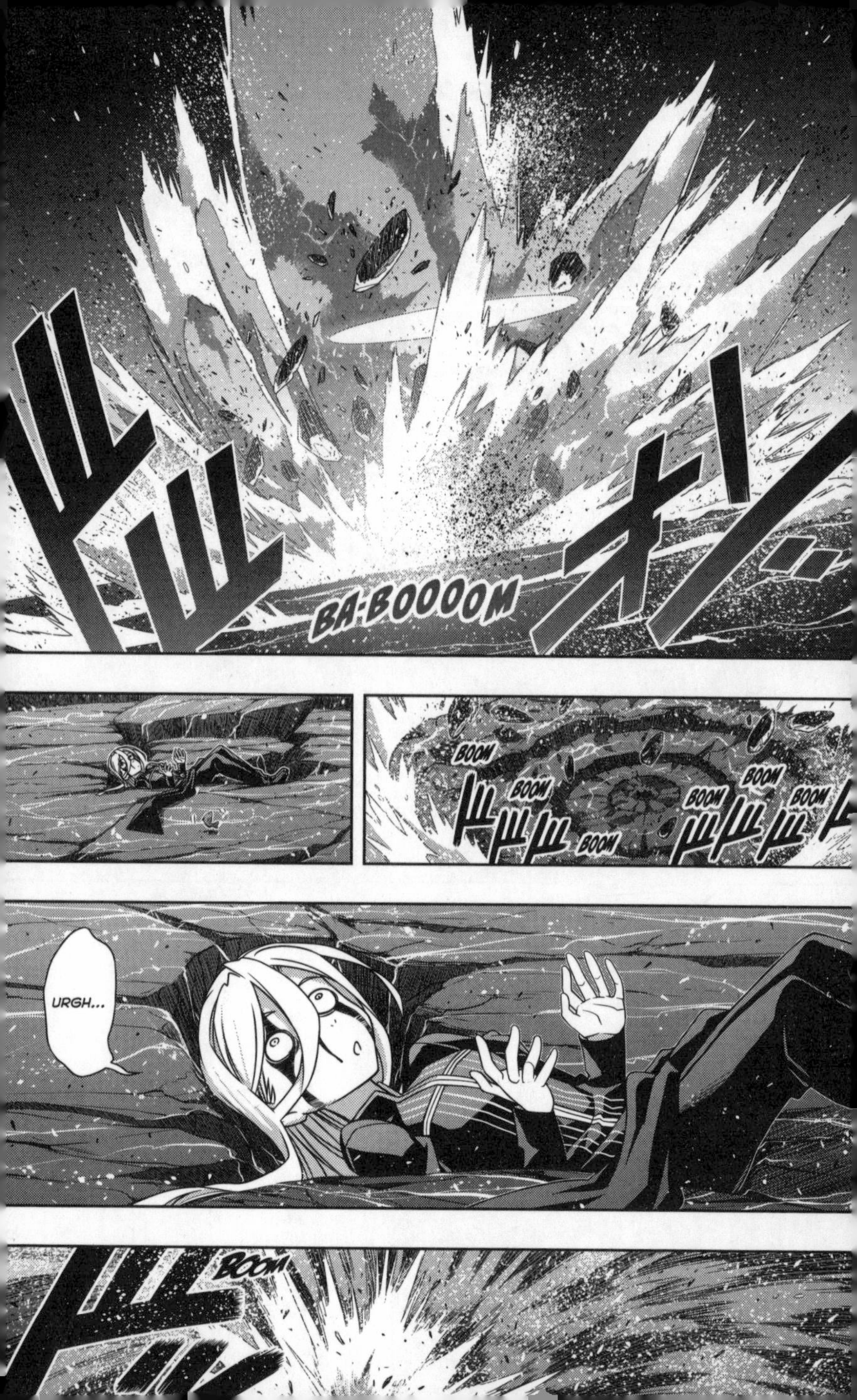
BA-BOOOOM
BOOM
BOOM
BOOM
BOOM
BOOM
BOOM
URGH...
BOOM

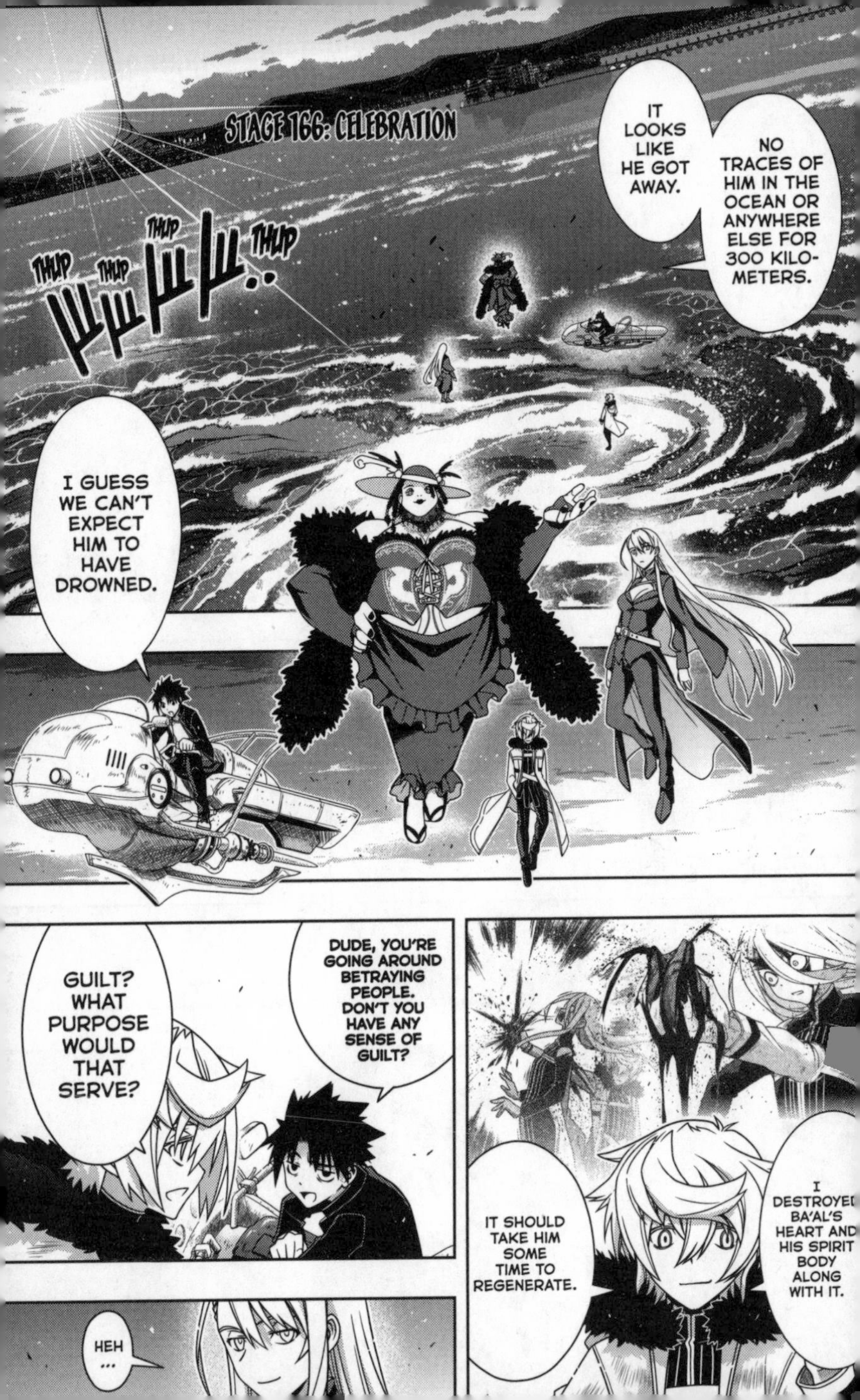
STAGE 166: CELEBRATION
THUP THUP THUP THUP
IT LOOKS LIKE HE GOT AWAY.
NO TRACES OF HIM IN THE OCEAN OR ANYWHERE ELSE FOR 300 KILO-METERS.
I GUESS WE CAN'T EXPECT HIM TO HAVE DROWNED.
I DESTROYE BA'AL'S HEART AND HIS SPIRIT BODY ALONG WITH IT.
IT SHOULD TAKE HIM SOME TIME TO REGENERATE.
DUDE, YOU'RE GOING AROUND BETRAYING PEOPLE. DON'T YOU HAVE ANY SENSE OF GUILT?
GUILT? WHAT PURPOSE WOULD THAT SERVE?
HEH ...

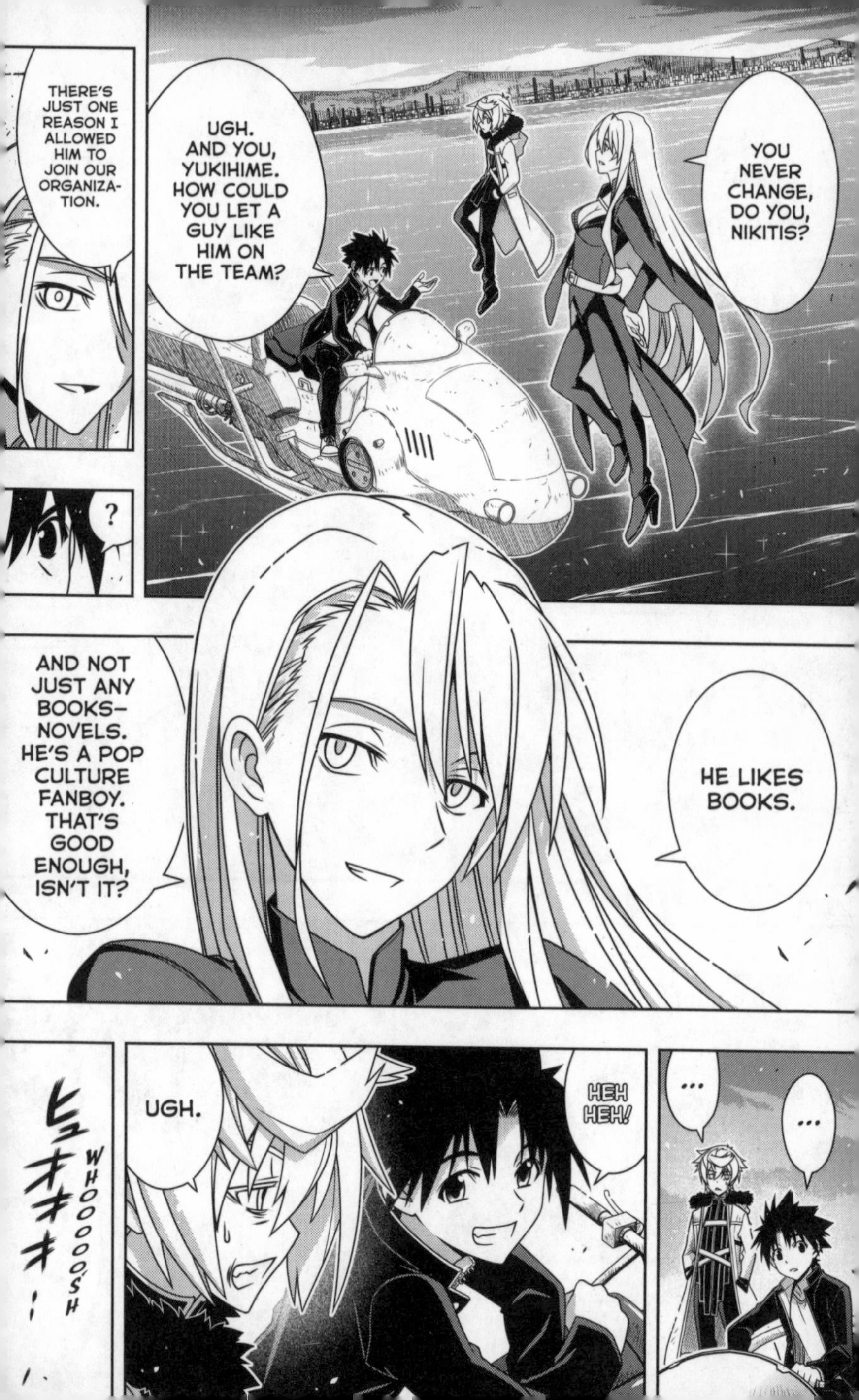
YOU NEVER CHANGE, DO YOU, NIKITIS?
UGH. AND YOU, YUKIHIME. HOW COULD YOU LET A GUY LIKE HIM ON THE TEAM?
THERE'S JUST ONE REASON I ALLOWED HIM TO JOIN OUR ORGANIZATION.
?
HE LIKES BOOKS.
AND NOT JUST ANY BOOKS—NOVELS. HE'S A POP CULTURE FANBOY. THAT'S GOOD ENOUGH, ISN'T IT?
...
...
HEH HEH!
UGH.
ヒュオオオ!!
WHOOOOOOSH

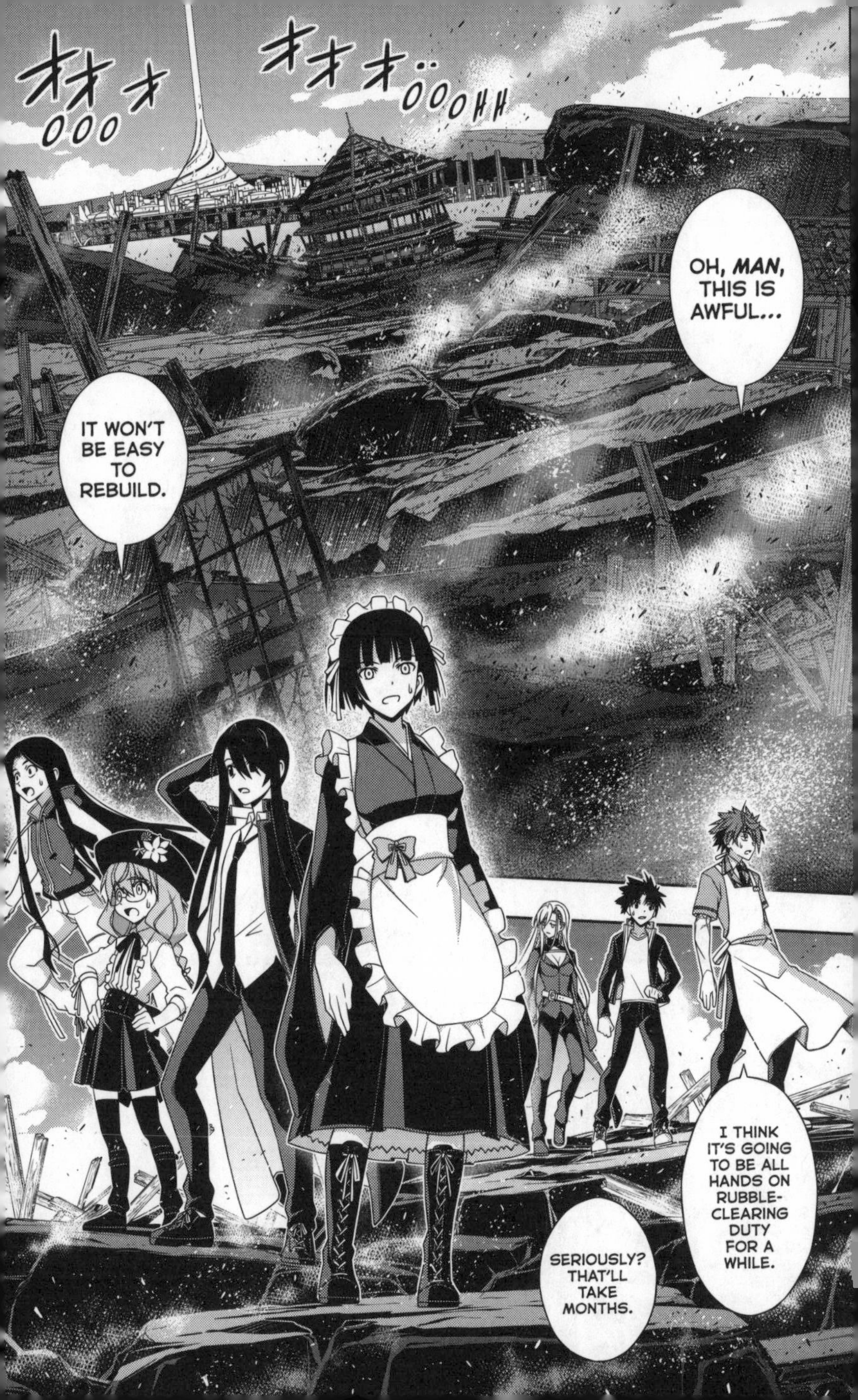
オオオ‥
OOOHH
オオオ
OOO
OH, *MAN*, THIS IS AWFUL...
IT WON'T BE EASY TO REBUILD.
I THINK IT'S GOING TO BE ALL HANDS ON RUBBLE-CLEARING DUTY FOR A WHILE.
SERIOUSLY? THAT'LL TAKE MONTHS.

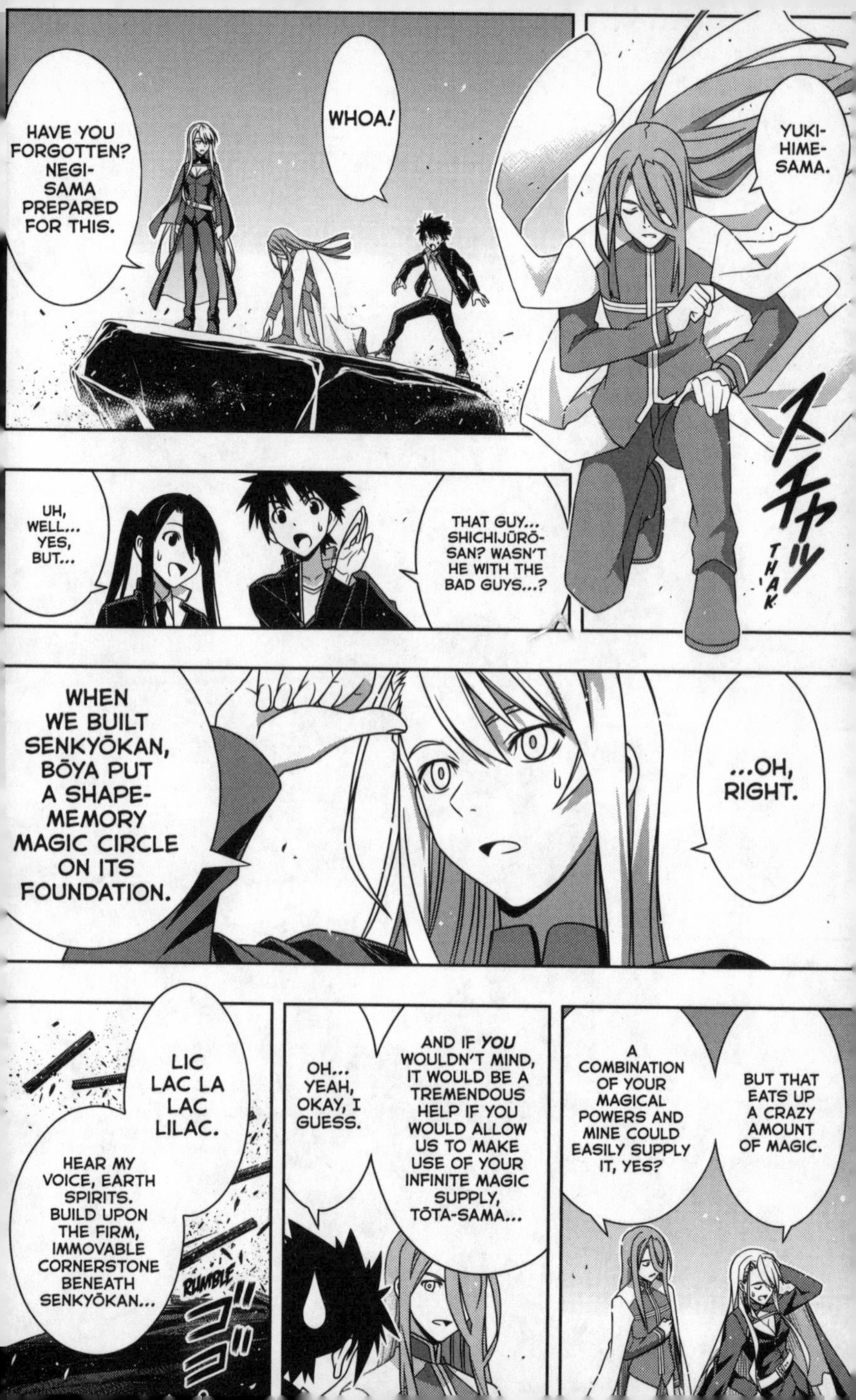
YUKI-HIME-SAMA.
THAK
WHOA!
HAVE YOU FORGOTTEN? NEGI-SAMA PREPARED FOR THIS.
THAT GUY... SHICHIJŪRŌ-SAN? WASN'T HE WITH THE BAD GUYS...?
UH, WELL... YES, BUT...
...OH, RIGHT.
WHEN WE BUILT SENKYŌKAN, BŌYA PUT A SHAPE-MEMORY MAGIC CIRCLE ON ITS FOUNDATION.
BUT THAT EATS UP A CRAZY AMOUNT OF MAGIC.
A COMBINATION OF YOUR MAGICAL POWERS AND MINE COULD EASILY SUPPLY IT, YES?
AND IF *YOU* WOULDN'T MIND, IT WOULD BE A TREMENDOUS HELP IF YOU WOULD ALLOW US TO MAKE USE OF YOUR INFINITE MAGIC SUPPLY, TŌTA-SAMA...
OH... YEAH, OKAY, I GUESS.
LIC LAC LA LAC LILAC.
HEAR MY VOICE, EARTH SPIRITS. BUILD UPON THE FIRM, IMMOVABLE CORNERSTONE BENEATH SENKYŌKAN...
RUMBLE

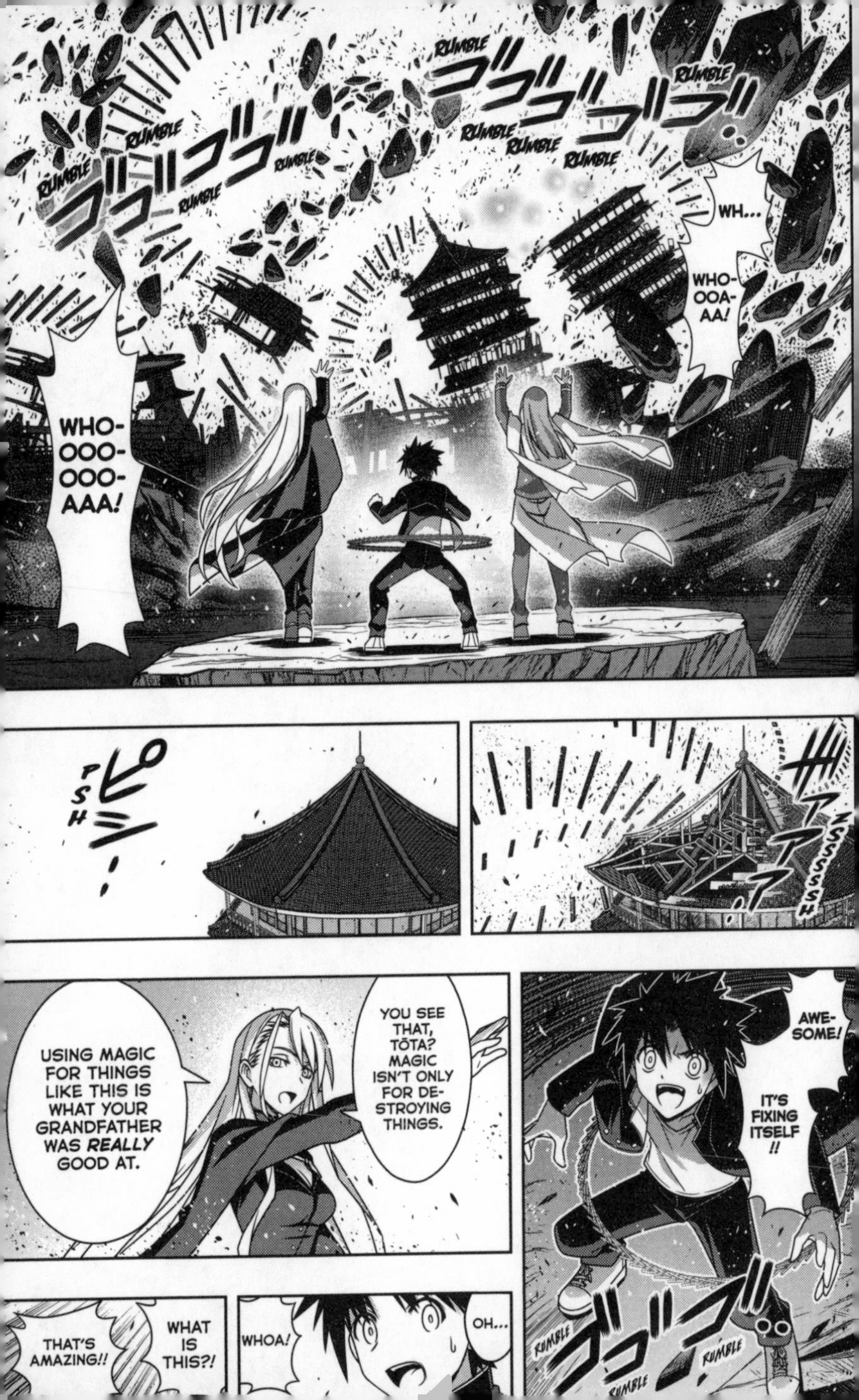
RUMBLE
RUMBLE
RUMBLE
RUMBLE
RUMBLE
RUMBLE
RUMBLE
RUMBLE
RUMBLE
WH...
WHO-OOA-AA!
WHO-OOO-OOO-AAA!
ZSSSSSSH
PSH
AWE-SOME!
IT'S FIXING ITSELF !!
RUMBLE
RUMBLE
RUMBLE
YOU SEE THAT, TŌTA? MAGIC ISN'T ONLY FOR DE-STROYING THINGS.
USING MAGIC FOR THINGS LIKE THIS IS WHAT YOUR GRANDFATHER WAS *REALLY* GOOD AT.
OH...
WHOA!
WHAT IS THIS?!
THAT'S AMAZING!!

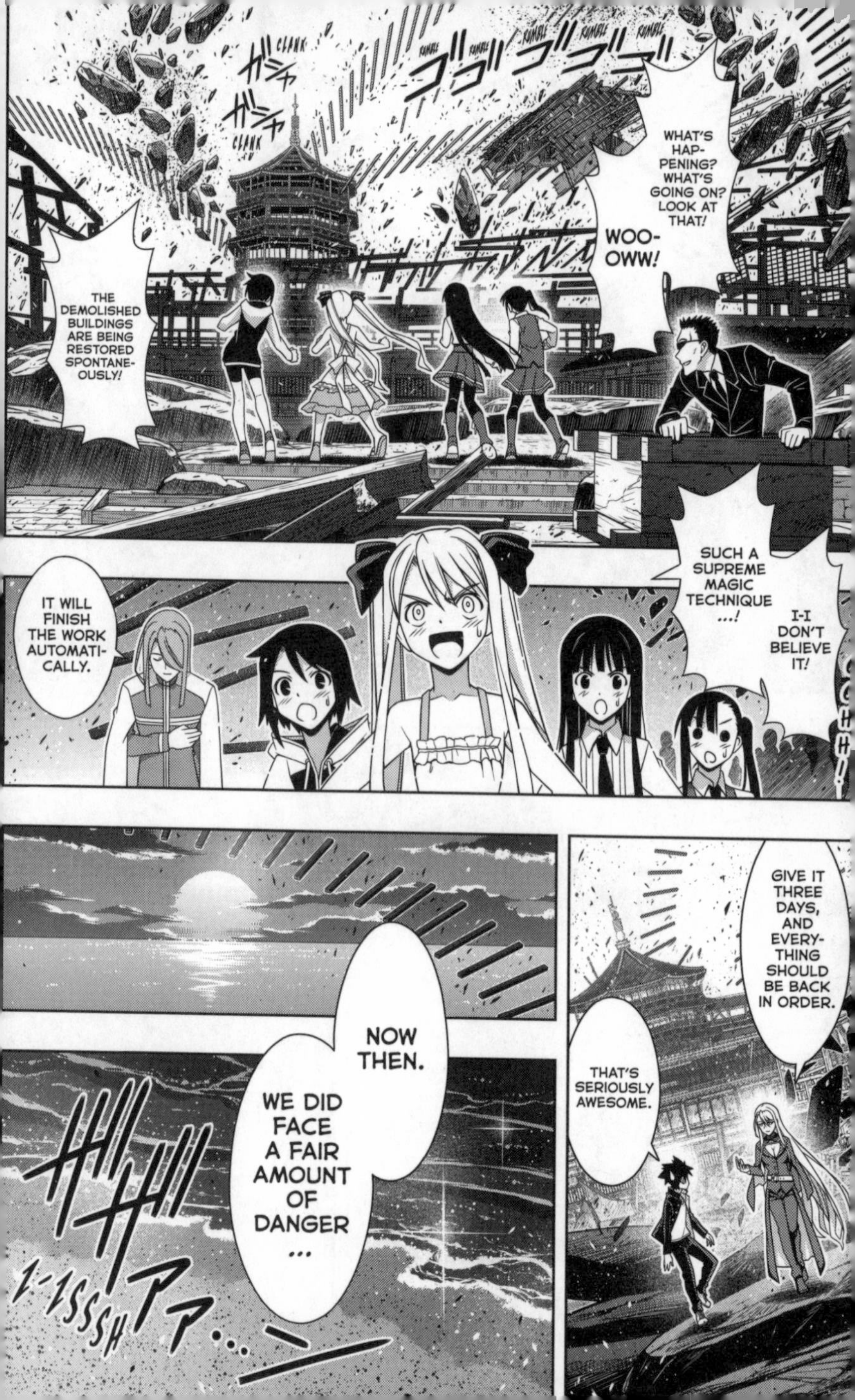
RUMBLE RUMBLE RUMBLE RUMBLE
CLANK CLANK
WHAT'S HAPPENING? WHAT'S GOING ON? LOOK AT THAT!
WOO-OWW!
THE DEMOLISHED BUILDINGS ARE BEING RESTORED SPONTANEOUSLY!
SUCH A SUPREME MAGIC TECHNIQUE ...!
I-I DON'T BELIEVE IT!
GGHH!
IT WILL FINISH THE WORK AUTOMATICALLY.
GIVE IT THREE DAYS, AND EVERYTHING SHOULD BE BACK IN ORDER.
THAT'S SERIOUSLY AWESOME.
NOW THEN.
WE DID FACE A FAIR AMOUNT OF DANGER ...
I-ISSSH

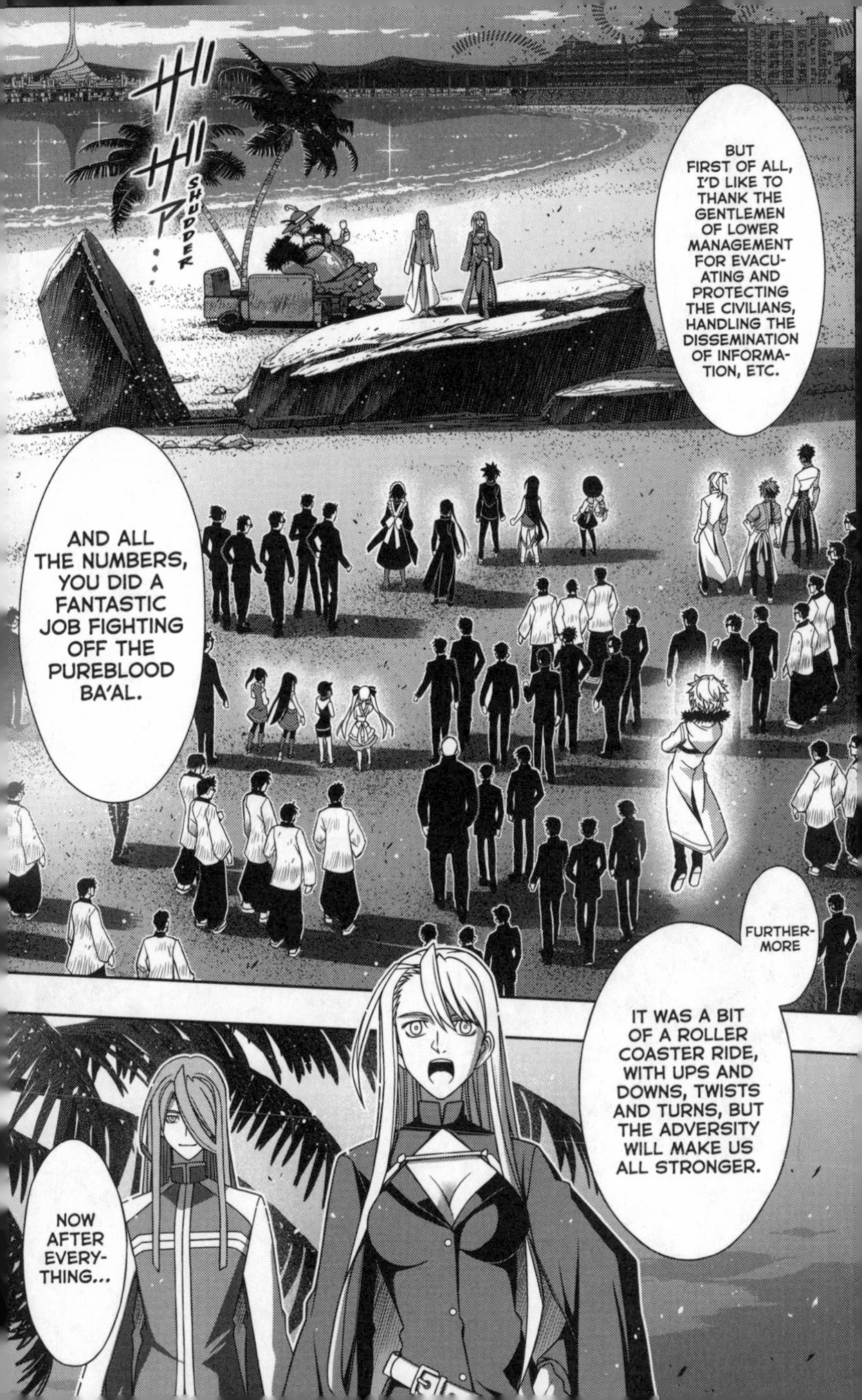
BUT FIRST OF ALL, I'D LIKE TO THANK THE GENTLEMEN OF LOWER MANAGEMENT FOR EVACU-ATING AND PROTECTING THE CIVILIANS, HANDLING THE DISSEMINATION OF INFORMA-TION, ETC.
SHUDDER...
AND ALL THE NUMBERS, YOU DID A FANTASTIC JOB FIGHTING OFF THE PUREBLOOD BA'AL.
FURTHER-MORE
IT WAS A BIT OF A ROLLER COASTER RIDE, WITH UPS AND DOWNS, TWISTS AND TURNS, BUT THE ADVERSITY WILL MAKE US ALL STRONGER.
NOW AFTER EVERY-THING...

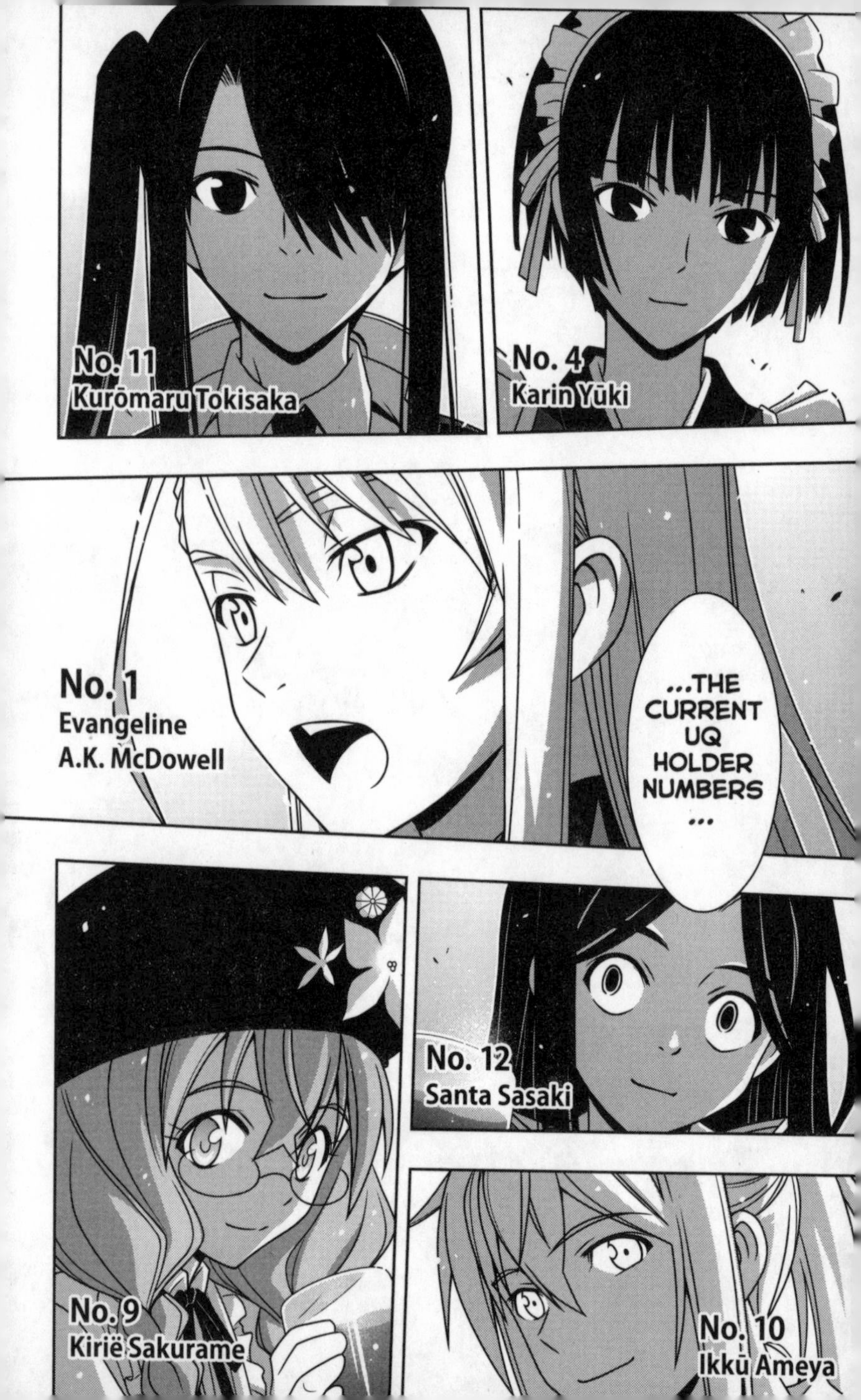
No. 4
Karin Yūki
No. 11
Kurōmaru Tokisaka
...THE CURRENT UQ HOLDER NUMBERS ...
No. 1
Evangeline A.K. McDowell
No. 12
Santa Sasaki
No. 10
Ikkū Ameya
No. 9
Kiriē Sakurame

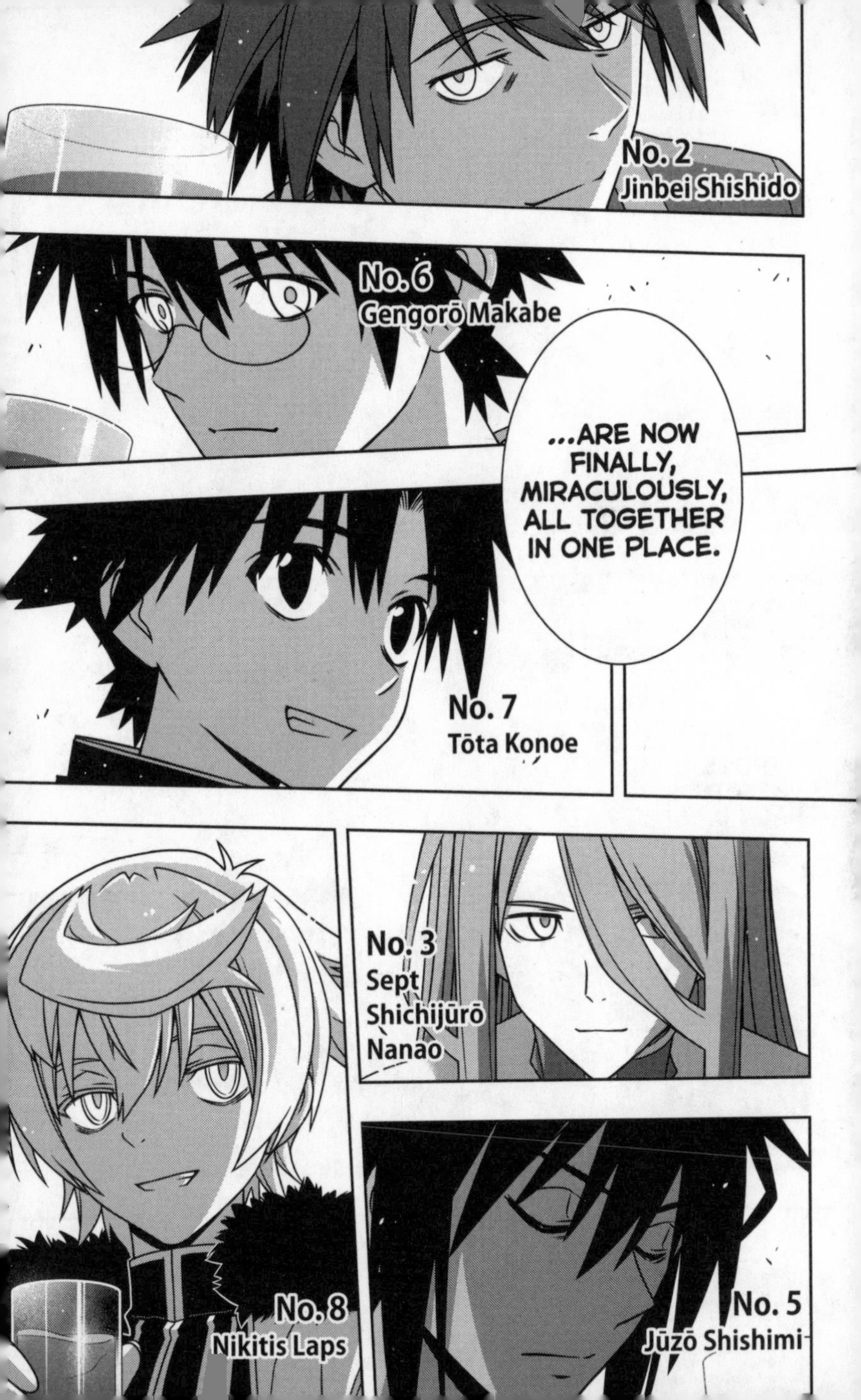
No. 2
Jinbei Shishido
No. 6
Gengorō Makabe
...ARE NOW FINALLY, MIRACULOUSLY, ALL TOGETHER IN ONE PLACE.
No. 7
Tōta Konoe
No. 3
Sept Shichijūrō Nanao
No. 5
Jūzō Shishimi
No. 8
Nikitis Laps

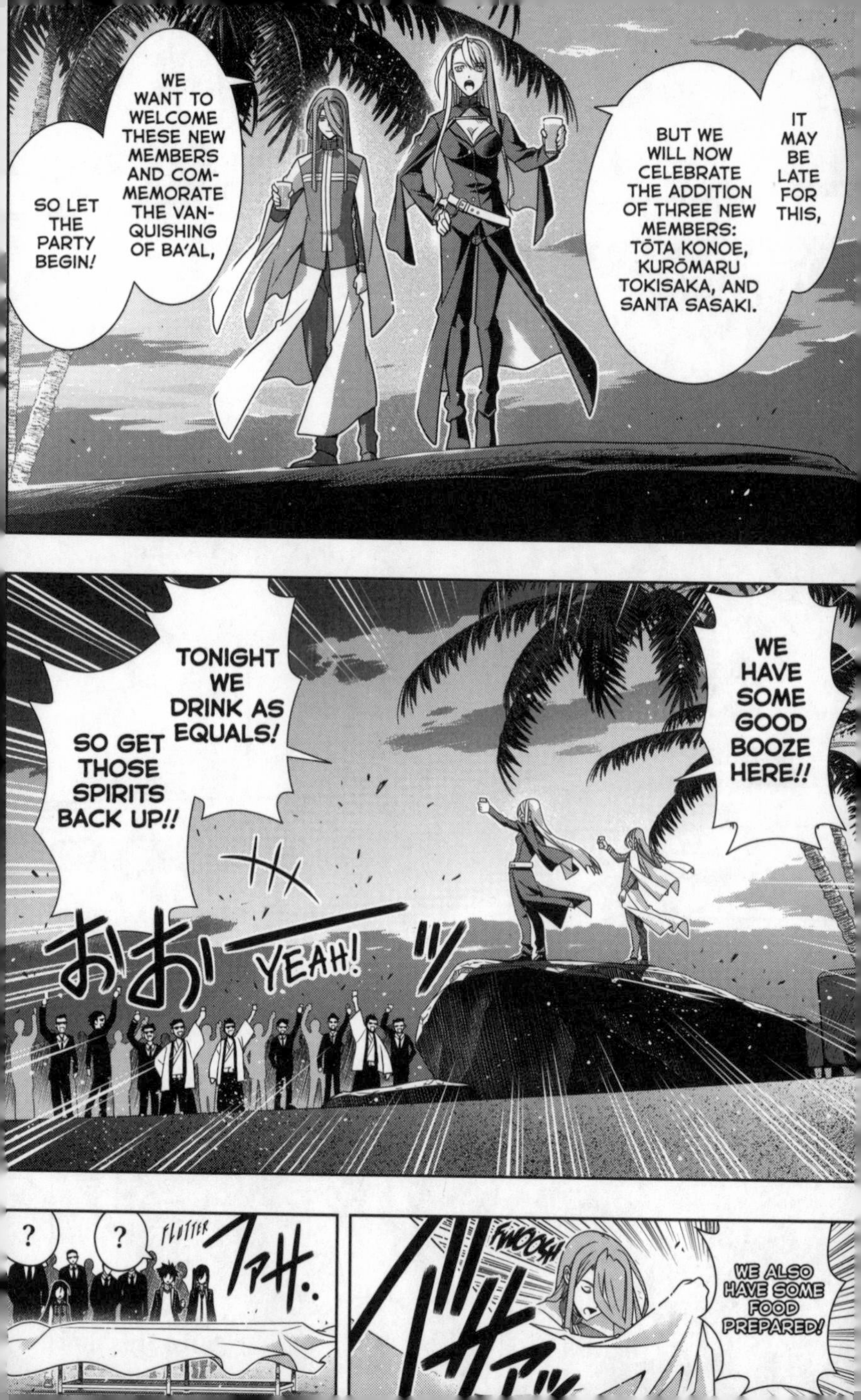
IT MAY BE LATE FOR THIS,
BUT WE WILL NOW CELEBRATE THE ADDITION OF THREE NEW MEMBERS: TŌTA KONOE, KURŌMARU TOKISAKA, AND SANTA SASAKI.
WE WANT TO WELCOME THESE NEW MEMBERS AND COMMEMORATE THE VANQUISHING OF BA'AL,
SO LET THE PARTY BEGIN!
WE HAVE SOME GOOD BOOZE HERE!!
TONIGHT WE DRINK AS EQUALS!
SO GET THOSE SPIRITS BACK UP!!
おおーーッ
YEAH!
FWOOSH
WE ALSO HAVE SOME FOOD PREPARED!
?
?
FLUTTER

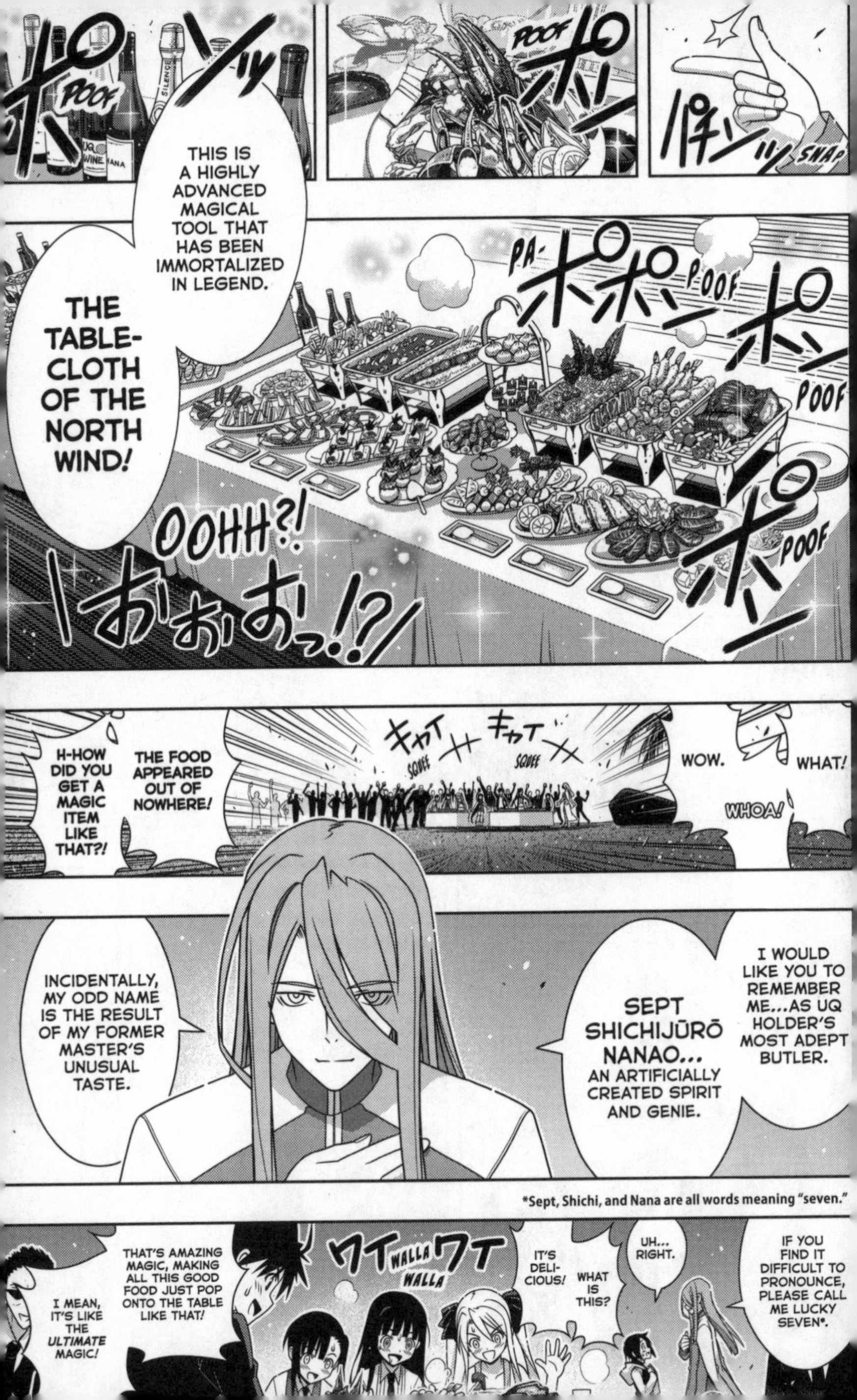
パチンッ SNAP
ポンッ POOF
ポンッ POOF
THIS IS A HIGHLY ADVANCED MAGICAL TOOL THAT HAS BEEN IMMORTALIZED IN LEGEND.
PA- ポポーン POOF
ポンッ POOF
ポッ POOF
THE TABLECLOTH OF THE NORTH WIND!
OOHH?! おぉおっ!?
WHAT!
WOW.
WHOA!
キャアキャア SQUEE SQUEE
THE FOOD APPEARED OUT OF NOWHERE!
H-HOW DID YOU GET A MAGIC ITEM LIKE THAT?!
I WOULD LIKE YOU TO REMEMBER ME...AS UQ HOLDER'S MOST ADEPT BUTLER.
SEPT SHICHIJŪRŌ NANAO... AN ARTIFICIALLY CREATED SPIRIT AND GENIE.
INCIDENTALLY, MY ODD NAME IS THE RESULT OF MY FORMER MASTER'S UNUSUAL TASTE.
*Sept, Shichi, and Nana are all words meaning "seven."
IF YOU FIND IT DIFFICULT TO PRONOUNCE, PLEASE CALL ME LUCKY SEVEN*.
UH... RIGHT.
WHAT IS THIS?
IT'S DELICIOUS!
ワイワイ WALLA WALLA
THAT'S AMAZING MAGIC, MAKING ALL THIS GOOD FOOD JUST POP ONTO THE TABLE LIKE THAT!
I MEAN, IT'S LIKE THE *ULTIMATE* MAGIC!

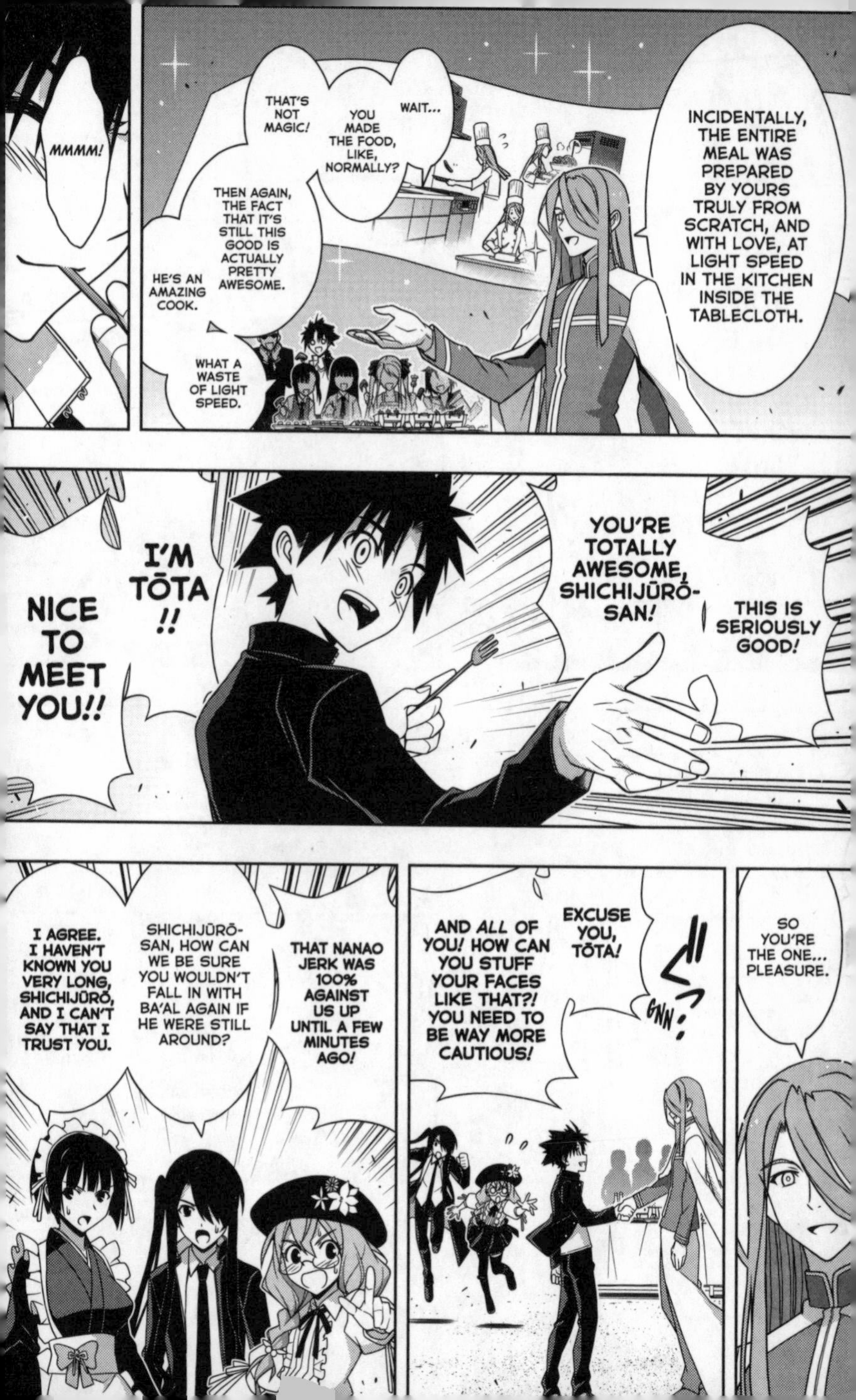
INCIDENTALLY, THE ENTIRE MEAL WAS PREPARED BY YOURS TRULY FROM SCRATCH, AND WITH LOVE, AT LIGHT SPEED IN THE KITCHEN INSIDE THE TABLECLOTH.
WAIT...
YOU MADE THE FOOD, LIKE, NORMALLY?
THAT'S NOT MAGIC!
THEN AGAIN, THE FACT THAT IT'S STILL THIS GOOD IS ACTUALLY PRETTY AWESOME.
HE'S AN AMAZING COOK.
WHAT A WASTE OF LIGHT SPEED.
MMMM!
THIS IS SERIOUSLY GOOD!
YOU'RE TOTALLY AWESOME, SHICHIJŪRŌ-SAN!
I'M TŌTA!!
NICE TO MEET YOU!!
SO YOU'RE THE ONE... PLEASURE.
EXCUSE YOU, TŌTA!
GNN
AND ALL OF YOU! HOW CAN YOU STUFF YOUR FACES LIKE THAT?! YOU NEED TO BE WAY MORE CAUTIOUS!
THAT NANAO JERK WAS 100% AGAINST US UP UNTIL A FEW MINUTES AGO!
SHICHIJŪRŌ-SAN, HOW CAN WE BE SURE YOU WOULDN'T FALL IN WITH BA'AL AGAIN IF HE WERE STILL AROUND?
I AGREE. I HAVEN'T KNOWN YOU VERY LONG, SHICHIJŪRŌ, AND I CAN'T SAY THAT I TRUST YOU.

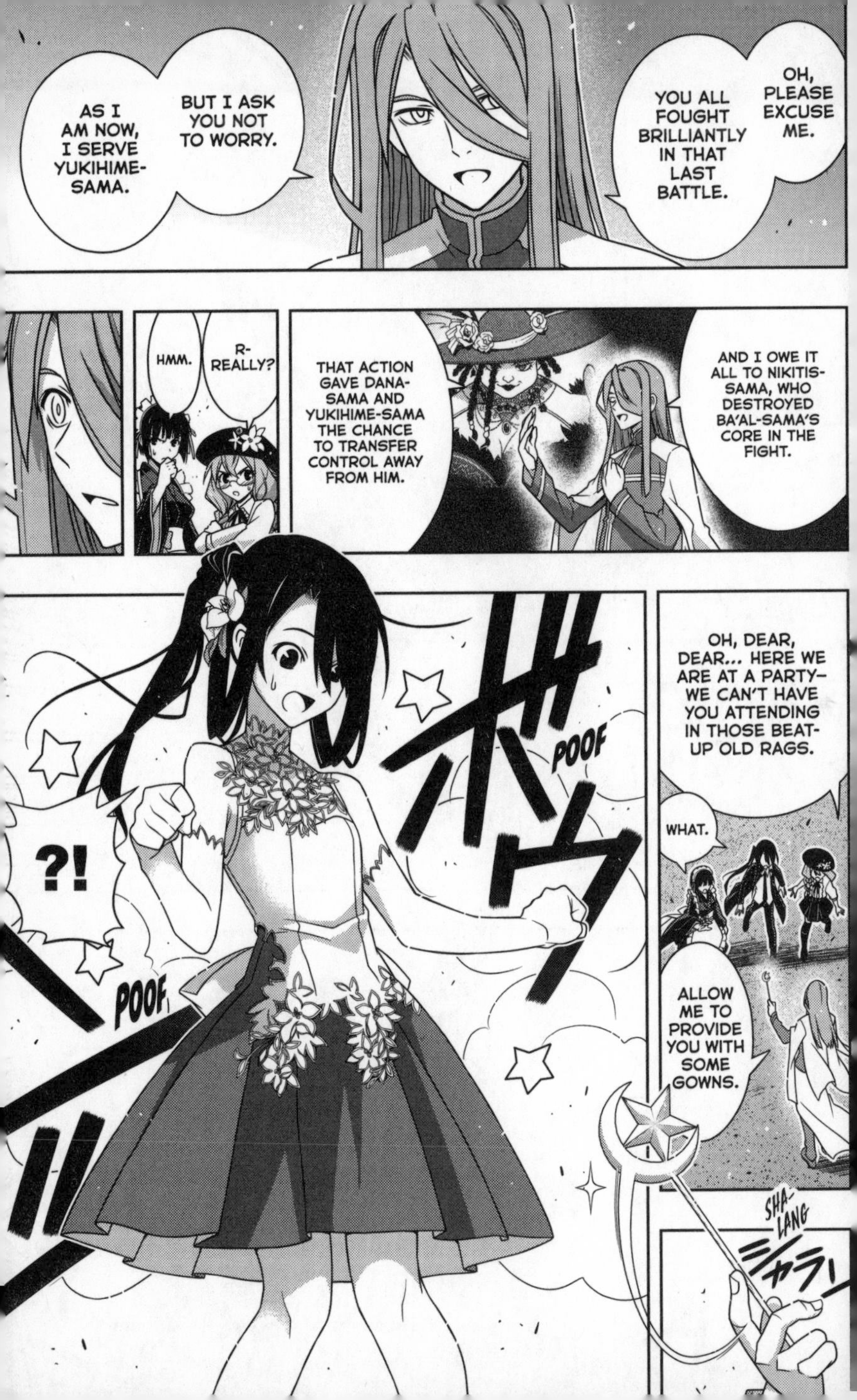
OH, PLEASE EXCUSE ME.
YOU ALL FOUGHT BRILLIANTLY IN THAT LAST BATTLE.
BUT I ASK YOU NOT TO WORRY.
AS I AM NOW, I SERVE YUKIHIME-SAMA.
AND I OWE IT ALL TO NIKITIS-SAMA, WHO DESTROYED BA'AL-SAMA'S CORE IN THE FIGHT.
THAT ACTION GAVE DANA-SAMA AND YUKIHIME-SAMA THE CHANCE TO TRANSFER CONTROL AWAY FROM HIM.
R-REALLY?
HMM.
OH, DEAR, DEAR... HERE WE ARE AT A PARTY—WE CAN'T HAVE YOU ATTENDING IN THOSE BEAT-UP OLD RAGS.
WHAT.
ALLOW ME TO PROVIDE YOU WITH SOME GOWNS.
SHA-LANG
POOF
?!
POOF

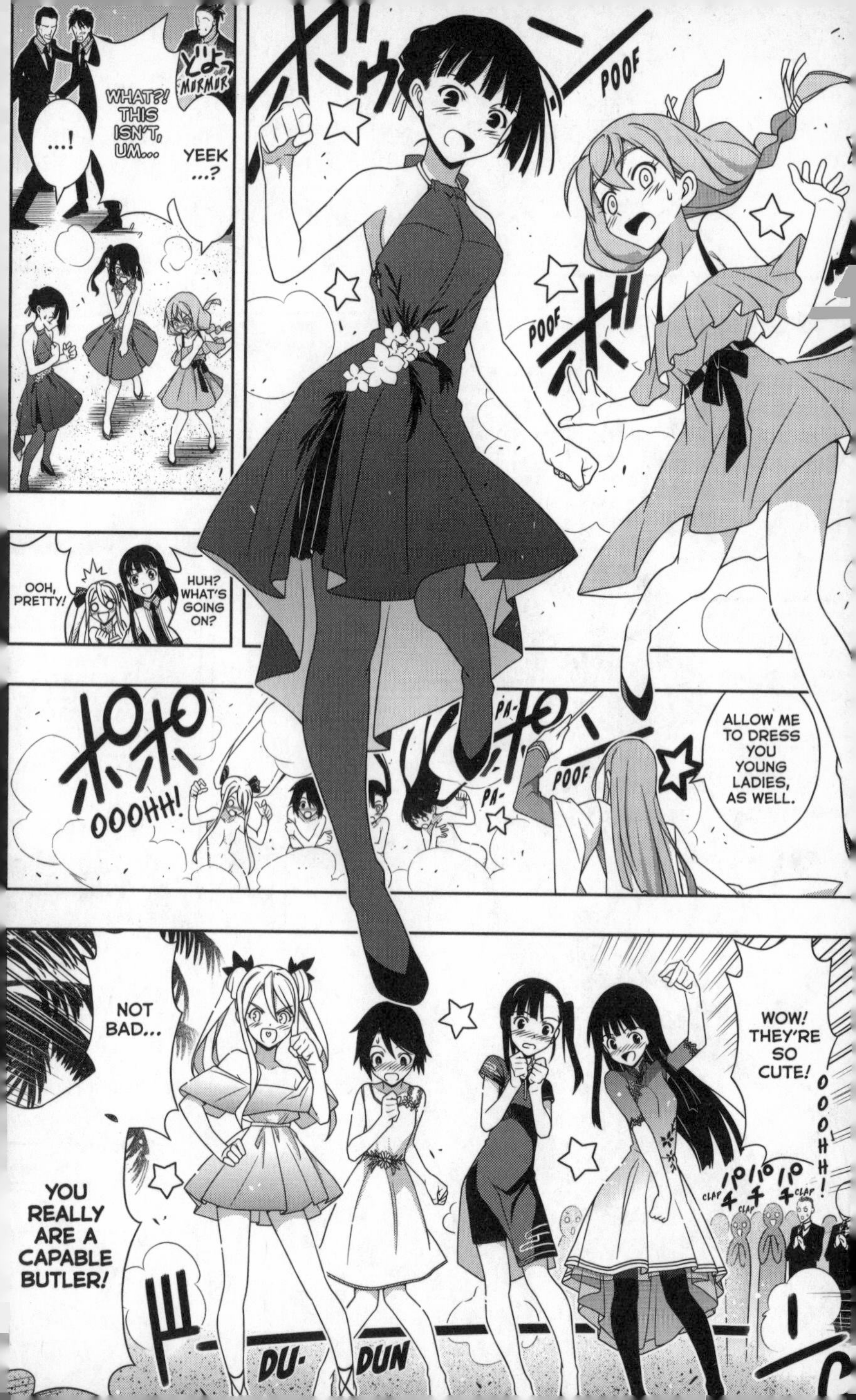
POOF
POOF
MURMUR
YEEK ...?
WHAT?! THIS ISN'T, UM...
...!
HUH? WHAT'S GOING ON?
OOH, PRETTY!
ALLOW ME TO DRESS YOU YOUNG LADIES, AS WELL.
POOF
PA-
PA-
OOOHH!
WOW! THEY'RE SO CUTE!
OOOHH!
CLAP
CLAP
CLAP
NOT BAD...
YOU REALLY ARE A CAPABLE BUTLER!
DU-
DUN

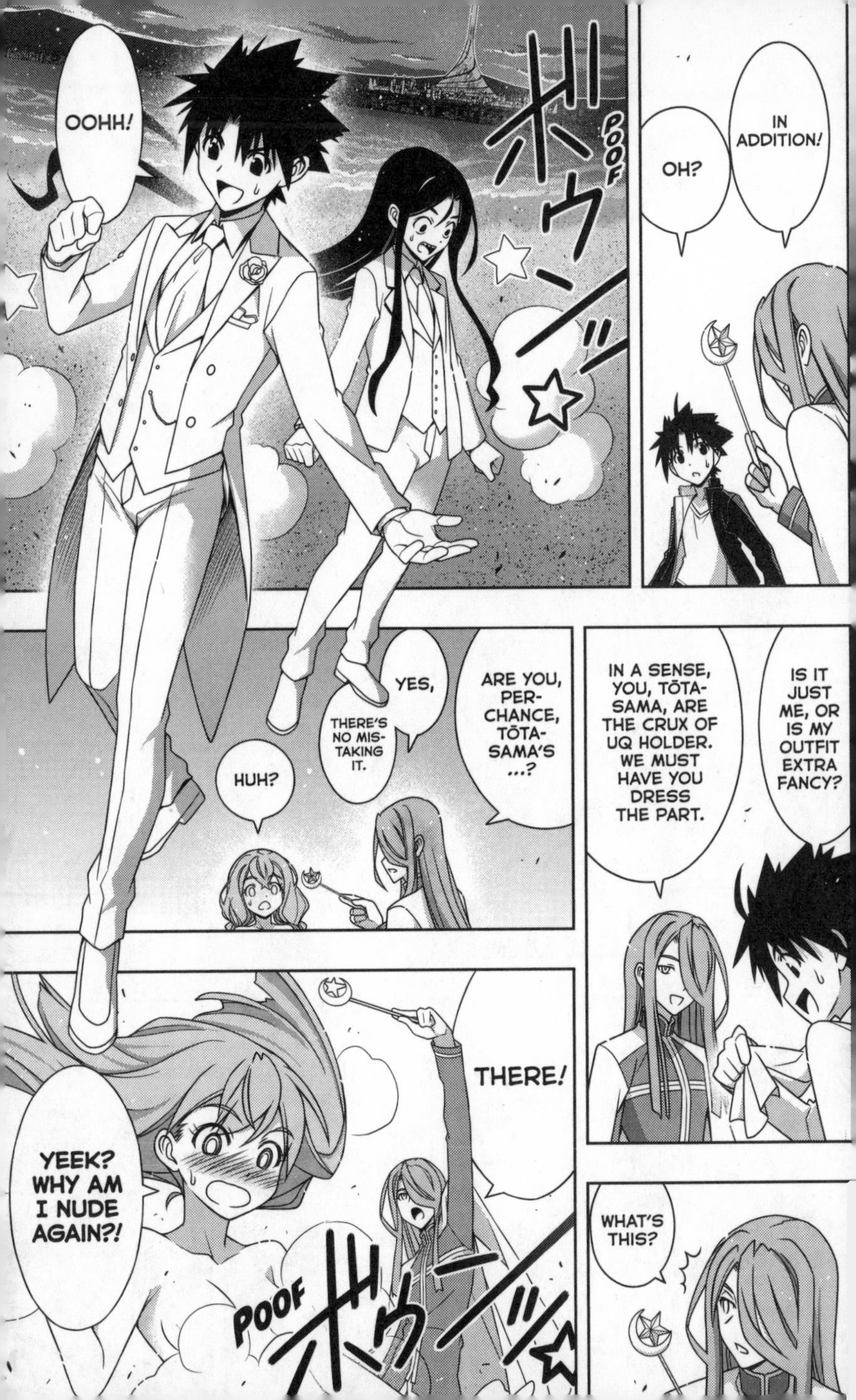
IN ADDITION!
OH?
POOF
OOHH!
IS IT JUST ME, OR IS MY OUTFIT EXTRA FANCY?
IN A SENSE, YOU, TŌTA-SAMA, ARE THE CRUX OF UQ HOLDER. WE MUST HAVE YOU DRESS THE PART.
ARE YOU, PER-CHANCE, TŌTA-SAMA'S ...?
YES,
THERE'S NO MIS-TAKING IT.
HUH?
WHAT'S THIS?
THERE!
POOF
YEEK? WHY AM I NUDE AGAIN?!

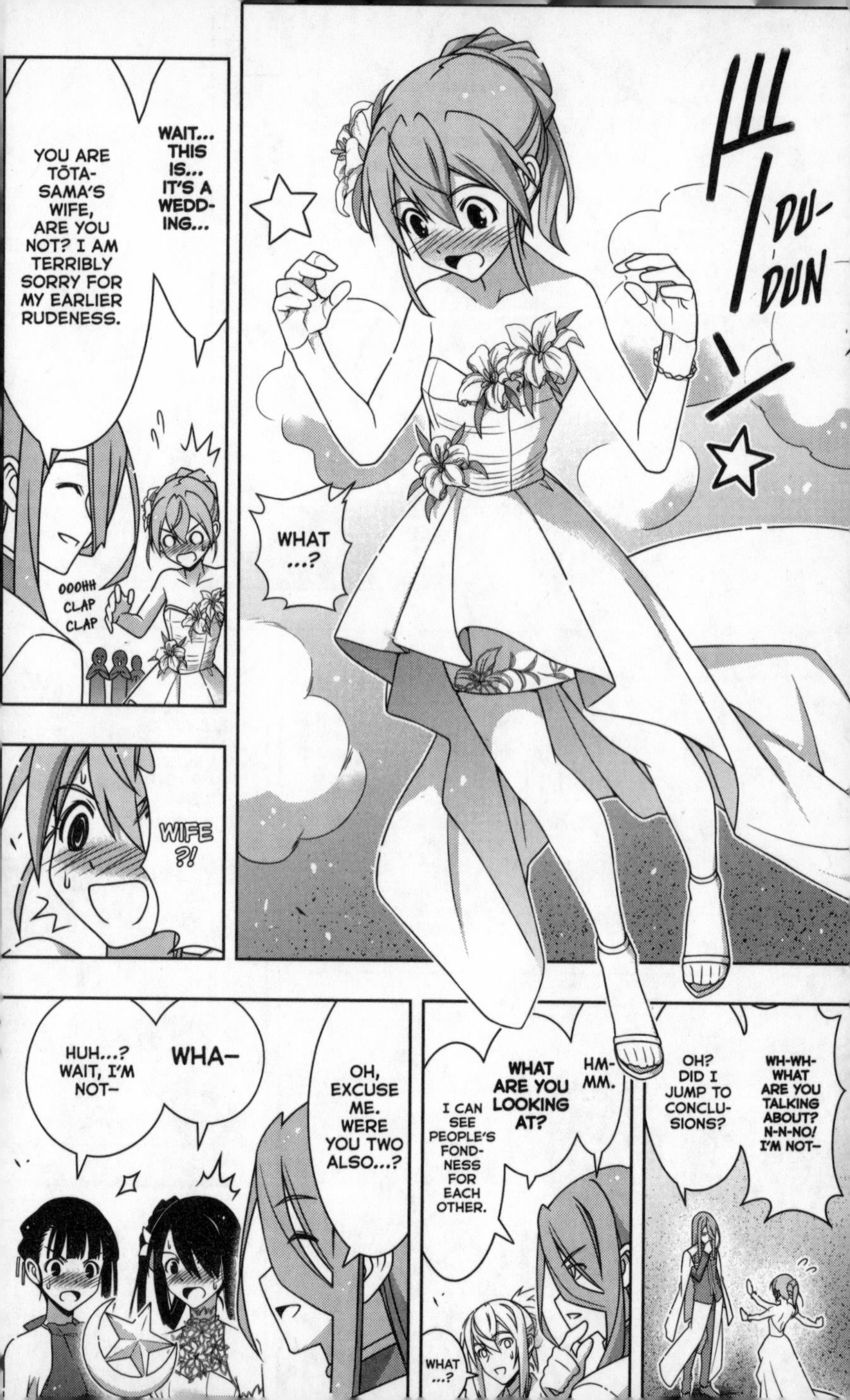
DU-DUN
WHAT...?
WAIT... THIS IS... IT'S A WEDDING...
YOU ARE TŌTA-SAMA'S WIFE, ARE YOU NOT? I AM TERRIBLY SORRY FOR MY EARLIER RUDENESS.
OOOHH CLAP CLAP
WIFE?!
WH-WH-WHAT ARE YOU TALKING ABOUT? N-N-NO! I'M NOT-
OH? DID I JUMP TO CONCLUSIONS?
HM-MM.
WHAT ARE YOU LOOKING AT?
I CAN SEE PEOPLE'S FONDNESS FOR EACH OTHER.
WHAT...?
OH, EXCUSE ME. WERE YOU TWO ALSO...?
WHA-
HUH...? WAIT, I'M NOT-

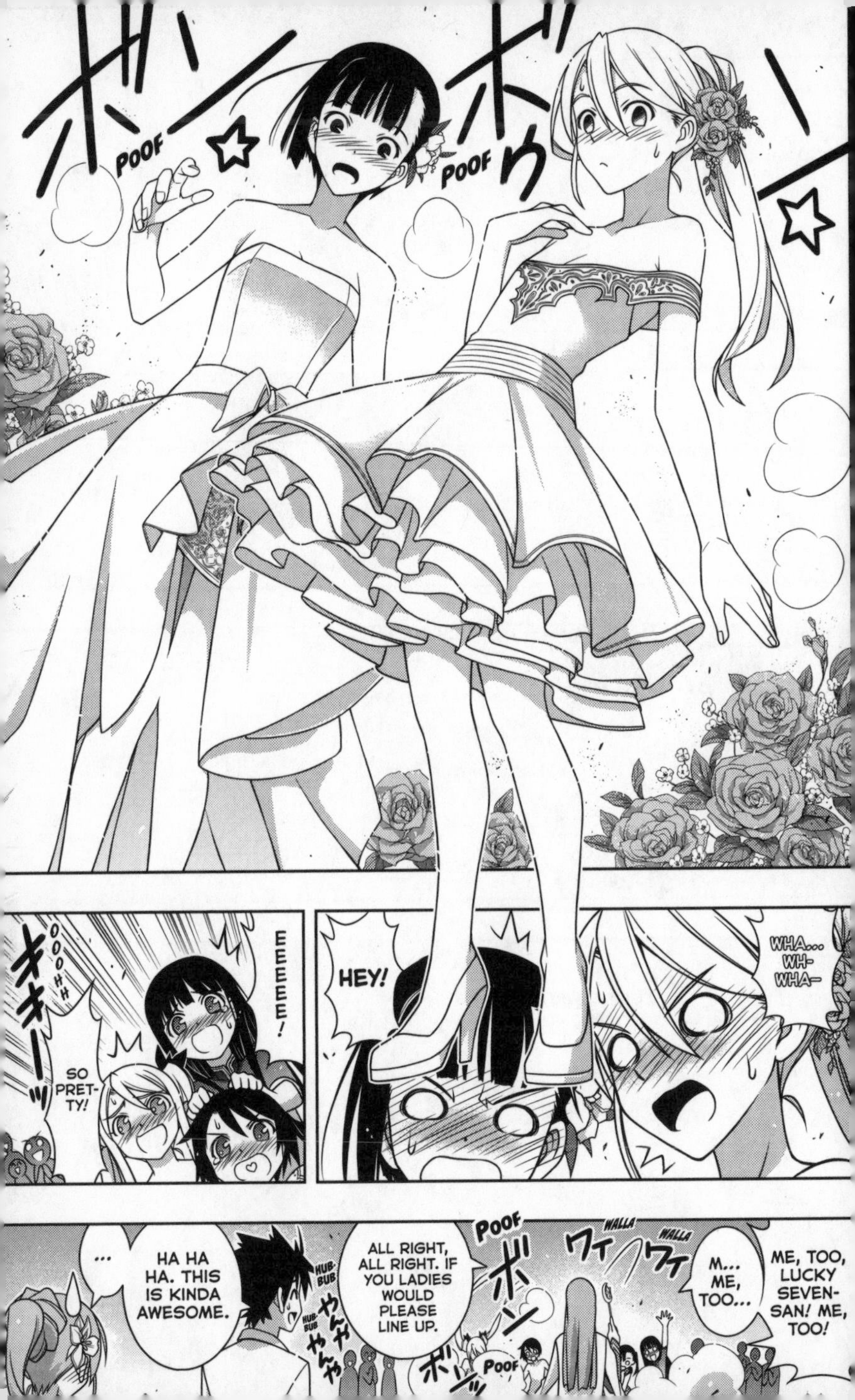
POOF
POOF
WHA... WH- WHA-
HEY!
EEEEEE!
SO PRET-TY!
OOOOHH
ME, TOO, LUCKY SEVEN-SAN! ME, TOO!
M... ME, TOO...
WALLA
WALLA
POOF
POOF
ALL RIGHT, ALL RIGHT. IF YOU LADIES WOULD PLEASE LINE UP.
HUB-BUB
HUB-BUB
HA HA HA. THIS IS KINDA AWESOME.
...

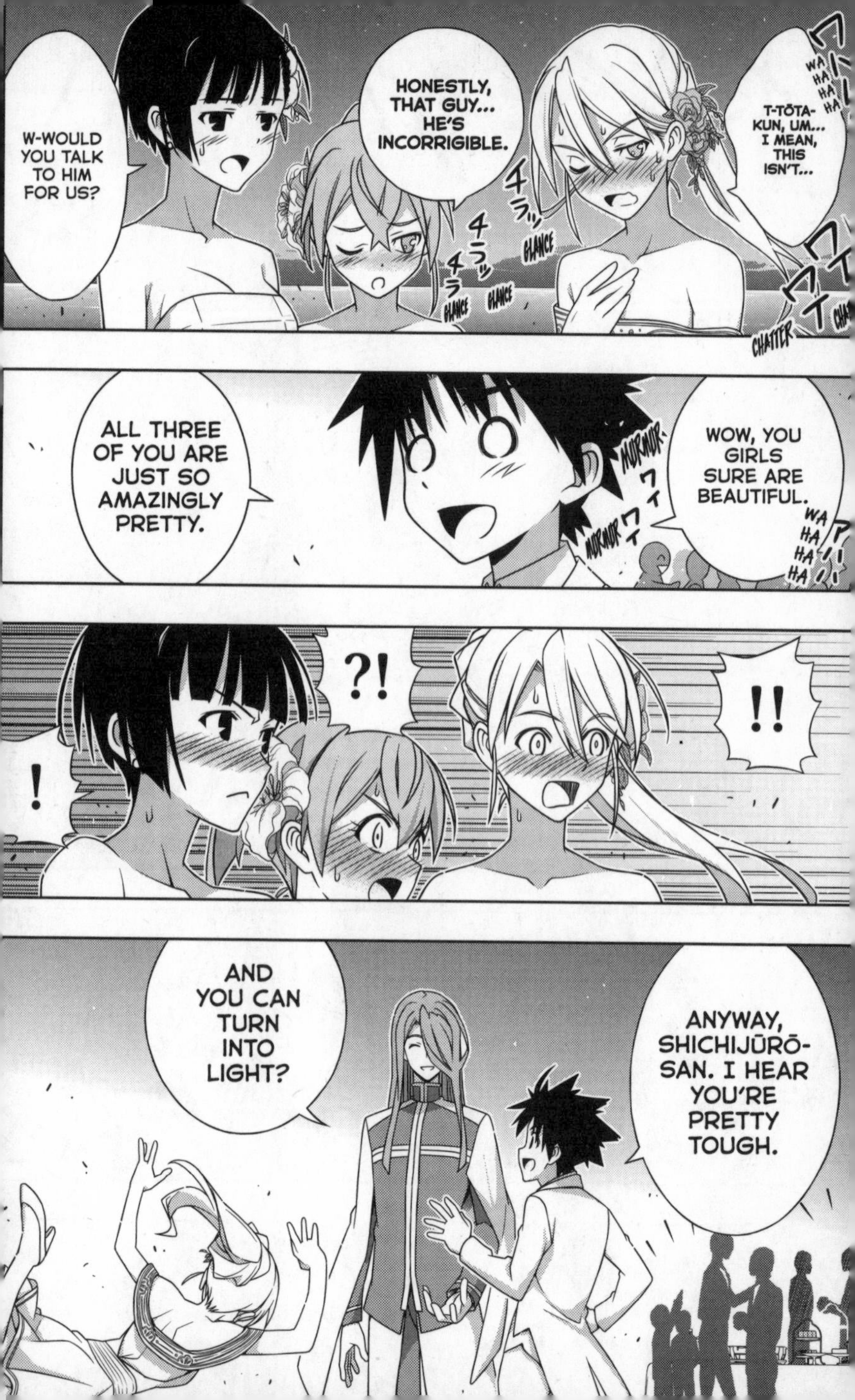

WA HA HA HA
T-TŌTA-KUN, UM... I MEAN, THIS ISN'T...
CHATTER
CHA
GLANCE
GLANCE
GLANCE
HONESTLY, THAT GUY... HE'S INCORRIGIBLE.
W-WOULD YOU TALK TO HIM FOR US?
WOW, YOU GIRLS SURE ARE BEAUTIFUL.
WA HA HA HA HA
MURMUR
MURMUR
ALL THREE OF YOU ARE JUST SO AMAZINGLY PRETTY.
!!
?!
!
ANYWAY, SHICHIJŪRŌ-SAN. I HEAR YOU'RE PRETTY TOUGH.
AND YOU CAN TURN INTO LIGHT?

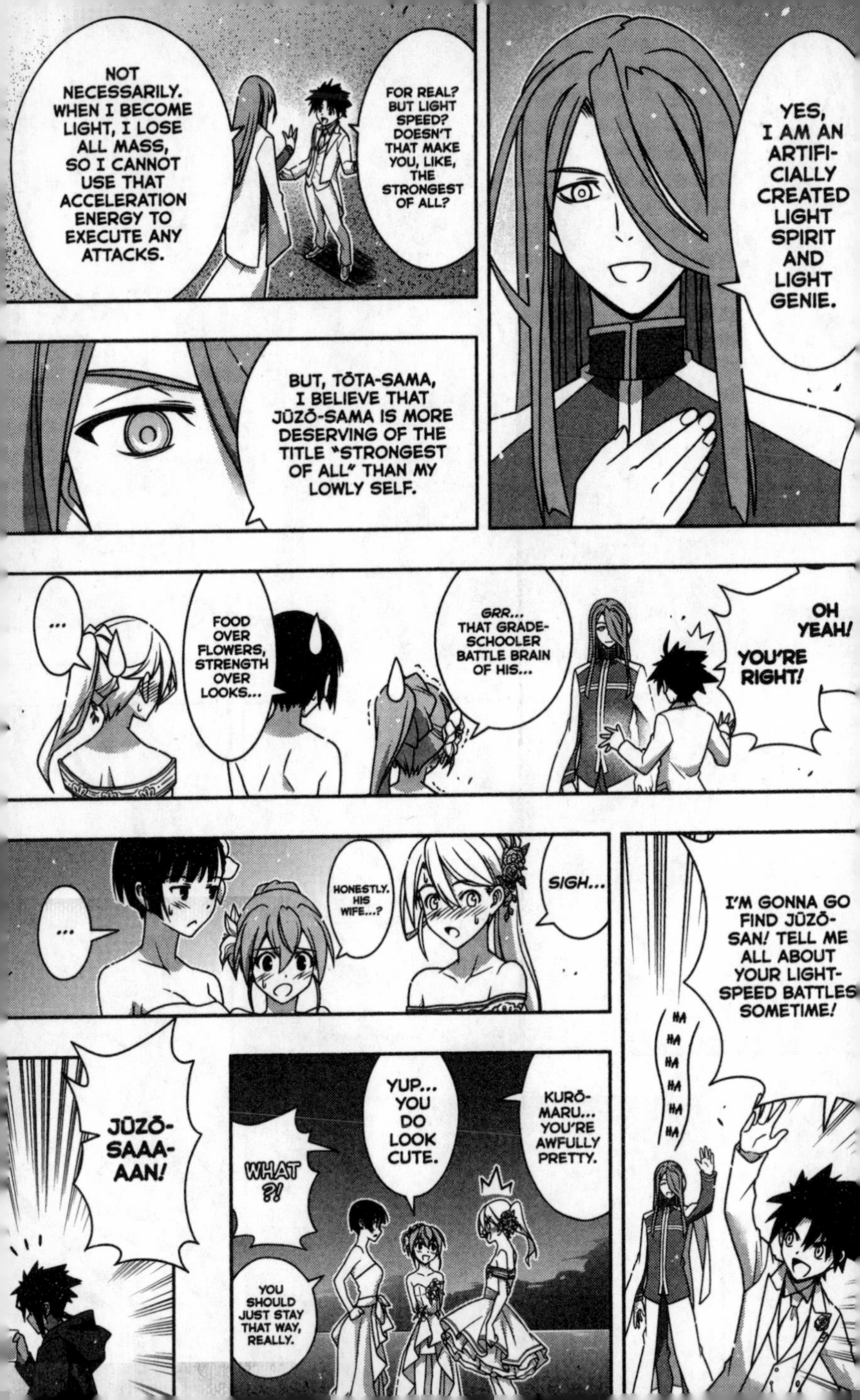
YES, I AM AN ARTIFICIALLY CREATED LIGHT SPIRIT AND LIGHT GENIE.
FOR REAL? BUT LIGHT SPEED? DOESN'T THAT MAKE YOU, LIKE, THE STRONGEST OF ALL?
NOT NECESSARILY. WHEN I BECOME LIGHT, I LOSE ALL MASS, SO I CANNOT USE THAT ACCELERATION ENERGY TO EXECUTE ANY ATTACKS.
BUT, TŌTA-SAMA, I BELIEVE THAT JŪZŌ-SAMA IS MORE DESERVING OF THE TITLE "STRONGEST OF ALL" THAN MY LOWLY SELF.
OH YEAH!
YOU'RE RIGHT!
GRR... THAT GRADE-SCHOOLER BATTLE BRAIN OF HIS...
FOOD OVER FLOWERS, STRENGTH OVER LOOKS...
...
I'M GONNA GO FIND JŪZŌ-SAN! TELL ME ALL ABOUT YOUR LIGHT-SPEED BATTLES SOMETIME!
HA HA HA HA HA HA
SIGH...
HONESTLY. HIS WIFE...?
...
KURŌ-MARU... YOU'RE AWFULLY PRETTY.
YUP... YOU DO LOOK CUTE.
WHAT?!
YOU SHOULD JUST STAY THAT WAY, REALLY.
JŪZŌ-SAAAAAN!

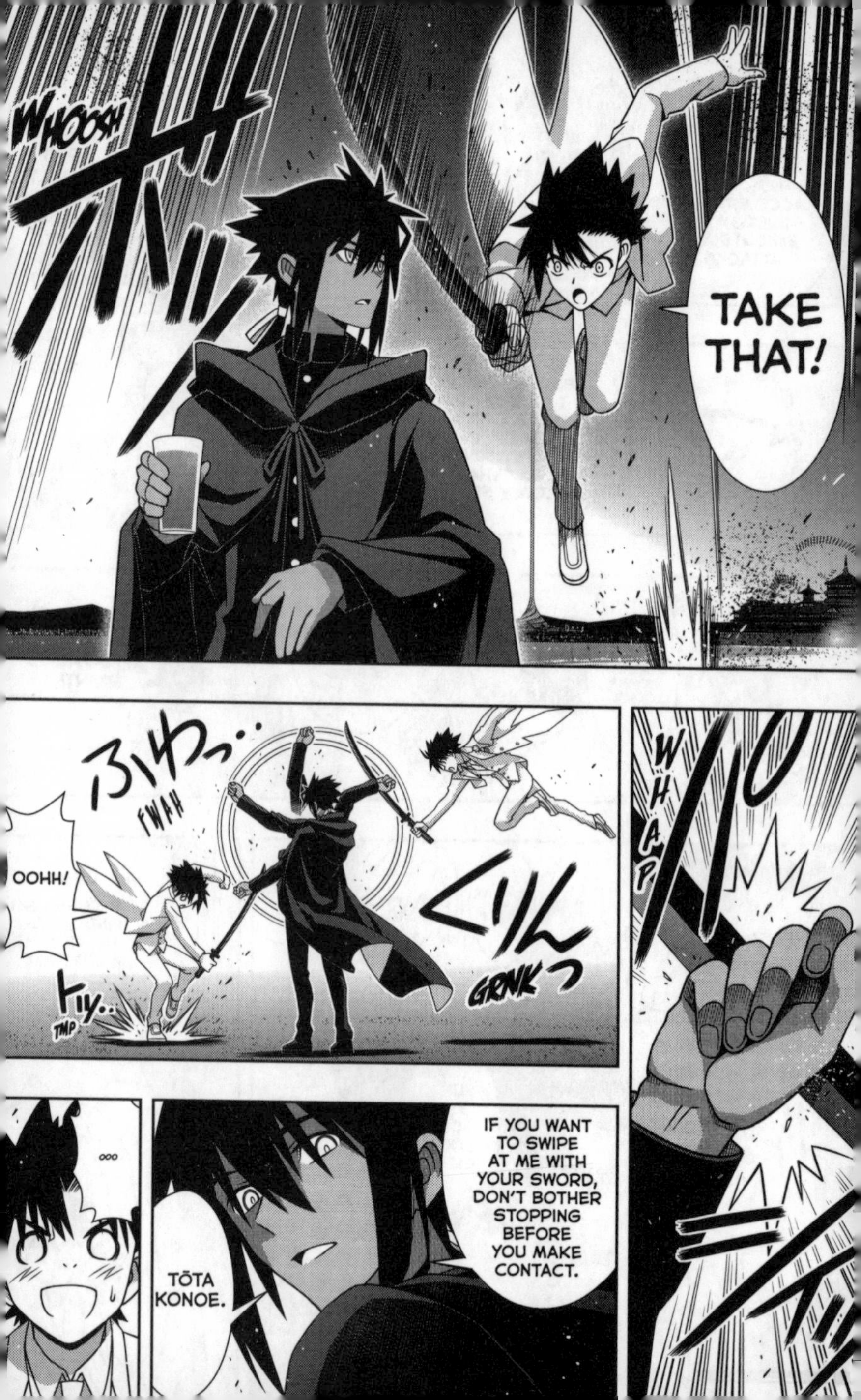
WHOOSH
TAKE THAT!
WHAP
FWAH
OOHH!
GRNK
TMP
IF YOU WANT TO SWIPE AT ME WITH YOUR SWORD, DON'T BOTHER STOPPING BEFORE YOU MAKE CONTACT.
TŌTA KONOE.
ooo

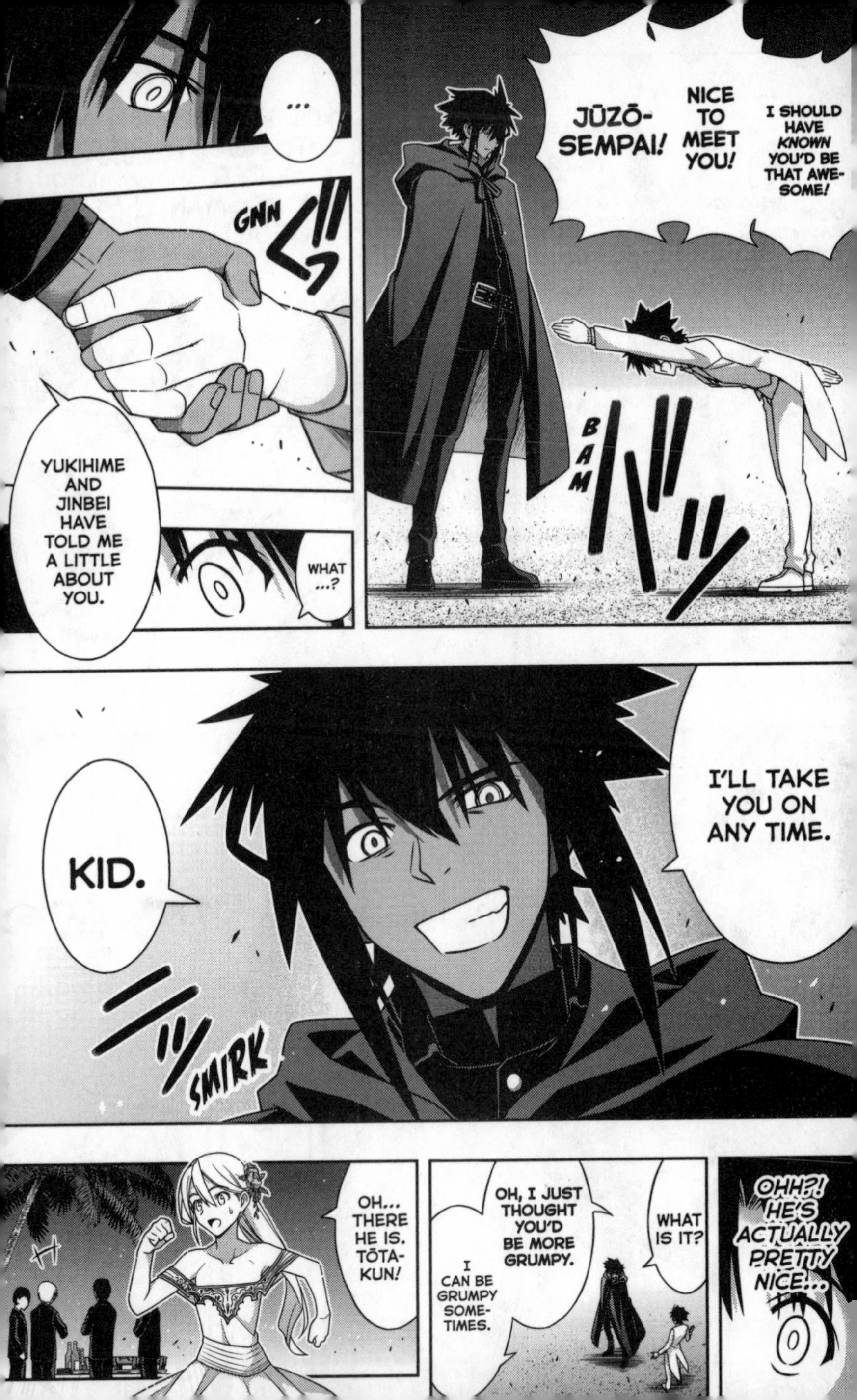
JŪZŌ-SEMPAI! NICE TO MEET YOU! I SHOULD HAVE KNOWN YOU'D BE THAT AWESOME!
BAM
...
GNN
YUKIHIME AND JINBEI HAVE TOLD ME A LITTLE ABOUT YOU.
WHAT ...?
I'LL TAKE YOU ON ANY TIME.
KID.
SMIRK
OHH?! HE'S ACTUALLY PRETTY NICE...
WHAT IS IT?
OH, I JUST THOUGHT YOU'D BE MORE GRUMPY.
I CAN BE GRUMPY SOME-TIMES.
OH... THERE HE IS. TŌTA-KUN!

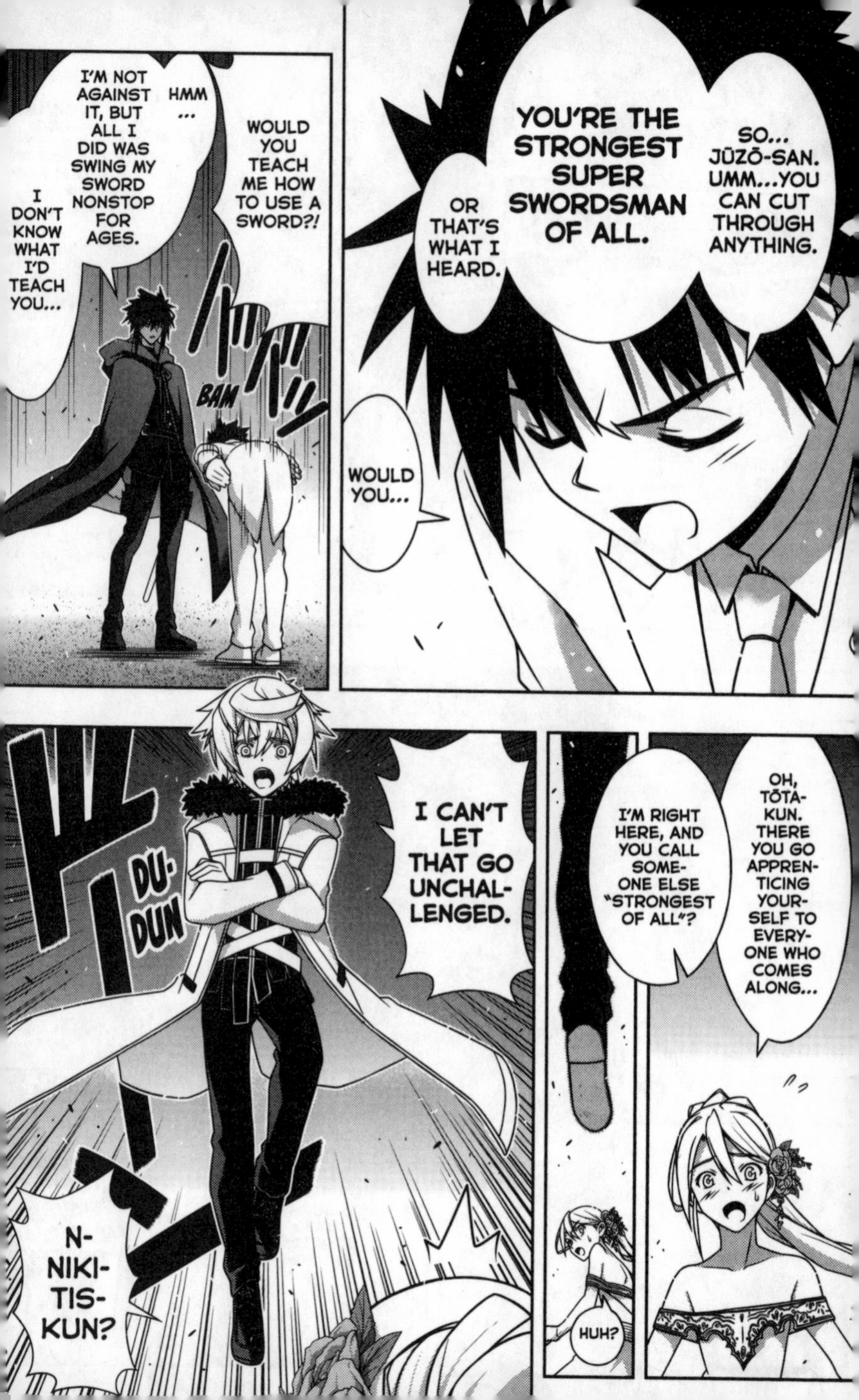
SO... JŪZŌ-SAN. UMM...YOU CAN CUT THROUGH ANYTHING.
YOU'RE THE STRONGEST SUPER SWORDSMAN OF ALL.
OR THAT'S WHAT I HEARD.
WOULD YOU...
WOULD YOU TEACH ME HOW TO USE A SWORD?!
BAM
HMM...
I'M NOT AGAINST IT, BUT ALL I DID WAS SWING MY SWORD NONSTOP FOR AGES.
I DON'T KNOW WHAT I'D TEACH YOU...
OH, TŌTA-KUN. THERE YOU GO APPRENTICING YOURSELF TO EVERYONE WHO COMES ALONG...
I'M RIGHT HERE, AND YOU CALL SOMEONE ELSE "STRONGEST OF ALL"?
HUH?
I CAN'T LET THAT GO UNCHALLENGED.
DU-DUN
N-NIKITIS-KUN?

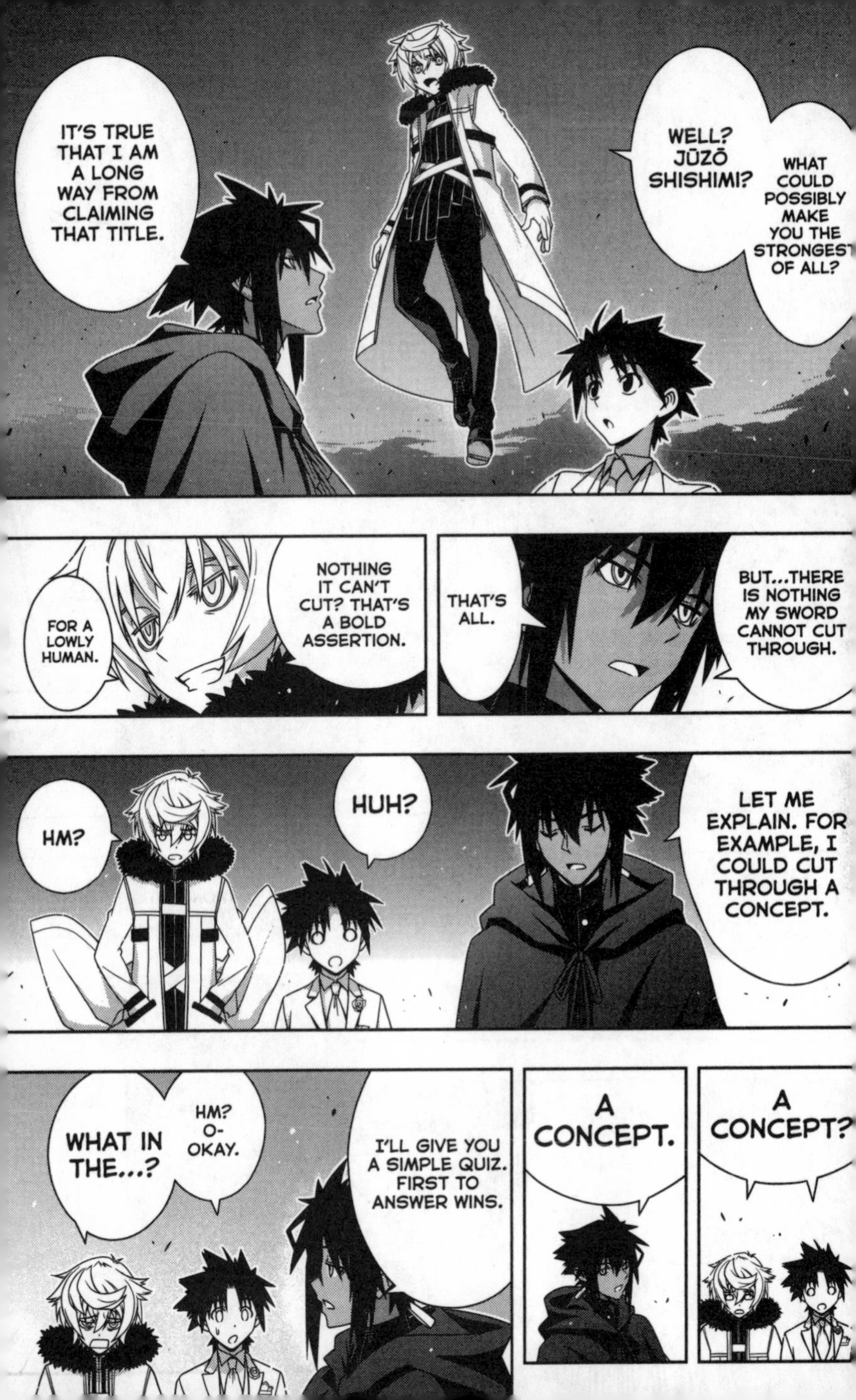
WELL? JŪZŌ SHISHIMI?
WHAT COULD POSSIBLY MAKE YOU THE STRONGEST OF ALL?
IT'S TRUE THAT I AM A LONG WAY FROM CLAIMING THAT TITLE.
BUT...THERE IS NOTHING MY SWORD CANNOT CUT THROUGH.
THAT'S ALL.
NOTHING IT CAN'T CUT? THAT'S A BOLD ASSERTION.
FOR A LOWLY HUMAN.
LET ME EXPLAIN. FOR EXAMPLE, I COULD CUT THROUGH A CONCEPT.
HUH?
HM?
A CONCEPT?
A CONCEPT.
I'LL GIVE YOU A SIMPLE QUIZ. FIRST TO ANSWER WINS.
HM? O-OKAY.
WHAT IN THE...?

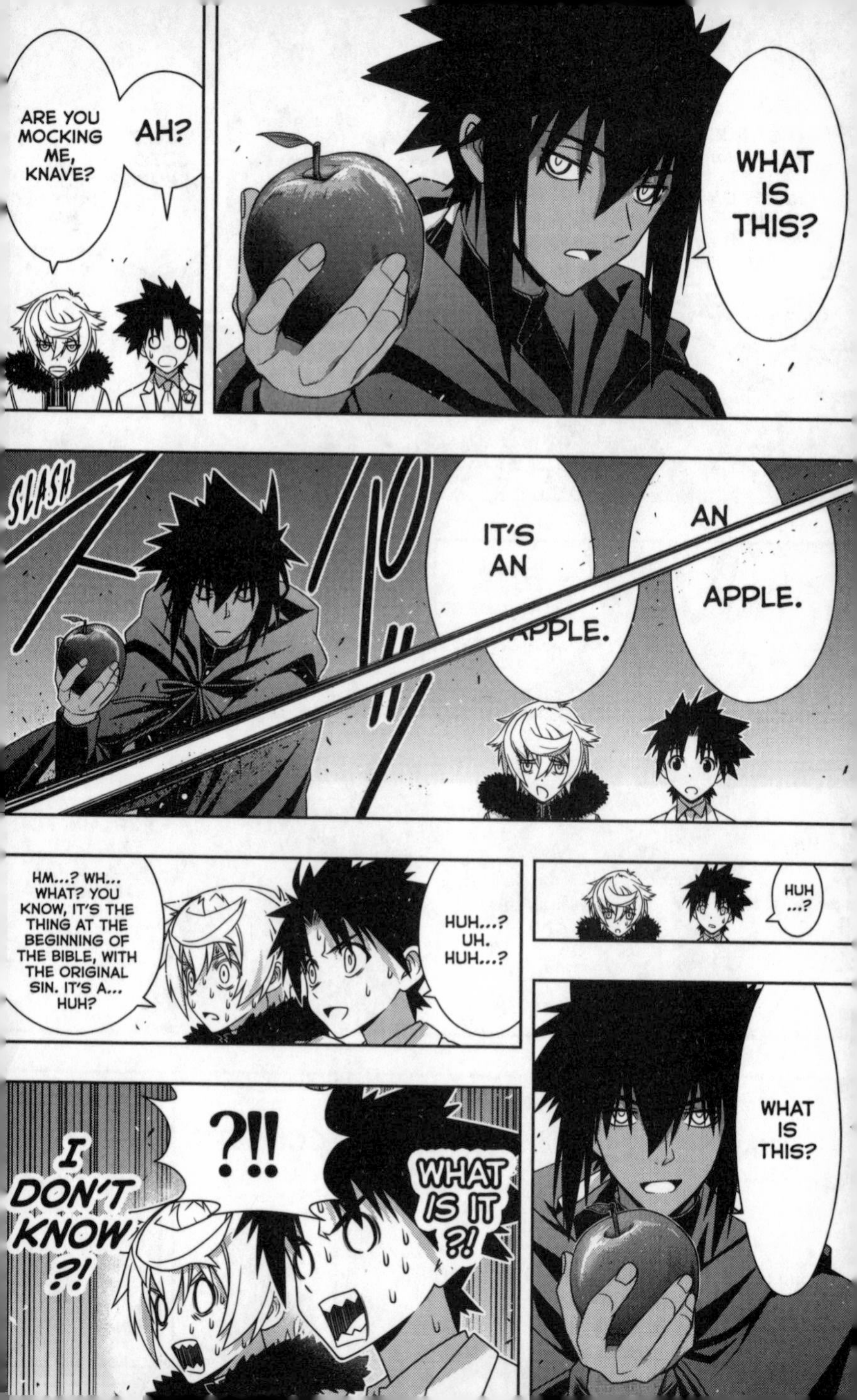
WHAT IS THIS?
AH?
ARE YOU MOCKING ME, KNAVE?
AN APPLE.
IT'S AN APPLE.
SLASH
HUH ...?
WHAT IS THIS?
HUH...? UH. HUH...?
HM...? WH... WHAT? YOU KNOW, IT'S THE THING AT THE BEGINNING OF THE BIBLE, WITH THE ORIGINAL SIN. IT'S A... HUH?
?!!
WHAT IS IT ?!
I DON'T KNOW ?!

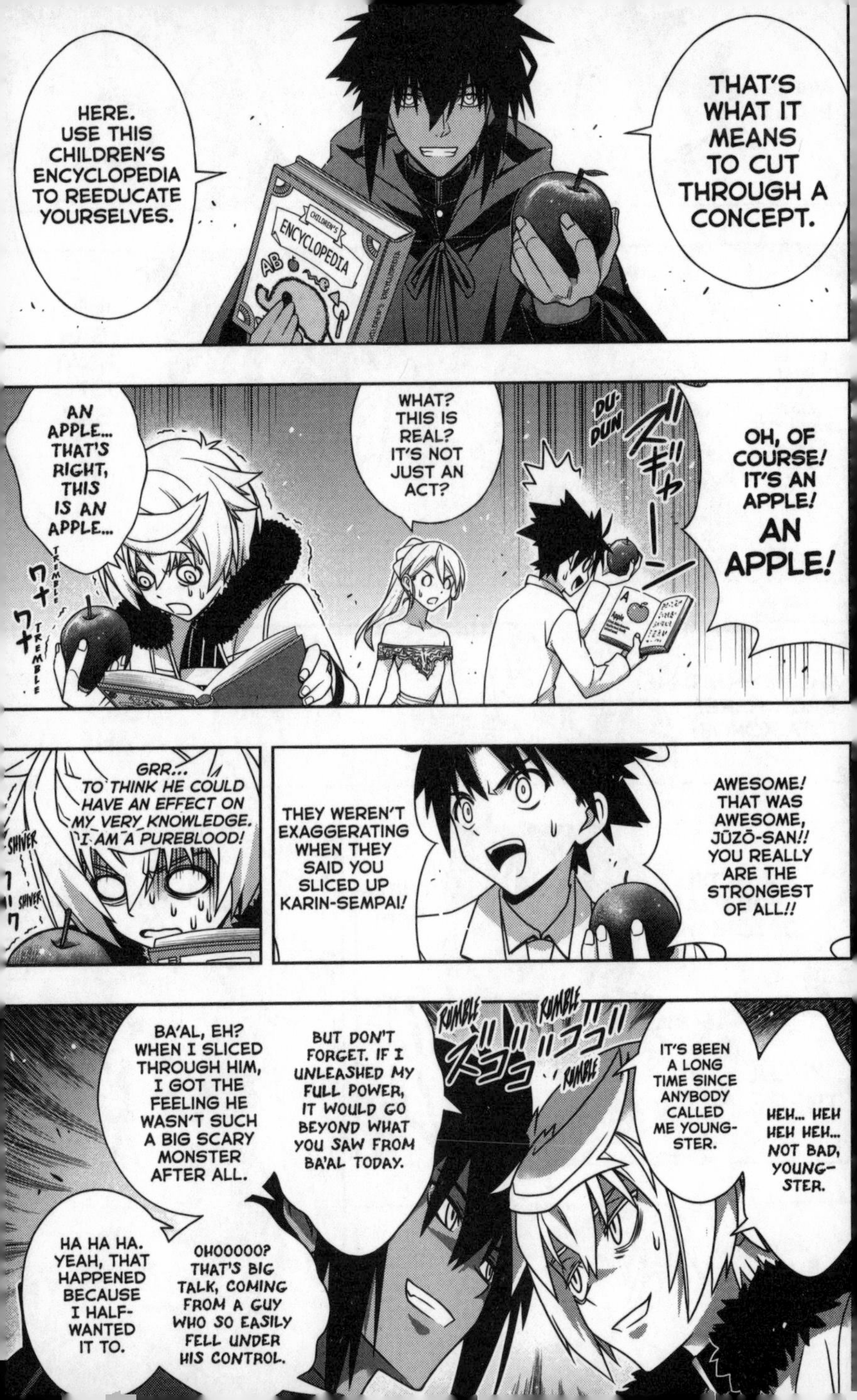
THAT'S WHAT IT MEANS TO CUT THROUGH A CONCEPT.
HERE. USE THIS CHILDREN'S ENCYCLOPEDIA TO REEDUCATE YOURSELVES.
CHILDREN'S ENCYCLOPEDIA
OH, OF COURSE! IT'S AN APPLE! AN APPLE!
DU-DUN
WHAT? THIS IS REAL? IT'S NOT JUST AN ACT?
AN APPLE... THAT'S RIGHT, THIS IS AN APPLE...
TREMBLE
TREMBLE
AWESOME! THAT WAS AWESOME, JŪZŌ-SAN!! YOU REALLY ARE THE STRONGEST OF ALL!!
THEY WEREN'T EXAGGERATING WHEN THEY SAID YOU SLICED UP KARIN-SEMPAI!
GRR... TO THINK HE COULD HAVE AN EFFECT ON MY VERY KNOWLEDGE. I AM A PUREBLOOD!
SHIVER
SHIVER
HEH... HEH HEH HEH... NOT BAD, YOUNGSTER.
IT'S BEEN A LONG TIME SINCE ANYBODY CALLED ME YOUNGSTER.
RUMBLE
RUMBLE
RUMBLE
BUT DON'T FORGET. IF I UNLEASHED MY FULL POWER, IT WOULD GO BEYOND WHAT YOU SAW FROM BA'AL TODAY.
BA'AL, EH? WHEN I SLICED THROUGH HIM, I GOT THE FEELING HE WASN'T SUCH A BIG SCARY MONSTER AFTER ALL.
OHOOOOO? THAT'S BIG TALK, COMING FROM A GUY WHO SO EASILY FELL UNDER HIS CONTROL.
HA HA HA. YEAH, THAT HAPPENED BECAUSE I HALF-WANTED IT TO.

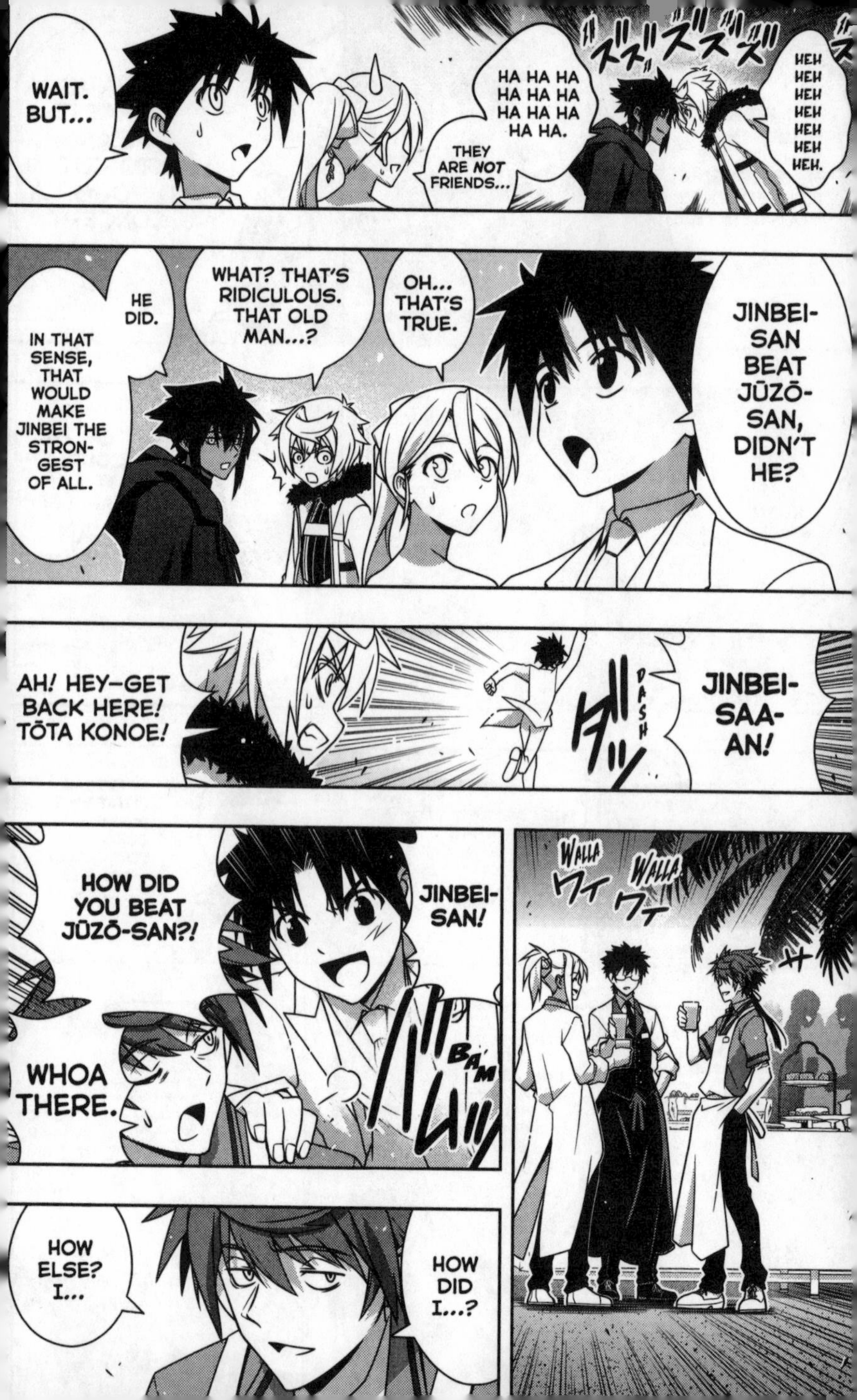
HEH HEH HEH HEH HEH HEH HEH.
HA HA HA HA HA HA HA HA HA HA HA.
THEY ARE *NOT* FRIENDS...
WAIT. BUT...
JINBEI-SAN BEAT JŪZŌ-SAN, DIDN'T HE?
OH... THAT'S TRUE.
WHAT? THAT'S RIDICULOUS. THAT OLD MAN...?
HE DID.
IN THAT SENSE, THAT WOULD MAKE JINBEI THE STRONGEST OF ALL.
JINBEI-SAAAN!
DASH
AH! HEY—GET BACK HERE! TŌTA KONOE!
WALLA
WALLA
JINBEI-SAN!
HOW DID YOU BEAT JŪZŌ-SAN?!
BAM
WHOA THERE.
HOW DID I...?
HOW ELSE? I...

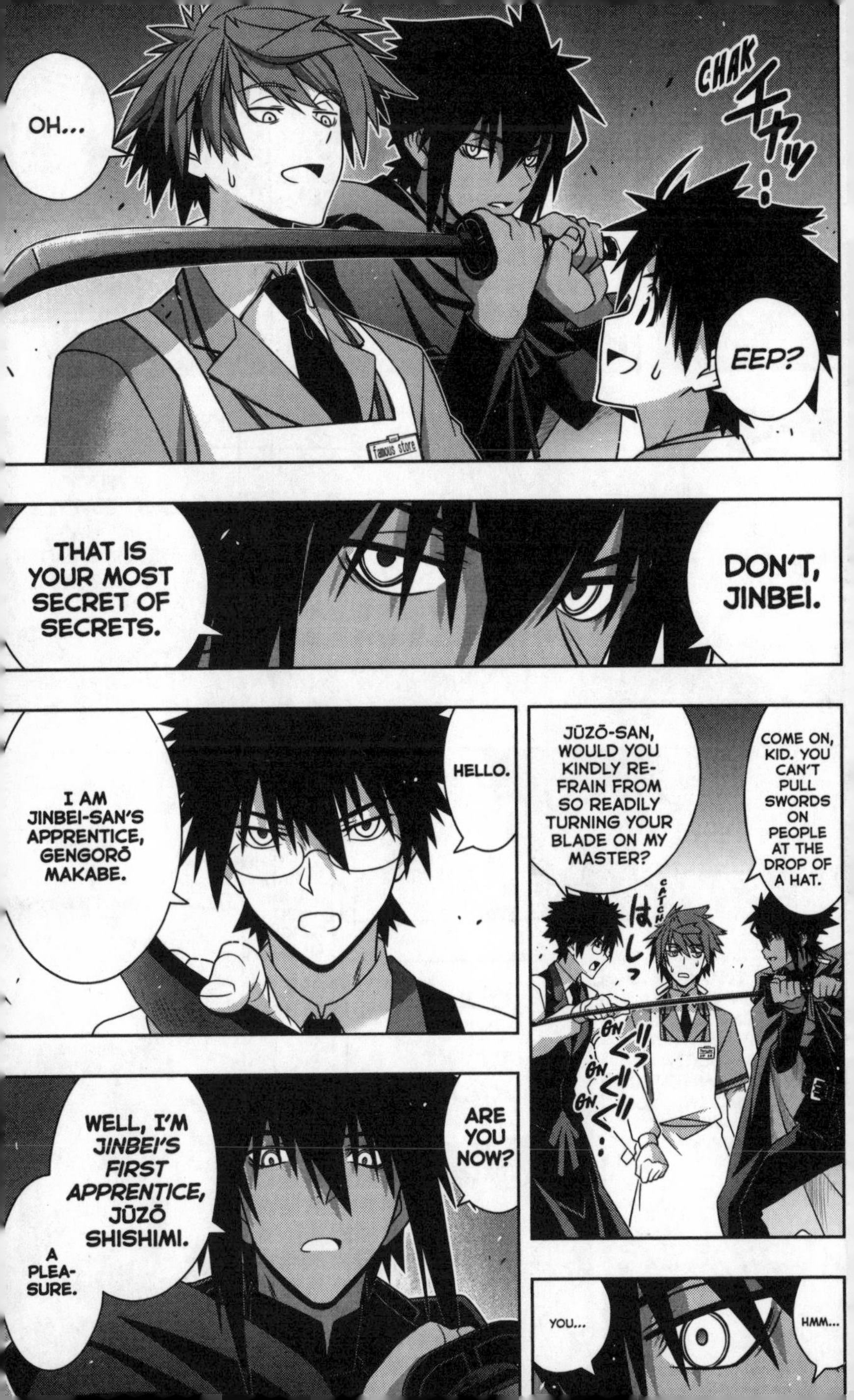
CHAK
チャッ
EEP?
OH...
DON'T, JINBEI.
THAT IS YOUR MOST SECRET OF SECRETS.
COME ON, KID. YOU CAN'T PULL SWORDS ON PEOPLE AT THE DROP OF A HAT.
JŪZŌ-SAN, WOULD YOU KINDLY RE-FRAIN FROM SO READILY TURNING YOUR BLADE ON MY MASTER?
CATCH
はしっ
GN
ぐっ
GN
ぐっ
GN
ぐっ
HELLO.
I AM JINBEI-SAN'S APPRENTICE, GENGORŌ MAKABE.
ARE YOU NOW?
WELL, I'M JINBEI'S FIRST APPRENTICE, JŪZŌ SHISHIMI.
A PLEA-SURE.
HMM...
YOU...

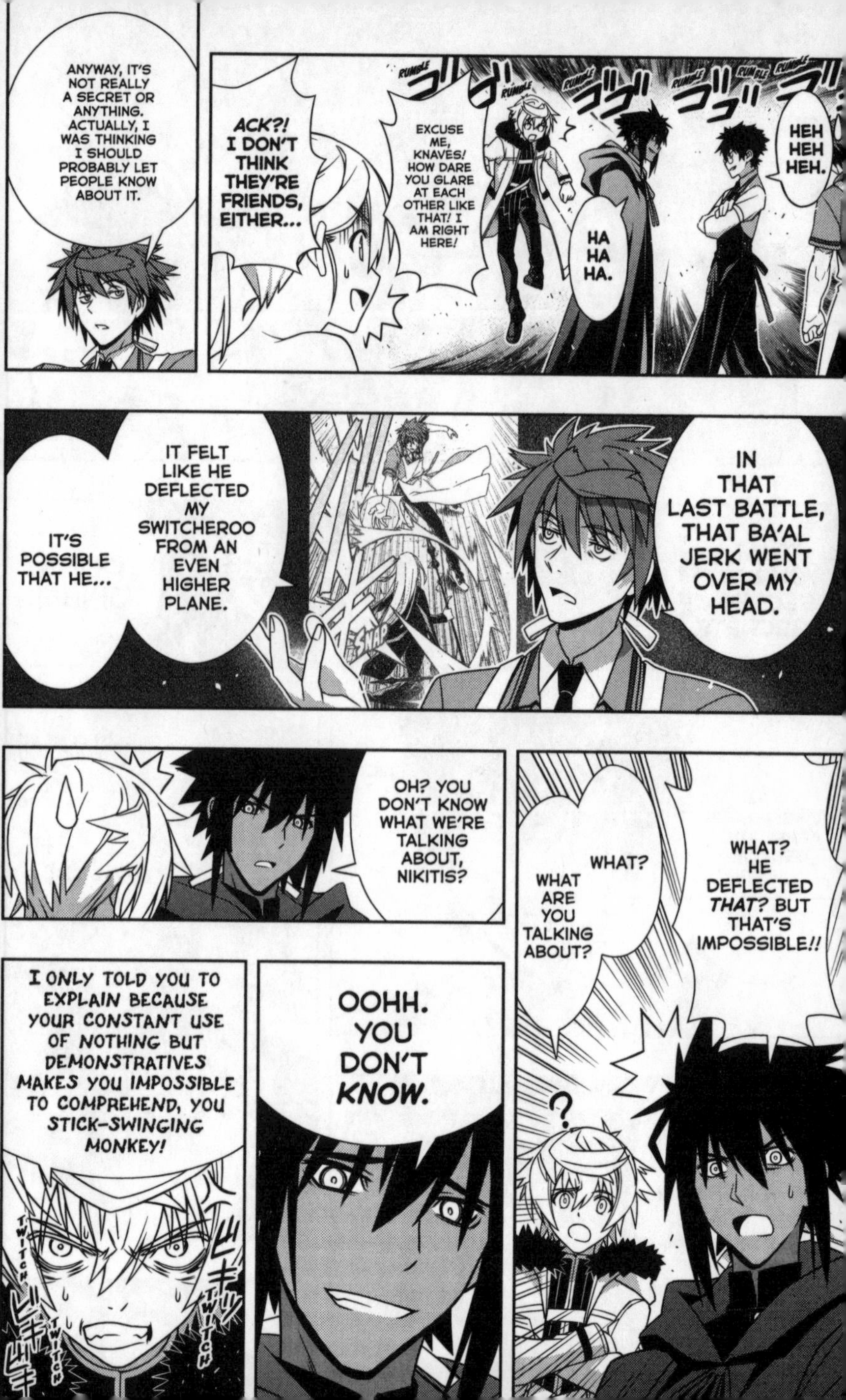
RUMBLE
RUMBLE
RUMBLE
RUMBLE
RUMBLE
RUMBLE
HEH HEH HEH.
HA HA HA.
EXCUSE ME, KNAVES! HOW DARE YOU GLARE AT EACH OTHER LIKE THAT! I AM RIGHT HERE!
ACK?! I DON'T THINK THEY'RE FRIENDS, EITHER...
ANYWAY, IT'S NOT REALLY A SECRET OR ANYTHING. ACTUALLY, I WAS THINKING I SHOULD PROBABLY LET PEOPLE KNOW ABOUT IT.
IN THAT LAST BATTLE, THAT BA'AL JERK WENT OVER MY HEAD.
SNAP
IT FELT LIKE HE DEFLECTED MY SWITCHEROO FROM AN EVEN HIGHER PLANE.
IT'S POSSIBLE THAT HE...
WHAT? HE DEFLECTED *THAT*? BUT THAT'S IMPOSSIBLE!!
WHAT?
WHAT ARE YOU TALKING ABOUT?
?
OH? YOU DON'T KNOW WHAT WE'RE TALKING ABOUT, NIKITIS?
OOHH. YOU DON'T *KNOW*.
I ONLY TOLD YOU TO EXPLAIN BECAUSE YOUR CONSTANT USE OF NOTHING BUT DEMONSTRATIVES MAKES YOU IMPOSSIBLE TO COMPREHEND, YOU STICK-SWINGING MONKEY!
TWITCH
TWITCH
TWITCH

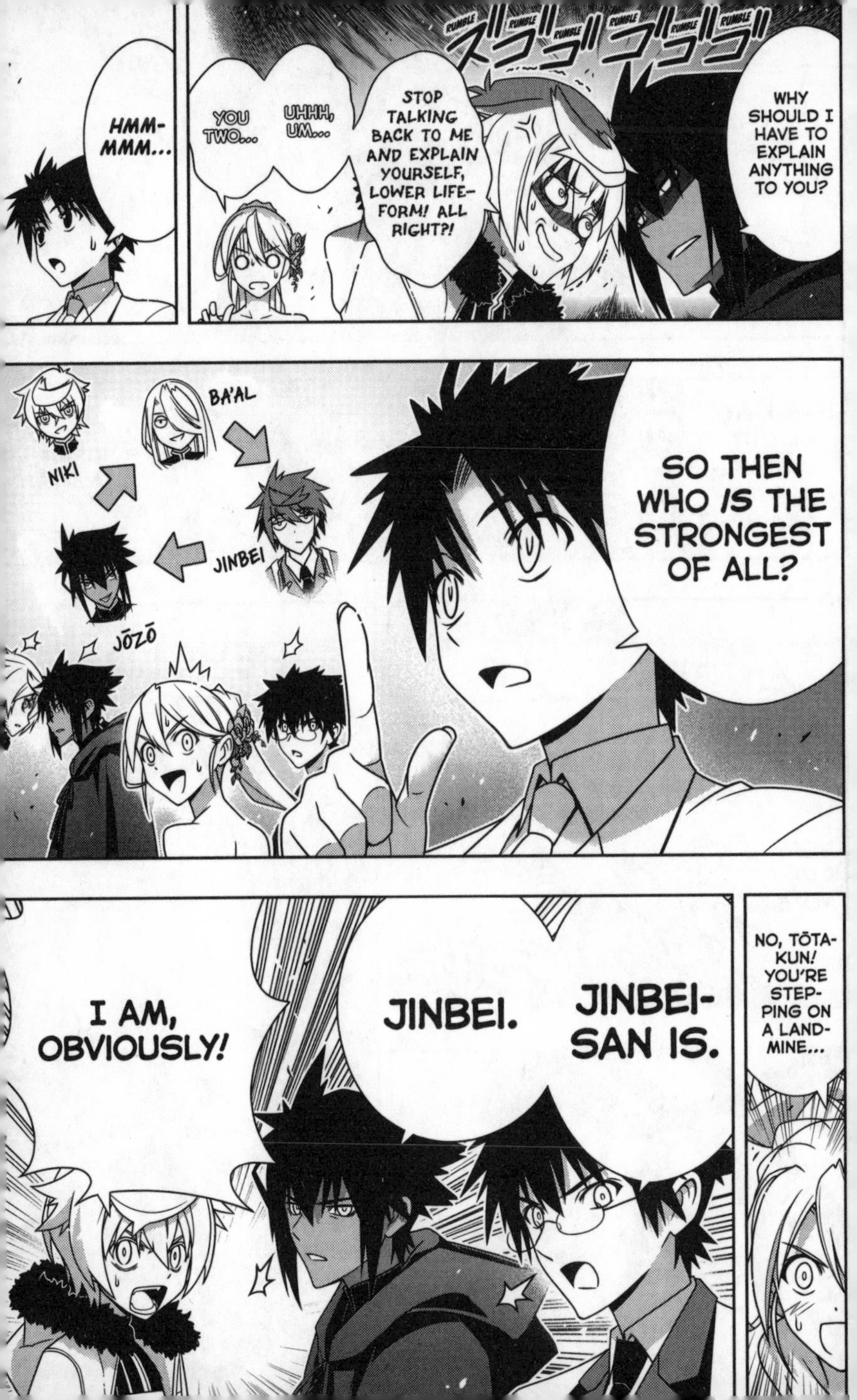
RUMBLE RUMBLE RUMBLE RUMBLE RUMBLE
WHY SHOULD I HAVE TO EXPLAIN ANYTHING TO YOU?
STOP TALKING BACK TO ME AND EXPLAIN YOURSELF, LOWER LIFE-FORM! ALL RIGHT?!
UHHH, UM...
YOU TWO...
HMM-MMM...
SO THEN WHO *IS* THE STRONGEST OF ALL?
BA'AL
NIKI
JINBEI
JŌZŌ
NO, TŌTA-KUN! YOU'RE STEP-PING ON A LAND-MINE...
JINBEI-SAN IS.
JINBEI.
I AM, OBVIOUSLY!

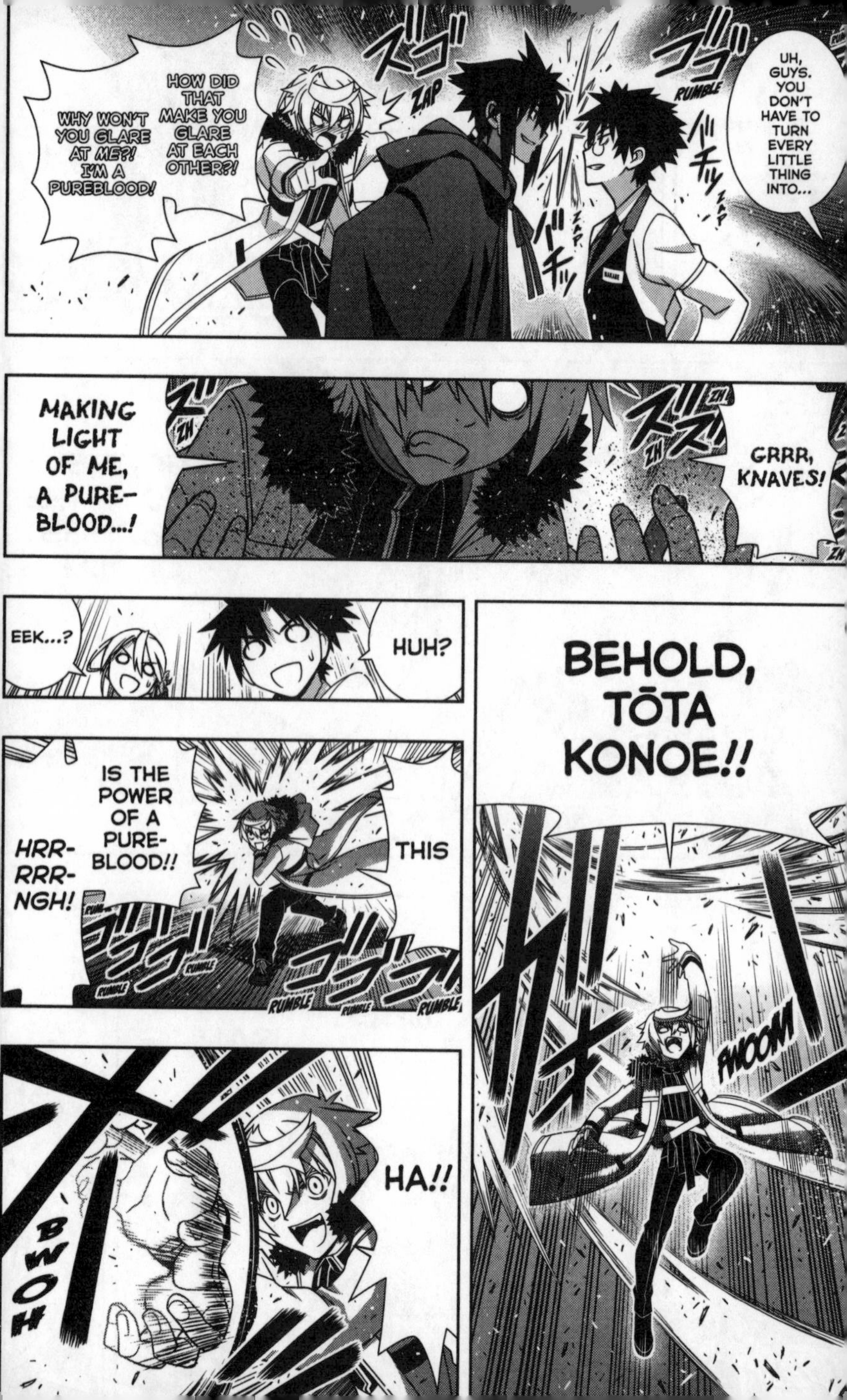
UH, GUYS. YOU DON'T HAVE TO TURN EVERY LITTLE THING INTO...
RUMBLE
ZAP
ZAP
ZAP
HOW DID THAT MAKE YOU GLARE AT EACH OTHER?!
WHY WON'T YOU GLARE AT *ME*?! I'M A PUREBLOOD!
ZH
ZH
GRRR, KNAVES!
ZH
ZH
MAKING LIGHT OF ME, A PURE-BLOOD...!
BEHOLD, TŌTA KONOE!!
PHOOM
HUH?
EEK...?
THIS
IS THE POWER OF A PURE-BLOOD!!
HRR-RRR-NGH!
RUMBLE
RUMBLE
RUMBLE
RUMBLE
RUMBLE
HA!!
BWOOH

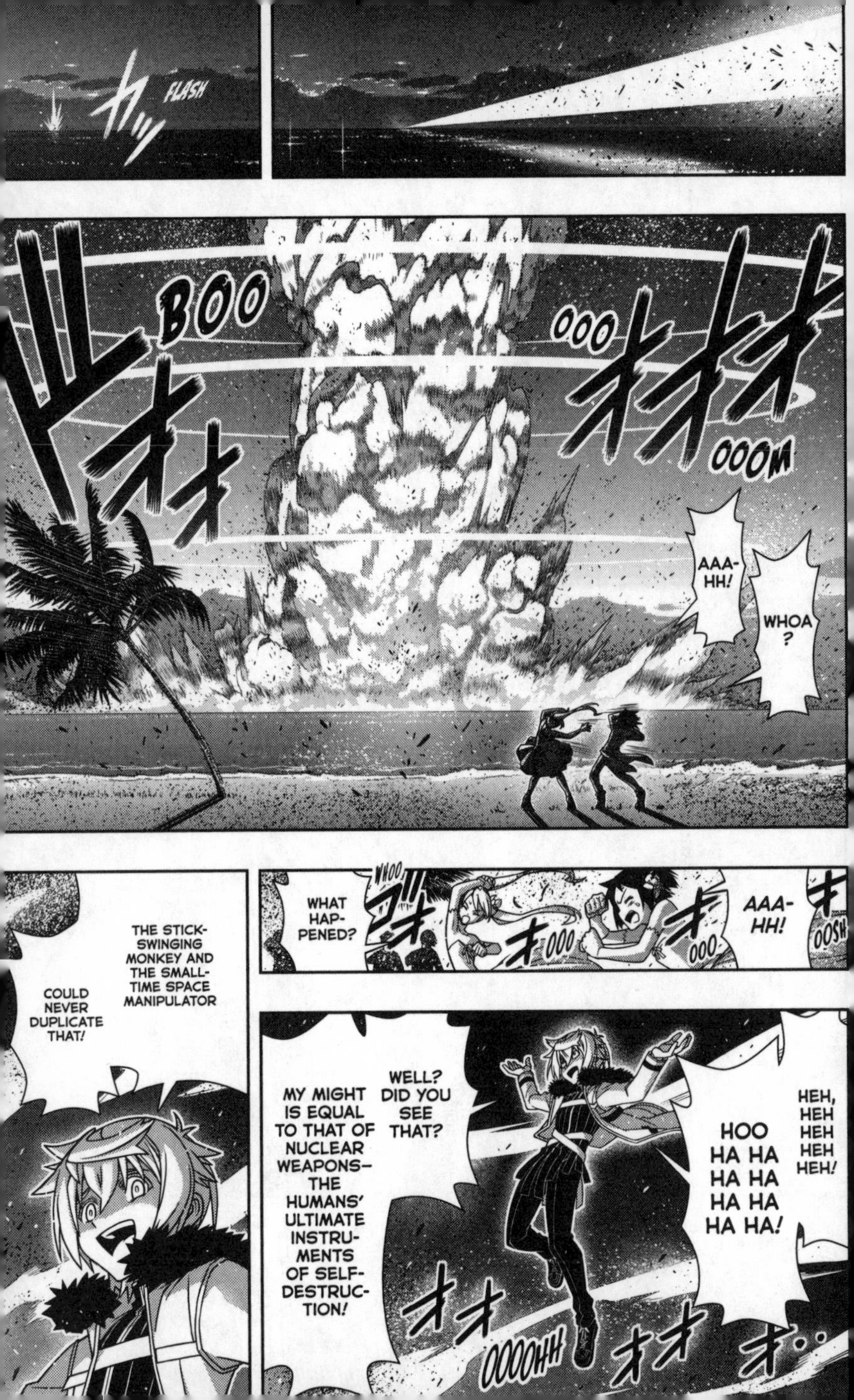

カッ
FLASH
ドオオ
BOO
OOO
オオオ
OOOM
WHOA?
AAA-HH!
オ
OOSH
AAA-HH!
オ
OOO
オ
OOO
ゴオ
WHOO
WHAT HAPPENED?
HEH, HEH HEH HEH HEH!
HOO HA HA HA HA HA HA HA HA!
WELL? DID YOU SEE THAT?
MY MIGHT IS EQUAL TO THAT OF NUCLEAR WEAPONS—THE HUMANS' ULTIMATE INSTRUMENTS OF SELF-DESTRUCTION!
オ..
オオ
オオ
OOOOHH
THE STICK-SWINGING MONKEY AND THE SMALL-TIME SPACE MANIPULATOR
COULD NEVER DUPLICATE THAT!

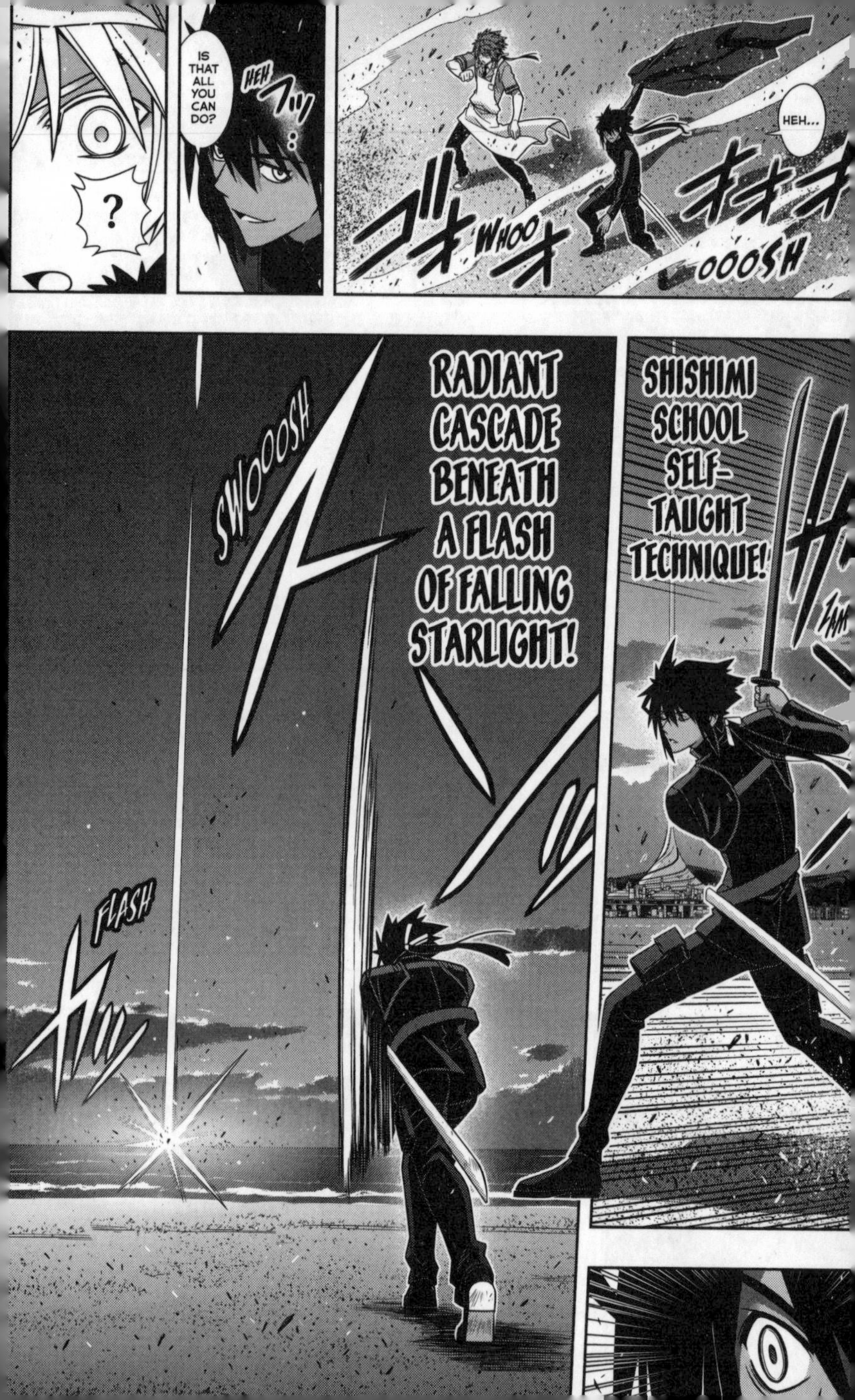

HEH...
WHOO
OOOSH
IS THAT ALL YOU CAN DO?
HEH
フッ
?
SHISHIMI SCHOOL SELF-TAUGHT TECHNIQUE!
ZAM
RADIANT CASCADE BENEATH A FLASH OF FALLING STARLIGHT!
SWOOOSH
FLASH

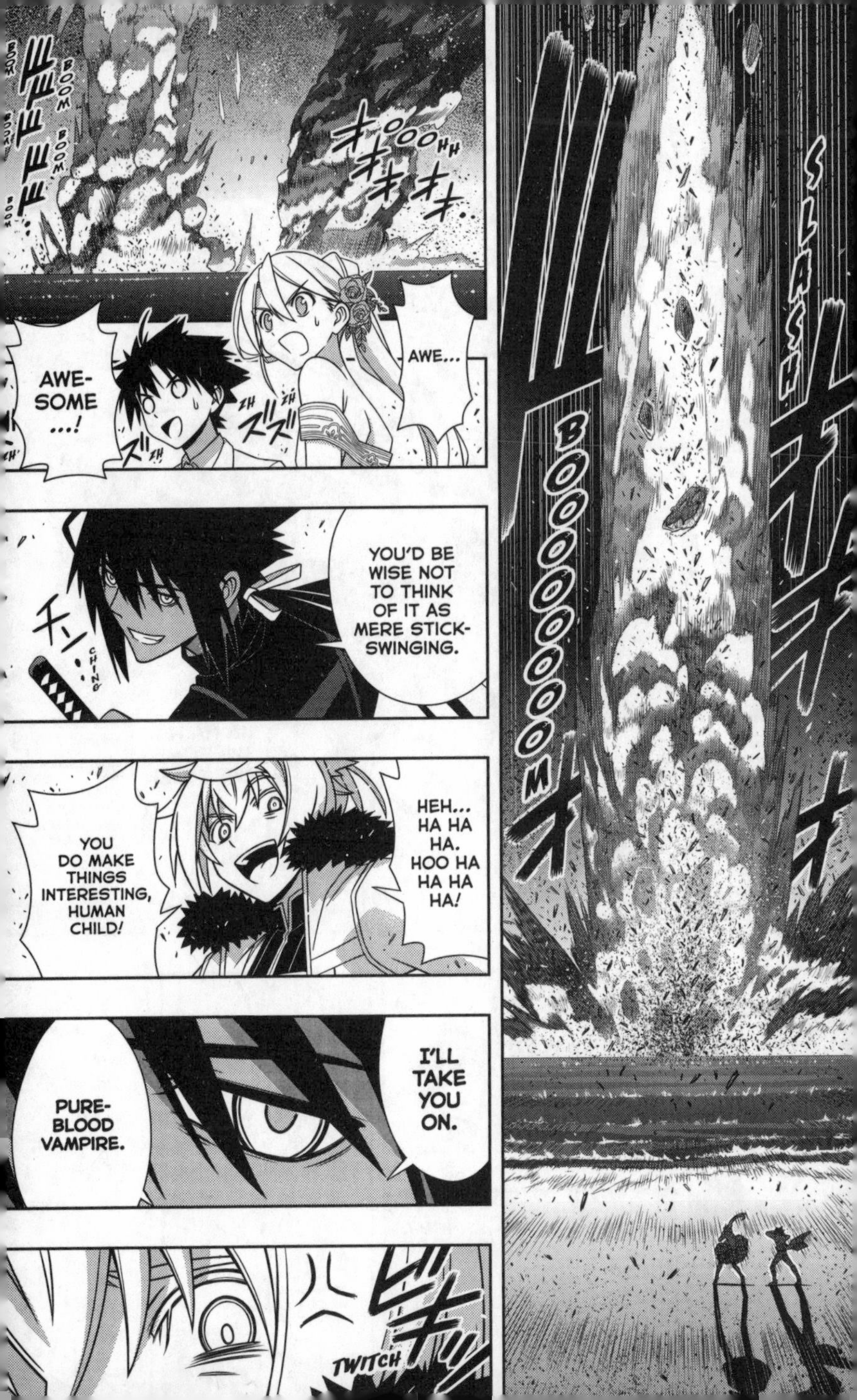
SLASH
BOOOOOOOOOOM
BOOM
BOOM
BOOM
BOOM
OOOOHH
AWE...
AWE-SOME ...!
ZH ZH ZH
YOU'D BE WISE NOT TO THINK OF IT AS MERE STICK-SWINGING.
CHING
HEH... HA HA HA. HOO HA HA HA HA HA!
YOU DO MAKE THINGS INTERESTING, HUMAN CHILD!
I'LL TAKE YOU ON.
PURE-BLOOD VAMPIRE.
TWITCH

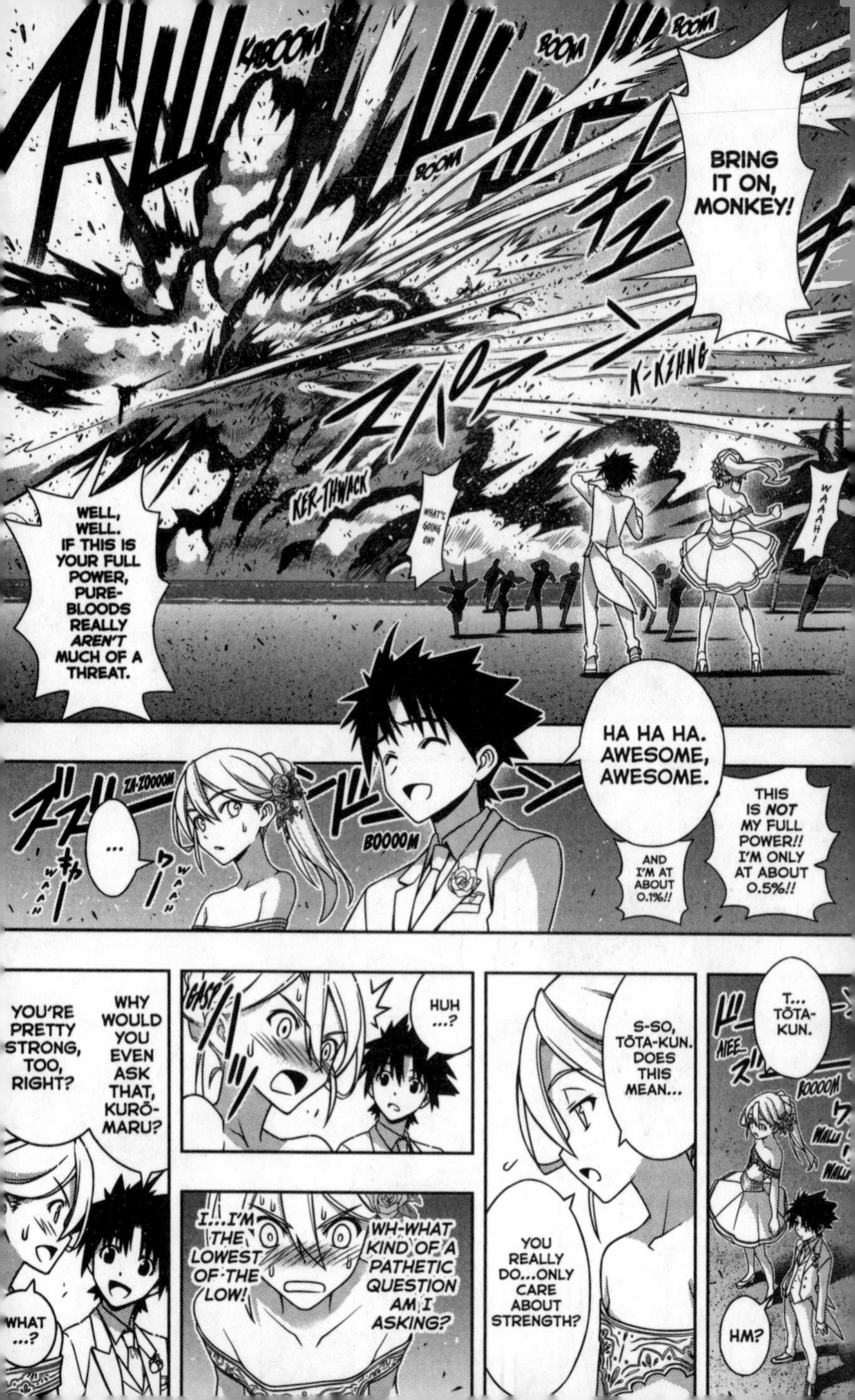
BOOM
BRING IT ON, MONKEY!
BOOM
KABOOM
BOOM
K-KZHNG
WAAAH!
WHAT'S GOING ON?
KER-THWACK
WELL, WELL. IF THIS IS YOUR FULL POWER, PURE-BLOODS REALLY *AREN'T* MUCH OF A THREAT.
HA HA HA. AWESOME, AWESOME.
THIS IS *NOT* MY FULL POWER!! I'M ONLY AT ABOUT 0.5%!!
AND I'M AT ABOUT 0.1%!!
BOOOOM
WAAAH
...
ZA-ZOOOOM
WAAAH
T... TŌTA-KUN.
AIEE...
BOOOOM
HM?
S-SO, TŌTA-KUN. DOES THIS MEAN...
YOU REALLY DO...ONLY CARE ABOUT STRENGTH?
HUH ...?
GASP!
WH-WHAT KIND OF A PATHETIC QUESTION AM I ASKING?
I...I'M THE LOWEST OF THE LOW!
WHY WOULD YOU EVEN ASK THAT, KURŌMARU?
YOU'RE PRETTY STRONG, TOO, RIGHT?
WHAT ...?

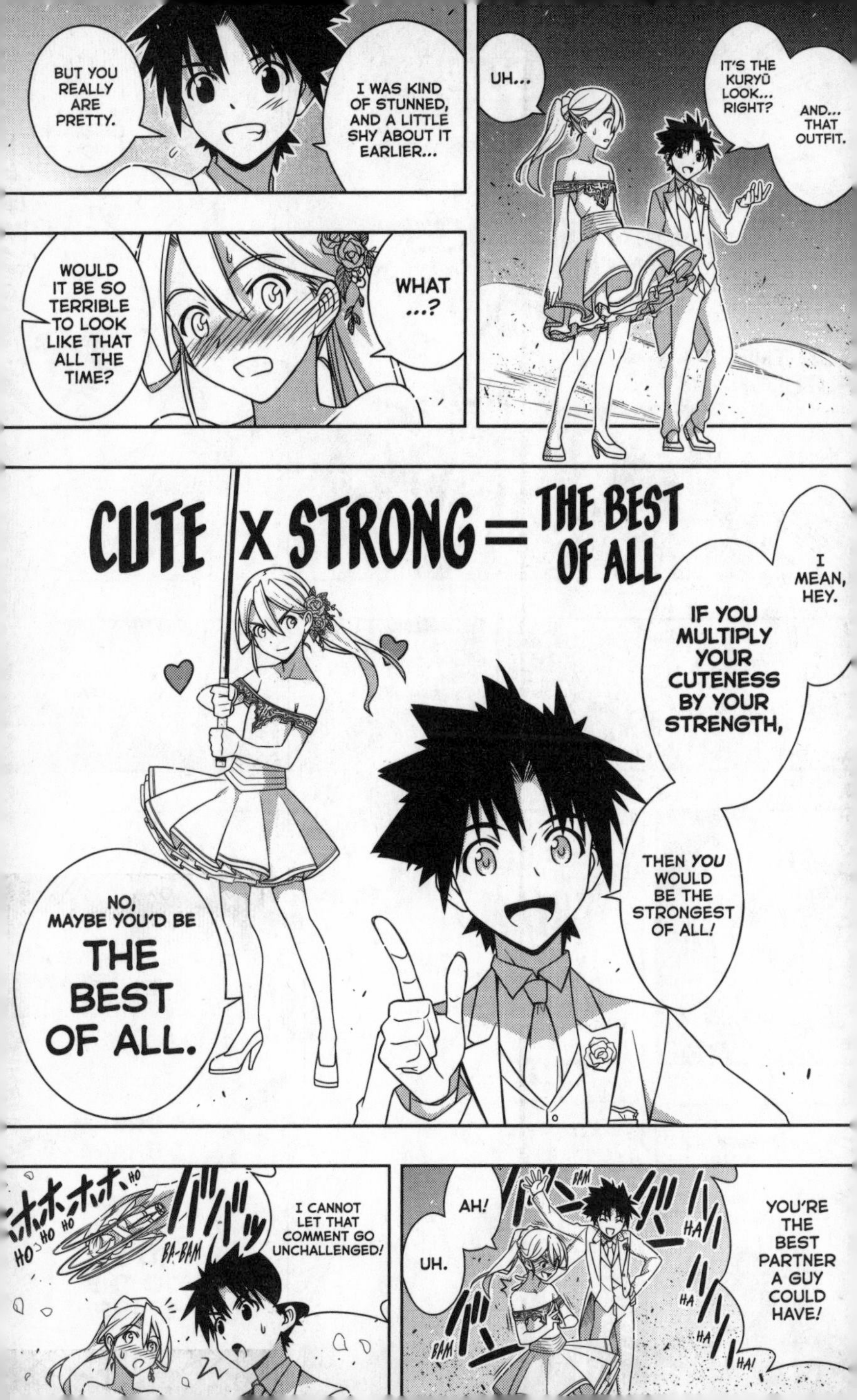

IT'S THE KURYŪ LOOK... RIGHT?
AND... THAT OUTFIT.
UH...
I WAS KIND OF STUNNED, AND A LITTLE SHY ABOUT IT EARLIER...
BUT YOU REALLY ARE PRETTY.
WHAT ...?
WOULD IT BE SO TERRIBLE TO LOOK LIKE THAT ALL THE TIME?
CUTE x STRONG = THE BEST OF ALL
I MEAN, HEY.
IF YOU MULTIPLY YOUR CUTENESS BY YOUR STRENGTH,
THEN *YOU* WOULD BE THE STRONGEST OF ALL!
NO, MAYBE YOU'D BE THE BEST OF ALL.
YOU'RE THE BEST PARTNER A GUY COULD HAVE!
BAM
HA HA HA HA HA!
AH!
UH.
BAM
I CANNOT LET THAT COMMENT GO UNCHALLENGED!
BA-BAM
HO HO HO HO

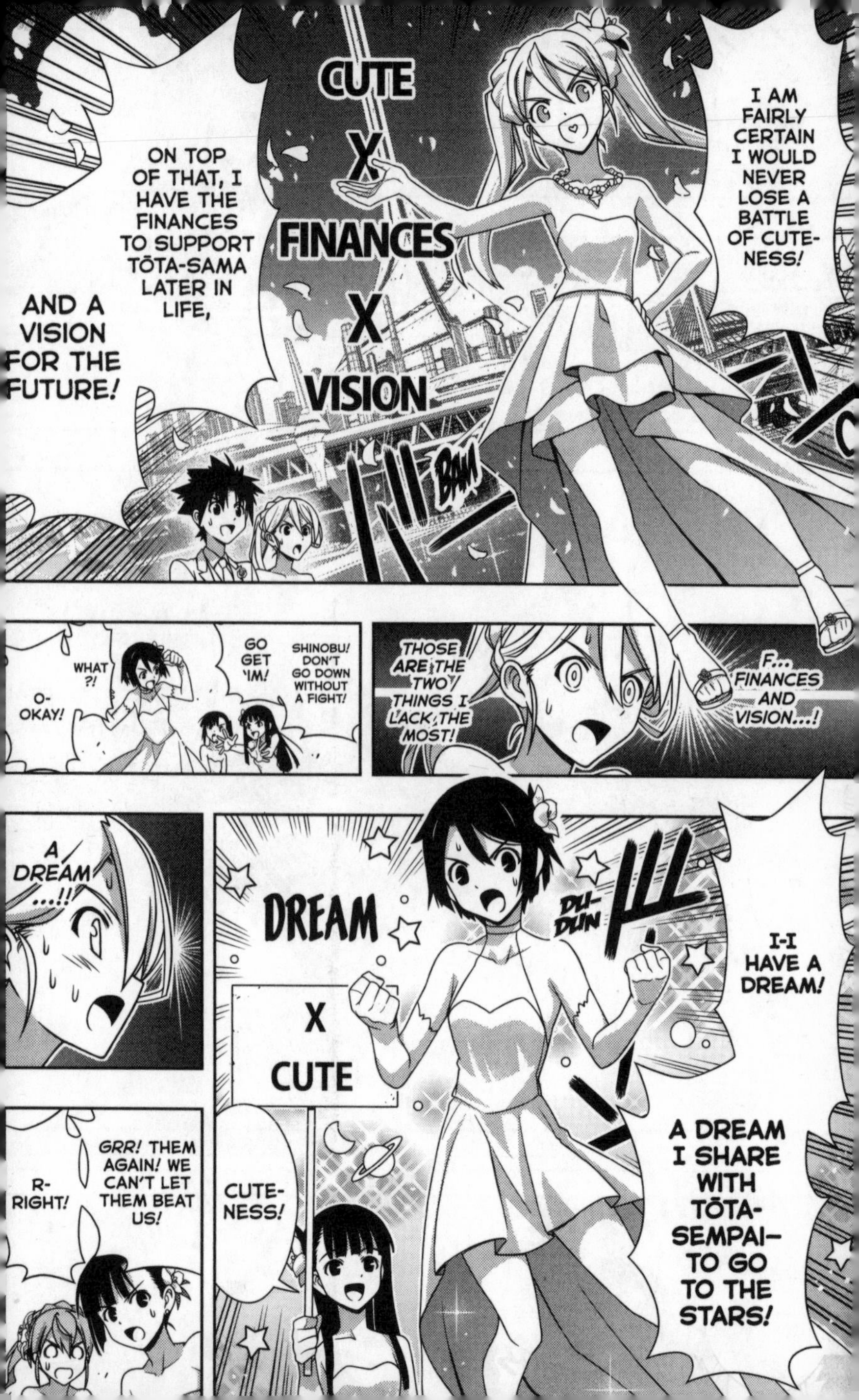
I AM FAIRLY CERTAIN I WOULD NEVER LOSE A BATTLE OF CUTE-NESS!
CUTE X FINANCES X VISION
ON TOP OF THAT, I HAVE THE FINANCES TO SUPPORT TŌTA-SAMA LATER IN LIFE,
AND A VISION FOR THE FUTURE!
BAM
F... FINANCES AND VISION...!
THOSE ARE THE TWO THINGS I LACK THE MOST!
SHINOBU! DON'T GO DOWN WITHOUT A FIGHT!
GO GET 'IM!
WHAT?!
O-OKAY!
I-I HAVE A DREAM!
DU-DUN
DREAM
X CUTE
A DREAM I SHARE WITH TŌTA-SEMPAI—TO GO TO THE STARS!
CUTE-NESS!
A DREAM...!!!
GRR! THEM AGAIN! WE CAN'T LET THEM BEAT US!
R-RIGHT!

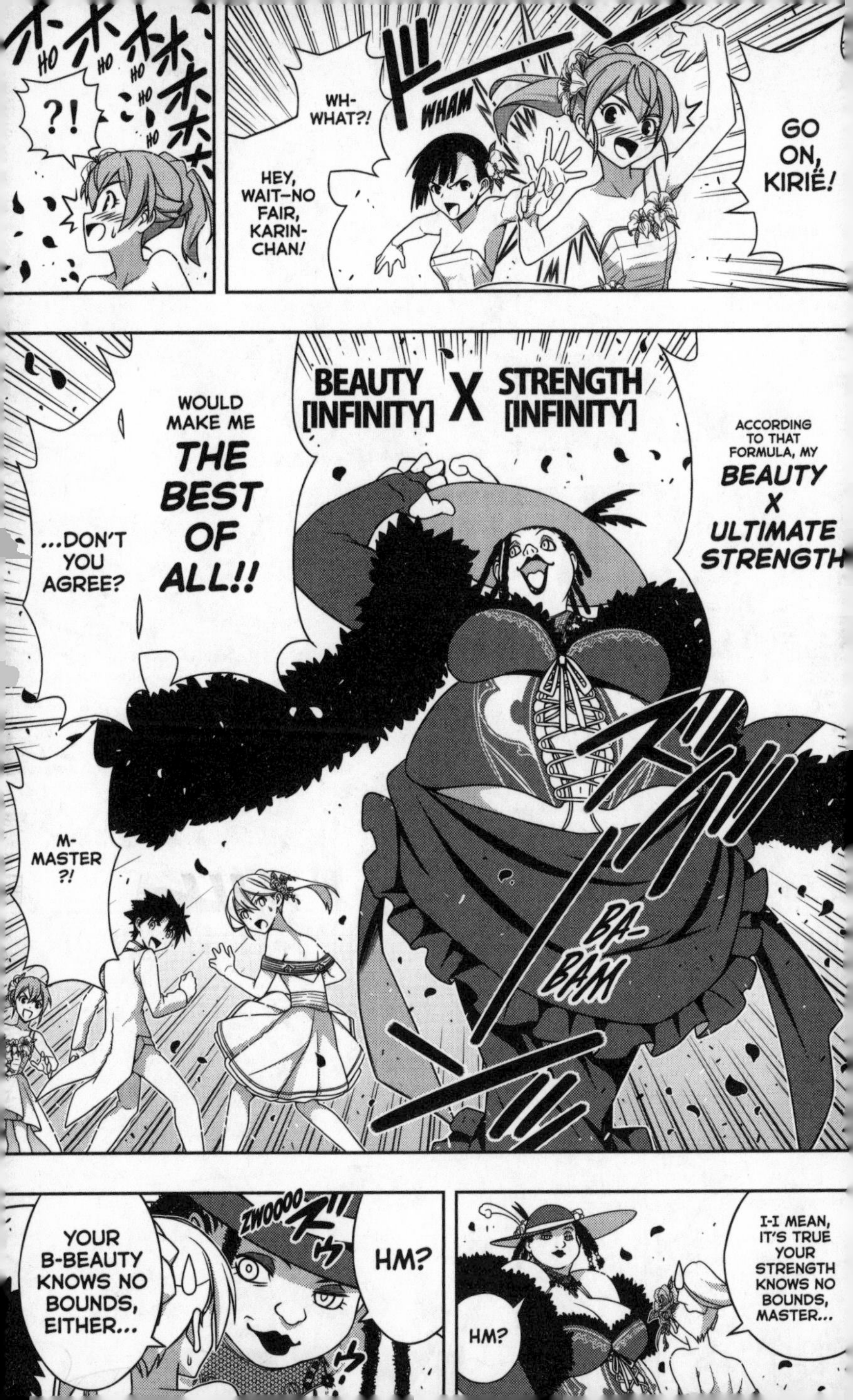
GO ON, KIRIË!
WHAM
WH- WHAT?!
HEY, WAIT—NO FAIR, KARIN-CHAN!
HO HO HO HO HO
?!
ACCORDING TO THAT FORMULA, MY BEAUTY X ULTIMATE STRENGTH
BEAUTY [INFINITY] X STRENGTH [INFINITY]
WOULD MAKE ME THE BEST OF ALL!!
...DON'T YOU AGREE?
BA-BAM
M-MASTER?!
I-I MEAN, IT'S TRUE YOUR STRENGTH KNOWS NO BOUNDS, MASTER...
HM?
ZWOOOO
HM?
YOUR B-BEAUTY KNOWS NO BOUNDS, EITHER...

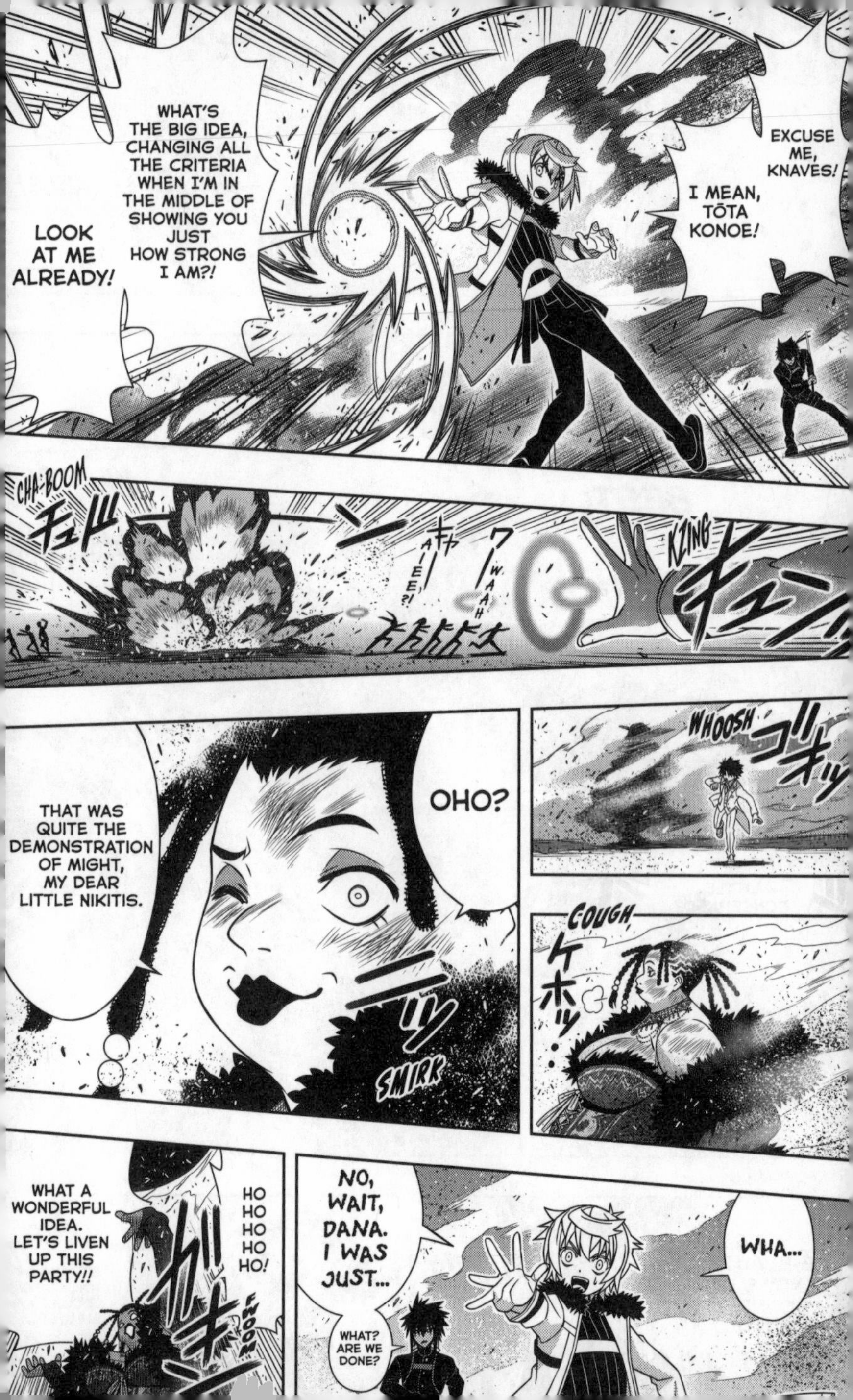
EXCUSE ME, KNAVES!
I MEAN, TŌTA KONOE!
WHAT'S THE BIG IDEA, CHANGING ALL THE CRITERIA WHEN I'M IN THE MIDDLE OF SHOWING YOU JUST HOW STRONG I AM?!
LOOK AT ME ALREADY!
KZING
WAAH
AIEE?!
CHA-BOOM
WHOOSH
COUGH
OHO?
THAT WAS QUITE THE DEMONSTRATION OF MIGHT, MY DEAR LITTLE NIKITIS.
SMIRK
WHA...
NO, WAIT, DANA. I WAS JUST...
WHAT? ARE WE DONE?
HO HO HO HO HO!
WHAT A WONDERFUL IDEA. LET'S LIVEN UP THIS PARTY!!
FWOOM

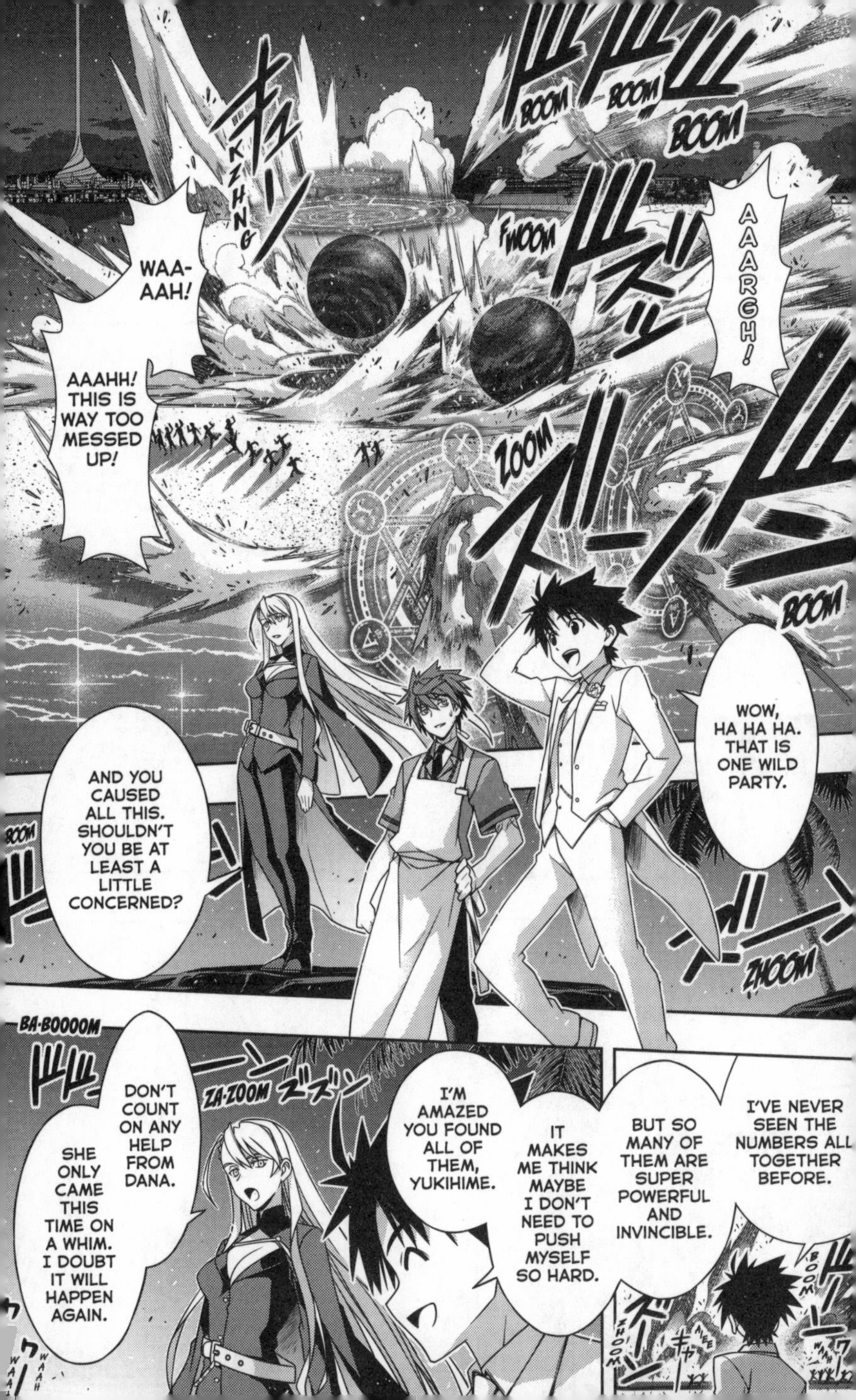
BOOM
BOOM
BOOM
AAAARGH!
FWOOM
KZHNG
WAA-AAH!
AAAHH! THIS IS WAY TOO MESSED UP!
ZOOM
BOOM
WOW, HA HA HA. THAT IS ONE WILD PARTY.
AND YOU CAUSED ALL THIS. SHOULDN'T YOU BE AT LEAST A LITTLE CONCERNED?
ZHOOM
BOOM
I'VE NEVER SEEN THE NUMBERS ALL TOGETHER BEFORE.
BUT SO MANY OF THEM ARE SUPER POWERFUL AND INVINCIBLE.
IT MAKES ME THINK MAYBE I DON'T NEED TO PUSH MYSELF SO HARD.
I'M AMAZED YOU FOUND ALL OF THEM, YUKIHIME.
ZA-ZOOM
BA-BOOOOM
DON'T COUNT ON ANY HELP FROM DANA.
SHE ONLY CAME THIS TIME ON A WHIM. I DOUBT IT WILL HAPPEN AGAIN.

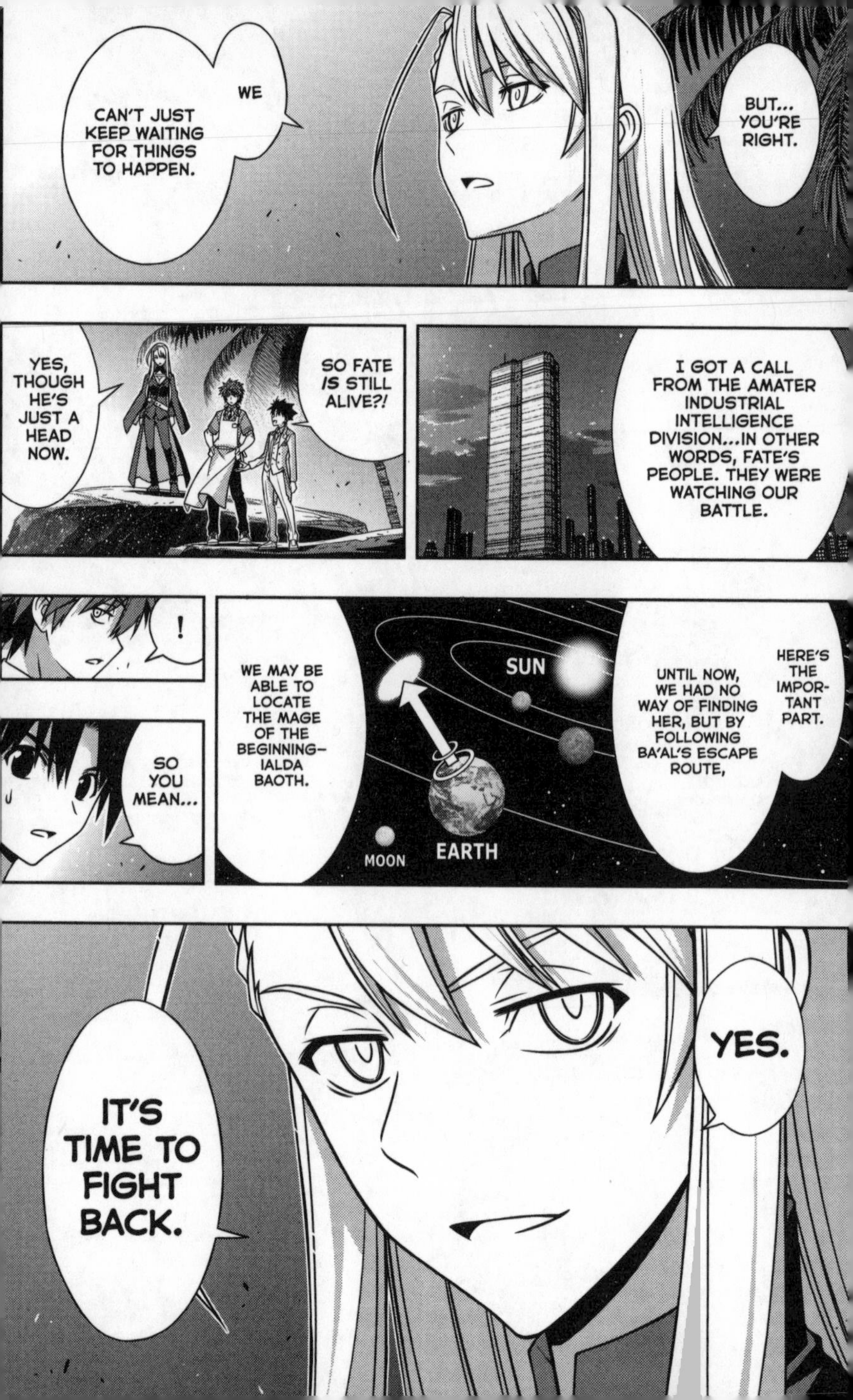
BUT... YOU'RE RIGHT.
WE CAN'T JUST KEEP WAITING FOR THINGS TO HAPPEN.
I GOT A CALL FROM THE AMATER INDUSTRIAL INTELLIGENCE DIVISION...IN OTHER WORDS, FATE'S PEOPLE. THEY WERE WATCHING OUR BATTLE.
SO FATE *IS* STILL ALIVE?!
YES, THOUGH HE'S JUST A HEAD NOW.
HERE'S THE IMPORTANT PART.
UNTIL NOW, WE HAD NO WAY OF FINDING HER, BUT BY FOLLOWING BA'AL'S ESCAPE ROUTE,
SUN
EARTH
MOON
WE MAY BE ABLE TO LOCATE THE MAGE OF THE BEGINNING—IALDA BAOTH.
!
SO YOU MEAN...
YES.
IT'S TIME TO FIGHT BACK.

UQ HOLDER!

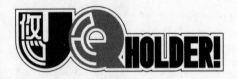

UQ HOLDER!

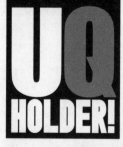

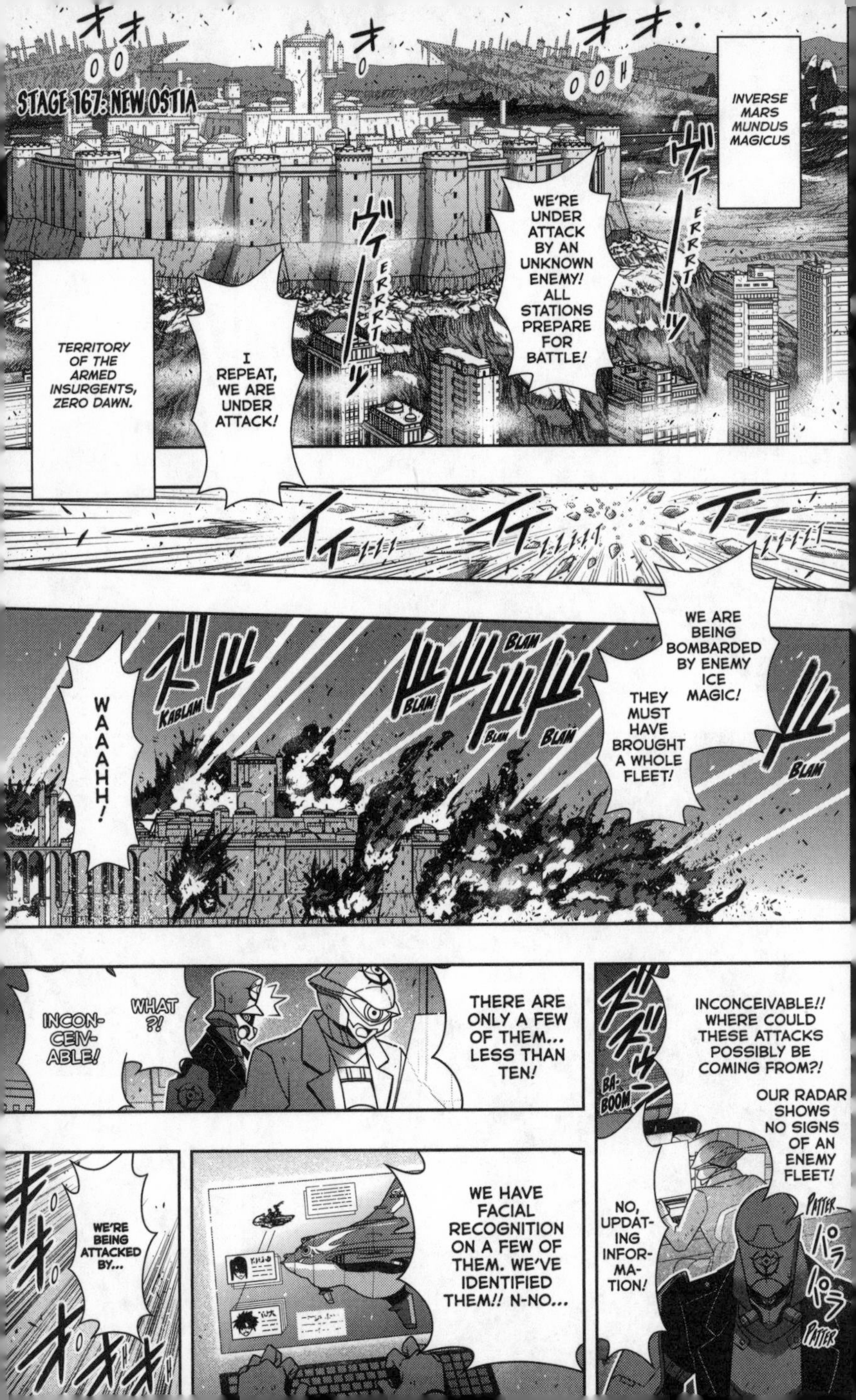

OOH
INVERSE MARS MUNDUS MAGICUS
ERRRT
WE'RE UNDER ATTACK BY AN UNKNOWN ENEMY! ALL STATIONS PREPARE FOR BATTLE!
ERRRT
OO
STAGE 167: NEW OSTIA
I REPEAT, WE ARE UNDER ATTACK!
TERRITORY OF THE ARMED INSURGENTS, ZERO DAWN.
WE ARE BEING BOMBARDED BY ENEMY ICE MAGIC!
THEY MUST HAVE BROUGHT A WHOLE FLEET!
BLAM
BLAM
BLAM
BLAM
BLAM
KABLAM
WAAAAHH!
INCONCEIVABLE!! WHERE COULD THESE ATTACKS POSSIBLY BE COMING FROM?!
BA-BOOM
OUR RADAR SHOWS NO SIGNS OF AN ENEMY FLEET!
NO, UPDATING INFORMATION!
PATTER
PATTER
THERE ARE ONLY A FEW OF THEM... LESS THAN TEN!
WHAT?!
INCONCEIVABLE!
WE HAVE FACIAL RECOGNITION ON A FEW OF THEM. WE'VE IDENTIFIED THEM!! N-NO...
WE'RE BEING ATTACKED BY...

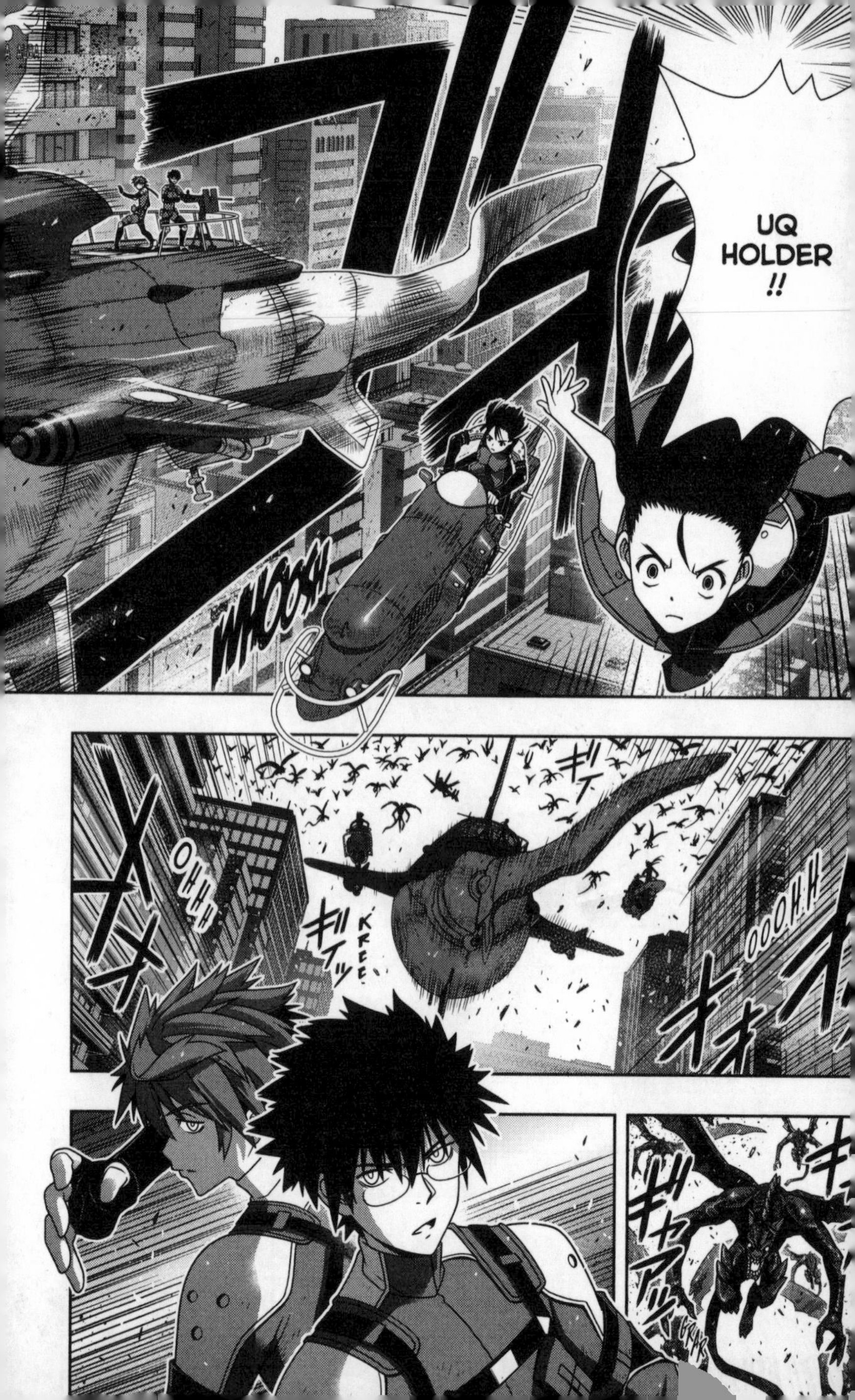
UQ HOLDER !!
WHOOSH
OOOHH
KREE
OHHH
GRAR

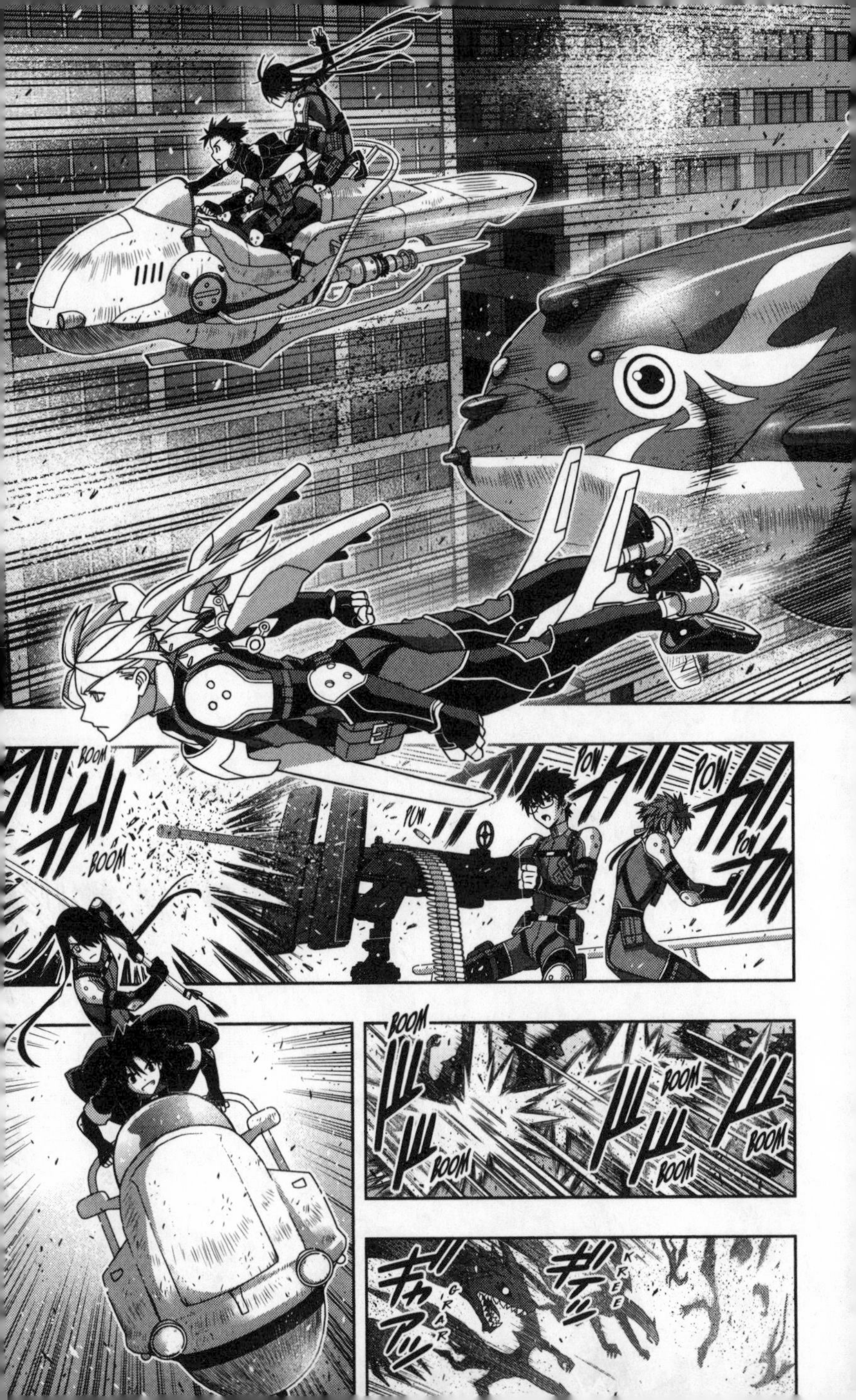
POW
POW
POW
POW
BOOM
BOOM
BOOM
BOOM
BOOM
BOOM
BOOM
KREE
GRAR

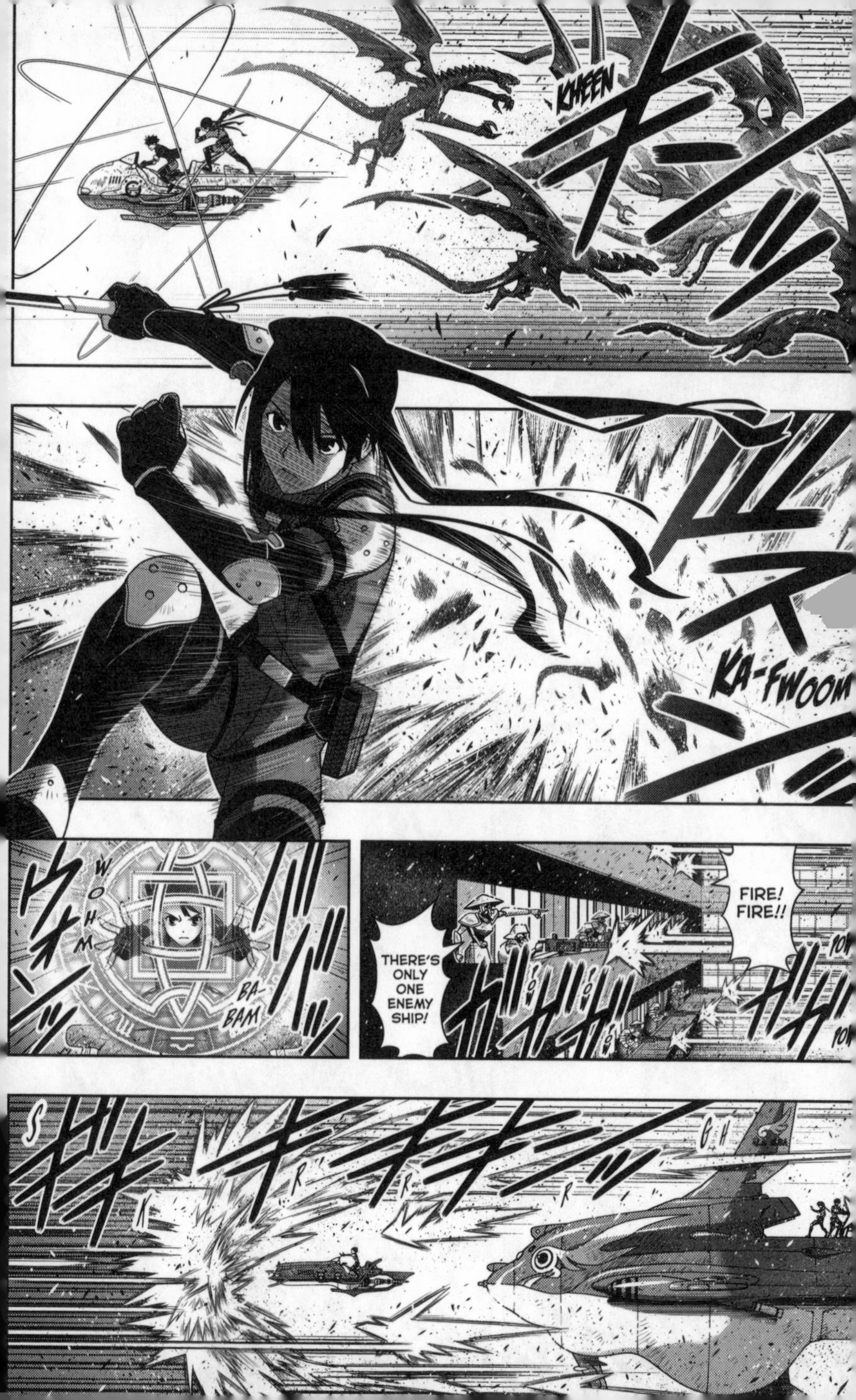
KHEEN
KA-FWOOM
FIRE! FIRE!!
THERE'S ONLY ONE ENEMY SHIP!
WOHM
BA-BAM

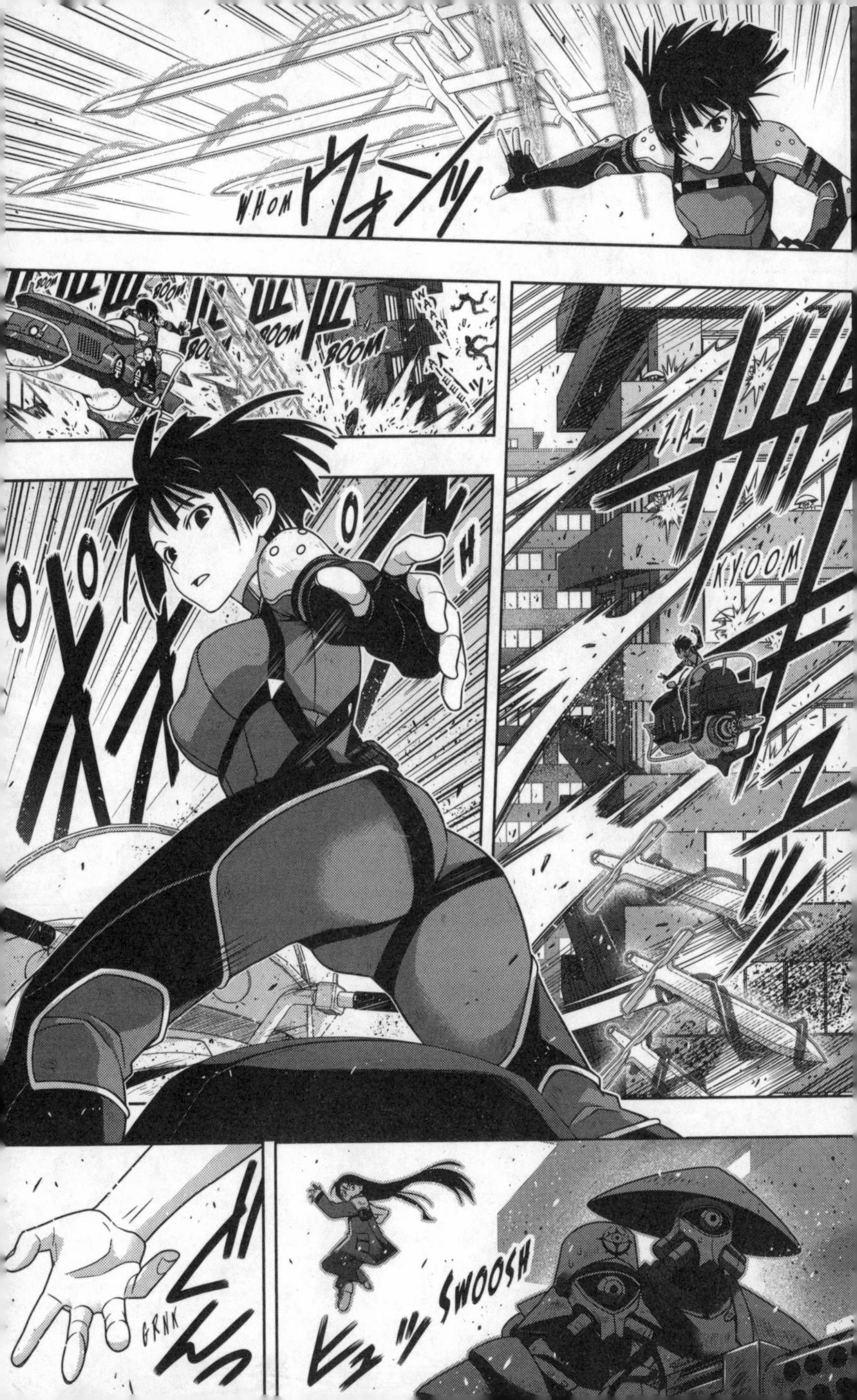
WHOM
ZA-
KYOOM
BOOM
BOOM
BOOM
BOOM
SWOOSH
GRNK

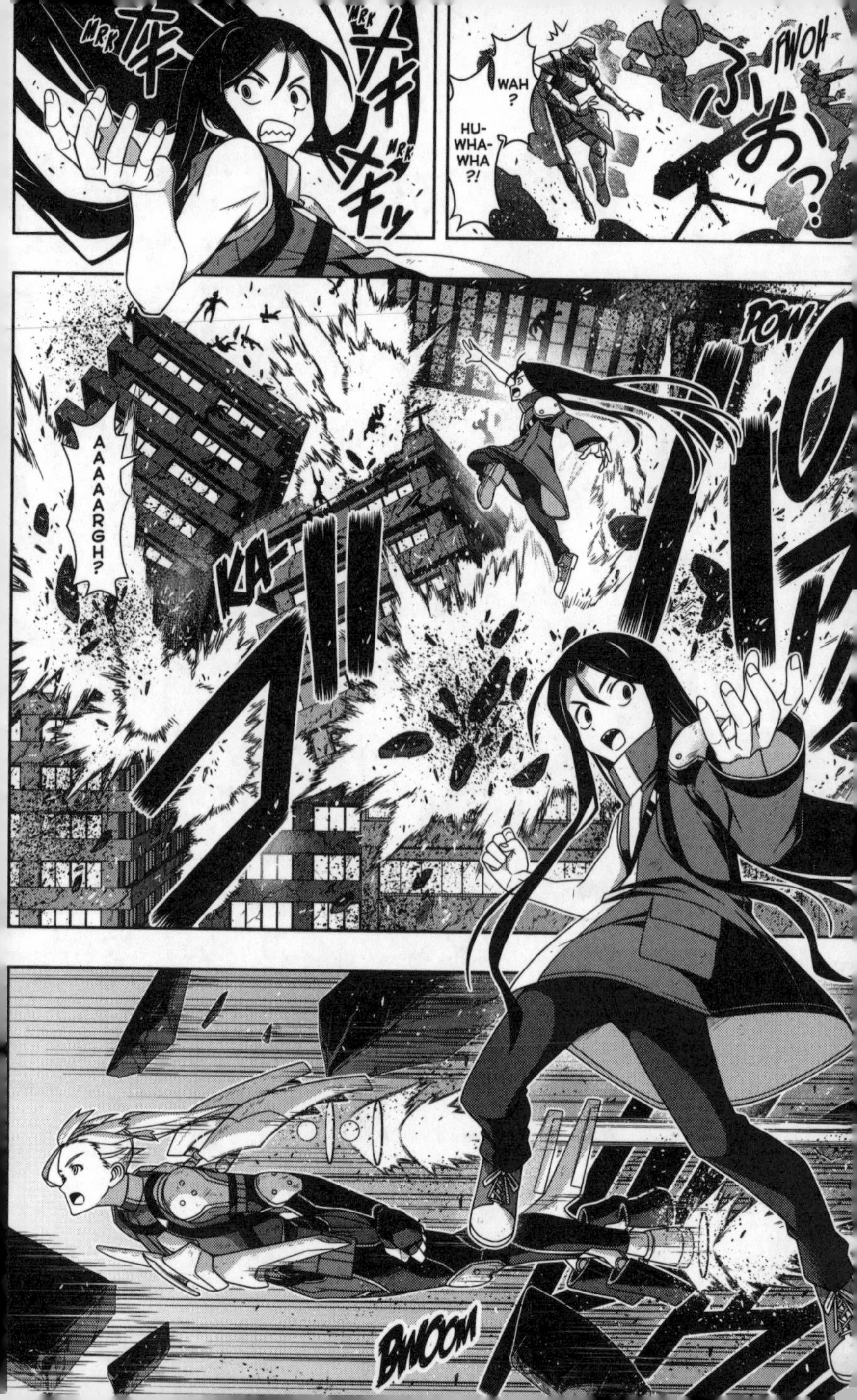
FWOH
WAH?
HU-WHA-WHA?!
MRK
MRK
MRK
POW
KA-
AAAAAARGH?
BWOOM

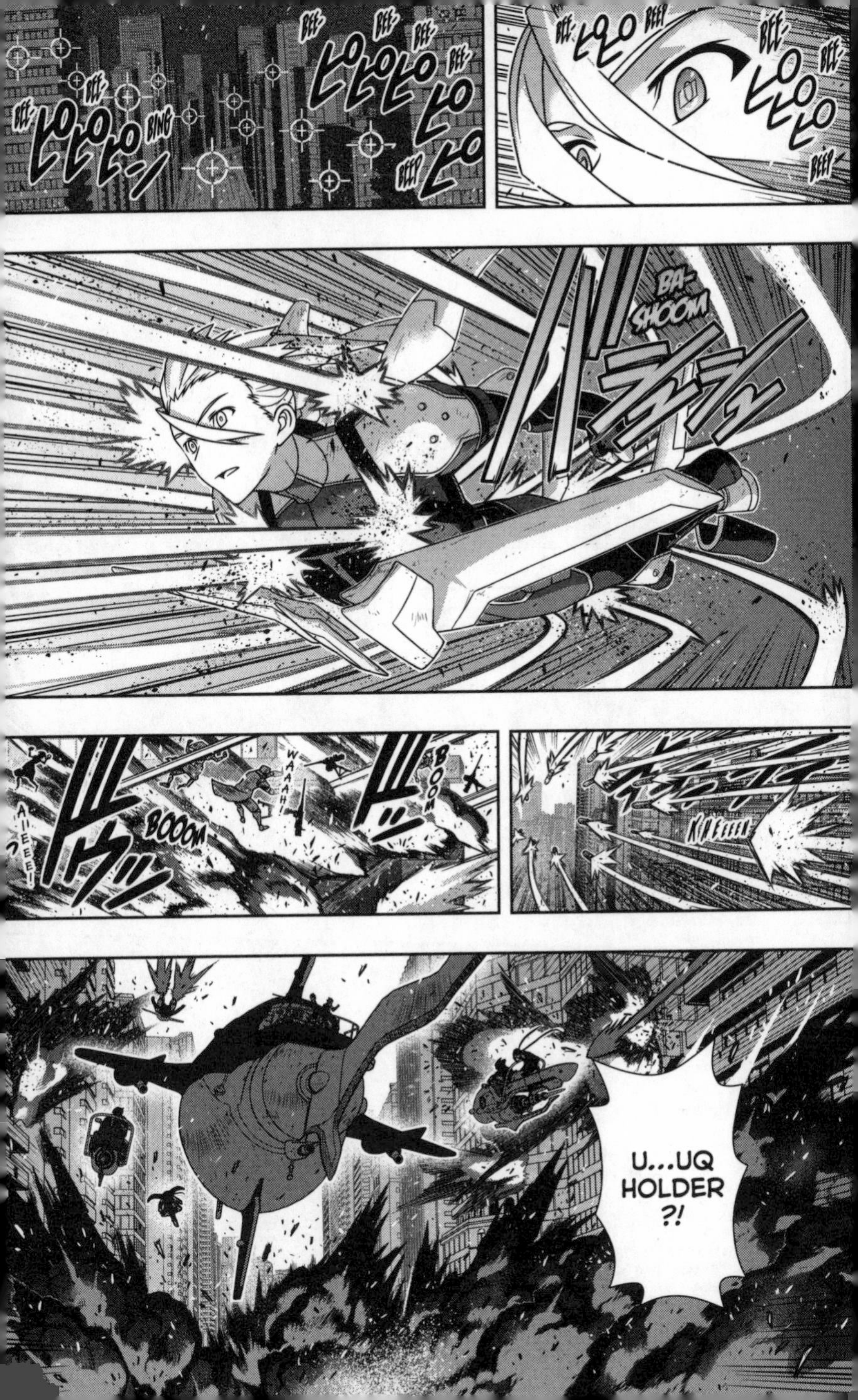
BEE- BEEP
BEE- BEE- BEEP
BEE- BEE- BEEP
BEE- BEE- BEING
BA-SHOOM
BOOM
WAAAH!
BOOOM
AIEEEE!
U...UQ HOLDER ?!

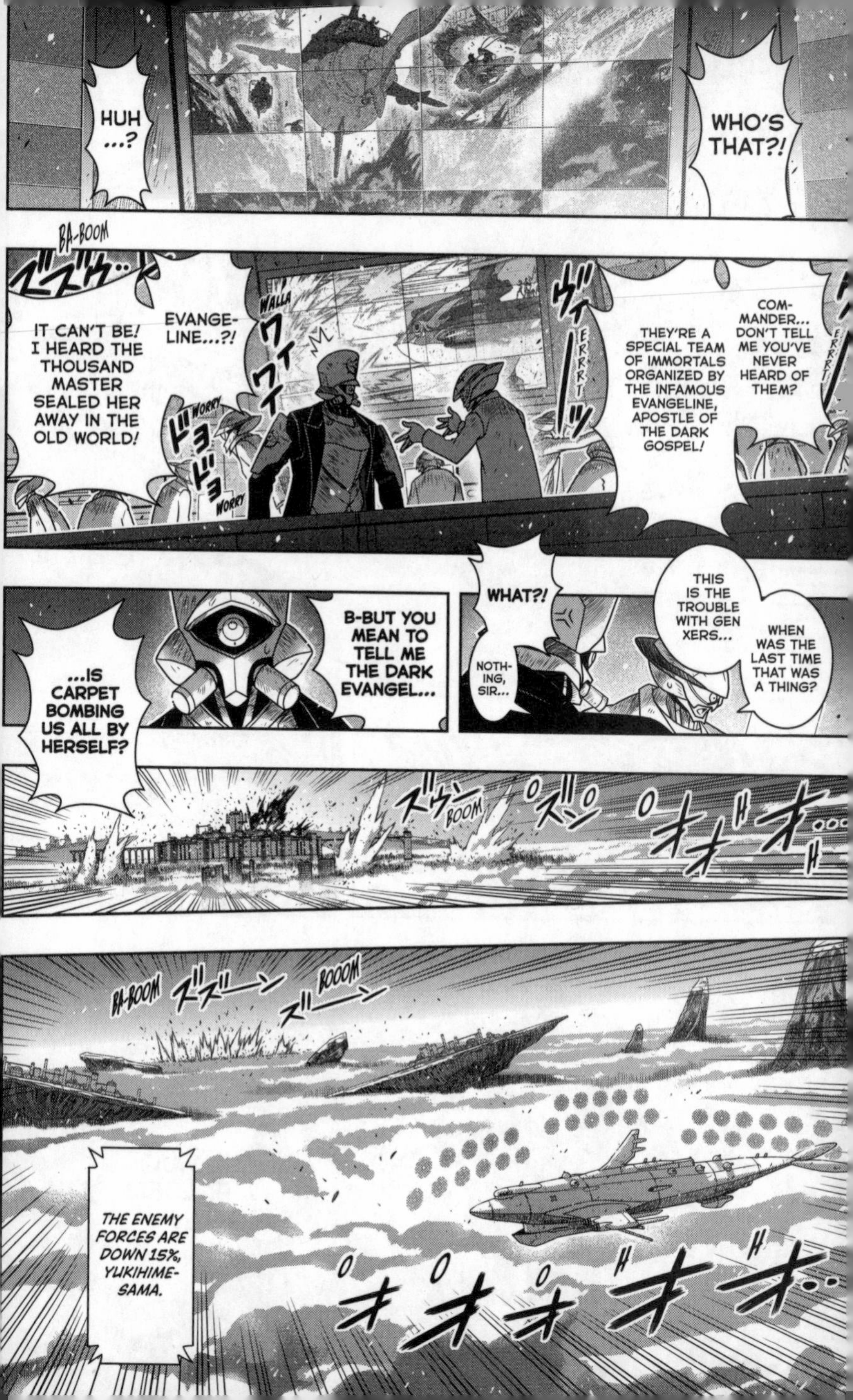
WHO'S THAT?!
HUH ...?
BA-BOOM
COMMANDER... DON'T TELL ME YOU'VE NEVER HEARD OF THEM?
ERRRT
THEY'RE A SPECIAL TEAM OF IMMORTALS ORGANIZED BY THE INFAMOUS EVANGELINE, APOSTLE OF THE DARK GOSPEL!
WALLA
EVANGELINE...?!
IT CAN'T BE! I HEARD THE THOUSAND MASTER SEALED HER AWAY IN THE OLD WORLD!
WORRY
WORRY
THIS IS THE TROUBLE WITH GEN XERS...
WHEN WAS THE LAST TIME THAT WAS A THING?
WHAT?!
NOTHING, SIR...
B-BUT YOU MEAN TO TELL ME THE DARK EVANGEL...
...IS CARPET BOMBING US ALL BY HERSELF?
BOOM
BA-BOOM
BOOOM
THE ENEMY FORCES ARE DOWN 15%, YUKIHIME-SAMA.

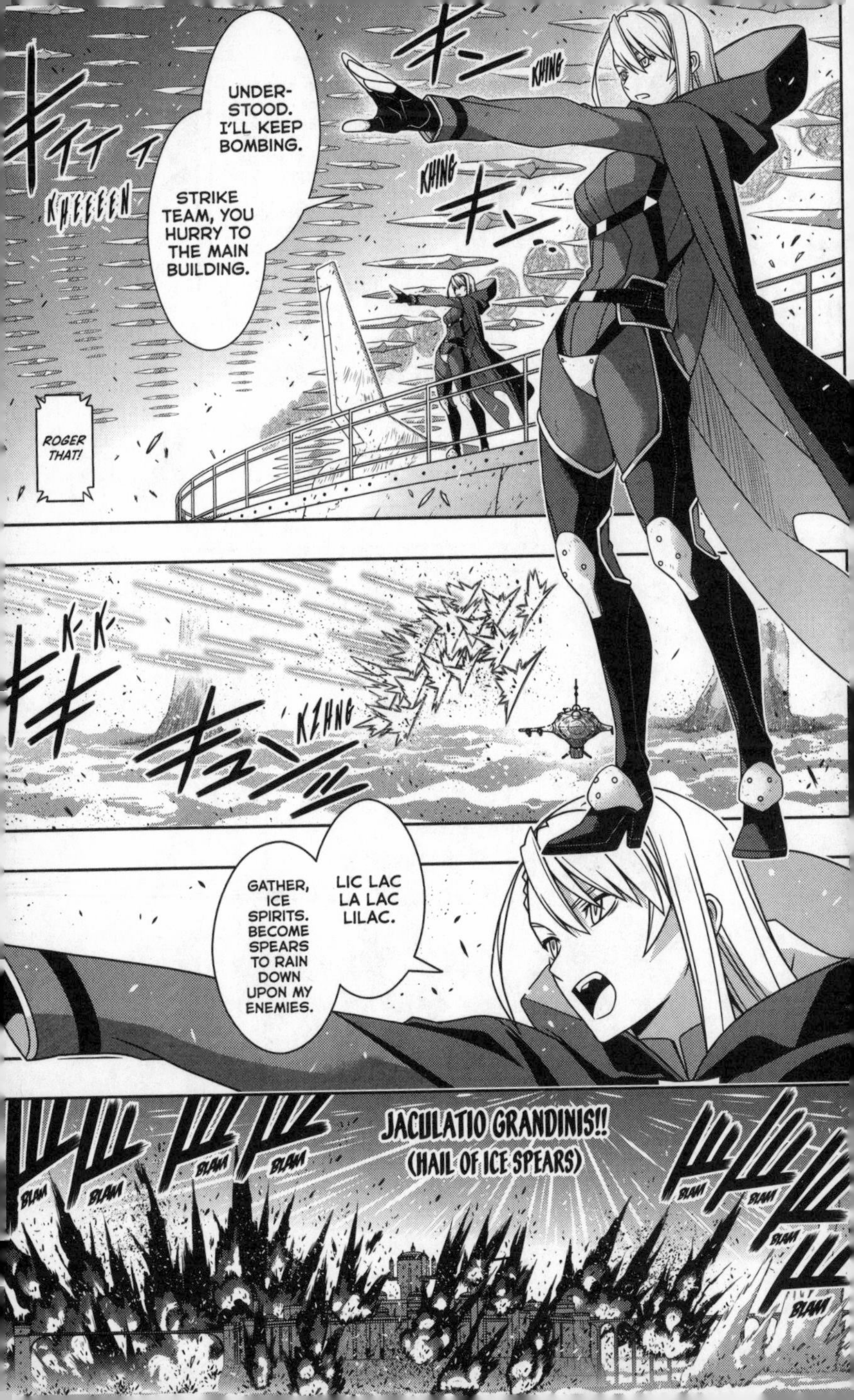
KHING
UNDER-STOOD. I'LL KEEP BOMBING.
STRIKE TEAM, YOU HURRY TO THE MAIN BUILDING.
KHING
KHEEEEN
ROGER THAT!
KZHNG
K-K-K
LIC LAC LA LAC LILAC.
GATHER, ICE SPIRITS. BECOME SPEARS TO RAIN DOWN UPON MY ENEMIES.
BLAM
BLAM
BLAM
JACULATIO GRANDINIS!!
(HAIL OF ICE SPEARS)
BLAM
BLAM
BLAM
BLAM
BLAM
BLAM

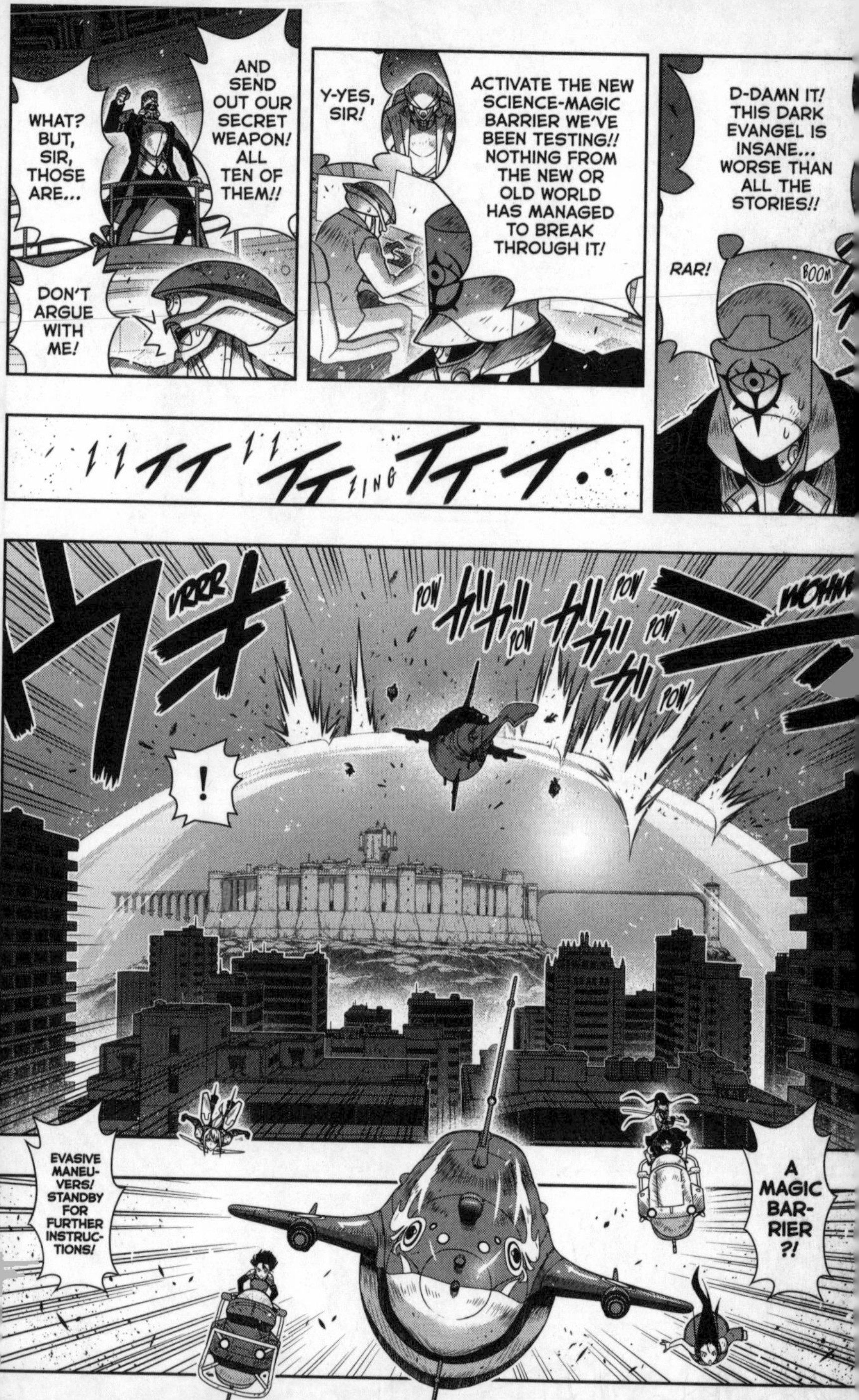
D-DAMN IT! THIS DARK EVANGEL IS INSANE... WORSE THAN ALL THE STORIES!!
RAR!
BOOM
ACTIVATE THE NEW SCIENCE-MAGIC BARRIER WE'VE BEEN TESTING!! NOTHING FROM THE NEW OR OLD WORLD HAS MANAGED TO BREAK THROUGH IT!
Y-YES, SIR!
AND SEND OUT OUR SECRET WEAPON! ALL TEN OF THEM!!
WHAT? BUT, SIR, THOSE ARE...
DON'T ARGUE WITH ME!
ZING
WOHM
POW
POW
POW
POW
POW
VRRR
!
A MAGIC BAR-RIER ?!
EVASIVE MANEU-VERS! STANDBY FOR FURTHER INSTRUC-TIONS!

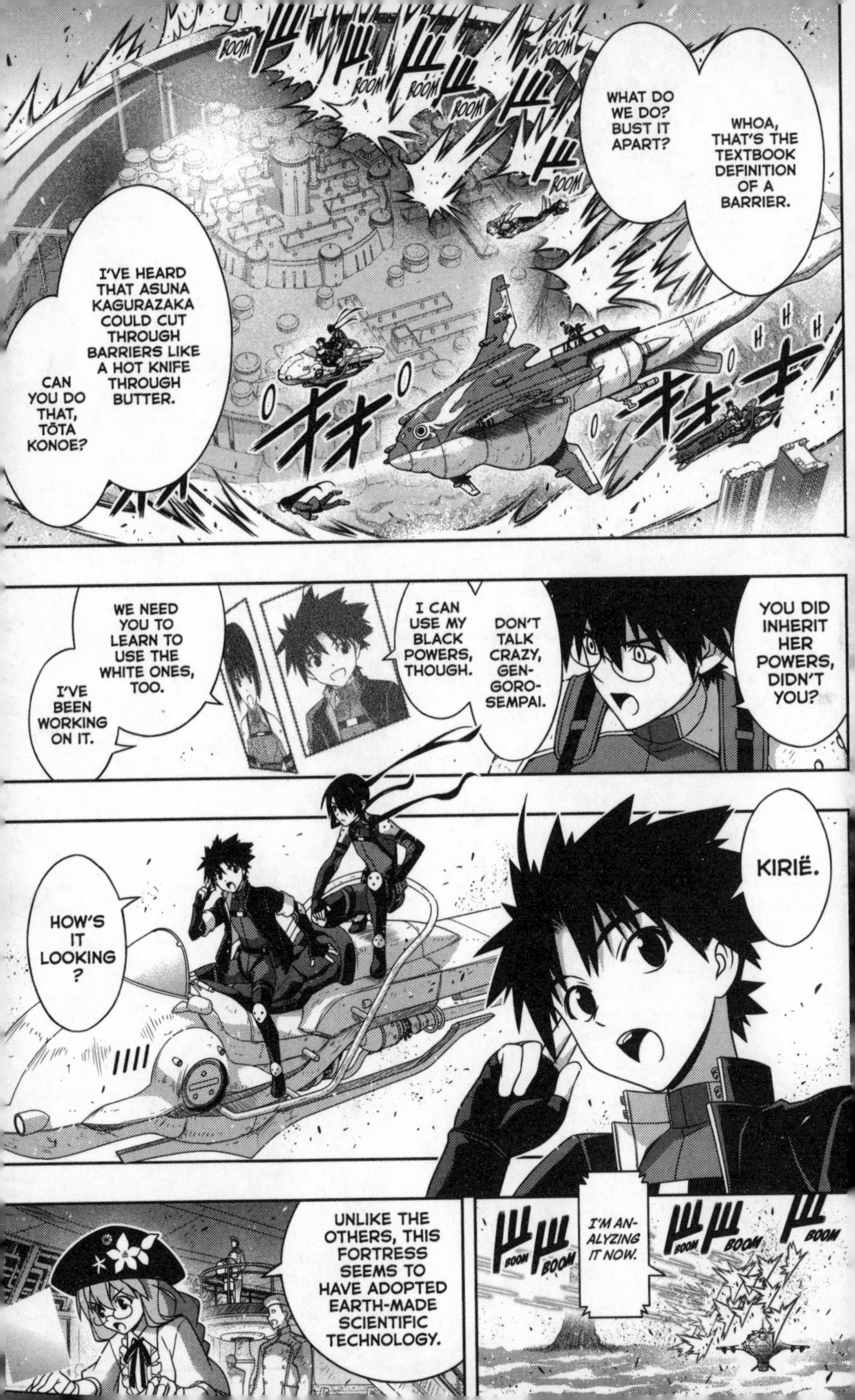
BOOM
BOOM
BOOM
BOOM
BOOM
BOOM
WHOA, THAT'S THE TEXTBOOK DEFINITION OF A BARRIER.
WHAT DO WE DO? BUST IT APART?
I'VE HEARD THAT ASUNA KAGURAZAKA COULD CUT THROUGH BARRIERS LIKE A HOT KNIFE THROUGH BUTTER.
CAN YOU DO THAT, TŌTA KONOE?
YOU DID INHERIT HER POWERS, DIDN'T YOU?
DON'T TALK CRAZY, GENGORO-SEMPAI.
I CAN USE MY BLACK POWERS, THOUGH.
WE NEED YOU TO LEARN TO USE THE WHITE ONES, TOO.
I'VE BEEN WORKING ON IT.
KIRIË.
HOW'S IT LOOKING?
BOOM
BOOM
BOOM
I'M AN-ALYZING IT NOW.
BOOM
BOOM
UNLIKE THE OTHERS, THIS FORTRESS SEEMS TO HAVE ADOPTED EARTH-MADE SCIENTIFIC TECHNOLOGY.

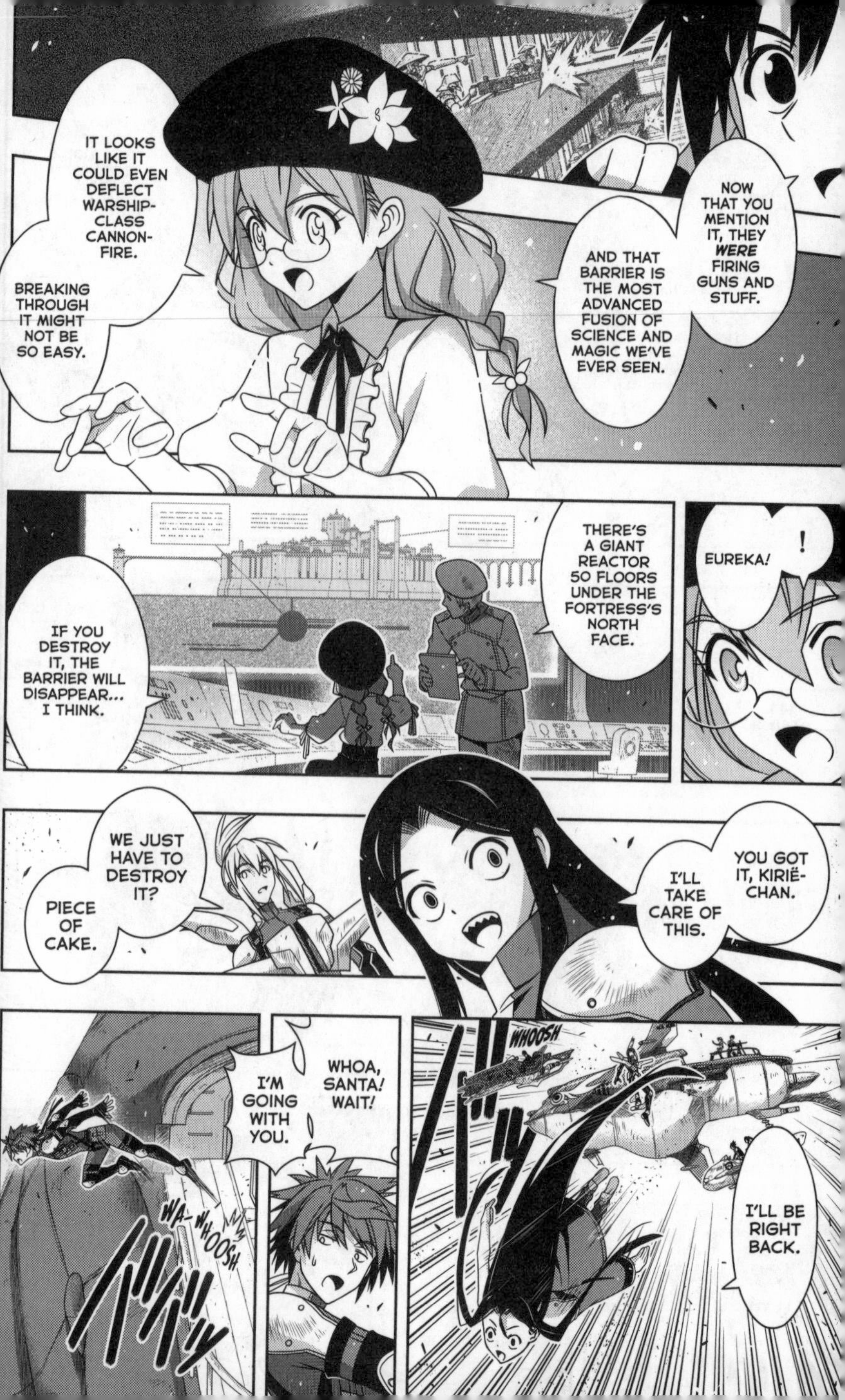
NOW THAT YOU MENTION IT, THEY *WERE* FIRING GUNS AND STUFF.
AND THAT BARRIER IS THE MOST ADVANCED FUSION OF SCIENCE AND MAGIC WE'VE EVER SEEN.
IT LOOKS LIKE IT COULD EVEN DEFLECT WARSHIP-CLASS CANNON-FIRE.
BREAKING THROUGH IT MIGHT NOT BE SO EASY.
!
EUREKA!
THERE'S A GIANT REACTOR 50 FLOORS UNDER THE FORTRESS'S NORTH FACE.
IF YOU DESTROY IT, THE BARRIER WILL DISAPPEAR... I THINK.
YOU GOT IT, KIRIË-CHAN.
I'LL TAKE CARE OF THIS.
WE JUST HAVE TO DESTROY IT?
PIECE OF CAKE.
WHOOSH
I'LL BE RIGHT BACK.
WHOA, SANTA! WAIT!
I'M GOING WITH YOU.
WA-WHOOSH

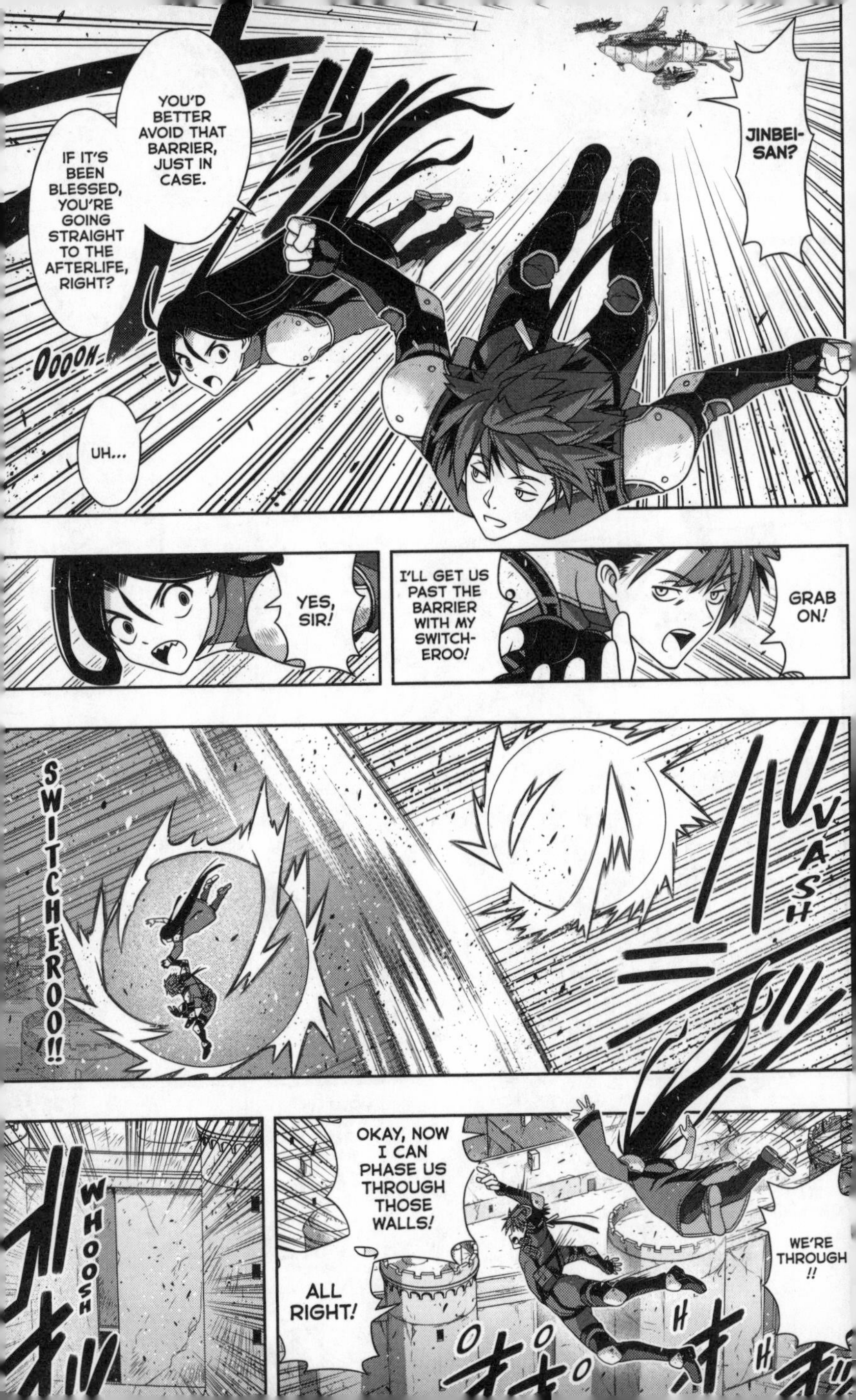
JINBEI-SAN?
YOU'D BETTER AVOID THAT BARRIER, JUST IN CASE.
IF IT'S BEEN BLESSED, YOU'RE GOING STRAIGHT TO THE AFTERLIFE, RIGHT?
OOOOH
UH...
GRAB ON!
I'LL GET US PAST THE BARRIER WITH MY SWITCH-EROO!
YES, SIR!
VASH
SWITCHEROO!!
WE'RE THROUGH!!
OKAY, NOW I CAN PHASE US THROUGH THOSE WALLS!
ALL RIGHT!
WHOOSH

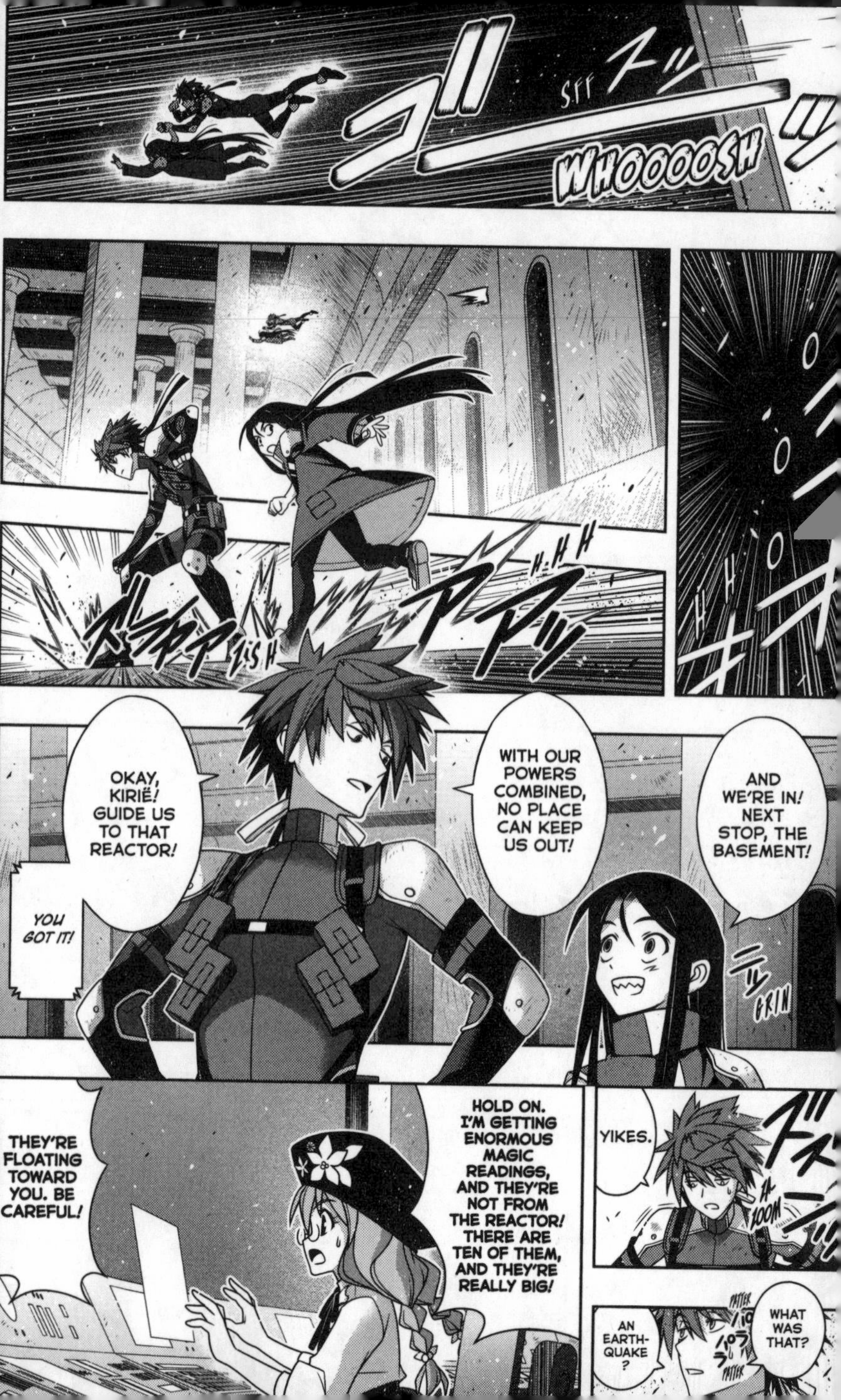

SFF
WHOOOOSH
HHH
ZISH
AND WE'RE IN! NEXT STOP, THE BASEMENT!
WITH OUR POWERS COMBINED, NO PLACE CAN KEEP US OUT!
OKAY, KIRIË! GUIDE US TO THAT REACTOR!
YOU GOT IT!
GRIN
YIKES.
ZOOM
WHAT WAS THAT?
AN EARTH-QUAKE?
PATTER
HOLD ON. I'M GETTING ENORMOUS MAGIC READINGS, AND THEY'RE NOT FROM THE REACTOR! THERE ARE TEN OF THEM, AND THEY'RE REALLY BIG!
THEY'RE FLOATING TOWARD YOU. BE CAREFUL!

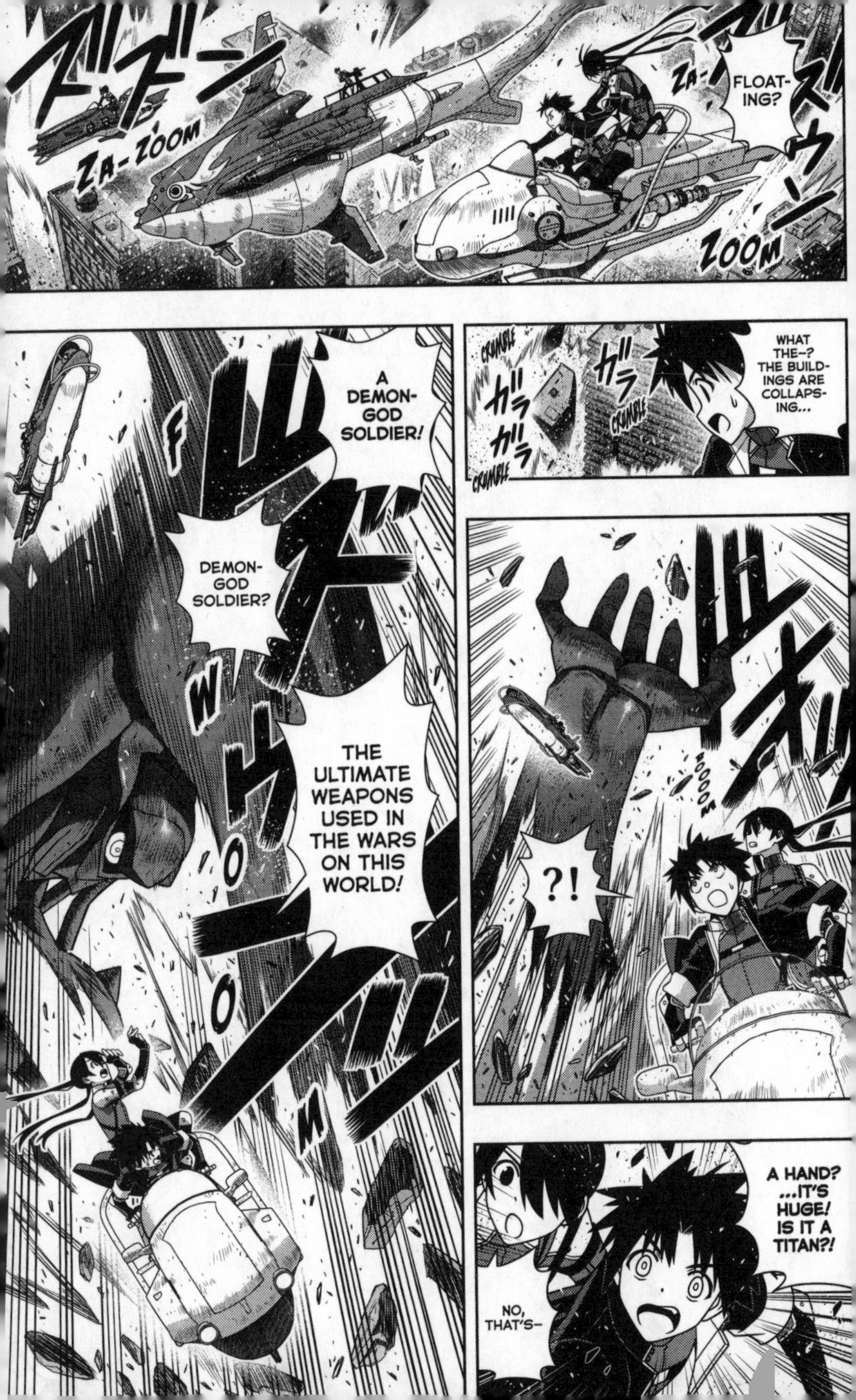

FLOAT-
ING?
ZA-
ZOOM
ZA-ZOOM
CRUMBLE
CRUMBLE
CRUMBLE
CRUMBLE
WHAT
THE-?
THE BUILD-
INGS ARE
COLLAPS-
ING...
ROOOOM
?!
A HAND?
...IT'S
HUGE!
IS IT A
TITAN?!
NO,
THAT'S–
A
DEMON-
GOD
SOLDIER!
DEMON-
GOD
SOLDIER?
THE
ULTIMATE
WEAPONS
USED IN
THE WARS
ON THIS
WORLD!
FWOOOM

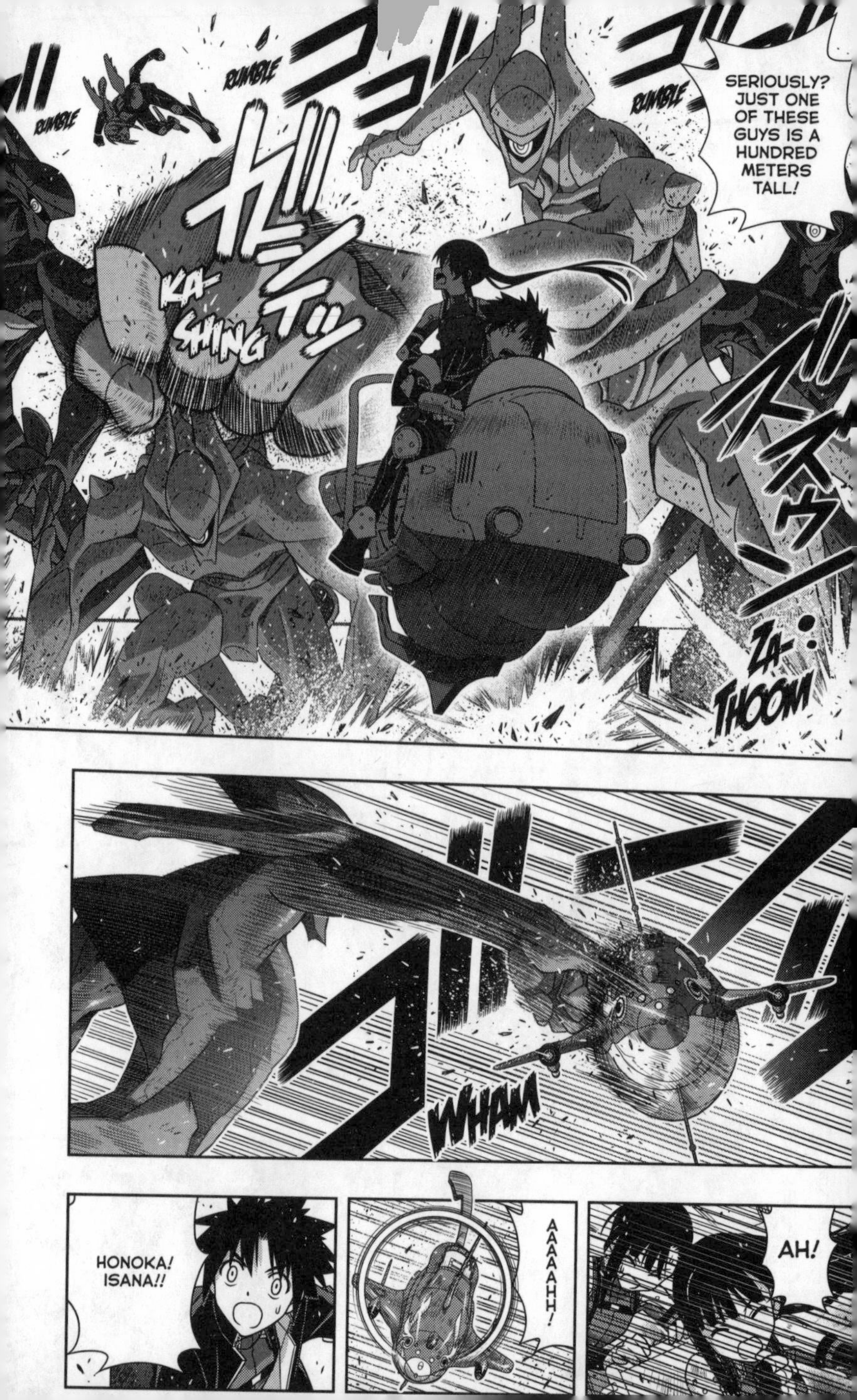
RUMBLE
SERIOUSLY? JUST ONE OF THESE GUYS IS A HUNDRED METERS TALL!
RUMBLE
RUMBLE
KA-SHING
ZA-THOOM
WHAM
AH!
AAAAAAHH!
HONOKA! ISANA!!

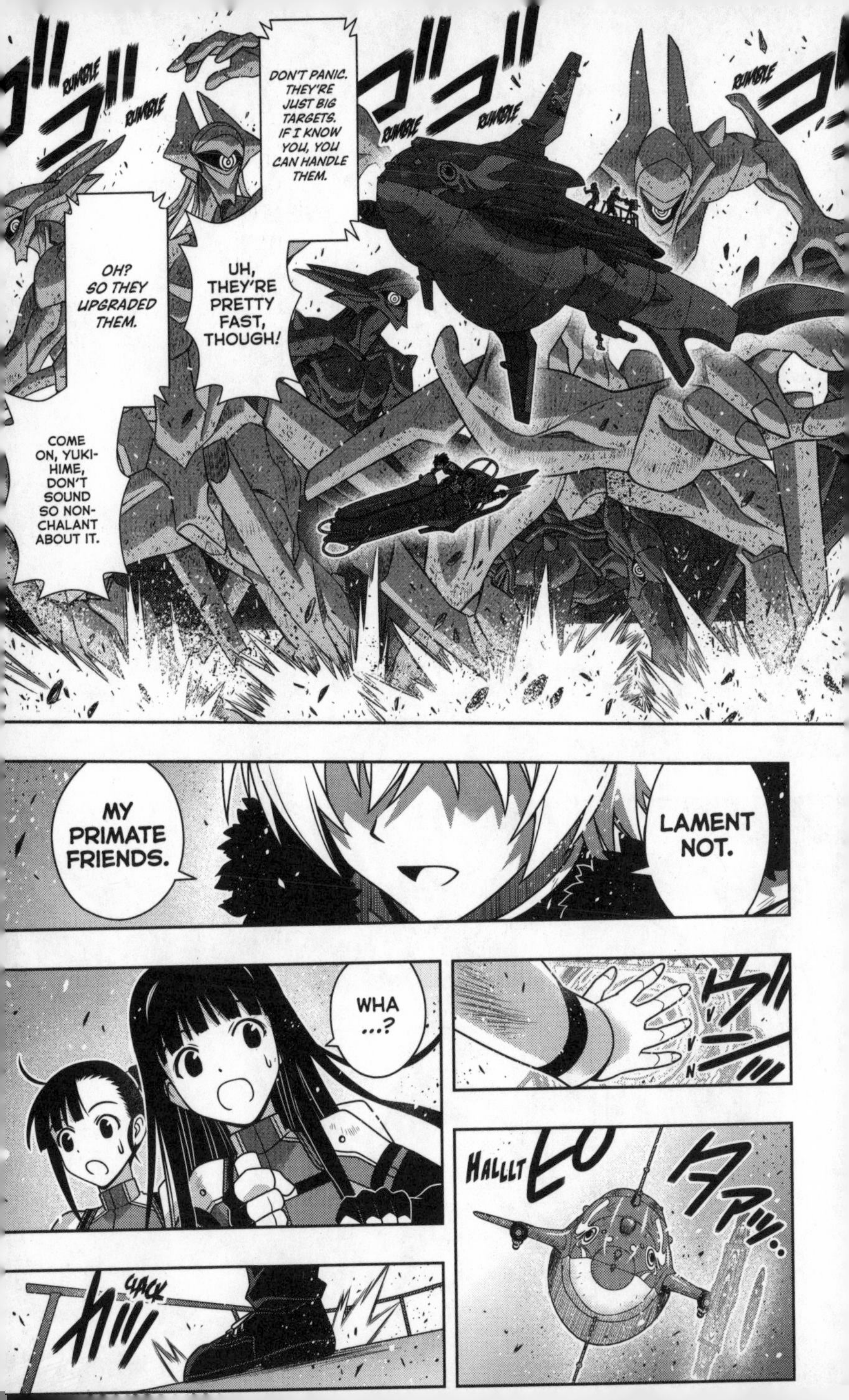
RUMBLE
RUMBLE
RUMBLE
DON'T PANIC. THEY'RE JUST BIG TARGETS. IF I KNOW YOU, YOU CAN HANDLE THEM.
RUMBLE
RUMBLE
UH, THEY'RE PRETTY FAST, THOUGH!
OH? SO THEY UPGRADED THEM.
COME ON, YUKI-HIME, DON'T SOUND SO NON-CHALANT ABOUT IT.
LAMENT NOT.
MY PRIMATE FRIENDS.
WHA ...?
HALLLT
CLACK

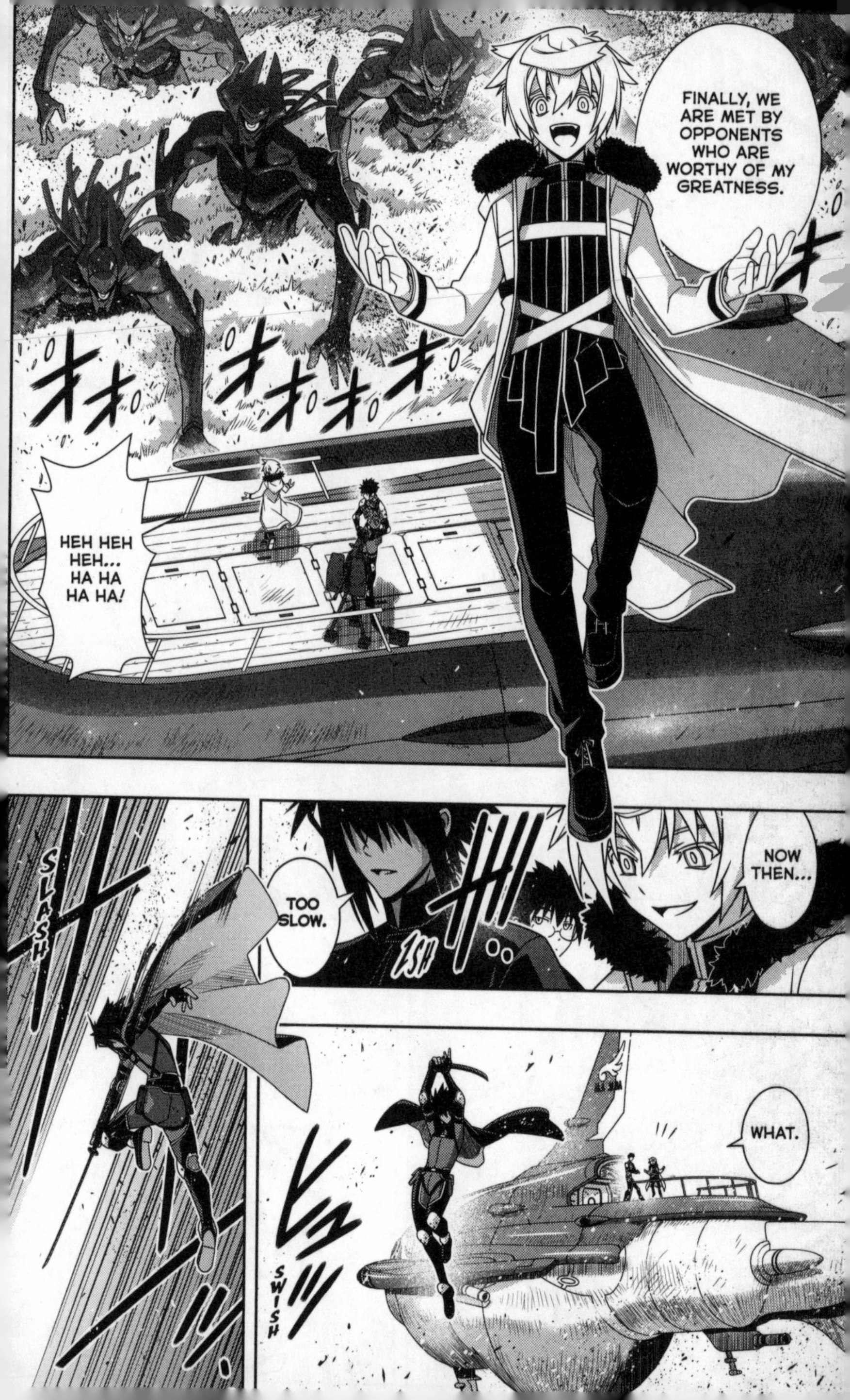
FINALLY, WE ARE MET BY OPPONENTS WHO ARE WORTHY OF MY GREATNESS.
HEH HEH HEH... HA HA HA HA!
NOW THEN...
TSH
TOO SLOW.
WHAT.
SWISH
SLASH

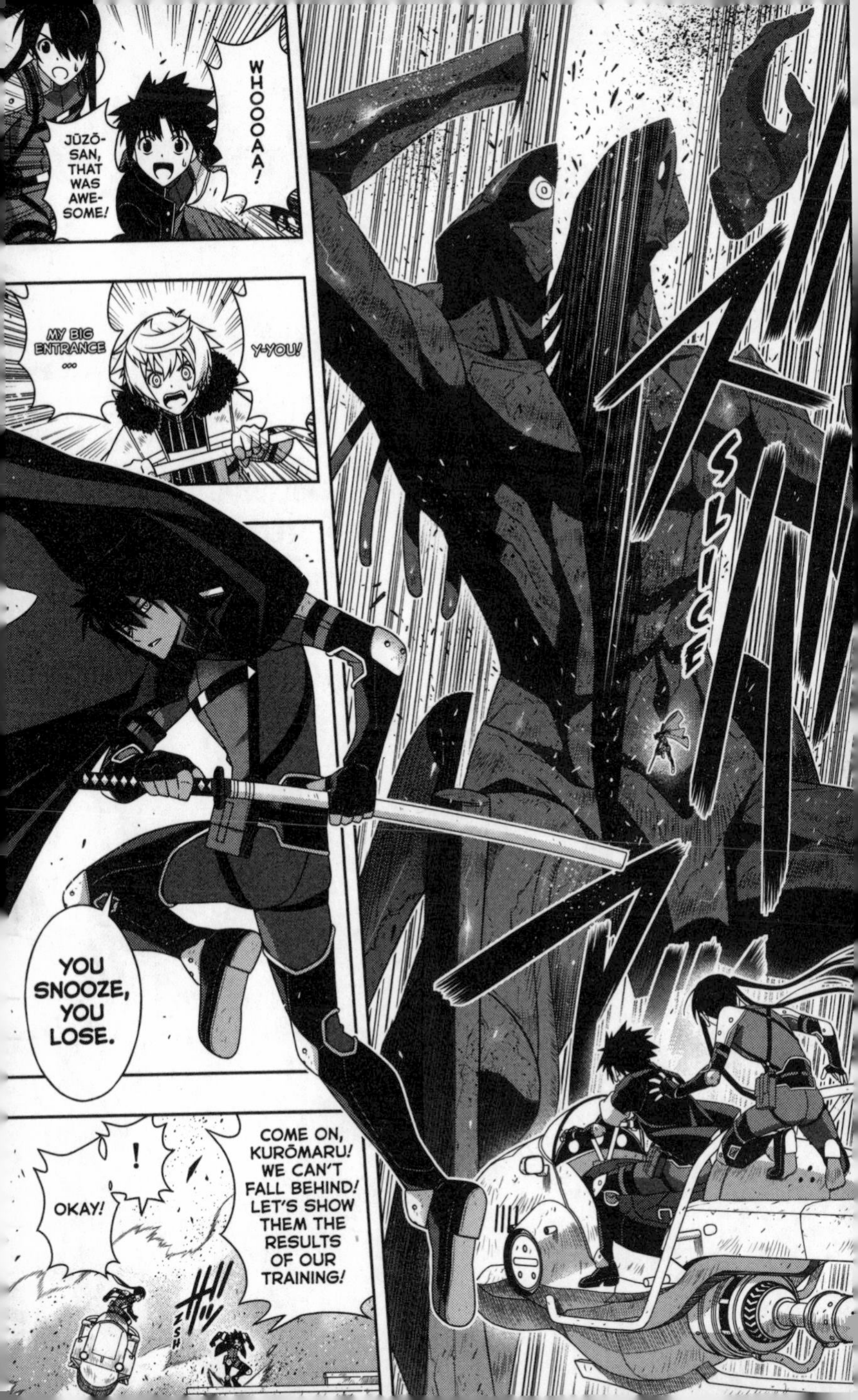
SLICE
WHOOOAA!
JŪZŌ-SAN, THAT WAS AWESOME!
Y-YOU!
MY BIG ENTRANCE ...
YOU SNOOZE, YOU LOSE.
COME ON, KURŌMARU! WE CAN'T FALL BEHIND! LET'S SHOW THEM THE RESULTS OF OUR TRAINING!
!
OKAY!
ZSH

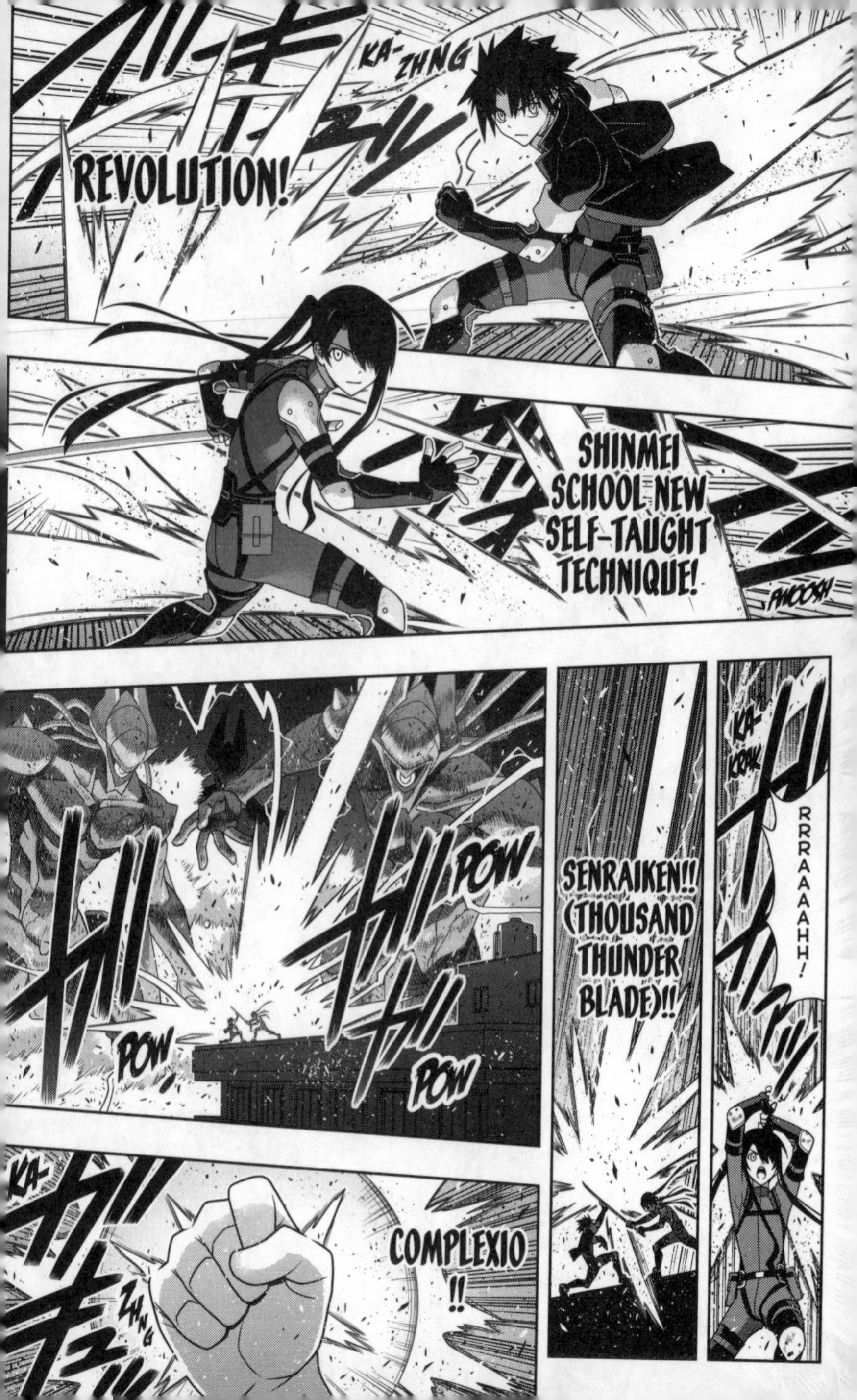
KA-ZHNG
REVOLUTION!
SHINMEI SCHOOL NEW SELF-TAUGHT TECHNIQUE!
FWOOSH
KA-KRAK
RRRAAAAAH!
SENRAIKEN!! (THOUSAND THUNDER BLADE)!!
POW
POW
POW
KA-ZHNG
COMPLEXIO !!

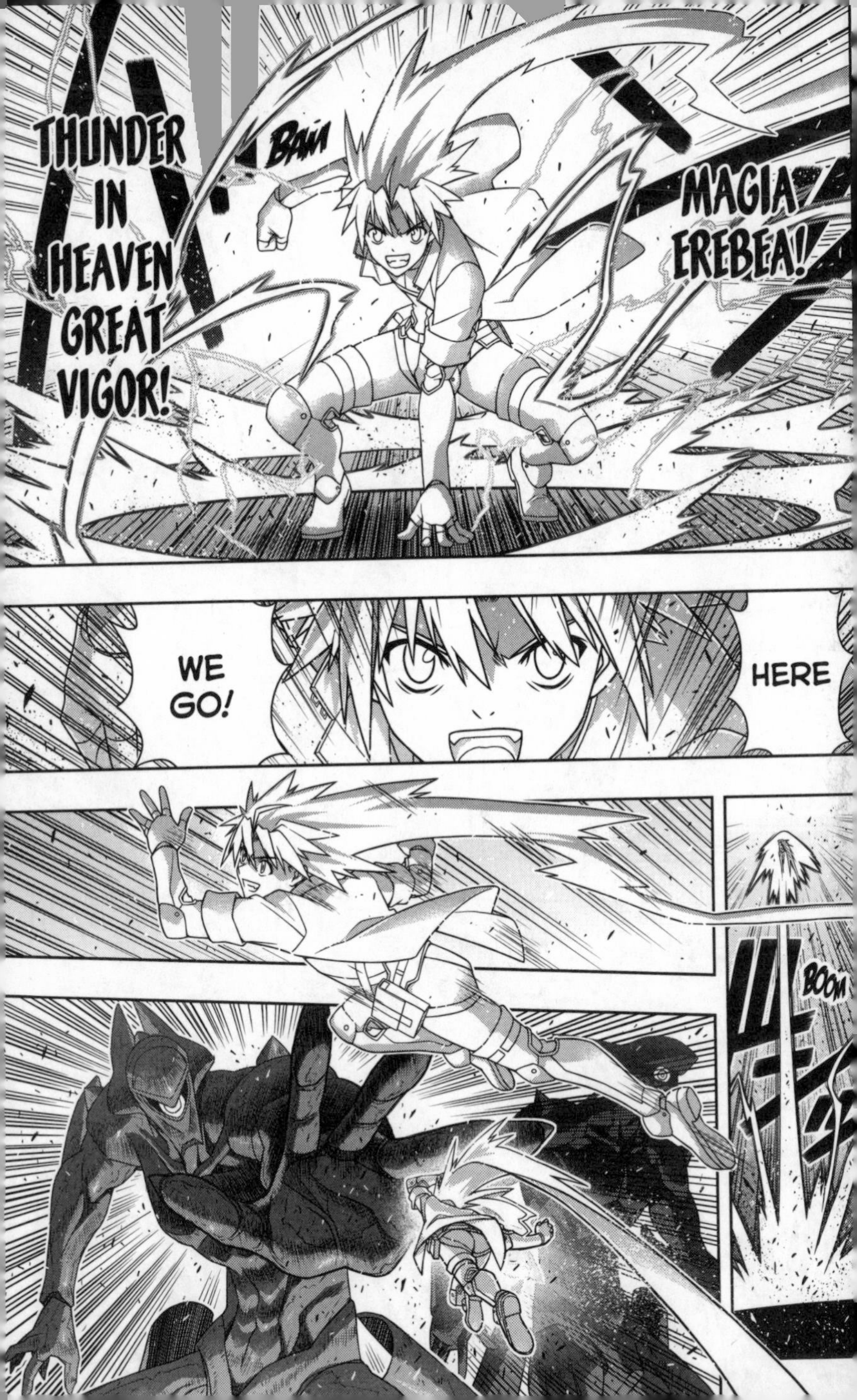
MAGIA EREBEA!
BAM
THUNDER IN HEAVEN GREAT VIGOR!
HERE
WE GO!
BOOM

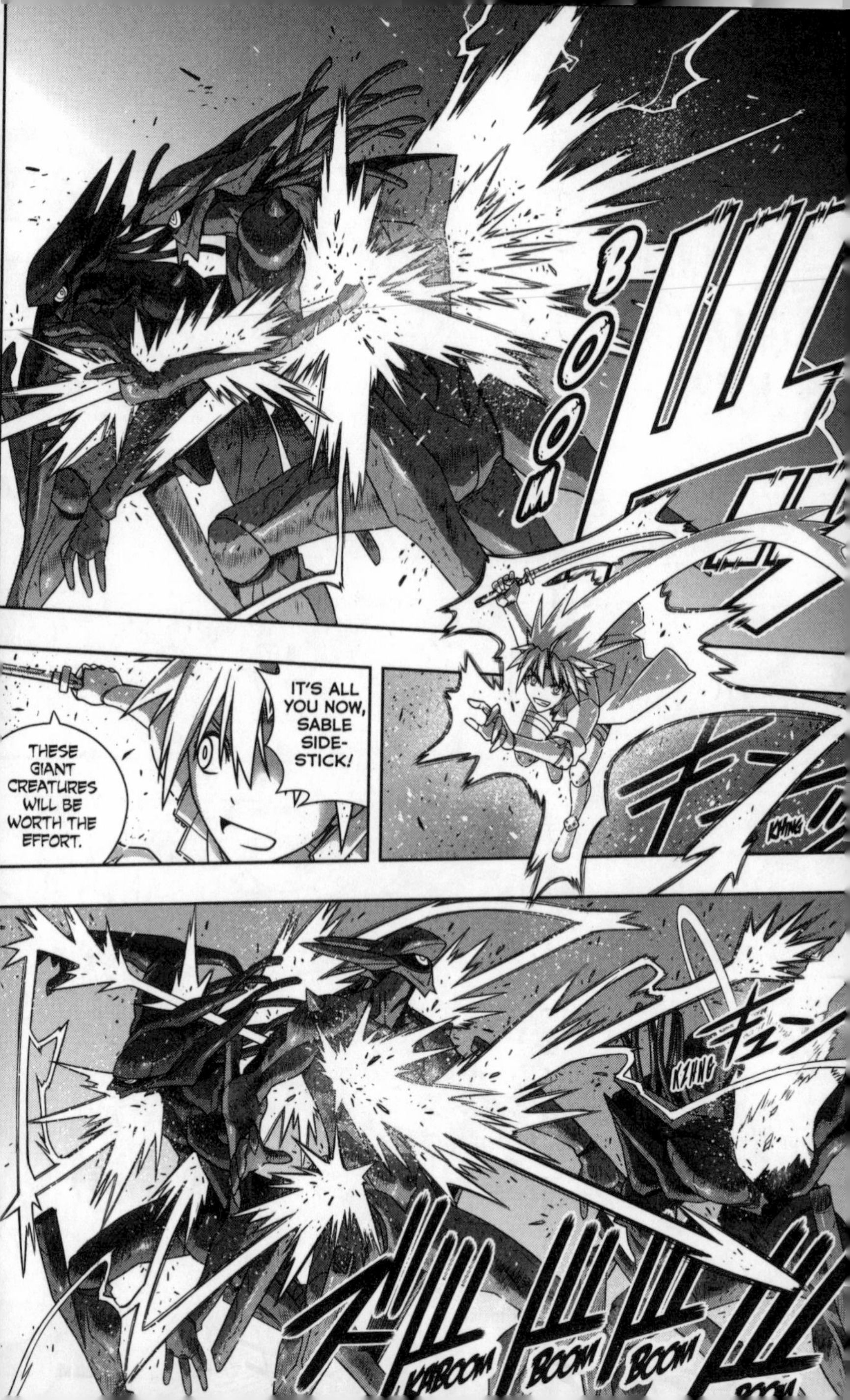

BOOOOOM
KYHING
IT'S ALL YOU NOW, SABLE SIDE-STICK!
THESE GIANT CREATURES WILL BE WORTH THE EFFORT.
KSHING
BOOM
BOOM
KABOOM

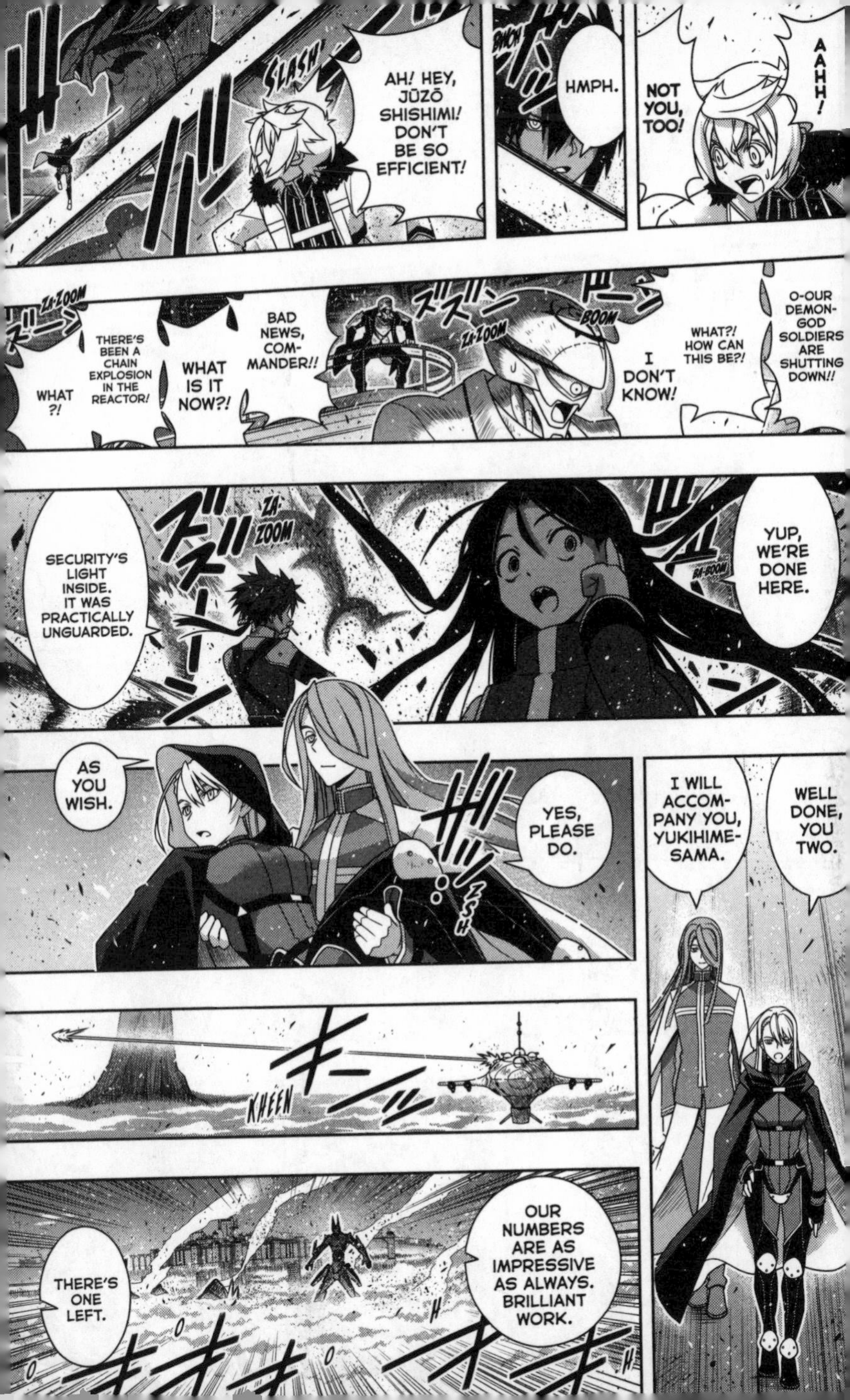
AAHH!
NOT YOU, TOO!
HMPH.
SLASH
AH! HEY, JŪZŌ SHISHIMI! DON'T BE SO EFFICIENT!
O-OUR DEMON-GOD SOLDIERS ARE SHUTTING DOWN!!
WHAT?! HOW CAN THIS BE?!
I DON'T KNOW!
BOOM
ZA-ZOOM
BAD NEWS, COMMANDER!!
WHAT IS IT NOW?!
THERE'S BEEN A CHAIN EXPLOSION IN THE REACTOR!
WHAT ?!
ZA-ZOOM
YUP, WE'RE DONE HERE.
BA-BOOM
ZA-ZOOM
SECURITY'S LIGHT INSIDE. IT WAS PRACTICALLY UNGUARDED.
WELL DONE, YOU TWO.
I WILL ACCOMPANY YOU, YUKIHIME-SAMA.
YES, PLEASE DO.
ZSSH
AS YOU WISH.
KHEEN
OUR NUMBERS ARE AS IMPRESSIVE AS ALWAYS. BRILLIANT WORK.
THERE'S ONE LEFT.

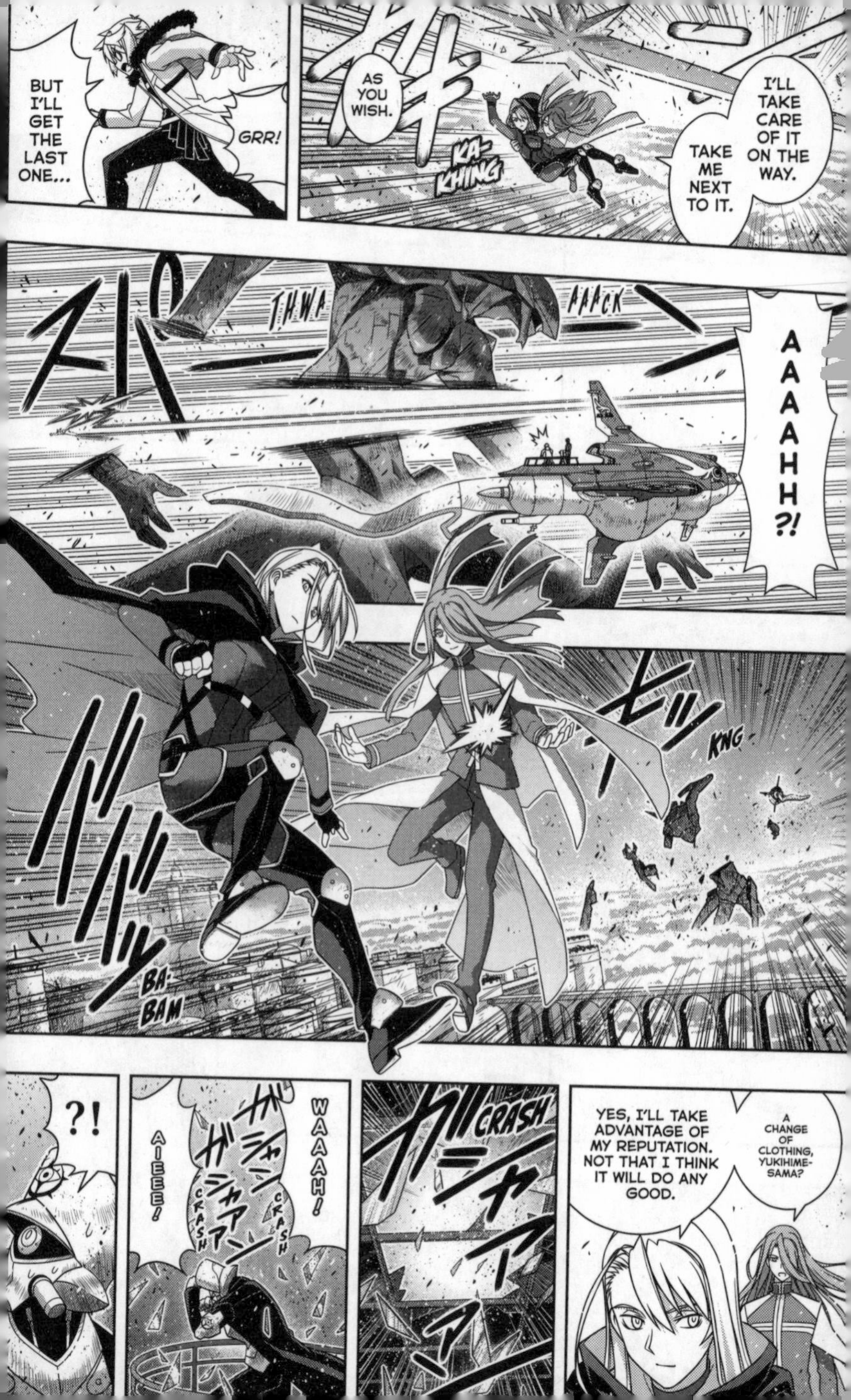
I'LL TAKE CARE OF IT ON THE WAY.
TAKE ME NEXT TO IT.
AS YOU WISH.
KA-KHING
GRR!
BUT I'LL GET THE LAST ONE...
AAAAAHH?!
THWAAAACK
KNG
BA-BAM
A CHANGE OF CLOTHING, YUKIHIME-SAMA?
YES, I'LL TAKE ADVANTAGE OF MY REPUTATION. NOT THAT I THINK IT WILL DO ANY GOOD.
CRASH
WAAAAH!
CRASH
CRASH
AIEEE!
?!

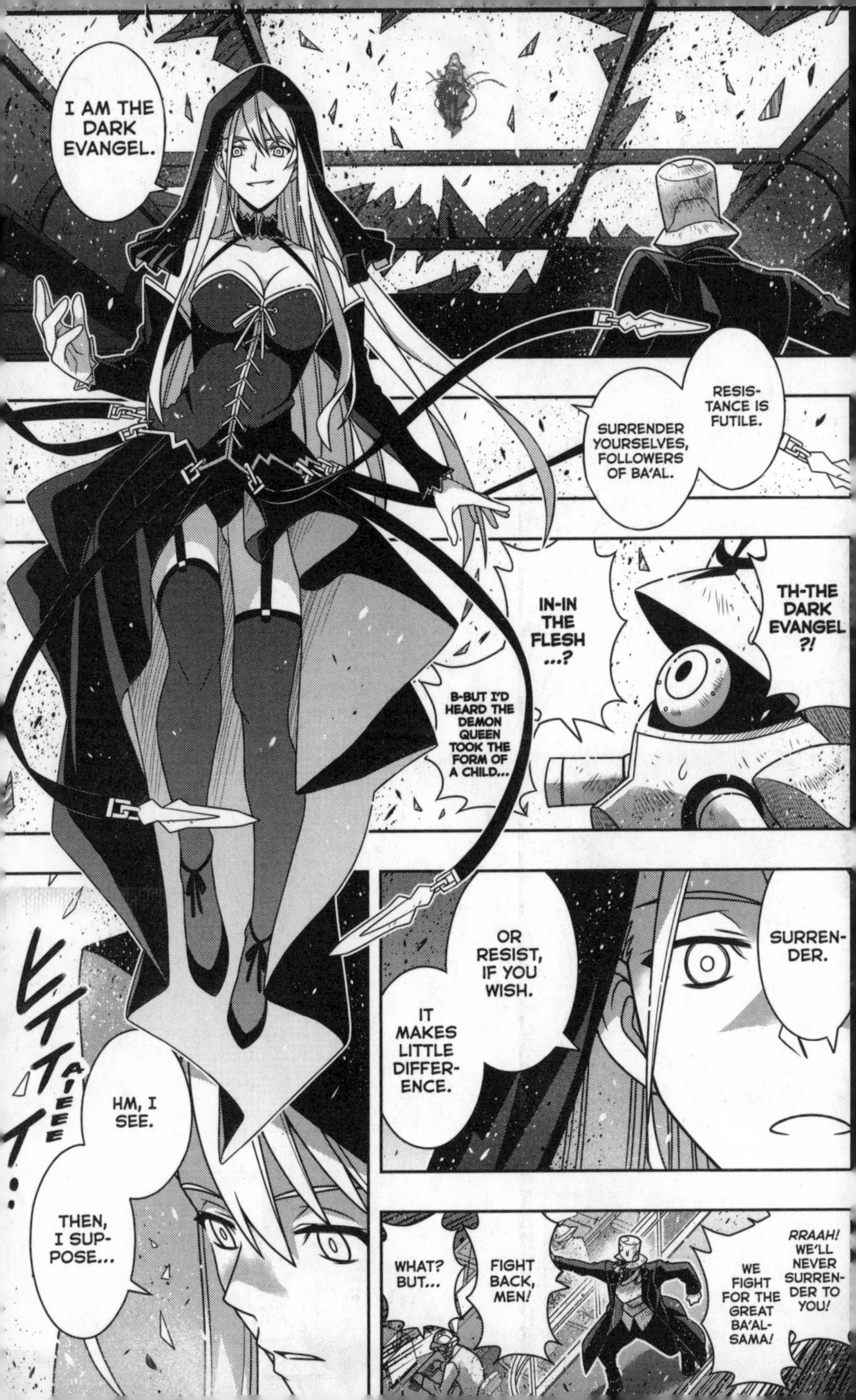
I AM THE DARK EVANGEL.
RESISTANCE IS FUTILE.
SURRENDER YOURSELVES, FOLLOWERS OF BA'AL.
TH-THE DARK EVANGEL?!
IN-IN THE FLESH...?
B-BUT I'D HEARD THE DEMON QUEEN TOOK THE FORM OF A CHILD...
SURRENDER.
OR RESIST, IF YOU WISH.
IT MAKES LITTLE DIFFERENCE.
RRAAH! WE'LL NEVER SURRENDER TO YOU!
WE FIGHT FOR THE GREAT BA'AL-SAMA!
FIGHT BACK, MEN!
WHAT? BUT...
HM, I SEE.
THEN, I SUPPOSE...
AIEEE

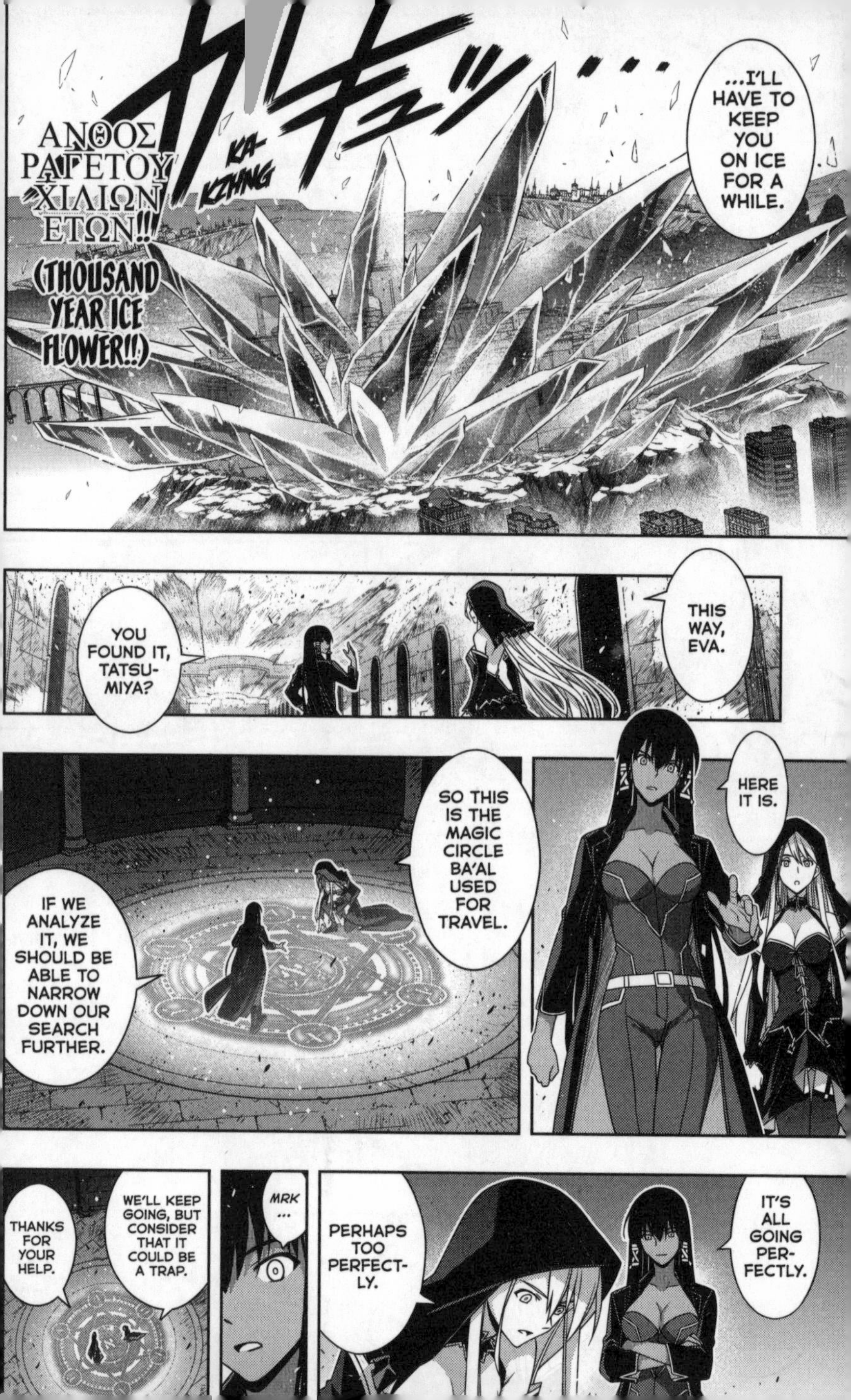
...I'LL HAVE TO KEEP YOU ON ICE FOR A WHILE.
KA-KZHING
ΑΝΘΟΣ ΡΑΓΕΤΟΥ ΧΙΛΙΩΝ ΕΤΩΝ!!
(THOUSAND YEAR ICE FLOWER!!)
THIS WAY, EVA.
YOU FOUND IT, TATSUMIYA?
HERE IT IS.
SO THIS IS THE MAGIC CIRCLE BA'AL USED FOR TRAVEL.
IF WE ANALYZE IT, WE SHOULD BE ABLE TO NARROW DOWN OUR SEARCH FURTHER.
IT'S ALL GOING PERFECTLY.
PERHAPS TOO PERFECTLY.
MRK...
WE'LL KEEP GOING, BUT CONSIDER THAT IT COULD BE A TRAP.
THANKS FOR YOUR HELP.

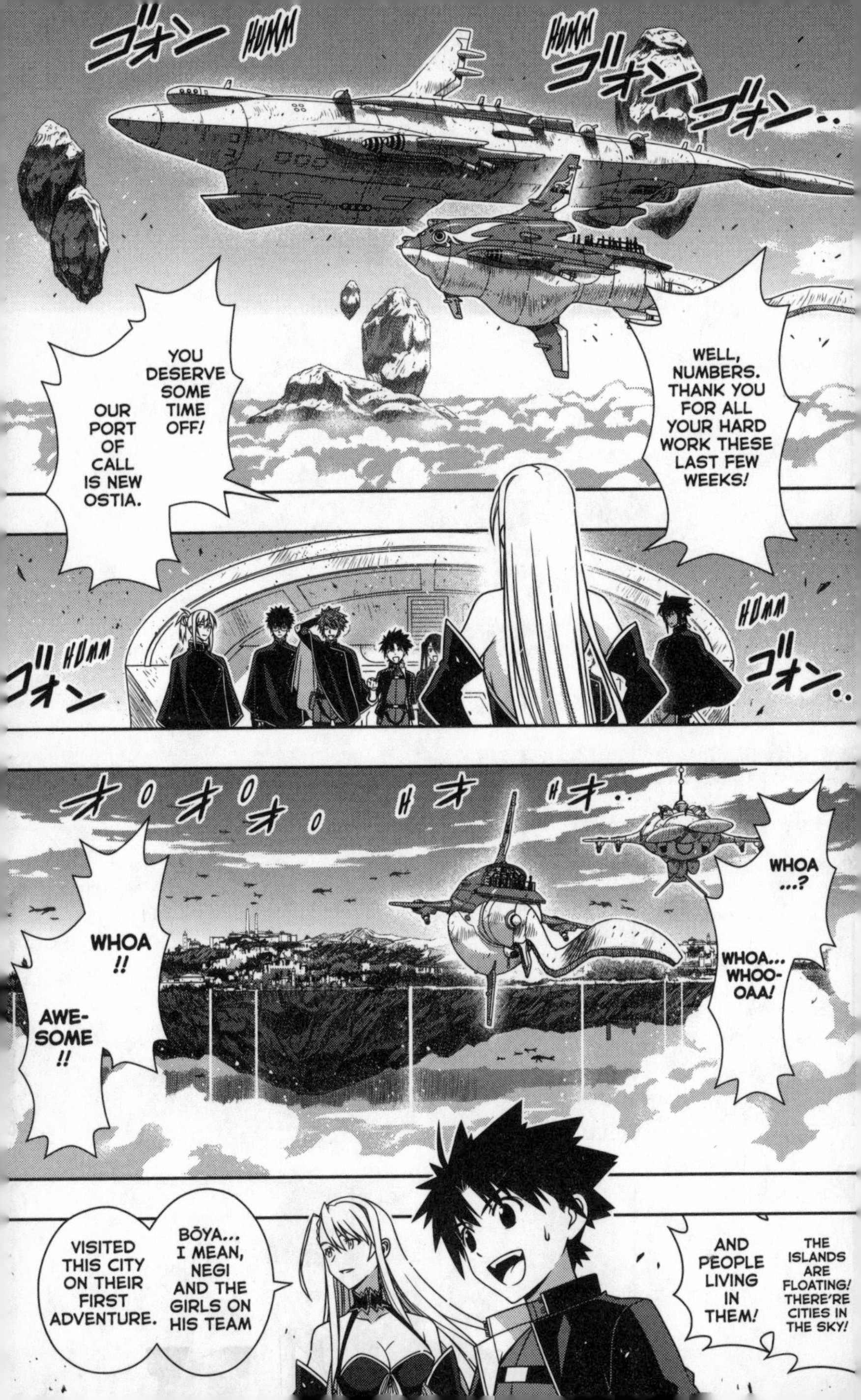
HUMM
ゴオンゴオン‥
ゴオン
HUMM
WELL, NUMBERS. THANK YOU FOR ALL YOUR HARD WORK THESE LAST FEW WEEKS!
YOU DESERVE SOME TIME OFF!
OUR PORT OF CALL IS NEW OSTIA.
HUMM
ゴオン‥
HUMM
ゴオン
H
オ
H
オ
O
オ
O
オ
O
オ
O
WHOA ...?
WHOA... WHOO-OAA!
WHOA !!
AWE-SOME !!
THE ISLANDS ARE FLOATING! THERE'RE CITIES IN THE SKY!
AND PEOPLE LIVING IN THEM!
BŌYA... I MEAN, NEGI AND THE GIRLS ON HIS TEAM
VISITED THIS CITY ON THEIR FIRST ADVENTURE.

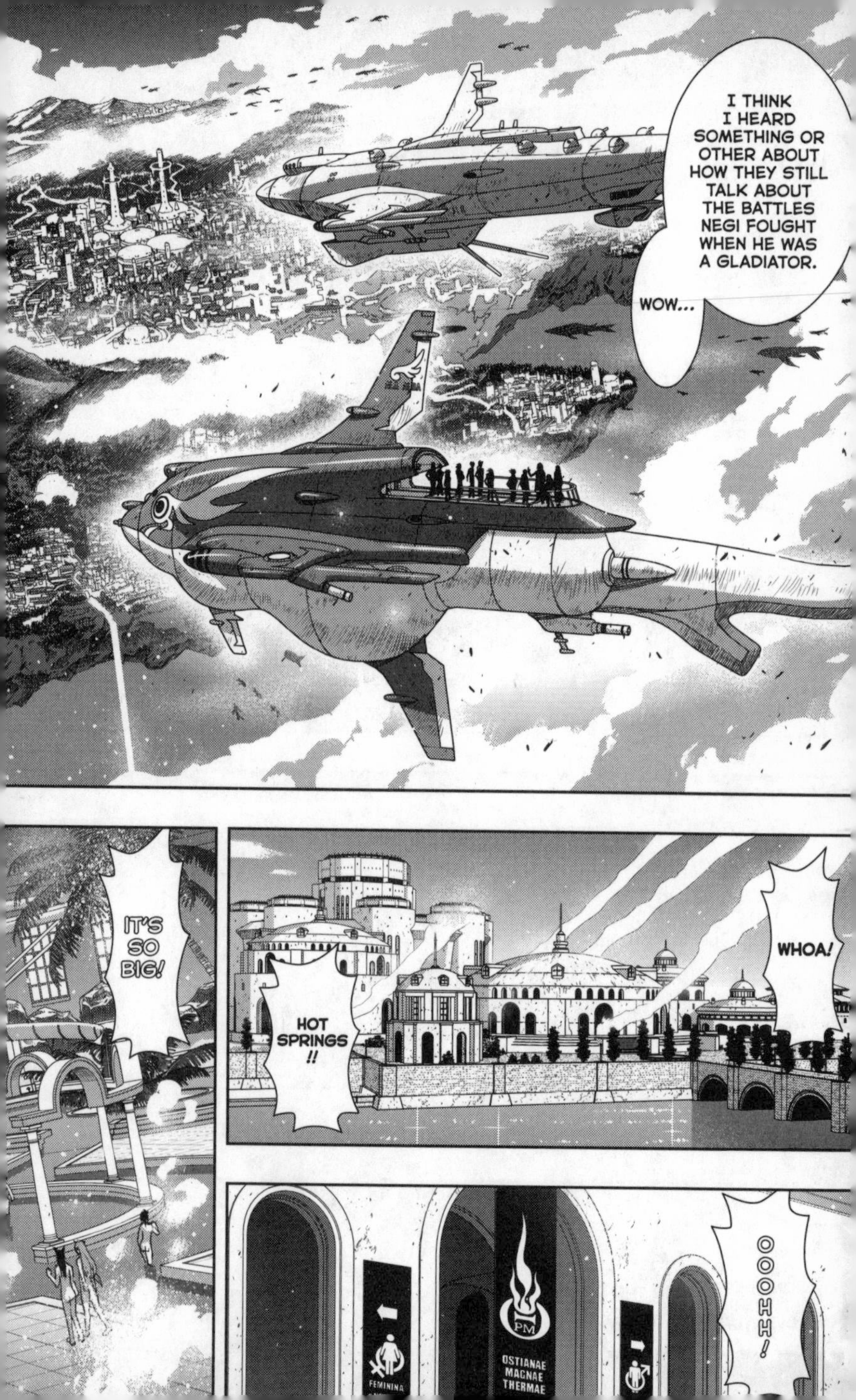
I THINK I HEARD SOMETHING OR OTHER ABOUT HOW THEY STILL TALK ABOUT THE BATTLES NEGI FOUGHT WHEN HE WAS A GLADIATOR.
WOW...
WHOA!
HOT SPRINGS!!
OOOHH!
PM
OSTIANAE MAGNAE THERMAE
FEMININA
IT'S SO BIG!

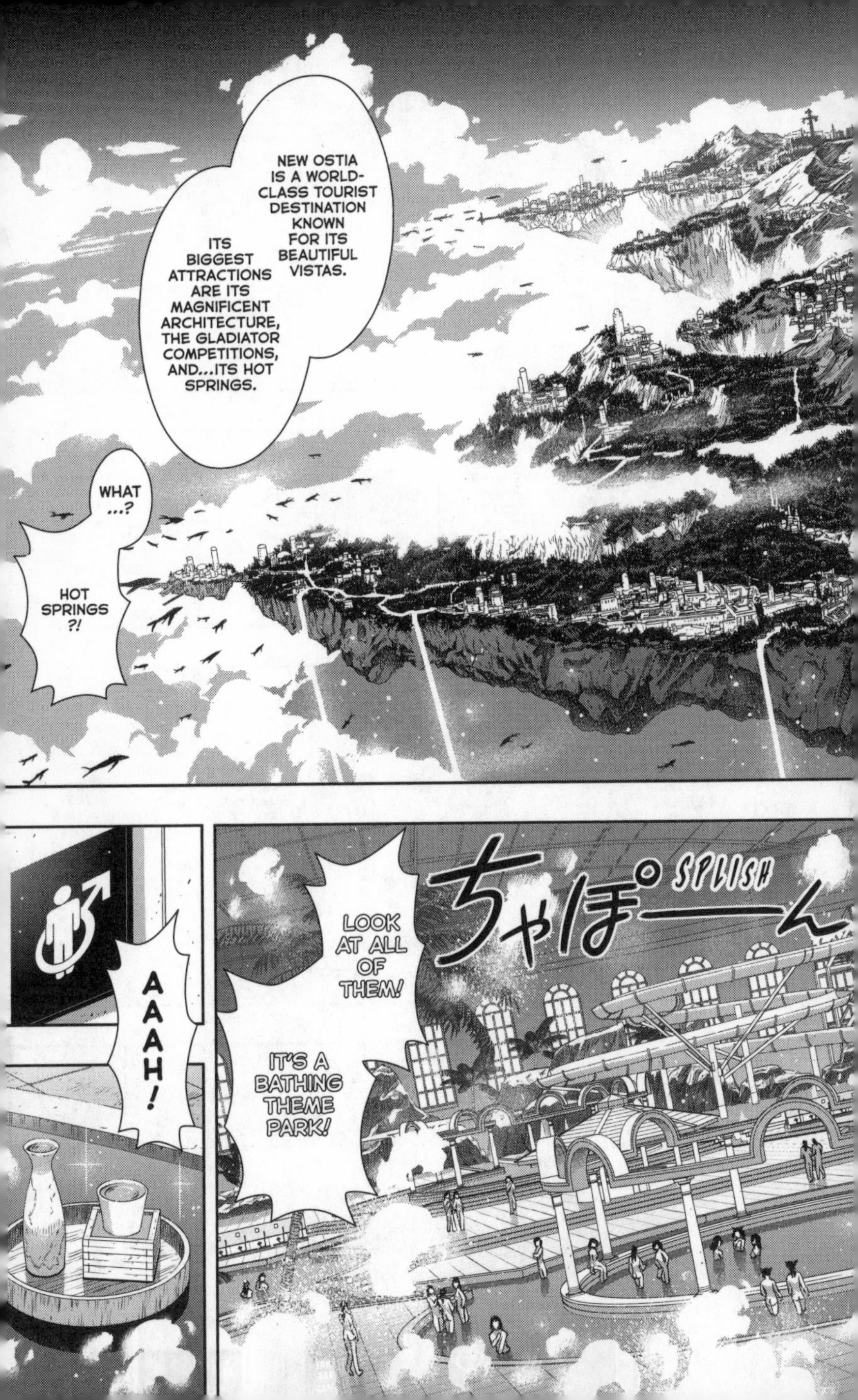
NEW OSTIA IS A WORLD-CLASS TOURIST DESTINATION KNOWN FOR ITS BEAUTIFUL VISTAS.
ITS BIGGEST ATTRACTIONS ARE ITS MAGNIFICENT ARCHITECTURE, THE GLADIATOR COMPETITIONS, AND...ITS HOT SPRINGS.
WHAT...?
HOT SPRINGS?!
ちゃぽーん
SPLISH
LOOK AT ALL OF THEM!
IT'S A BATHING THEME PARK!
AAAAH!

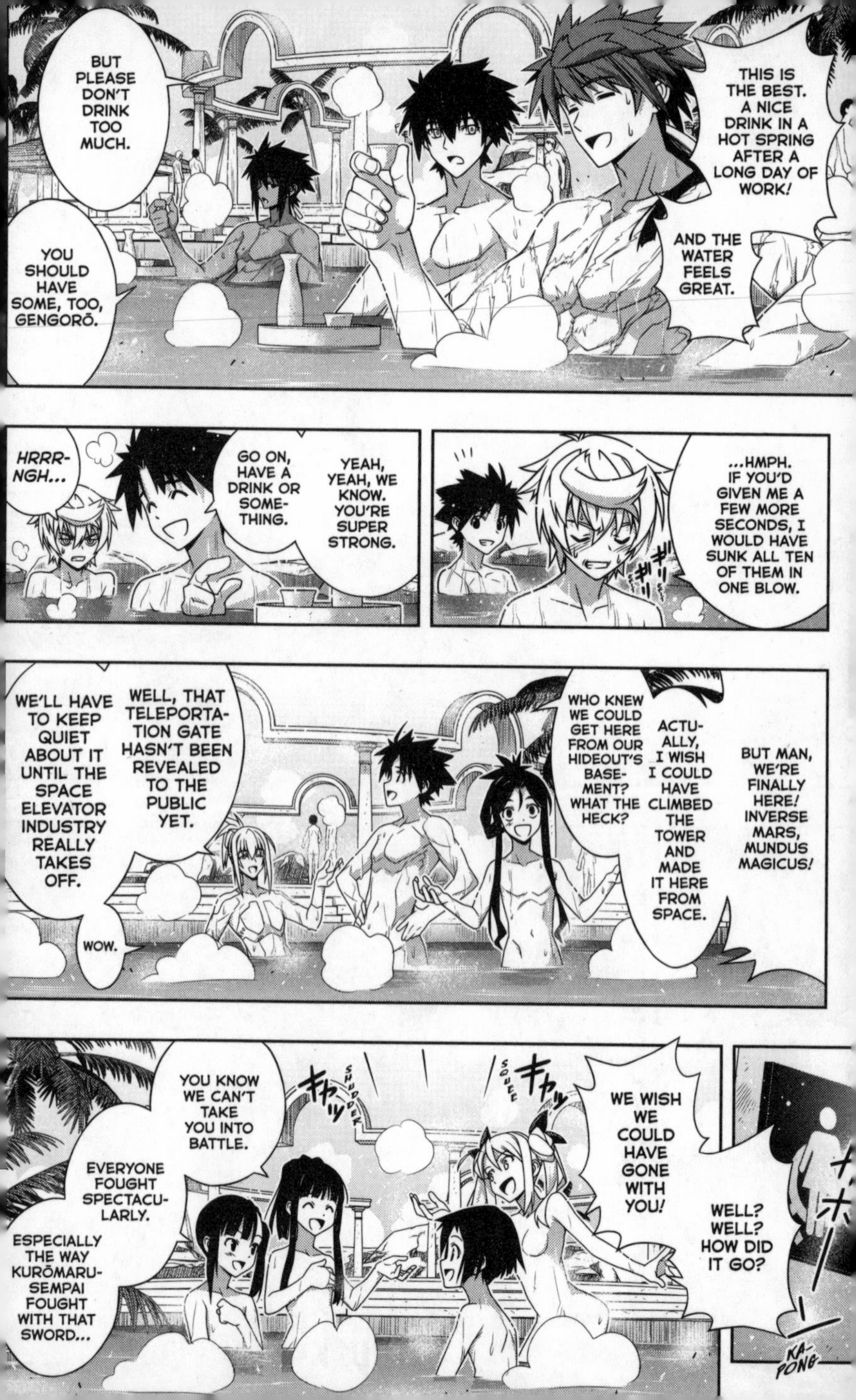
THIS IS THE BEST. A NICE DRINK IN A HOT SPRING AFTER A LONG DAY OF WORK!
AND THE WATER FEELS GREAT.
BUT PLEASE DON'T DRINK TOO MUCH.
YOU SHOULD HAVE SOME, TOO, GENGORŌ.
...HMPH. IF YOU'D GIVEN ME A FEW MORE SECONDS, I WOULD HAVE SUNK ALL TEN OF THEM IN ONE BLOW.
YEAH, YEAH, WE KNOW. YOU'RE SUPER STRONG.
GO ON, HAVE A DRINK OR SOMETHING.
HRRRNGH...
BUT MAN, WE'RE FINALLY HERE! INVERSE MARS, MUNDUS MAGICUS!
ACTUALLY, I WISH I COULD HAVE CLIMBED THE TOWER AND MADE IT HERE FROM SPACE.
WHO KNEW WE COULD GET HERE FROM OUR HIDEOUT'S BASEMENT? WHAT THE HECK?
WELL, THAT TELEPORTATION GATE HASN'T BEEN REVEALED TO THE PUBLIC YET.
WE'LL HAVE TO KEEP QUIET ABOUT IT UNTIL THE SPACE ELEVATOR INDUSTRY REALLY TAKES OFF.
WOW.
KA-PONG
WELL? WELL? HOW DID IT GO?
WE WISH WE COULD HAVE GONE WITH YOU!
SQUEE
SHUDDER
YOU KNOW WE CAN'T TAKE YOU INTO BATTLE.
EVERYONE FOUGHT SPECTACULARLY.
ESPECIALLY THE WAY KURŌMARU-SEMPAI FOUGHT WITH THAT SWORD...

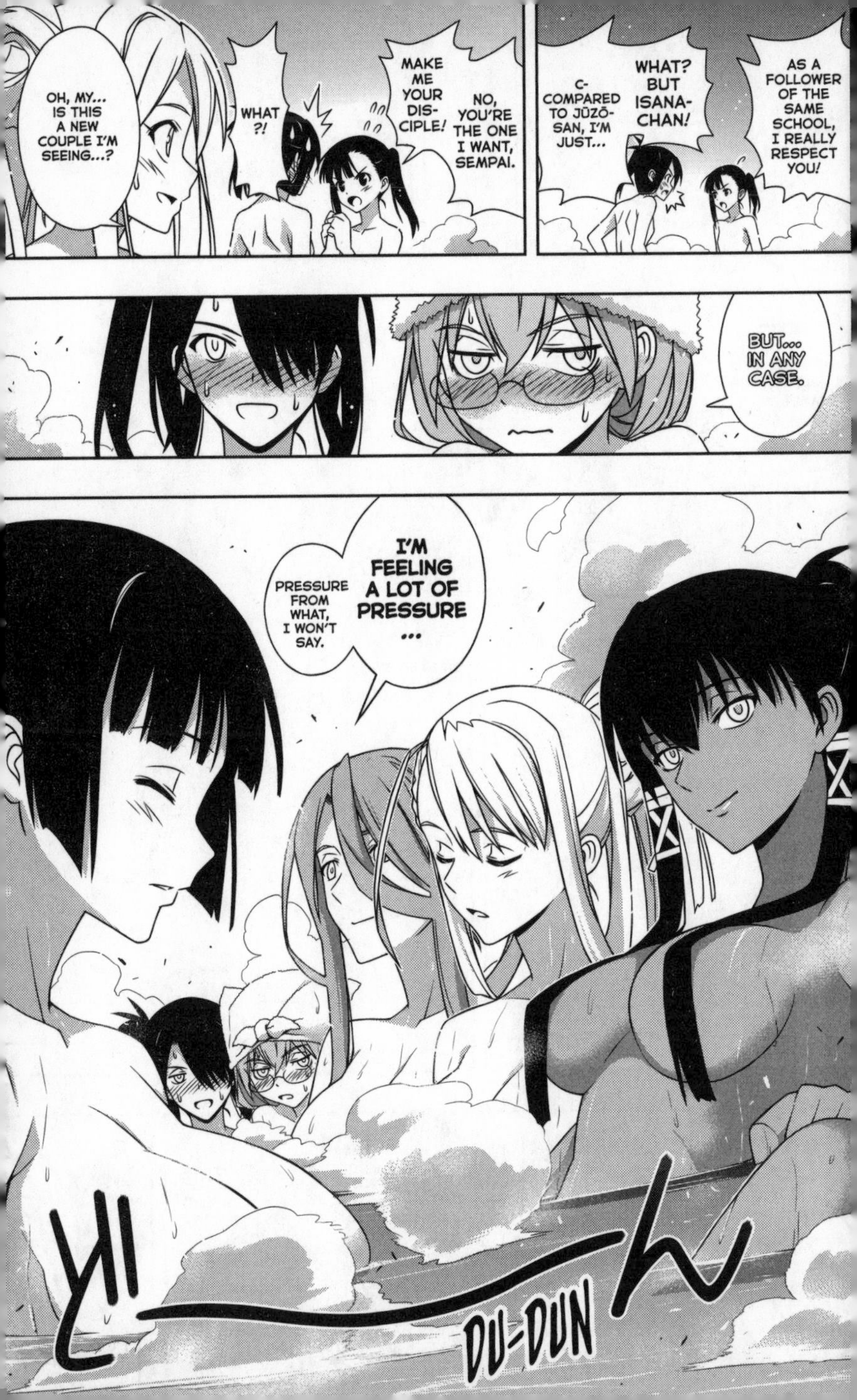
AS A FOLLOWER OF THE SAME SCHOOL, I REALLY RESPECT YOU!
WHAT? BUT ISANA-CHAN!
C-COMPARED TO JŪZŌ-SAN, I'M JUST...
MAKE ME YOUR DISCIPLE!
NO, YOU'RE THE ONE I WANT, SEMPAI.
WHAT ?!
OH, MY... IS THIS A NEW COUPLE I'M SEEING...?
BUT... IN ANY CASE.
I'M FEELING A LOT OF PRESSURE ...
PRESSURE FROM WHAT, I WON'T SAY.
DU-DUN

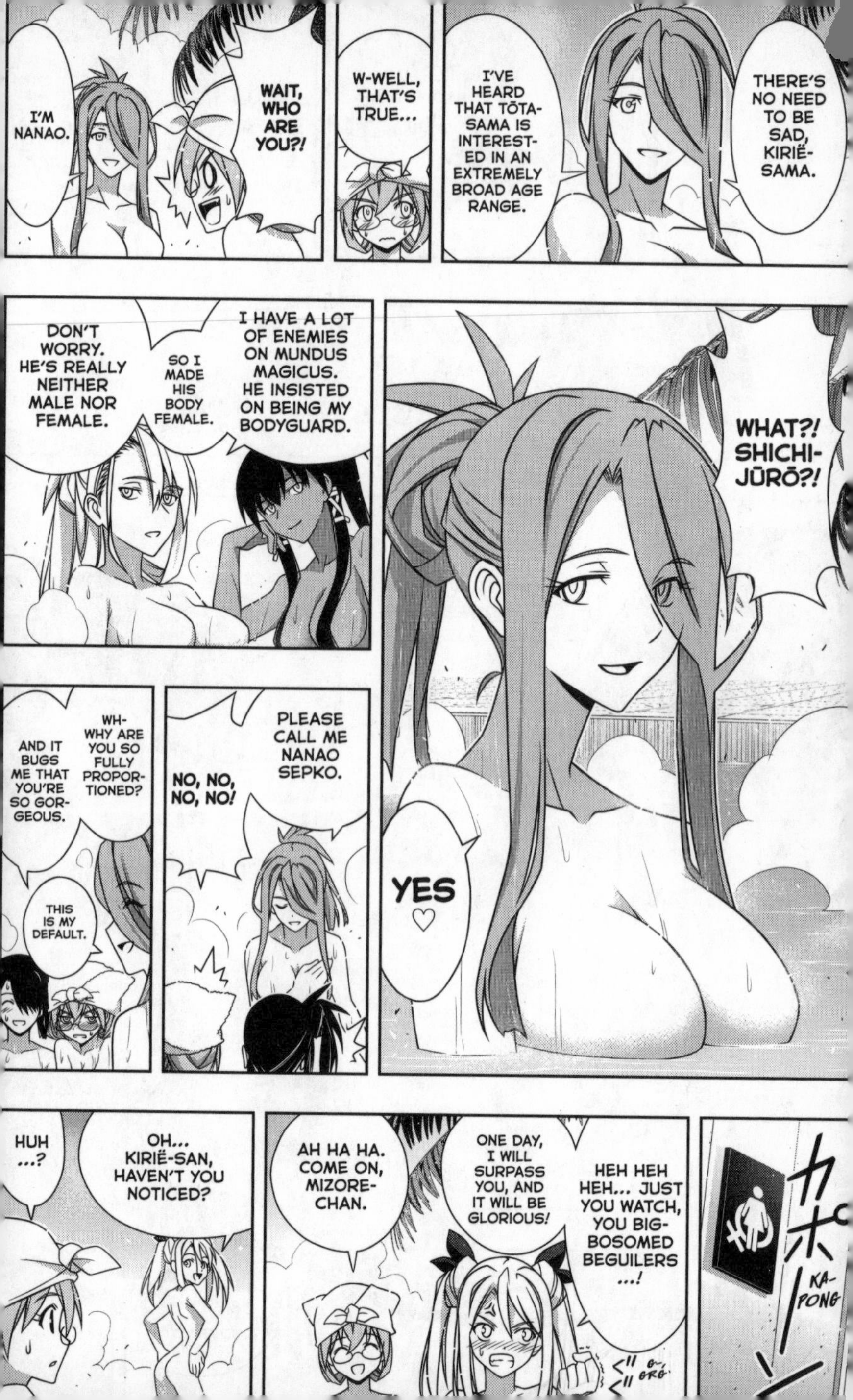
THERE'S NO NEED TO BE SAD, KIRIË-SAMA.
I'VE HEARD THAT TŌTA-SAMA IS INTEREST-ED IN AN EXTREMELY BROAD AGE RANGE.
W-WELL, THAT'S TRUE...
WAIT, WHO ARE YOU?!
I'M NANAO.
WHAT?! SHICHI-JŪRŌ?!
YES ♡
I HAVE A LOT OF ENEMIES ON MUNDUS MAGICUS. HE INSISTED ON BEING MY BODYGUARD.
SO I MADE HIS BODY FEMALE.
DON'T WORRY. HE'S REALLY NEITHER MALE NOR FEMALE.
PLEASE CALL ME NANAO SEPKO.
NO, NO, NO, NO!
WH- WHY ARE YOU SO FULLY PROPOR-TIONED?
AND IT BUGS ME THAT YOU'RE SO GOR-GEOUS.
THIS IS MY DEFAULT.
KA-PONG
HEH HEH HEH... JUST YOU WATCH, YOU BIG-BOSOMED BEGUILERS ...!
ONE DAY, I WILL SURPASS YOU, AND IT WILL BE GLORIOUS!
AH HA HA. COME ON, MIZORE-CHAN.
OH... KIRIË-SAN, HAVEN'T YOU NOTICED?
HUH ...?

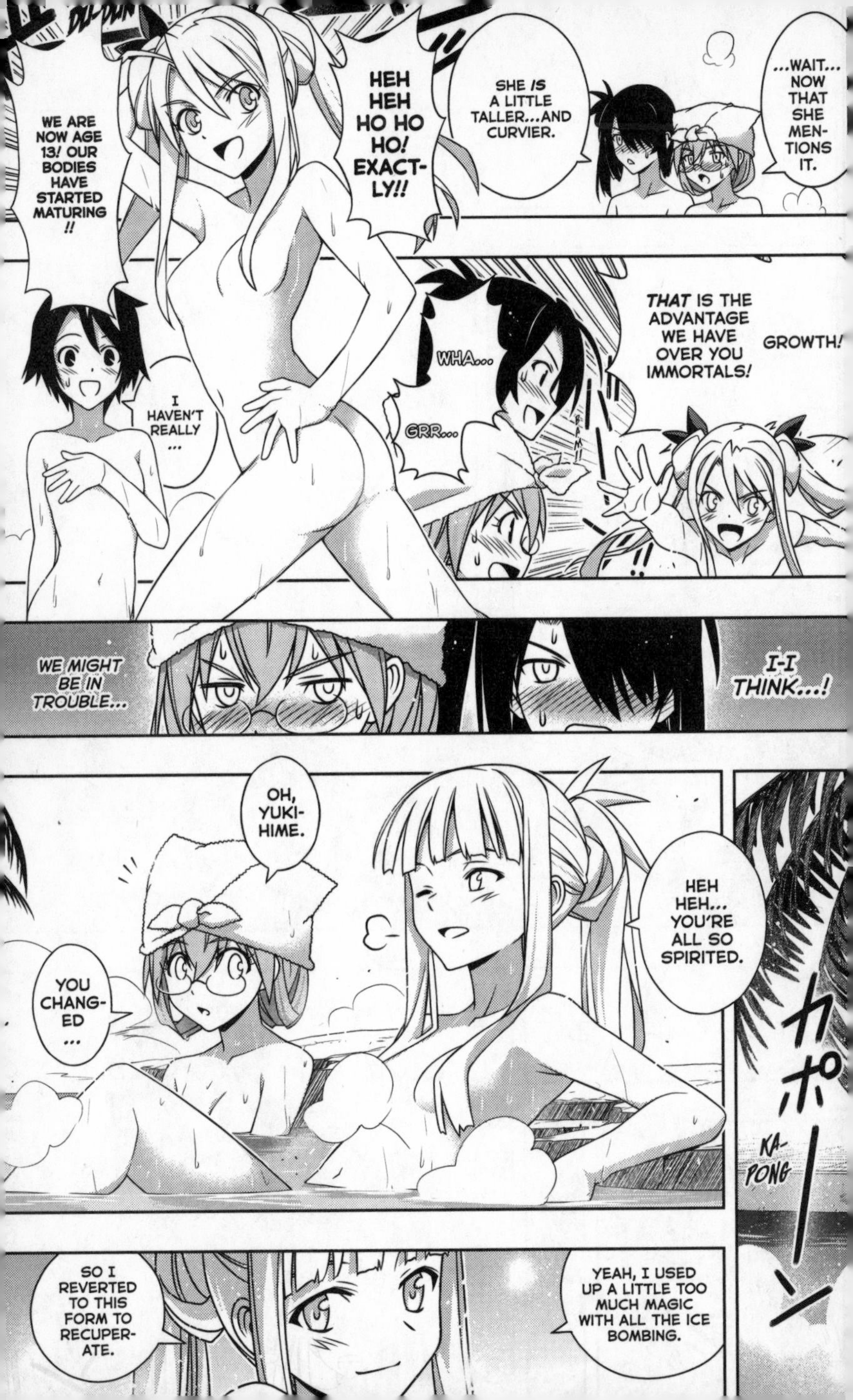
...WAIT... NOW THAT SHE MEN-TIONS IT.
SHE IS A LITTLE TALLER...AND CURVIER.
THAT IS THE ADVANTAGE WE HAVE OVER YOU IMMORTALS!
GROWTH!
WHA...
GRR...
DU-DUN
HEH HEH HO HO HO! EXACT-LY!!
WE ARE NOW AGE 13! OUR BODIES HAVE STARTED MATURING!!
I HAVEN'T REALLY...
I-I THINK...!
WE MIGHT BE IN TROUBLE...
KA-PONG
OH, YUKI-HIME.
HEH HEH... YOU'RE ALL SO SPIRITED.
YOU CHANG-ED...
YEAH, I USED UP A LITTLE TOO MUCH MAGIC WITH ALL THE ICE BOMBING.
SO I REVERTED TO THIS FORM TO RECUPER-ATE.

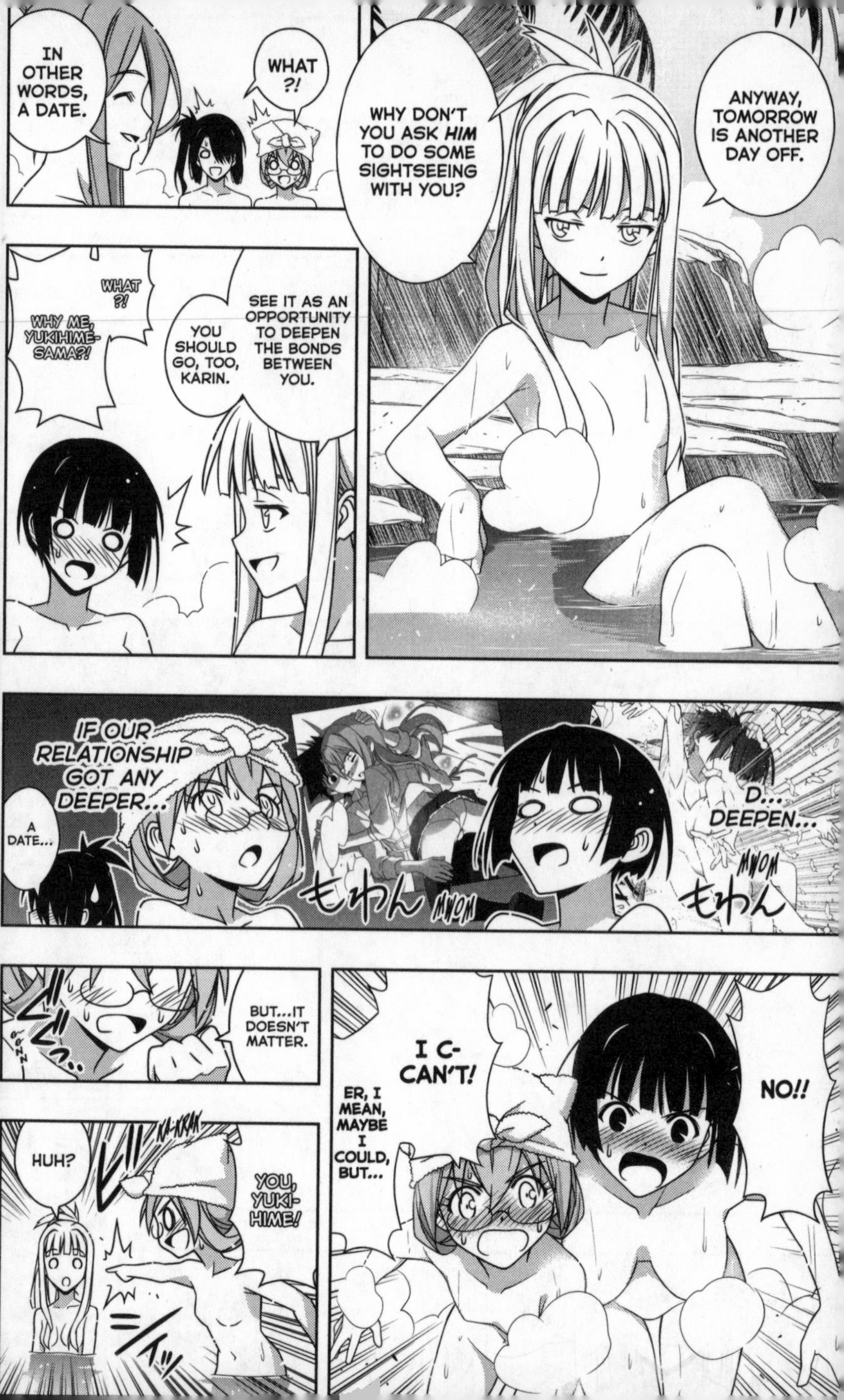
ANYWAY, TOMORROW IS ANOTHER DAY OFF.
WHY DON'T YOU ASK *HIM* TO DO SOME SIGHTSEEING WITH YOU?
WHAT ?!
IN OTHER WORDS, A DATE.
SEE IT AS AN OPPORTUNITY TO DEEPEN THE BONDS BETWEEN YOU.
YOU SHOULD GO, TOO, KARIN.
WHAT ?!
WHY ME, YUKIHIME-SAMA?!
D... DEEPEN...
MWOM
もわん
もわん
MWOM
IF OUR RELATIONSHIP GOT ANY DEEPER...
A DATE...
NO!!
I C-CAN'T!
ER, I MEAN, MAYBE I COULD, BUT...
BUT...IT DOESN'T MATTER.
KA-KRAK
YOU, YUKI-HIME!
HUH?

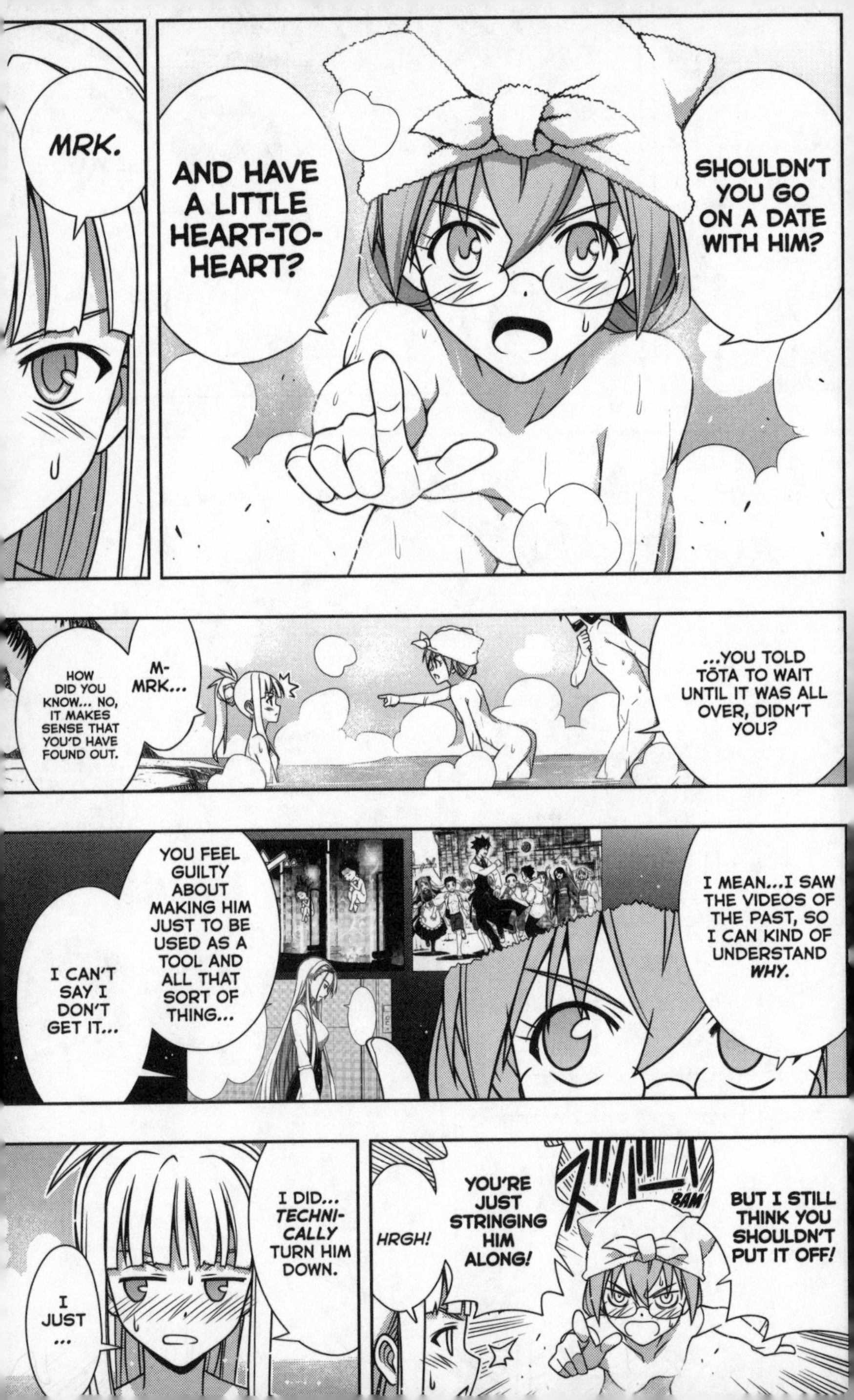

SHOULDN'T YOU GO ON A DATE WITH HIM?
AND HAVE A LITTLE HEART-TO-HEART?
MRK.
...YOU TOLD TŌTA TO WAIT UNTIL IT WAS ALL OVER, DIDN'T YOU?
M-MRK...
HOW DID YOU KNOW... NO, IT MAKES SENSE THAT YOU'D HAVE FOUND OUT.
I MEAN...I SAW THE VIDEOS OF THE PAST, SO I CAN KIND OF UNDERSTAND *WHY.*
YOU FEEL GUILTY ABOUT MAKING HIM JUST TO BE USED AS A TOOL AND ALL THAT SORT OF THING...
I CAN'T SAY I DON'T GET IT...
BUT I STILL THINK YOU SHOULDN'T PUT IT OFF!
BAM
YOU'RE JUST STRINGING HIM ALONG!
HRGH!
I DID... *TECHNICALLY* TURN HIM DOWN.
I JUST ...

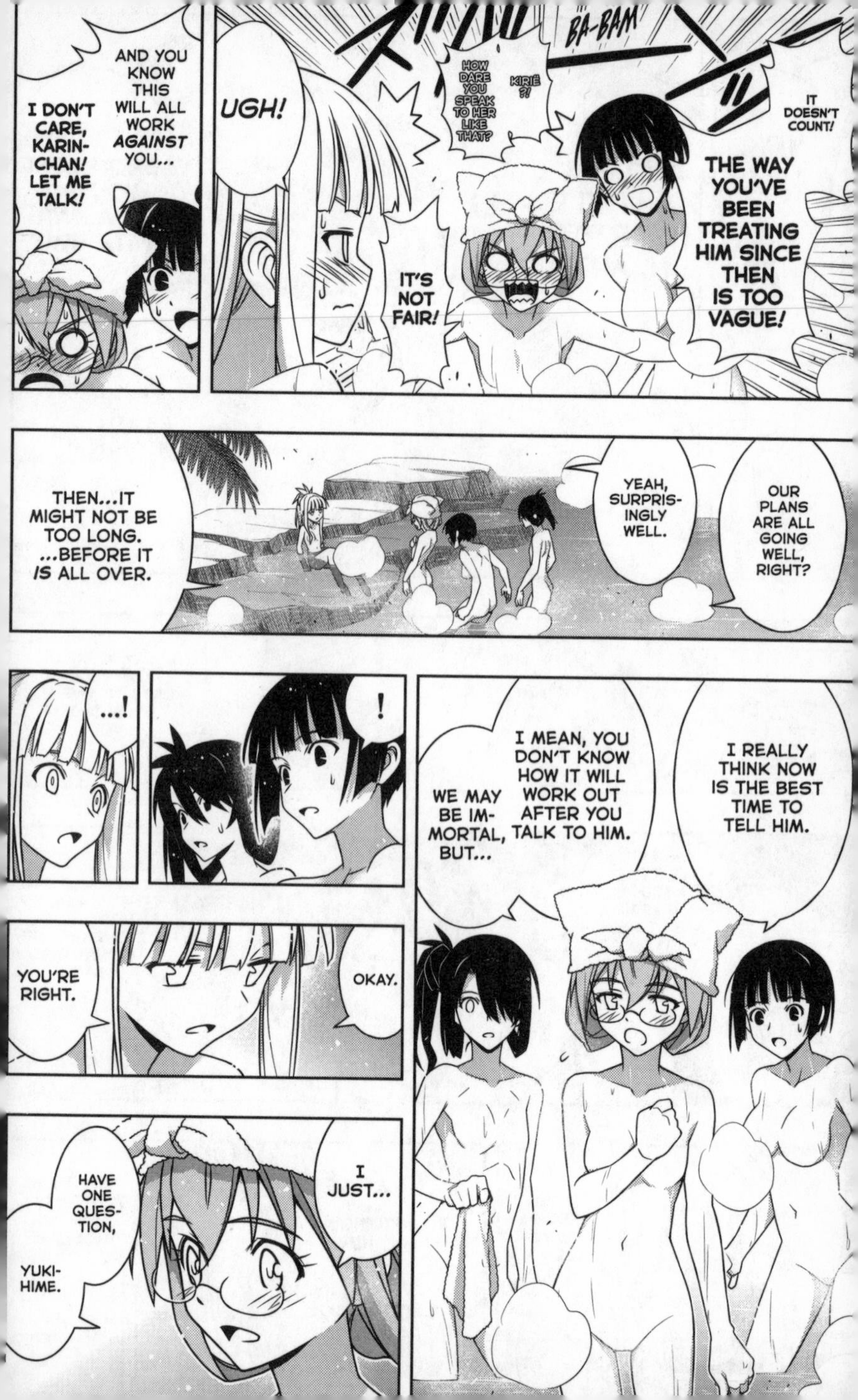
IT DOESN'T COUNT!
THE WAY YOU'VE BEEN TREATING HIM SINCE THEN IS TOO VAGUE!
BA-BAM
KIRIË ?!
HOW DARE YOU SPEAK TO HER LIKE THAT?
IT'S NOT FAIR!
UGH!
AND YOU KNOW THIS WILL ALL WORK AGAINST YOU...
I DON'T CARE, KARIN-CHAN! LET ME TALK!
OUR PLANS ARE ALL GOING WELL, RIGHT?
YEAH, SURPRISINGLY WELL.
THEN...IT MIGHT NOT BE TOO LONG. ...BEFORE IT IS ALL OVER.
I REALLY THINK NOW IS THE BEST TIME TO TELL HIM.
I MEAN, YOU DON'T KNOW HOW IT WILL WORK OUT AFTER YOU TALK TO HIM.
WE MAY BE IMMORTAL, BUT...
!
...!
OKAY.
YOU'RE RIGHT.
I JUST...
HAVE ONE QUESTION, YUKI-HIME.

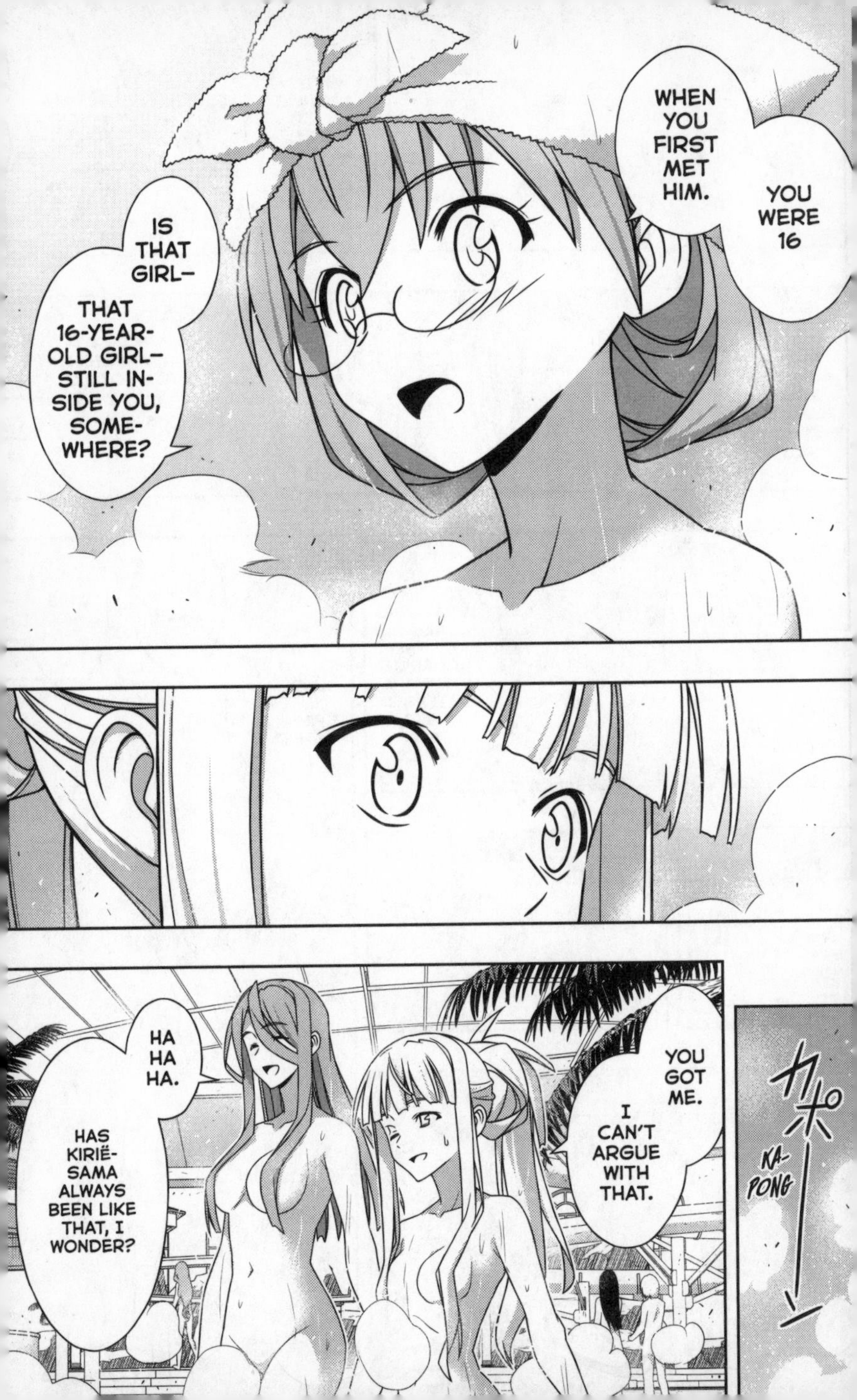
YOU WERE 16
WHEN YOU FIRST MET HIM.
IS THAT GIRL—
THAT 16-YEAR-OLD GIRL—STILL INSIDE YOU, SOMEWHERE?
KA-PONG
YOU GOT ME.
I CAN'T ARGUE WITH THAT.
HA HA HA.
HAS KIRIË-SAMA ALWAYS BEEN LIKE THAT, I WONDER?

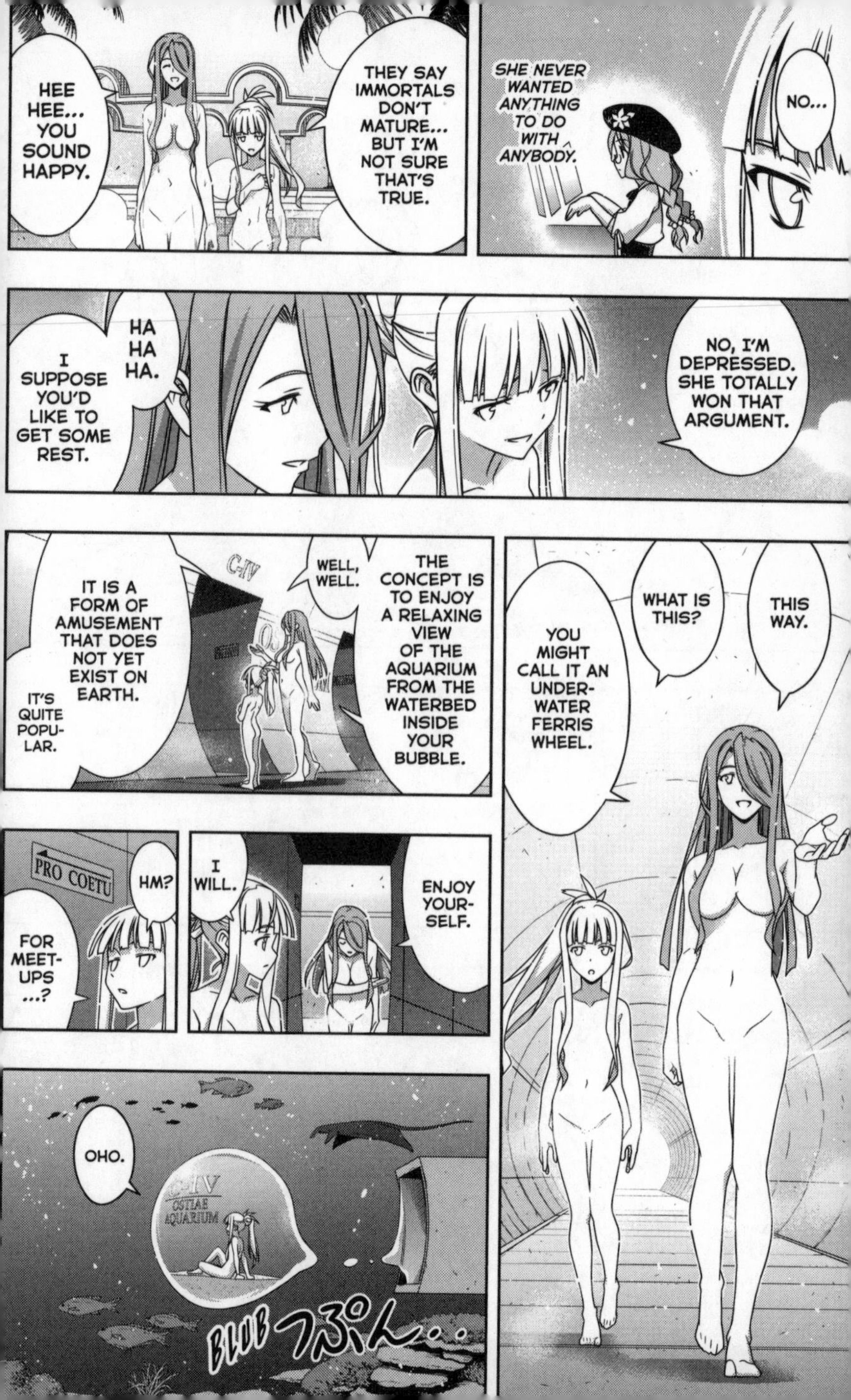
NO...
SHE NEVER WANTED ANYTHING TO DO WITH ANYBODY.
THEY SAY IMMORTALS DON'T MATURE... BUT I'M NOT SURE THAT'S TRUE.
HEE HEE... YOU SOUND HAPPY.
NO, I'M DEPRESSED. SHE TOTALLY WON THAT ARGUMENT.
HA HA HA.
I SUPPOSE YOU'D LIKE TO GET SOME REST.
THIS WAY.
WHAT IS THIS?
YOU MIGHT CALL IT AN UNDER-WATER FERRIS WHEEL.
C-IV
WELL, WELL.
THE CONCEPT IS TO ENJOY A RELAXING VIEW OF THE AQUARIUM FROM THE WATERBED INSIDE YOUR BUBBLE.
IT IS A FORM OF AMUSEMENT THAT DOES NOT YET EXIST ON EARTH.
IT'S QUITE POPU-LAR.
ENJOY YOUR-SELF.
I WILL.
HM?
PRO COETU
FOR MEET-UPS ...?
OHO.
C-IV
OSTIAE AQUARIUM
BLUB つぷん・・

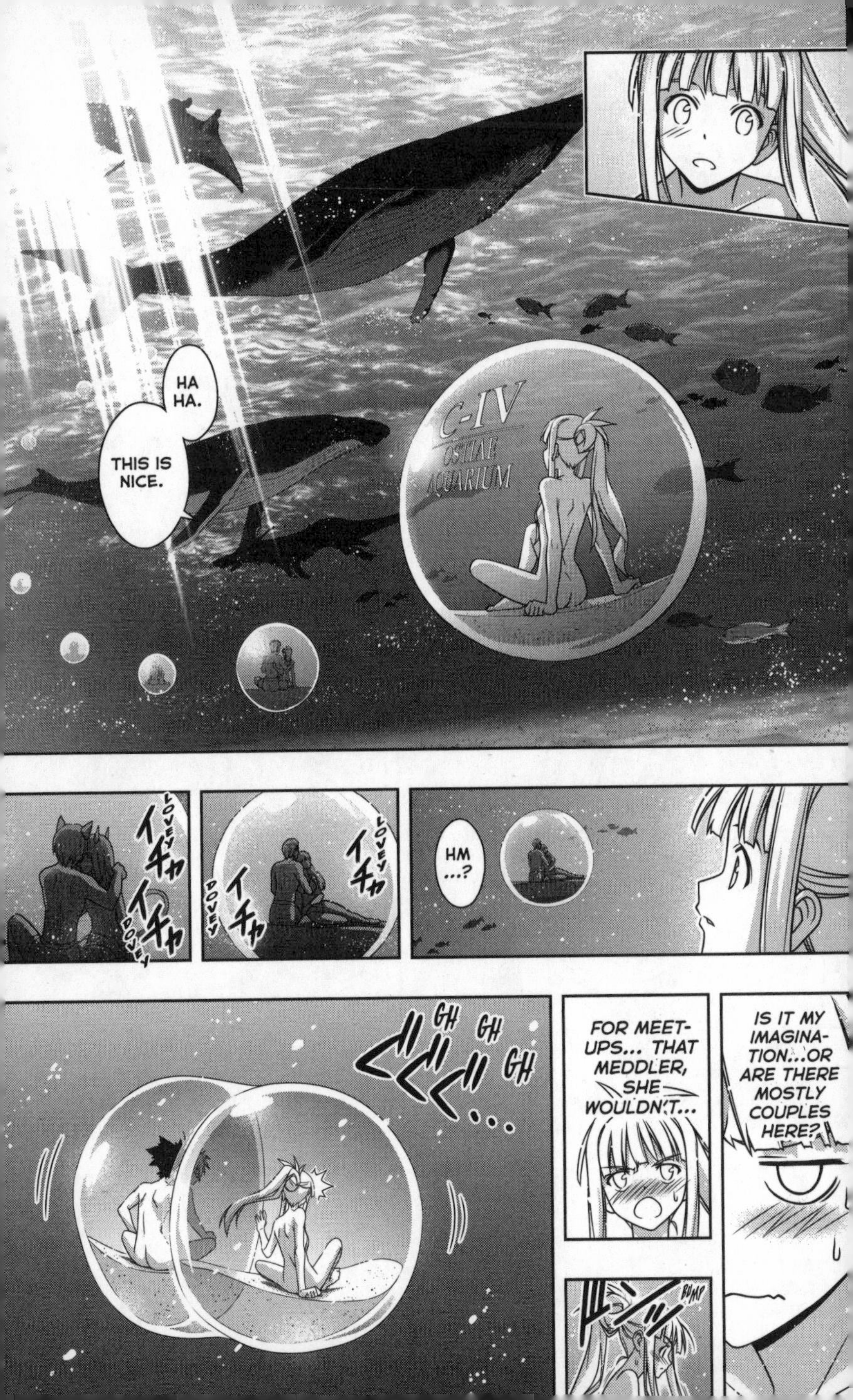
HA HA.
THIS IS NICE.
C-IV
OSTIAE AQUARIUM
HM ...?
イチャ LOVEY
イチャ DOVEY
イチャ LOVEY
イチャ DOVEY
IS IT MY IMAGINATION...OR ARE THERE MOSTLY COUPLES HERE?
FOR MEET-UPS... THAT MEDDLER, SHE WOULDN'T...
BUMP
GH GH GH
ぐぐぐ...

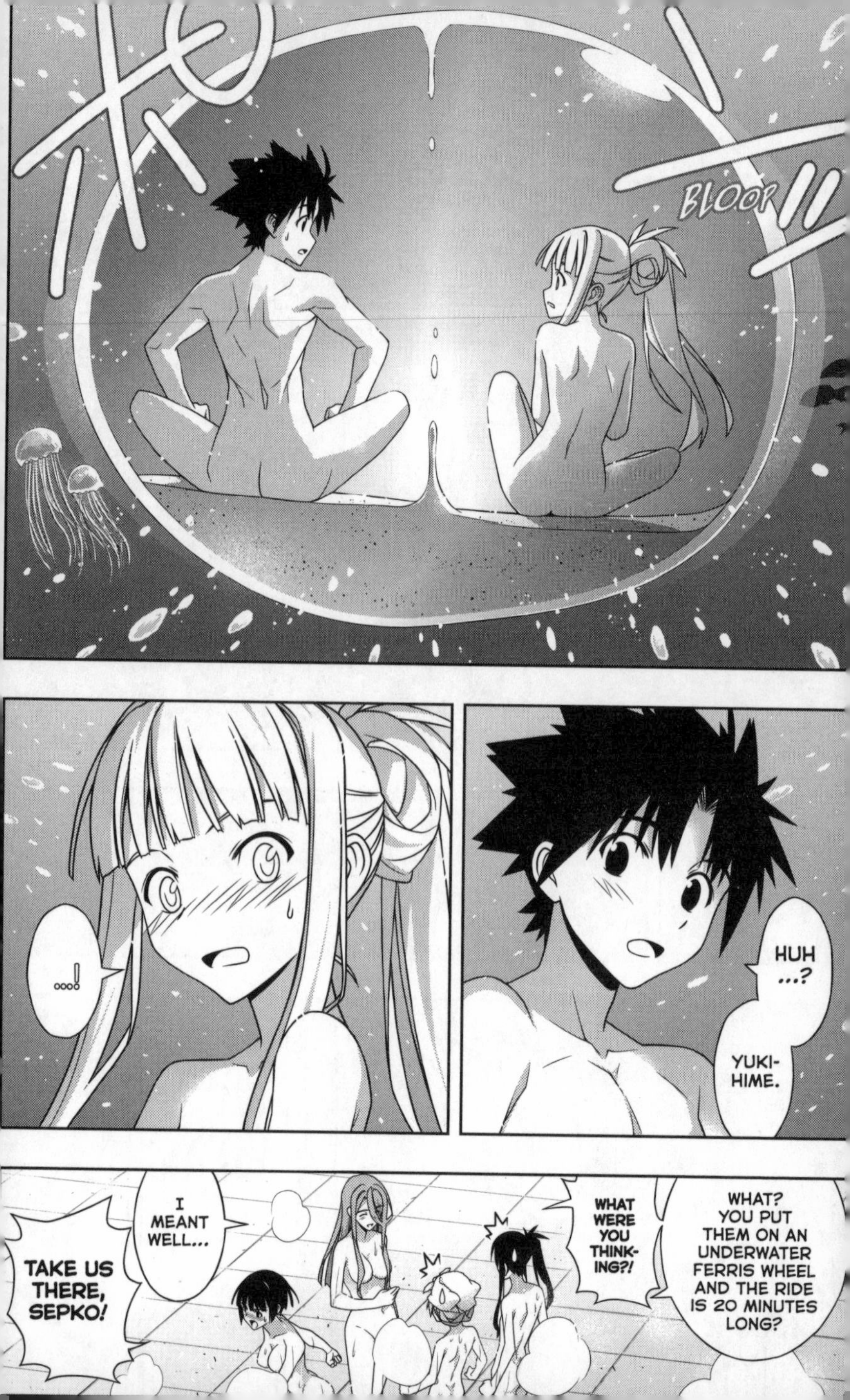
BLOOP!!
HUH ...?
YUKI-HIME.
...!
WHAT? YOU PUT THEM ON AN UNDERWATER FERRIS WHEEL AND THE RIDE IS 20 MINUTES LONG?
WHAT WERE YOU THINKING?!
I MEANT WELL...
TAKE US THERE, SEPKO!

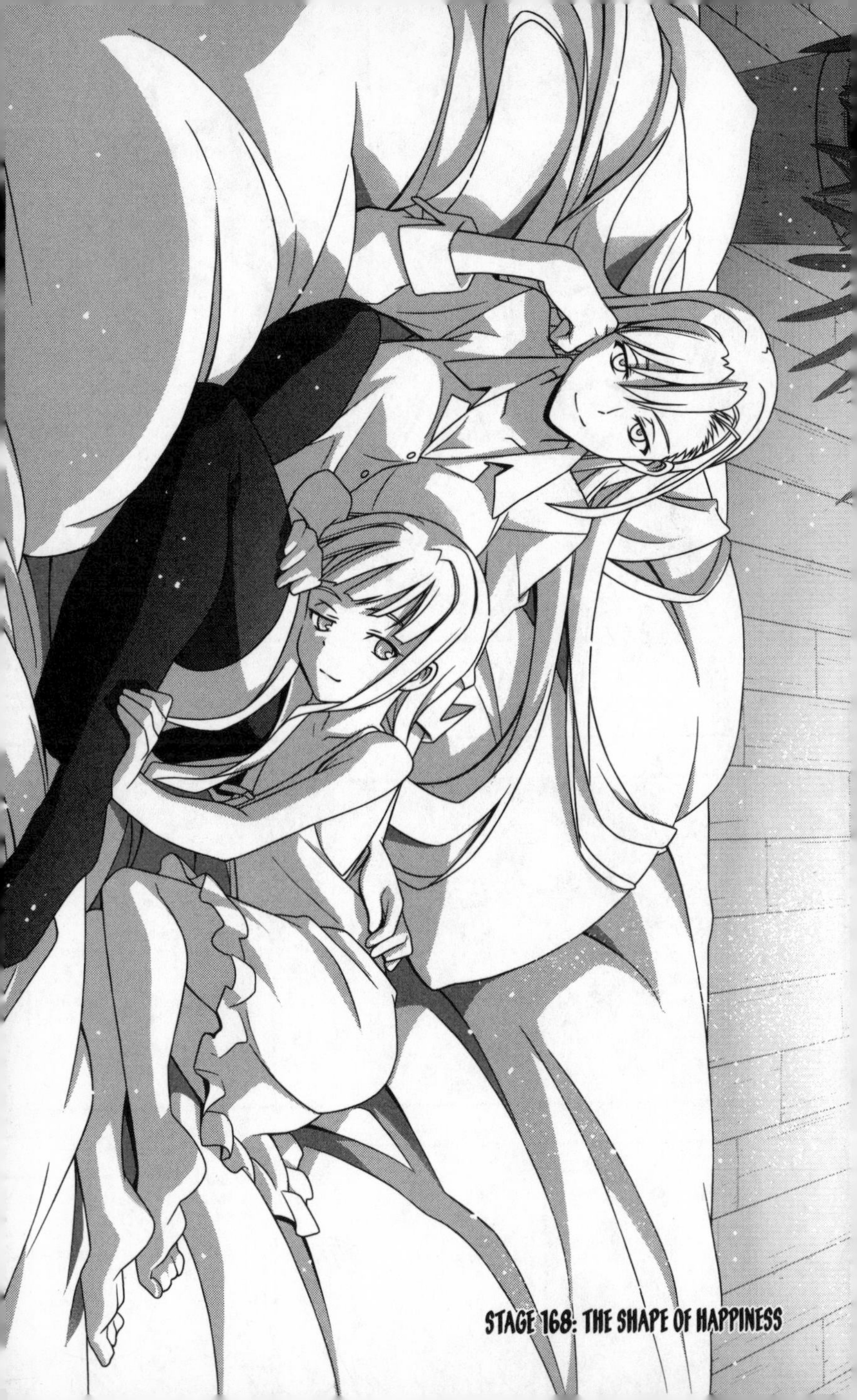

STAGE 168: THE SHAPE OF HAPPINESS

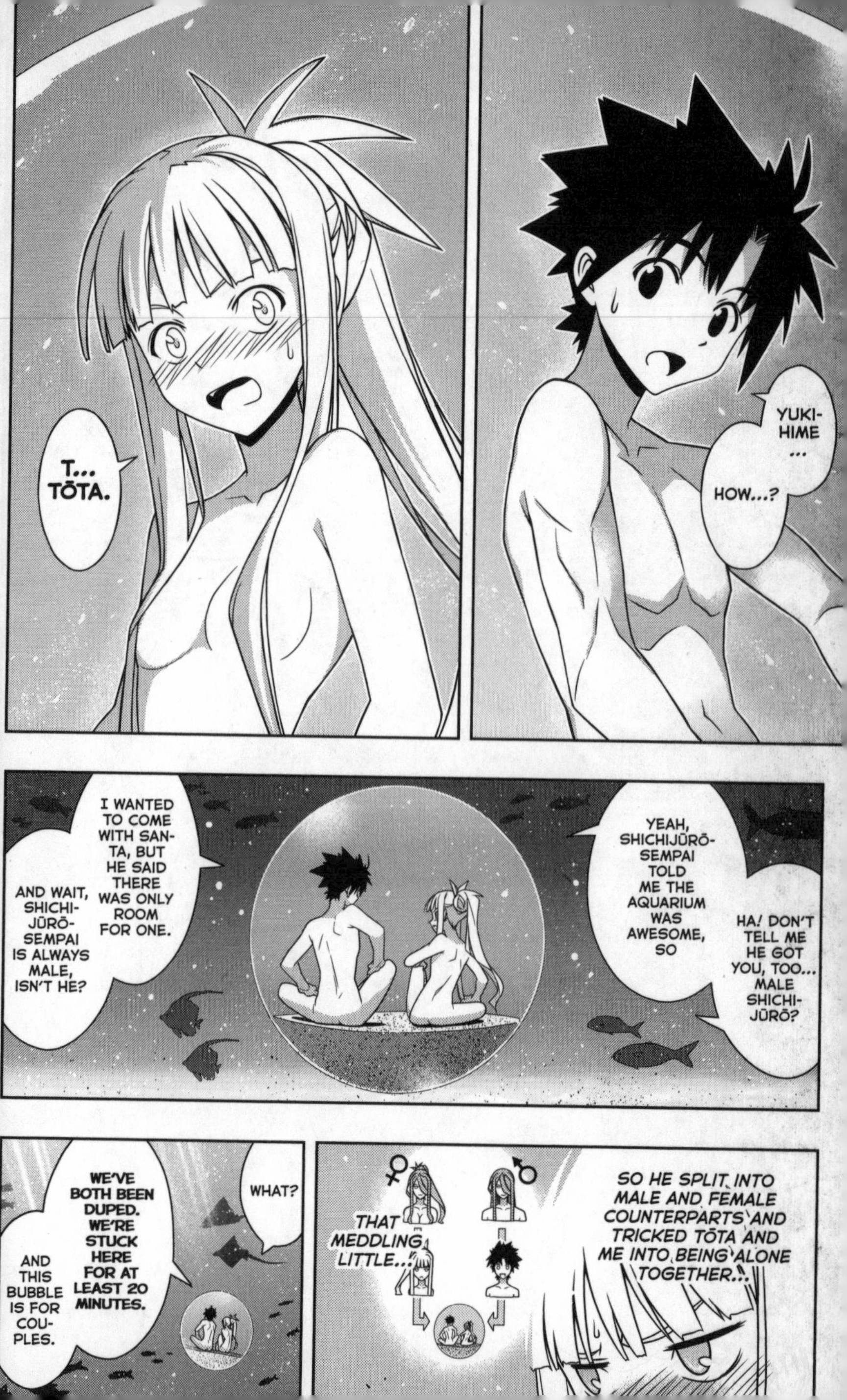

YUKI-HIME ...
HOW...?
T... TŌTA.
YEAH, SHICHIJŪRŌ-SEMPAI TOLD ME THE AQUARIUM WAS AWESOME, SO
HA! DON'T TELL ME HE GOT YOU, TOO... MALE SHICHIJŪRŌ?
I WANTED TO COME WITH SANTA, BUT HE SAID THERE WAS ONLY ROOM FOR ONE.
AND WAIT, SHICHIJŪRŌ-SEMPAI IS ALWAYS MALE, ISN'T HE?
SO HE SPLIT INTO MALE AND FEMALE COUNTERPARTS AND TRICKED TŌTA AND ME INTO BEING ALONE TOGETHER...
THAT MEDDLING LITTLE...!
WHAT?
WE'VE BOTH BEEN DUPED. WE'RE STUCK HERE FOR AT LEAST 20 MINUTES.
AND THIS BUBBLE IS FOR COUPLES.

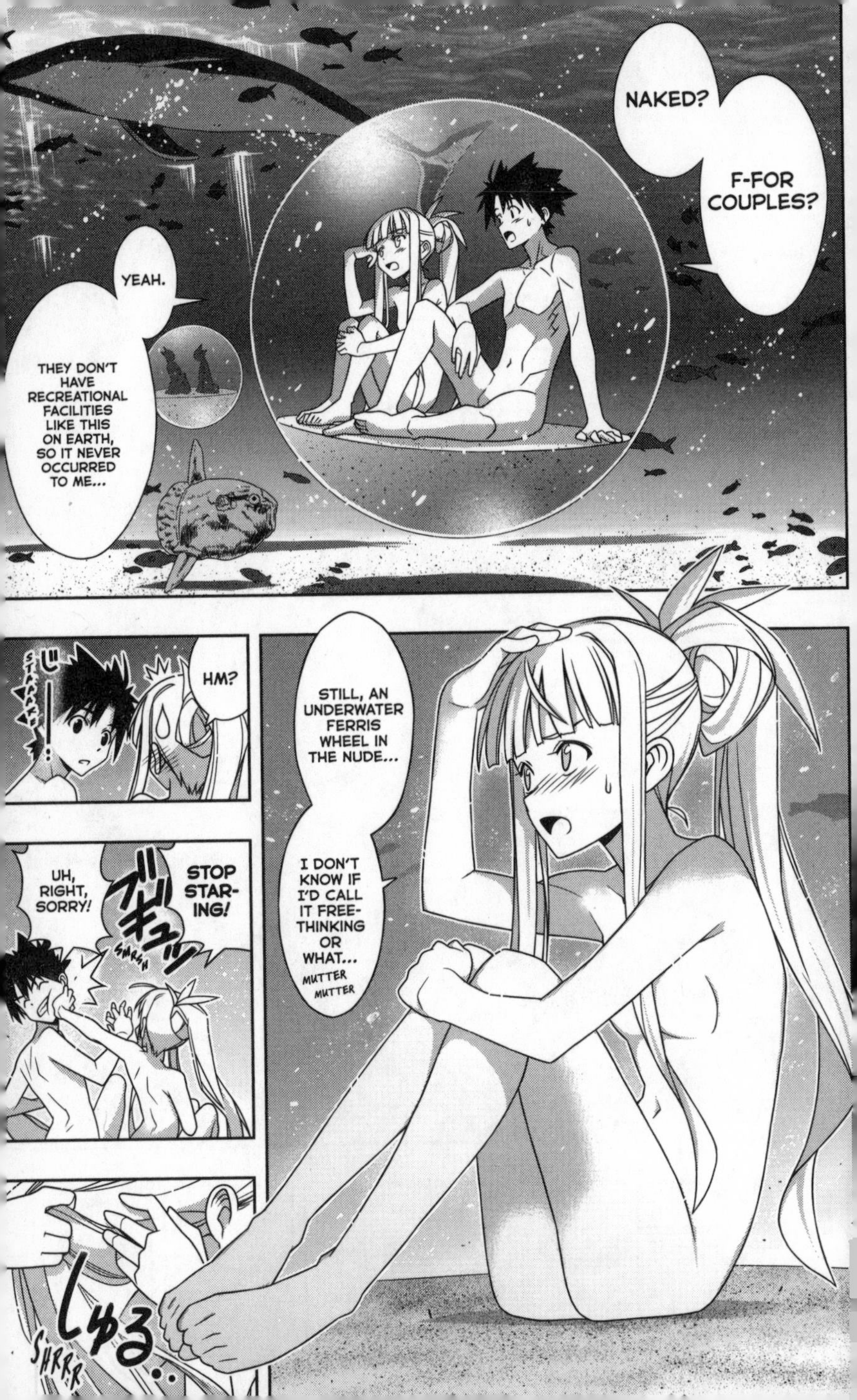
NAKED?
F-FOR COUPLES?
YEAH.
THEY DON'T HAVE RECREATIONAL FACILITIES LIKE THIS ON EARTH, SO IT NEVER OCCURRED TO ME...
STILL, AN UNDERWATER FERRIS WHEEL IN THE NUDE...
I DON'T KNOW IF I'D CALL IT FREE-THINKING OR WHAT... MUTTER MUTTER
HM?
STOP STARING!
UH, RIGHT, SORRY!
SMASH
しゅる

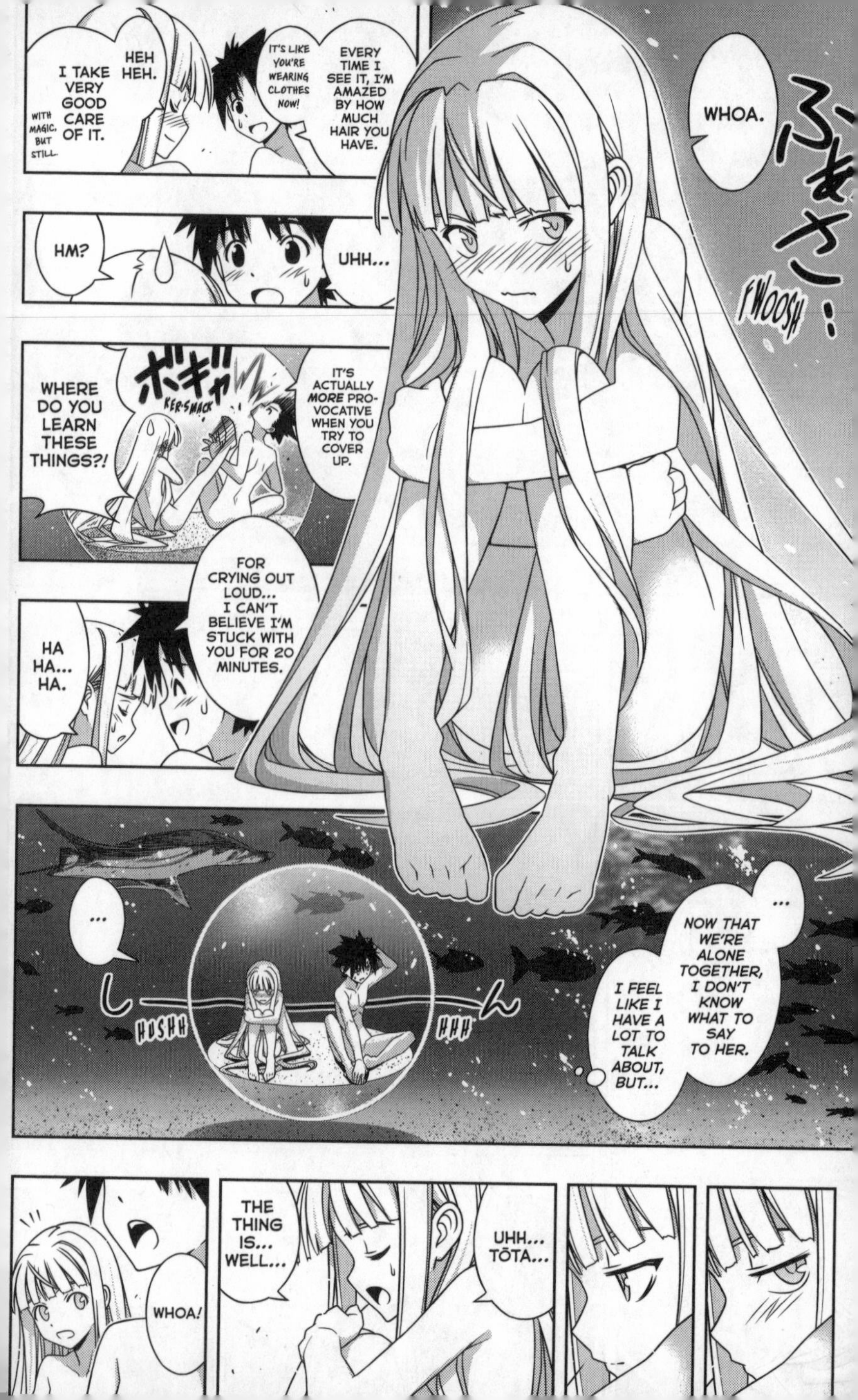
WHOA.
ふぁさ…
FWOOSH
EVERY TIME I SEE IT, I'M AMAZED BY HOW MUCH HAIR YOU HAVE.
IT'S LIKE YOU'RE WEARING CLOTHES NOW!
HEH HEH.
I TAKE VERY GOOD CARE OF IT.
WITH MAGIC, BUT STILL.
UHH...
HM?
IT'S ACTUALLY MORE PROVOCATIVE WHEN YOU TRY TO COVER UP.
ボギャ
KER-SMACK
WHERE DO YOU LEARN THESE THINGS?!
FOR CRYING OUT LOUD... I CAN'T BELIEVE I'M STUCK WITH YOU FOR 20 MINUTES.
HA HA... HA.
...
NOW THAT WE'RE ALONE TOGETHER, I DON'T KNOW WHAT TO SAY TO HER.
I FEEL LIKE I HAVE A LOT TO TALK ABOUT, BUT...
しーーん
HUSHHHH
...
UHH... TŌTA...
THE THING IS... WELL...
WHOA!

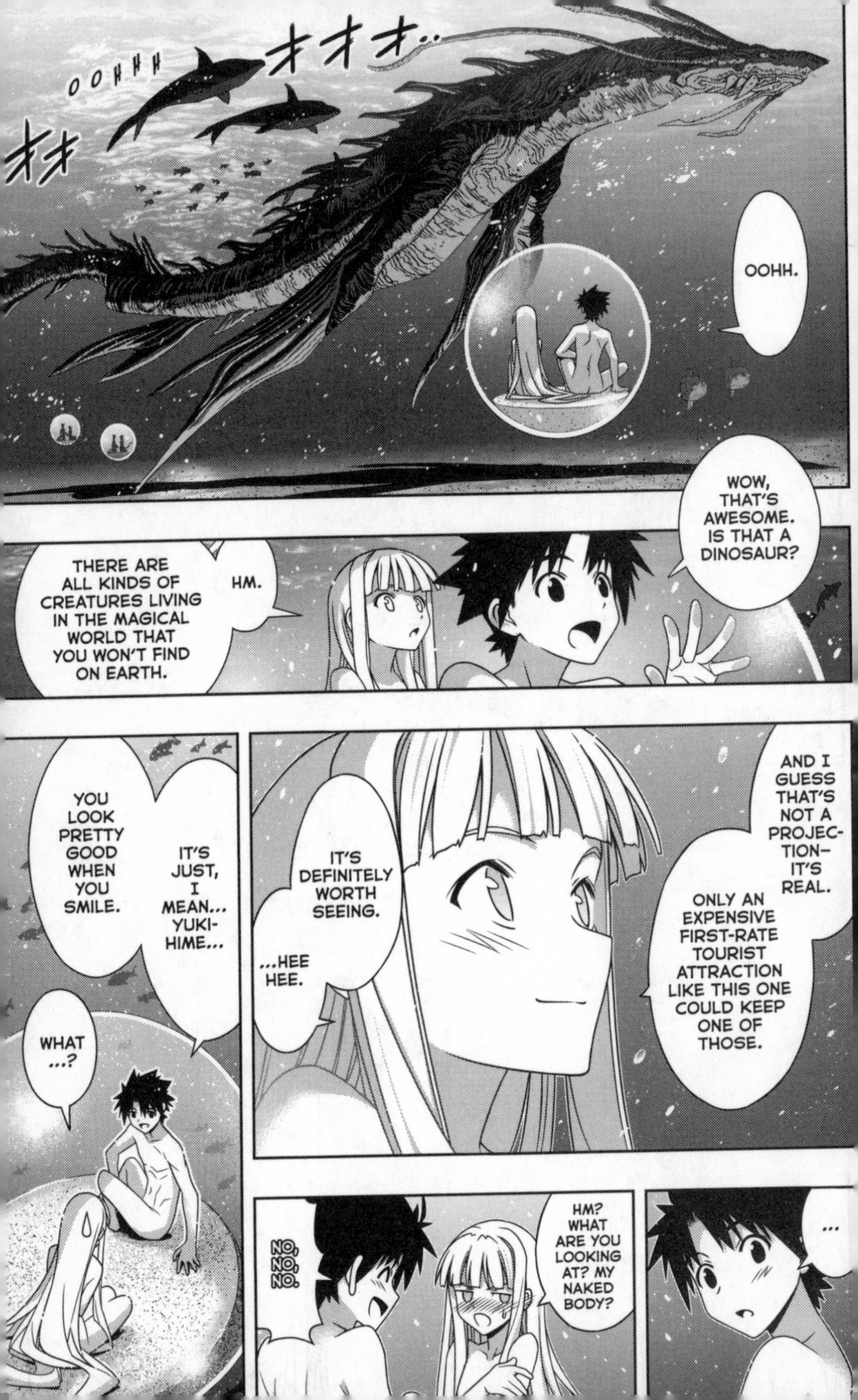
オオオ..
OOHHH
オオ
OOHH.
WOW, THAT'S AWESOME. IS THAT A DINOSAUR?
HM.
THERE ARE ALL KINDS OF CREATURES LIVING IN THE MAGICAL WORLD THAT YOU WON'T FIND ON EARTH.
AND I GUESS THAT'S NOT A PROJECTION—IT'S REAL.
ONLY AN EXPENSIVE FIRST-RATE TOURIST ATTRACTION LIKE THIS ONE COULD KEEP ONE OF THOSE.
IT'S DEFINITELY WORTH SEEING.
...HEE HEE.
...
HM? WHAT ARE YOU LOOKING AT? MY NAKED BODY?
NO, NO, NO.
IT'S JUST, I MEAN... YUKI-HIME...
YOU LOOK PRETTY GOOD WHEN YOU SMILE.
WHAT ...?

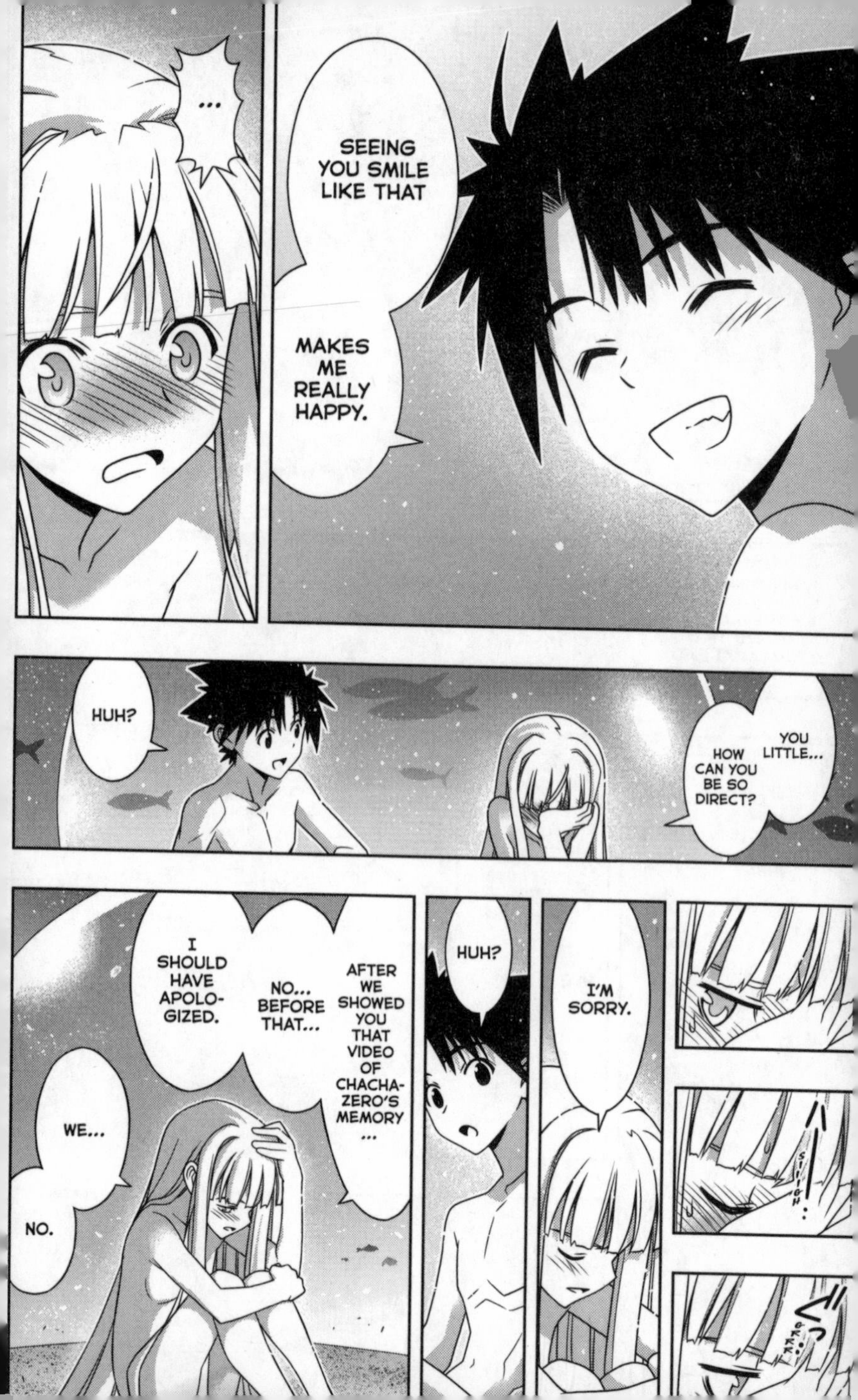
SEEING YOU SMILE LIKE THAT
MAKES ME REALLY HAPPY.
...
YOU LITTLE... HOW CAN YOU BE SO DIRECT?
HUH?
SIIIGH
GRKK
I'M SORRY.
HUH?
AFTER WE SHOWED YOU THAT VIDEO OF CHACHA-ZERO'S MEMORY...
NO... BEFORE THAT...
I SHOULD HAVE APOLO-GIZED.
WE...
NO.

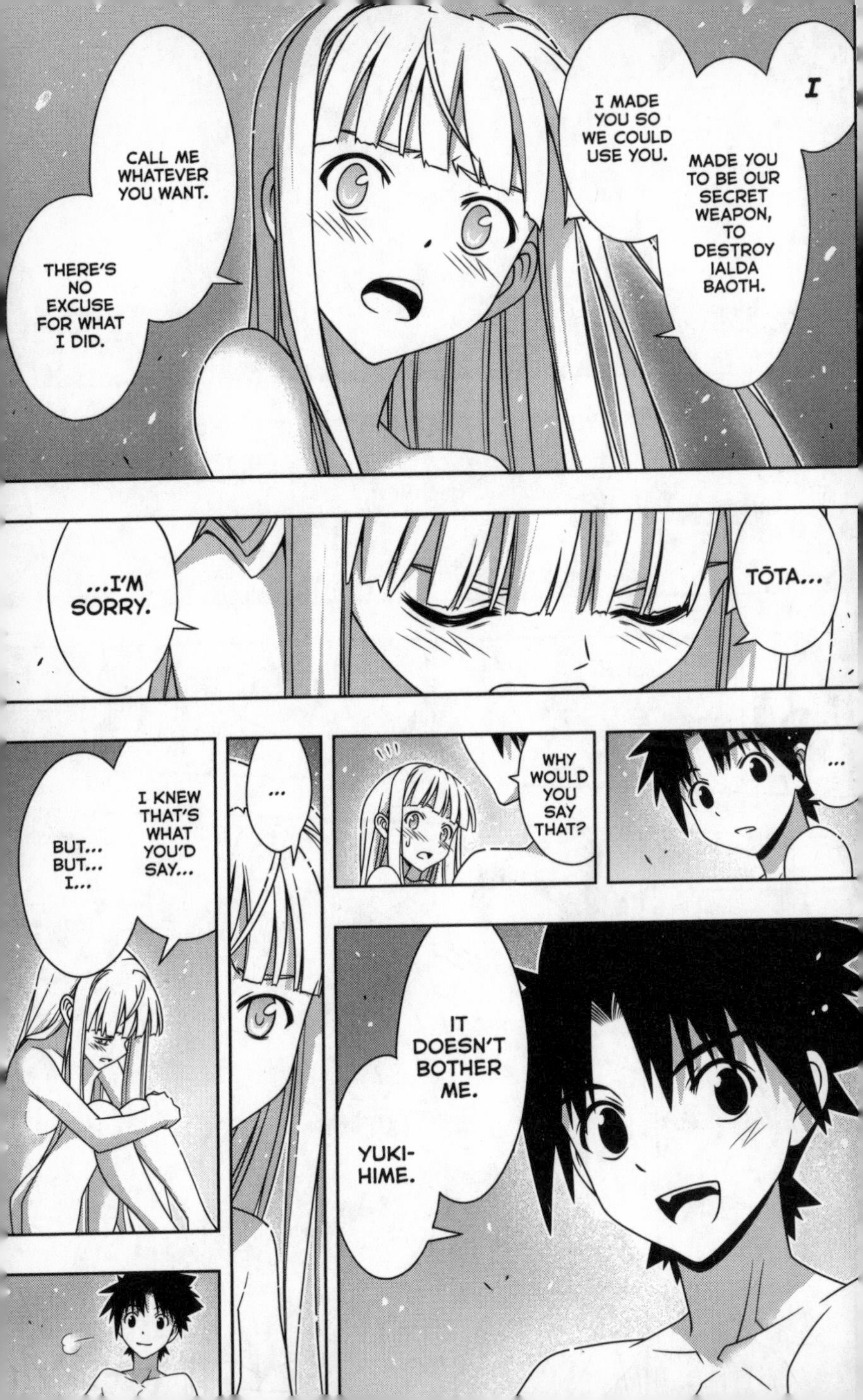

I
MADE YOU TO BE OUR SECRET WEAPON, TO DESTROY IALDA BAOTH.
I MADE YOU SO WE COULD USE YOU.
CALL ME WHATEVER YOU WANT.
THERE'S NO EXCUSE FOR WHAT I DID.
TŌTA...
...I'M SORRY.
...
WHY WOULD YOU SAY THAT?
...
I KNEW THAT'S WHAT YOU'D SAY...
BUT... BUT... I...
IT DOESN'T BOTHER ME.
YUKI-HIME.

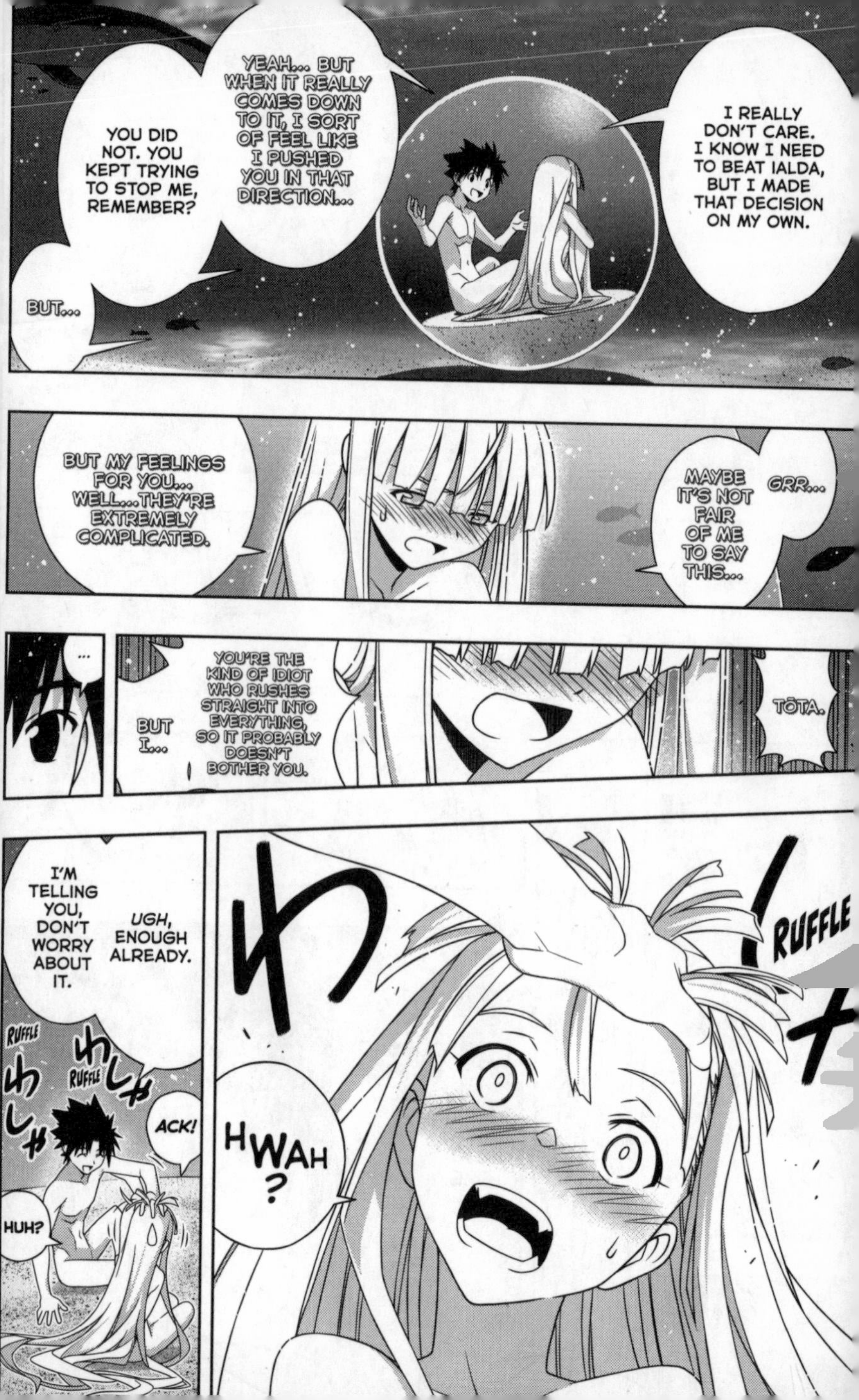
I REALLY DON'T CARE. I KNOW I NEED TO BEAT IALDA, BUT I MADE THAT DECISION ON MY OWN.
YEAH... BUT WHEN IT REALLY COMES DOWN TO IT, I SORT OF FEEL LIKE I PUSHED YOU IN THAT DIRECTION...
YOU DID NOT. YOU KEPT TRYING TO STOP ME, REMEMBER?
BUT...
GRR...
MAYBE IT'S NOT FAIR OF ME TO SAY THIS...
BUT MY FEELINGS FOR YOU... WELL...THEY'RE EXTREMELY COMPLICATED.
TŌTA.
YOU'RE THE KIND OF IDIOT WHO RUSHES STRAIGHT INTO EVERYTHING, SO IT PROBABLY DOESN'T BOTHER YOU.
BUT I...
...
RUFFLE
HWAH?
I'M TELLING YOU, DON'T WORRY ABOUT IT.
UGH, ENOUGH ALREADY.
RUFFLE
RUFFLE
ACK!
HUH?

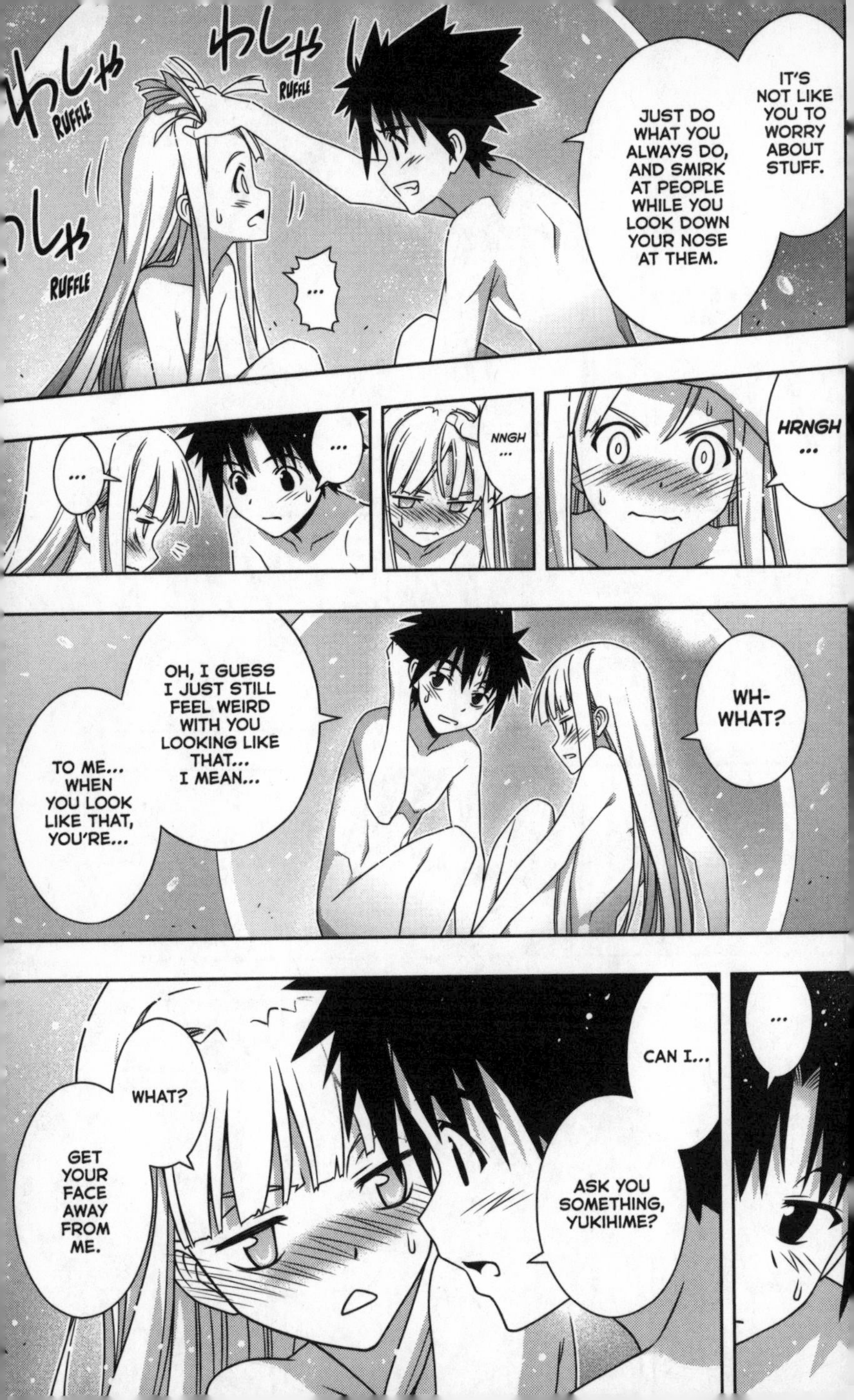
IT'S NOT LIKE YOU TO WORRY ABOUT STUFF.
JUST DO WHAT YOU ALWAYS DO, AND SMIRK AT PEOPLE WHILE YOU LOOK DOWN YOUR NOSE AT THEM.
わしゃ RUFFLE
わしゃ RUFFLE
わしゃ RUFFLE
...
HRNGH ...
NNGH ...
...
...
WH- WHAT?
OH, I GUESS I JUST STILL FEEL WEIRD WITH YOU LOOKING LIKE THAT... I MEAN...
TO ME... WHEN YOU LOOK LIKE THAT, YOU'RE...
...
CAN I...
ASK YOU SOMETHING, YUKIHIME?
WHAT?
GET YOUR FACE AWAY FROM ME.

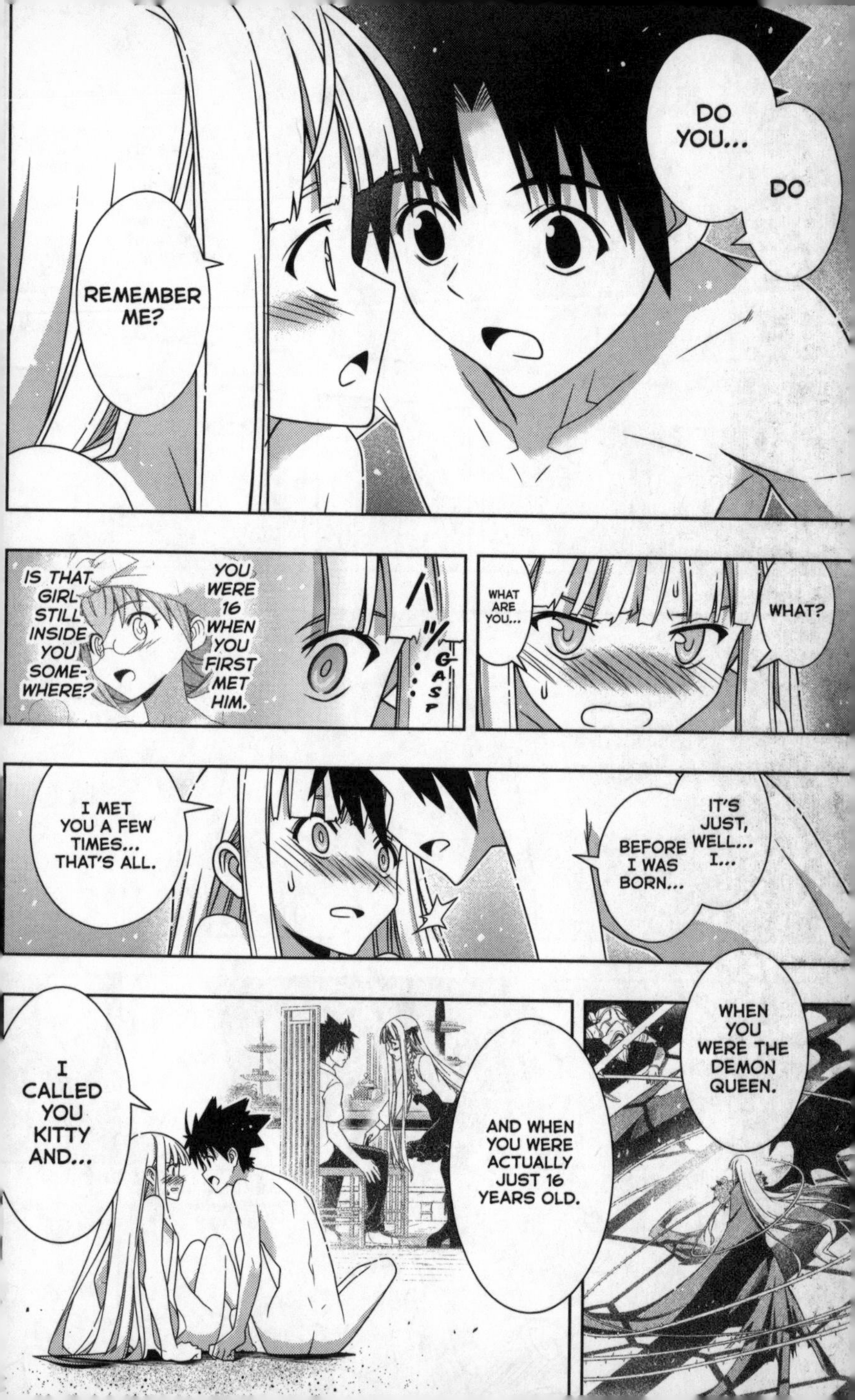
DO YOU... DO
REMEMBER ME?
WHAT?
WHAT ARE YOU...
GASP
YOU WERE 16 WHEN YOU FIRST MET HIM.
IS THAT GIRL STILL INSIDE YOU SOMEWHERE?
IT'S JUST, WELL... I...
BEFORE I WAS BORN...
I MET YOU A FEW TIMES... THAT'S ALL.
WHEN YOU WERE THE DEMON QUEEN.
AND WHEN YOU WERE ACTUALLY JUST 16 YEARS OLD.
I CALLED YOU KITTY AND...

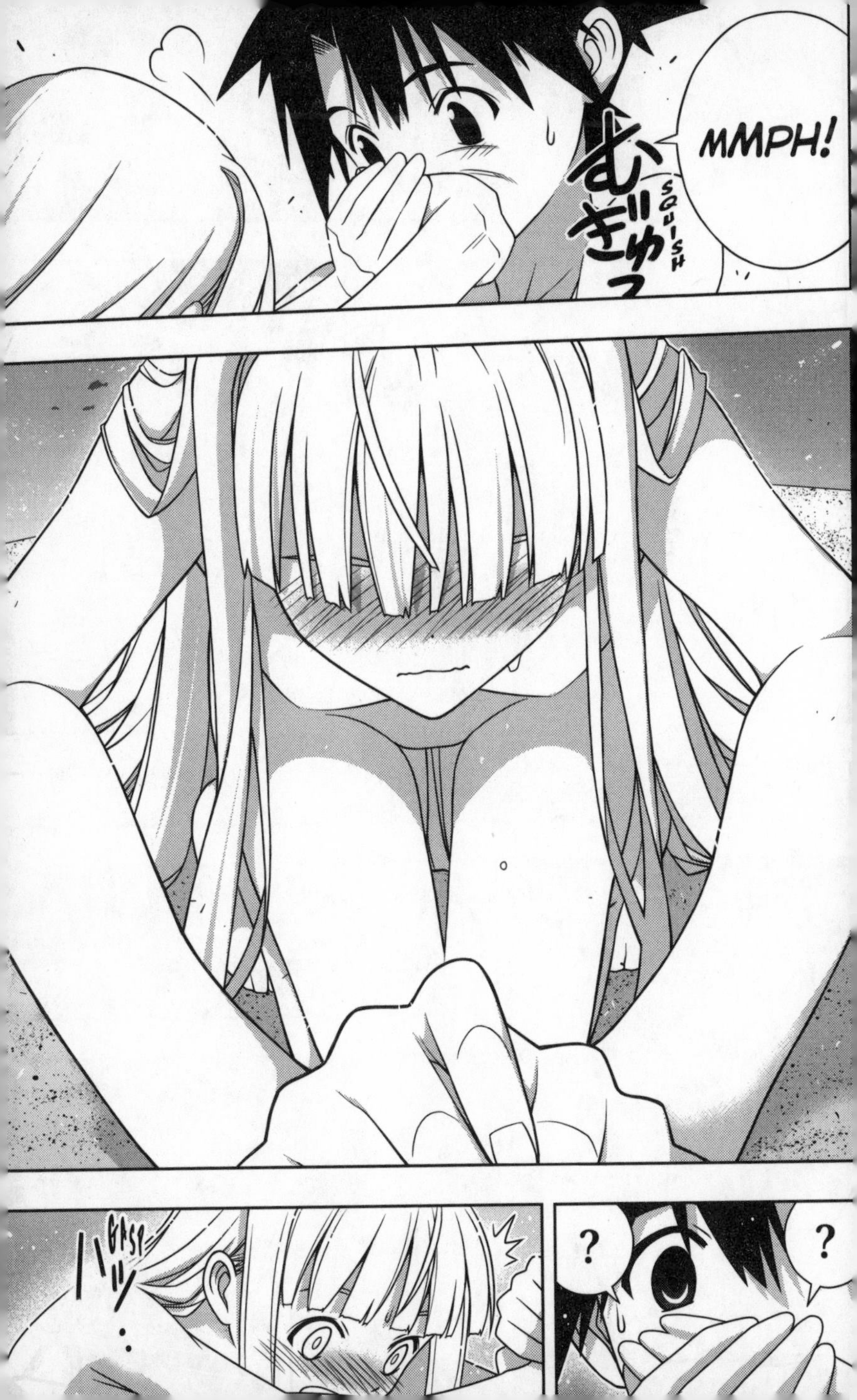

MMPH!
むぎゅ
SQUISH
?
?
GASP
ハッ

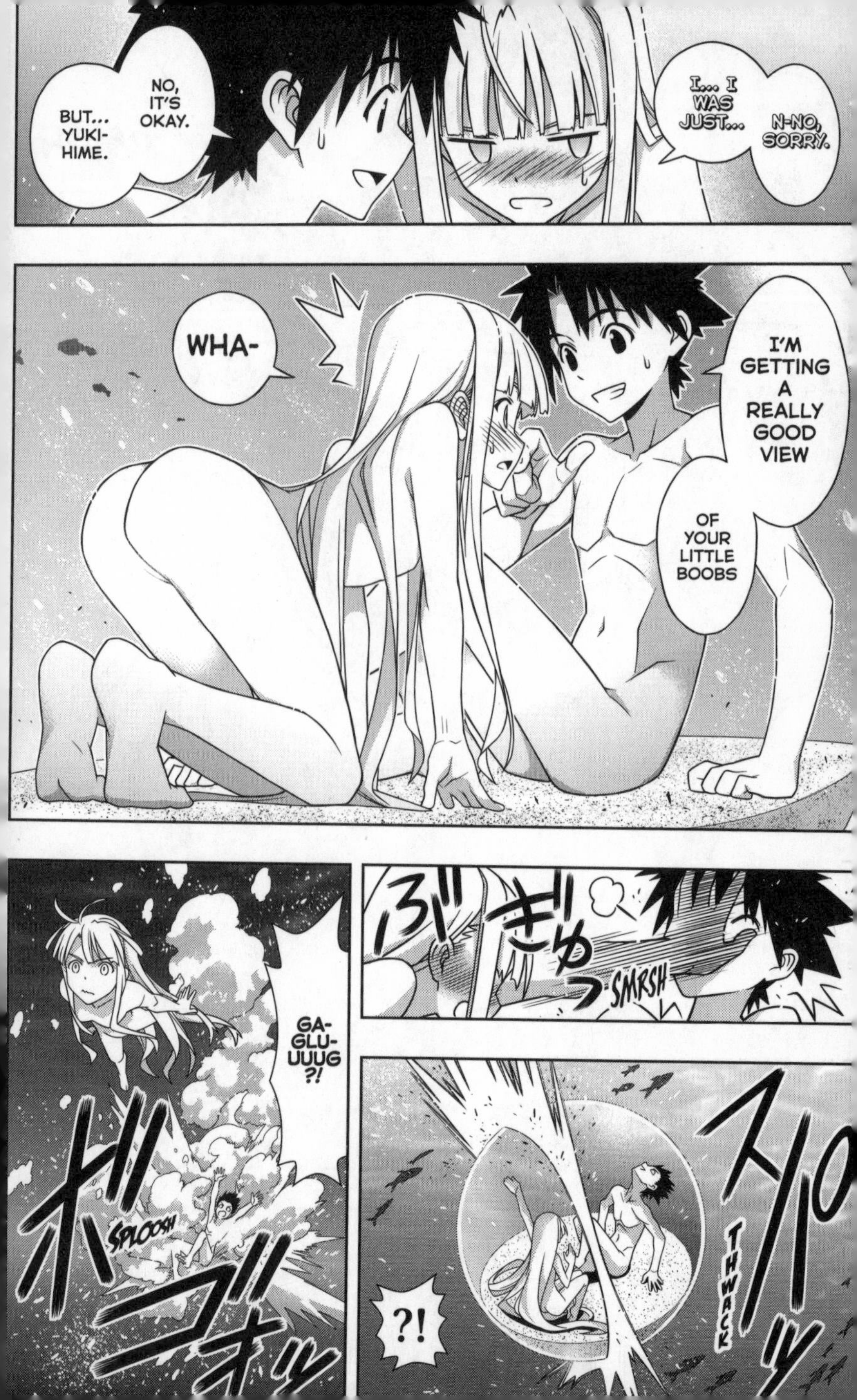

I... I WAS JUST...
N-NO, SORRY.
NO, IT'S OKAY.
BUT... YUKI-HIME.
I'M GETTING A REALLY GOOD VIEW
OF YOUR LITTLE BOOBS
WHA-
SMRSH
THWACK
?!
GA-GLU-UUUG?!
SPLOOSH

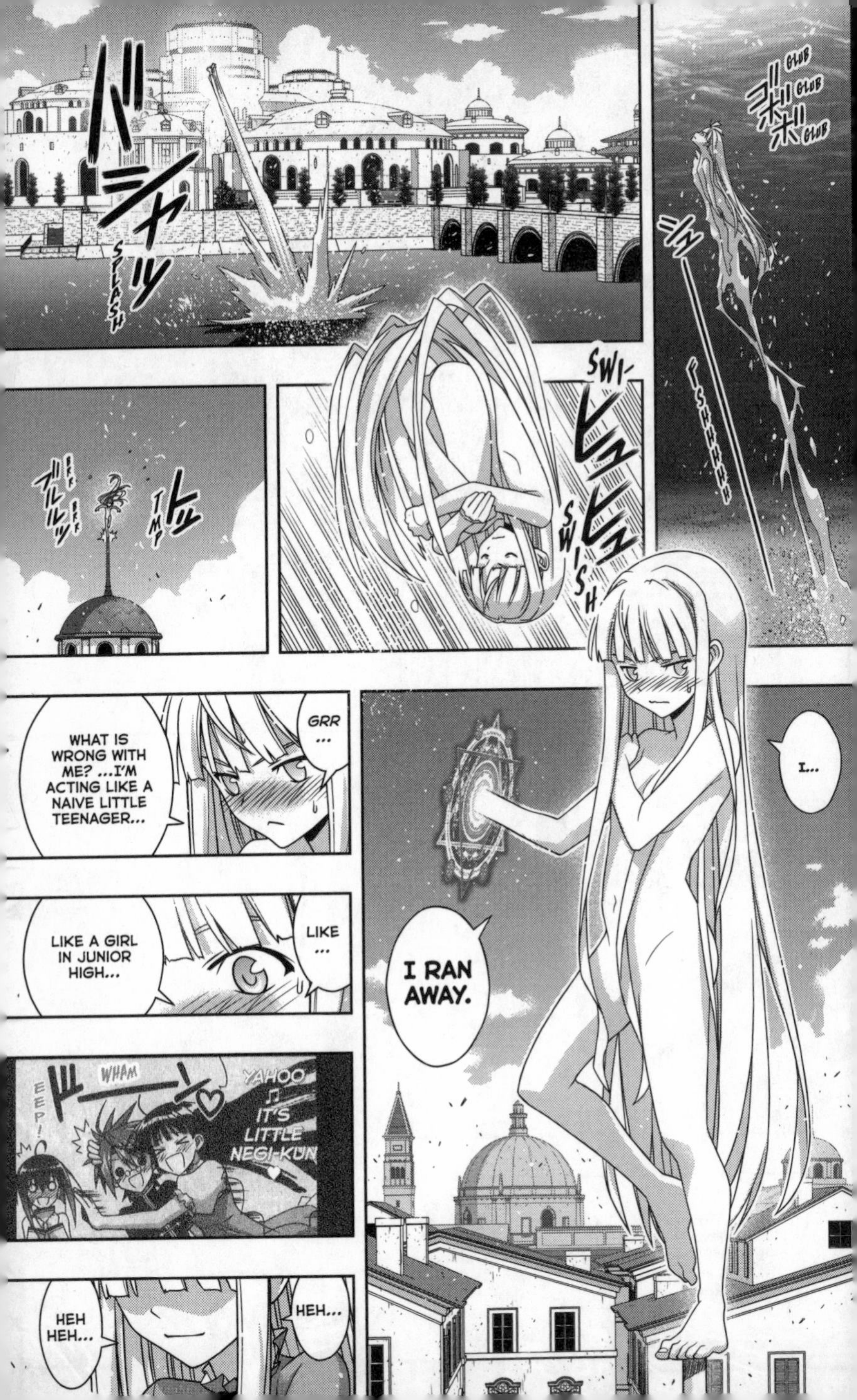
GLUB GLUB GLUB
FSHHHHH
SPLASH
SWISH
SWI-
TMP
BRR BRR
I...
I RAN AWAY.
GRR...
WHAT IS WRONG WITH ME? ...I'M ACTING LIKE A NAIVE LITTLE TEENAGER...
LIKE...
LIKE A GIRL IN JUNIOR HIGH...
YAHOO ♫ IT'S LITTLE NEGI-KUN
WHAM
EEP!
HEH...
HEH HEH...

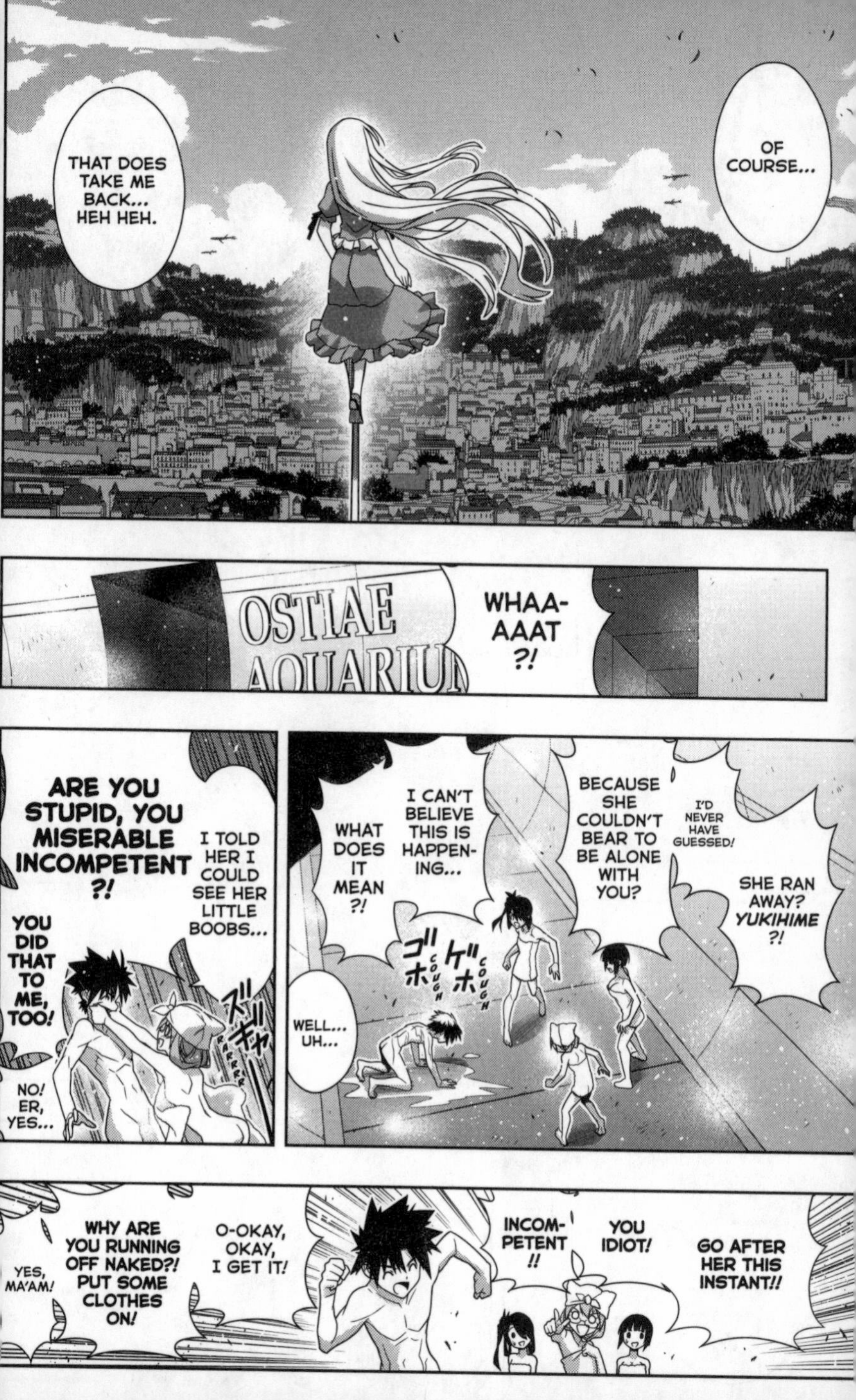

OF COURSE...
THAT DOES TAKE ME BACK... HEH HEH.
OSTIAE
WHAA-AAAT ?!
SHE RAN AWAY? YUKIHIME ?!
I'D NEVER HAVE GUESSED!
BECAUSE SHE COULDN'T BEAR TO BE ALONE WITH YOU?
I CAN'T BELIEVE THIS IS HAPPEN-ING...
WHAT DOES IT MEAN ?!
ゲホ COUGH
ゴホ COUGH
WELL... UH...
I TOLD HER I COULD SEE HER LITTLE BOOBS...
ARE YOU STUPID, YOU MISERABLE INCOMPETENT ?!
ズギャ RARRRR
YOU DID THAT TO ME, TOO!
NO! ER, YES...
GO AFTER HER THIS INSTANT!!
YOU IDIOT!
INCOM-PETENT !!
O-OKAY, OKAY, I GET IT!
WHY ARE YOU RUNNING OFF NAKED?! PUT SOME CLOTHES ON!
YES, MA'AM!

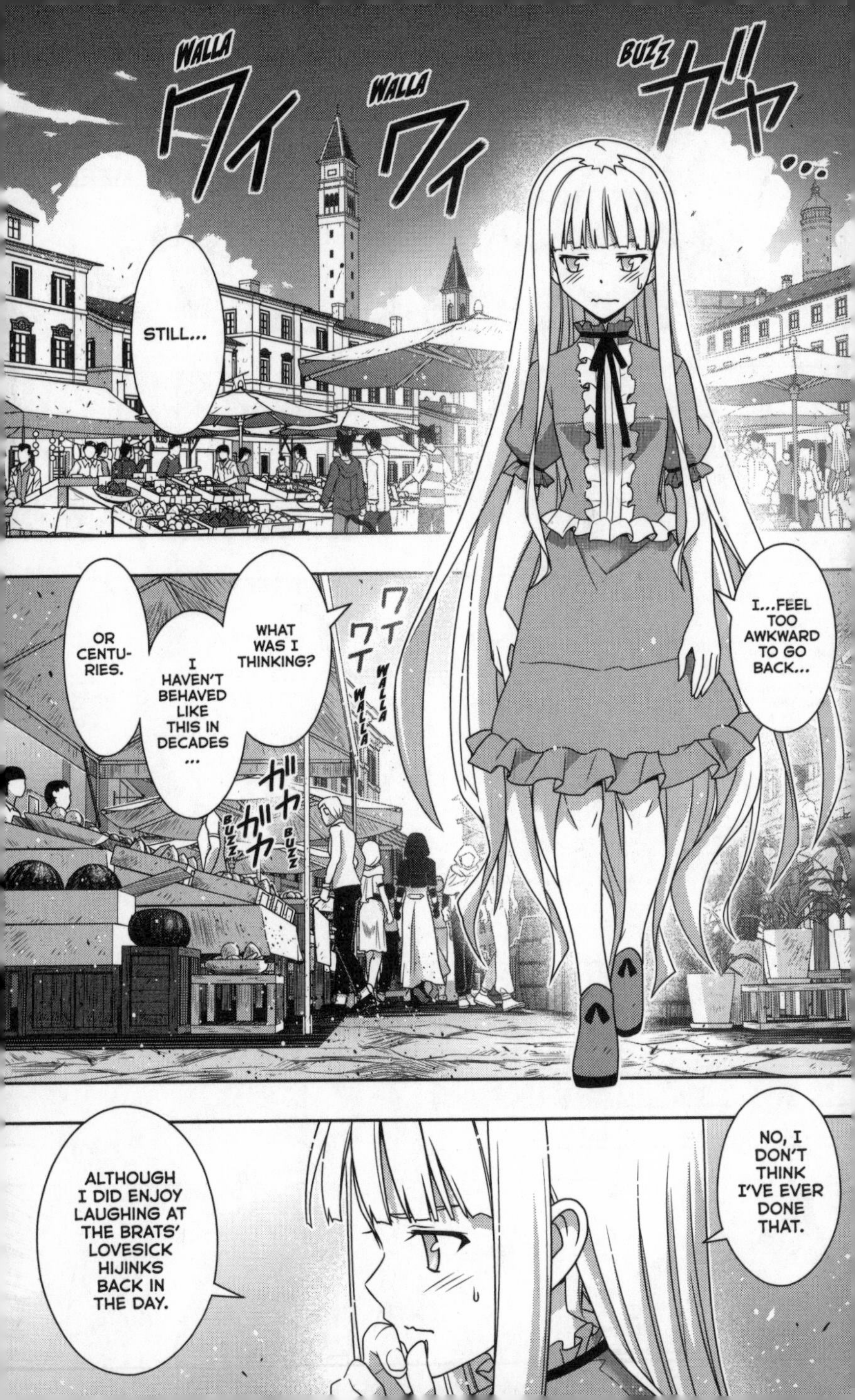
BUZZ
ガヤ…
WALLA
ワイ
WALLA
ワイ
STILL…
I…FEEL TOO AWKWARD TO GO BACK…
WHAT WAS I THINKING?
I HAVEN'T BEHAVED LIKE THIS IN DECADES…
OR CENTU-RIES.
ワイワイ
WALLA WALLA
ガヤガヤ
BUZZ BUZZ
NO, I DON'T THINK I'VE EVER DONE THAT.
ALTHOUGH I DID ENJOY LAUGHING AT THE BRATS' LOVESICK HIJINKS BACK IN THE DAY.

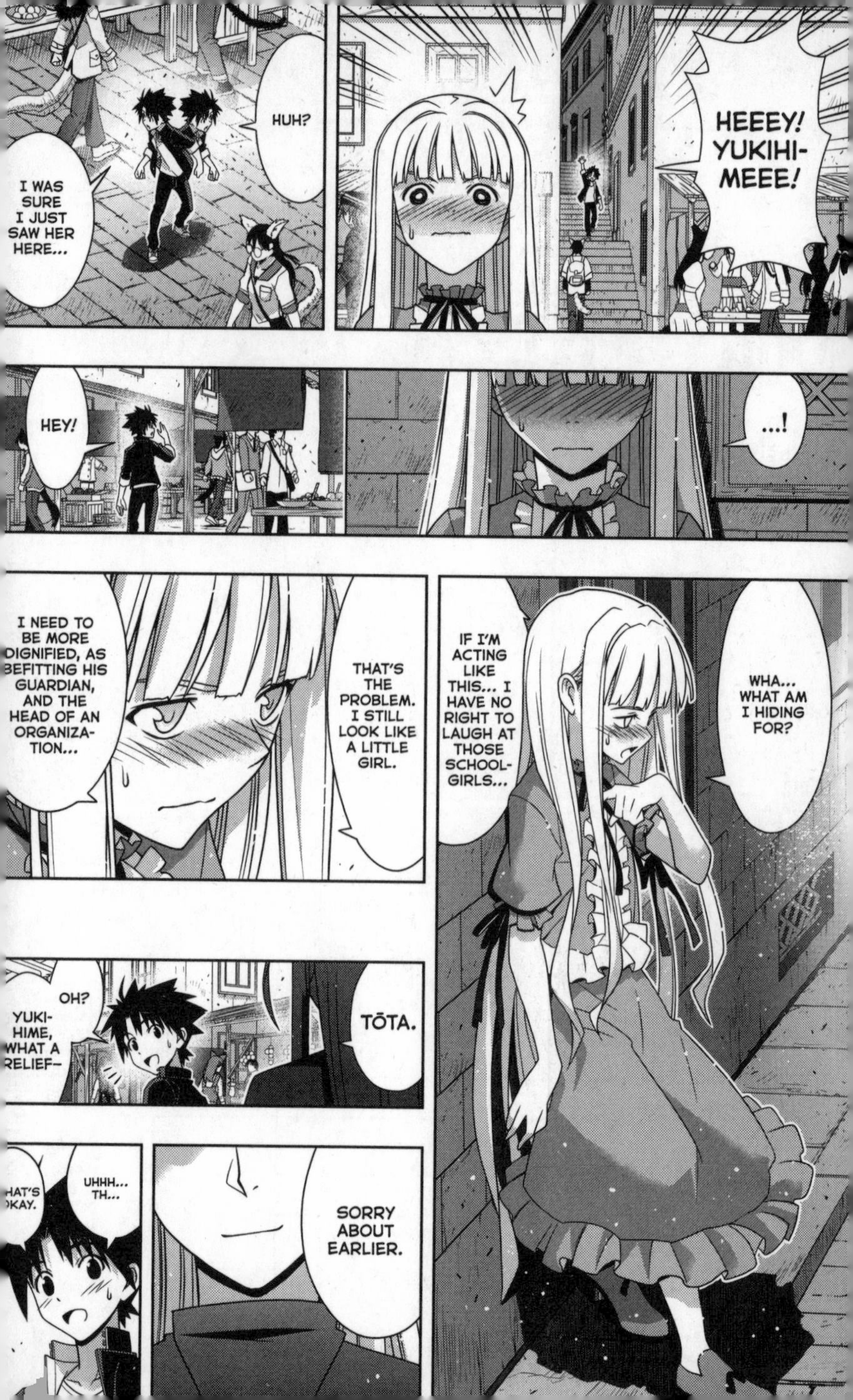
HEEEY! YUKIHI-MEEE!
HUH?
I WAS SURE I JUST SAW HER HERE...
...!
HEY!
WHA... WHAT AM I HIDING FOR?
IF I'M ACTING LIKE THIS... I HAVE NO RIGHT TO LAUGH AT THOSE SCHOOL-GIRLS...
THAT'S THE PROBLEM. I STILL LOOK LIKE A LITTLE GIRL.
I NEED TO BE MORE DIGNIFIED, AS BEFITTING HIS GUARDIAN, AND THE HEAD OF AN ORGANIZA-TION...
TŌTA.
OH? YUKI-HIME, WHAT A RELIEF–
SORRY ABOUT EARLIER.
UHHH... TH...
HAT'S KAY.

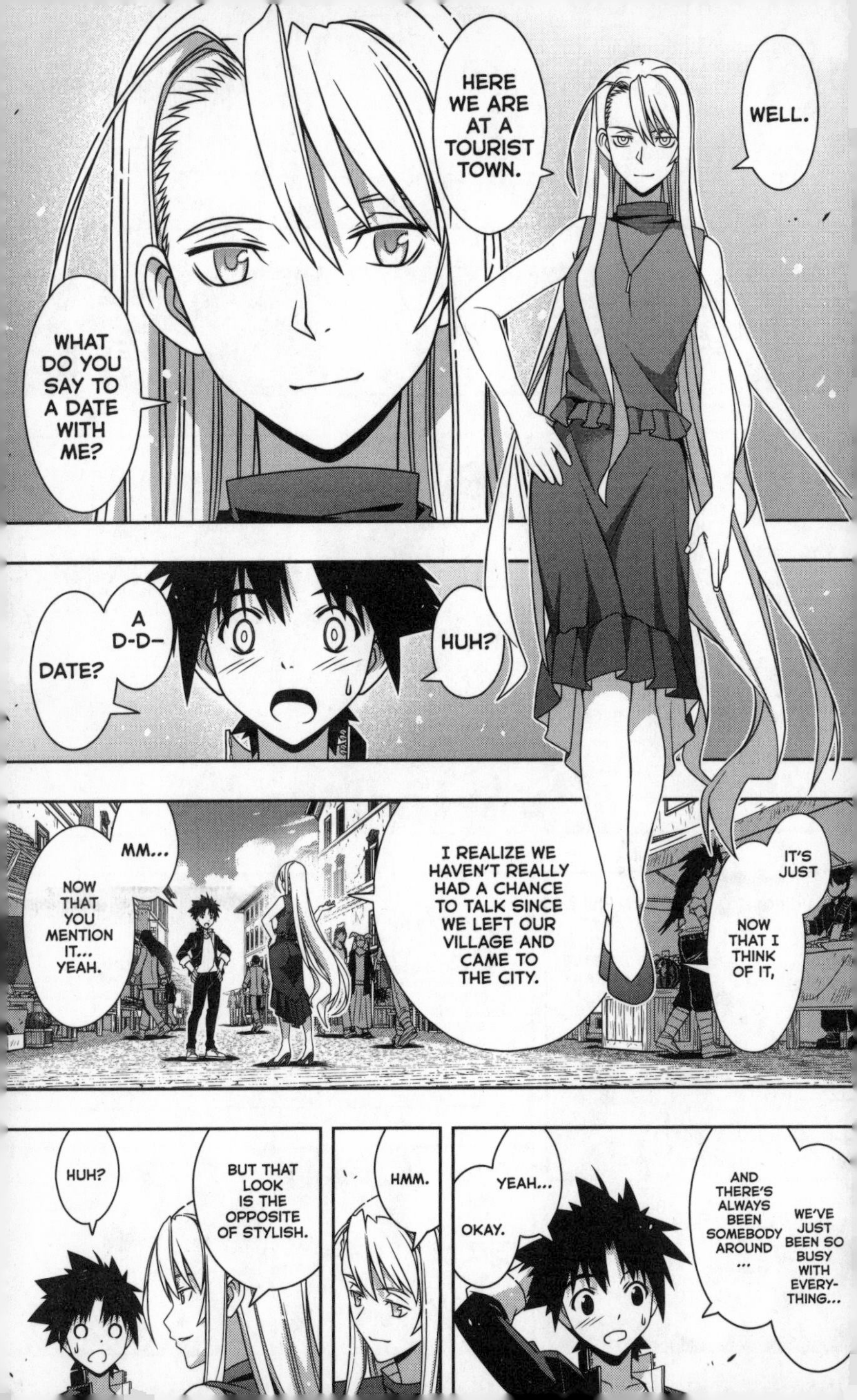
WELL.
HERE WE ARE AT A TOURIST TOWN.
WHAT DO YOU SAY TO A DATE WITH ME?
HUH?
A D-D- DATE?
IT'S JUST NOW THAT I THINK OF IT,
I REALIZE WE HAVEN'T REALLY HAD A CHANCE TO TALK SINCE WE LEFT OUR VILLAGE AND CAME TO THE CITY.
MM... NOW THAT YOU MENTION IT... YEAH.
WE'VE JUST BEEN SO BUSY WITH EVERY-THING...
AND THERE'S ALWAYS BEEN SOMEBODY AROUND...
YEAH... OKAY.
HMM.
BUT THAT LOOK IS THE OPPOSITE OF STYLISH.
HUH?

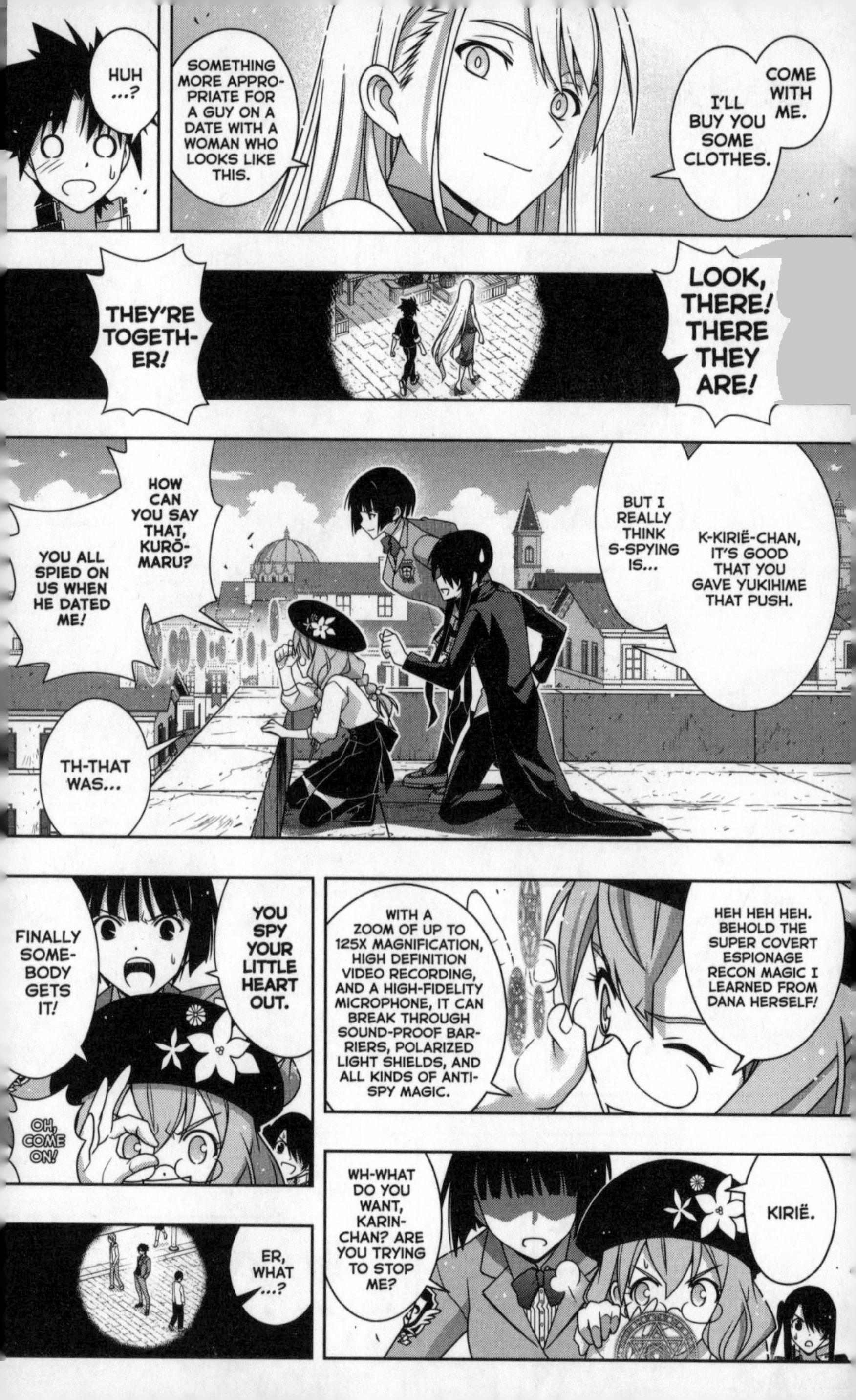
COME WITH ME.
I'LL BUY YOU SOME CLOTHES.
SOMETHING MORE APPROPRIATE FOR A GUY ON A DATE WITH A WOMAN WHO LOOKS LIKE THIS.
HUH ...?
LOOK, THERE! THERE THEY ARE!
THEY'RE TOGETH-ER!
K-KIRIË-CHAN, IT'S GOOD THAT YOU GAVE YUKIHIME THAT PUSH.
BUT I REALLY THINK S-SPYING IS...
HOW CAN YOU SAY THAT, KURŌMARU?
YOU ALL SPIED ON US WHEN HE DATED ME!
TH-THAT WAS...
HEH HEH HEH. BEHOLD THE SUPER COVERT ESPIONAGE RECON MAGIC I LEARNED FROM DANA HERSELF!
WITH A ZOOM OF UP TO 125X MAGNIFICATION, HIGH DEFINITION VIDEO RECORDING, AND A HIGH-FIDELITY MICROPHONE, IT CAN BREAK THROUGH SOUND-PROOF BARRIERS, POLARIZED LIGHT SHIELDS, AND ALL KINDS OF ANTI-SPY MAGIC.
YOU SPY YOUR LITTLE HEART OUT.
FINALLY SOMEBODY GETS IT!
OH, COME ON!
KIRIË.
WH-WHAT DO YOU WANT, KARIN-CHAN? ARE YOU TRYING TO STOP ME?
ER, WHAT ...?

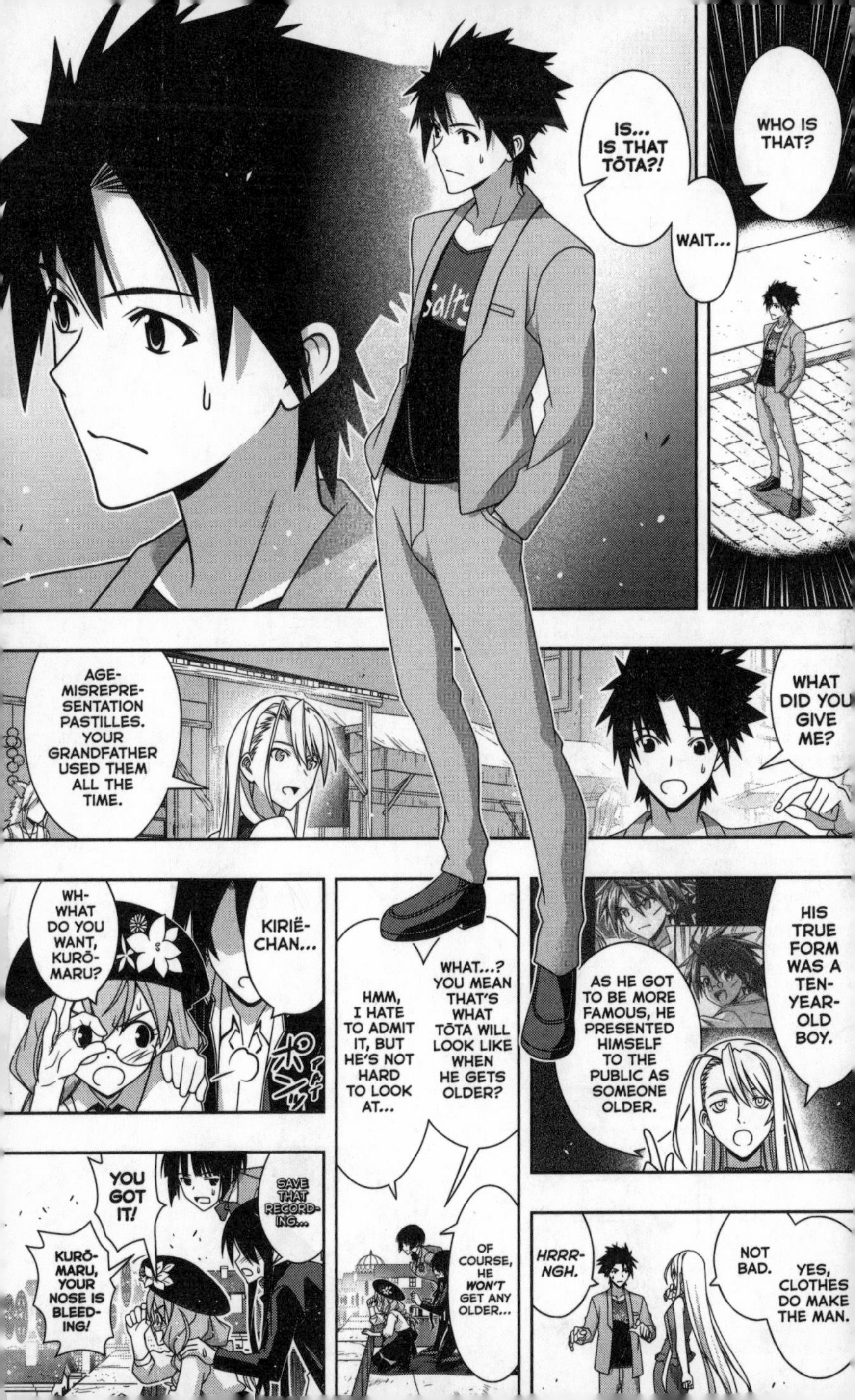
WHO IS THAT?
WAIT...
IS... IS THAT TŌTA?!
WHAT DID YOU GIVE ME?
AGE-MISREPRESENTATION PASTILLES. YOUR GRANDFATHER USED THEM ALL THE TIME.
HIS TRUE FORM WAS A TEN-YEAR-OLD BOY.
AS HE GOT TO BE MORE FAMOUS, HE PRESENTED HIMSELF TO THE PUBLIC AS SOMEONE OLDER.
WHAT...? YOU MEAN THAT'S WHAT TŌTA WILL LOOK LIKE WHEN HE GETS OLDER?
HMM, I HATE TO ADMIT IT, BUT HE'S NOT HARD TO LOOK AT...
KIRIË-CHAN...
PAT
WH-WHAT DO YOU WANT, KURŌMARU?
YES, CLOTHES DO MAKE THE MAN.
NOT BAD.
HRRR-NGH.
OF COURSE, HE *WON'T* GET ANY OLDER...
SAVE THAT RECORDING...
YOU GOT IT!
KURŌMARU, YOUR NOSE IS BLEEDING!

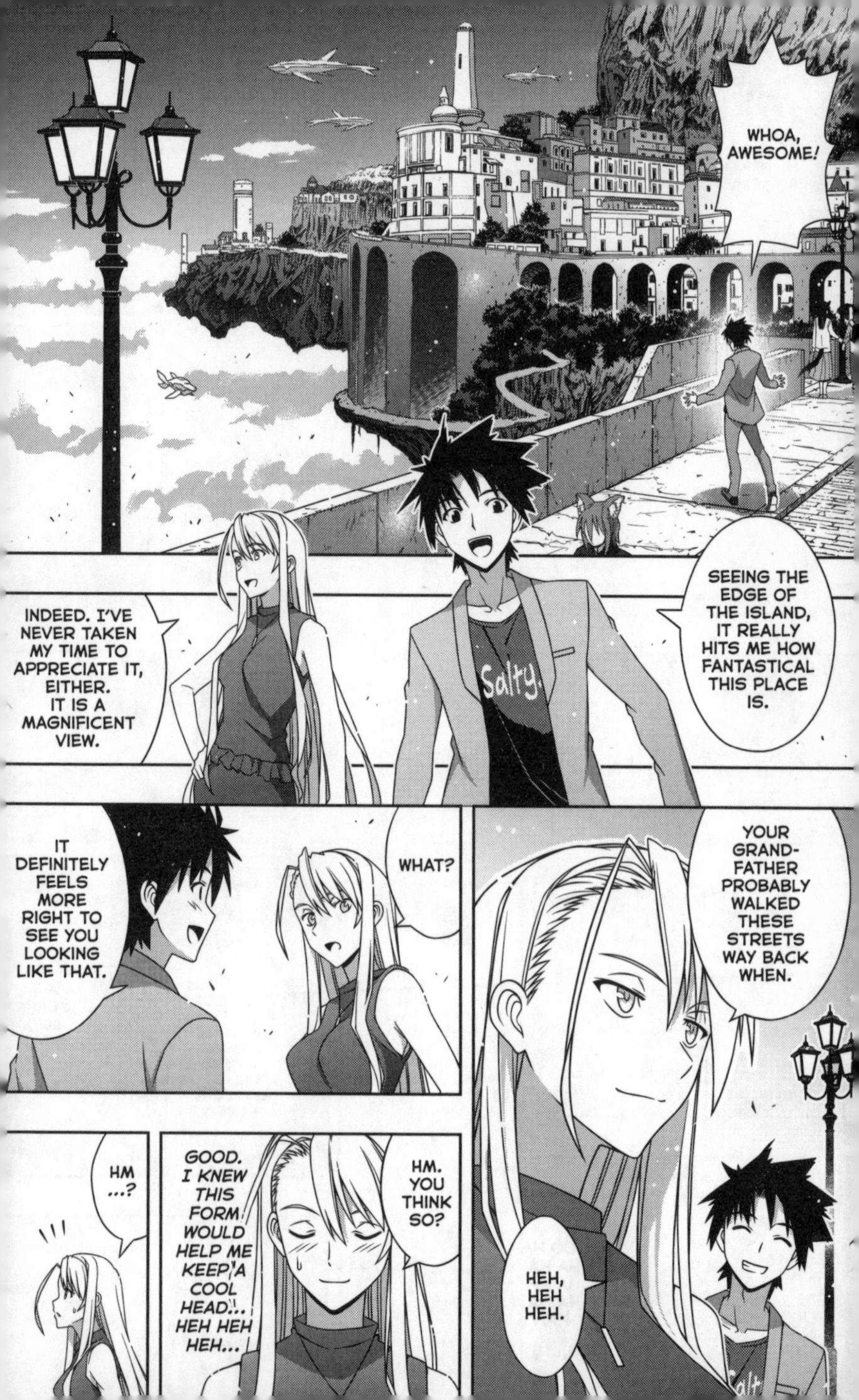
WHOA, AWESOME!
SEEING THE EDGE OF THE ISLAND, IT REALLY HITS ME HOW FANTASTICAL THIS PLACE IS.
INDEED. I'VE NEVER TAKEN MY TIME TO APPRECIATE IT, EITHER. IT IS A MAGNIFICENT VIEW.
YOUR GRAND-FATHER PROBABLY WALKED THESE STREETS WAY BACK WHEN.
HEH, HEH HEH.
IT DEFINITELY FEELS MORE RIGHT TO SEE YOU LOOKING LIKE THAT.
WHAT?
HM. YOU THINK SO?
GOOD. I KNEW THIS FORM WOULD HELP ME KEEP A COOL HEAD... HEH HEH HEH...
HM ...?

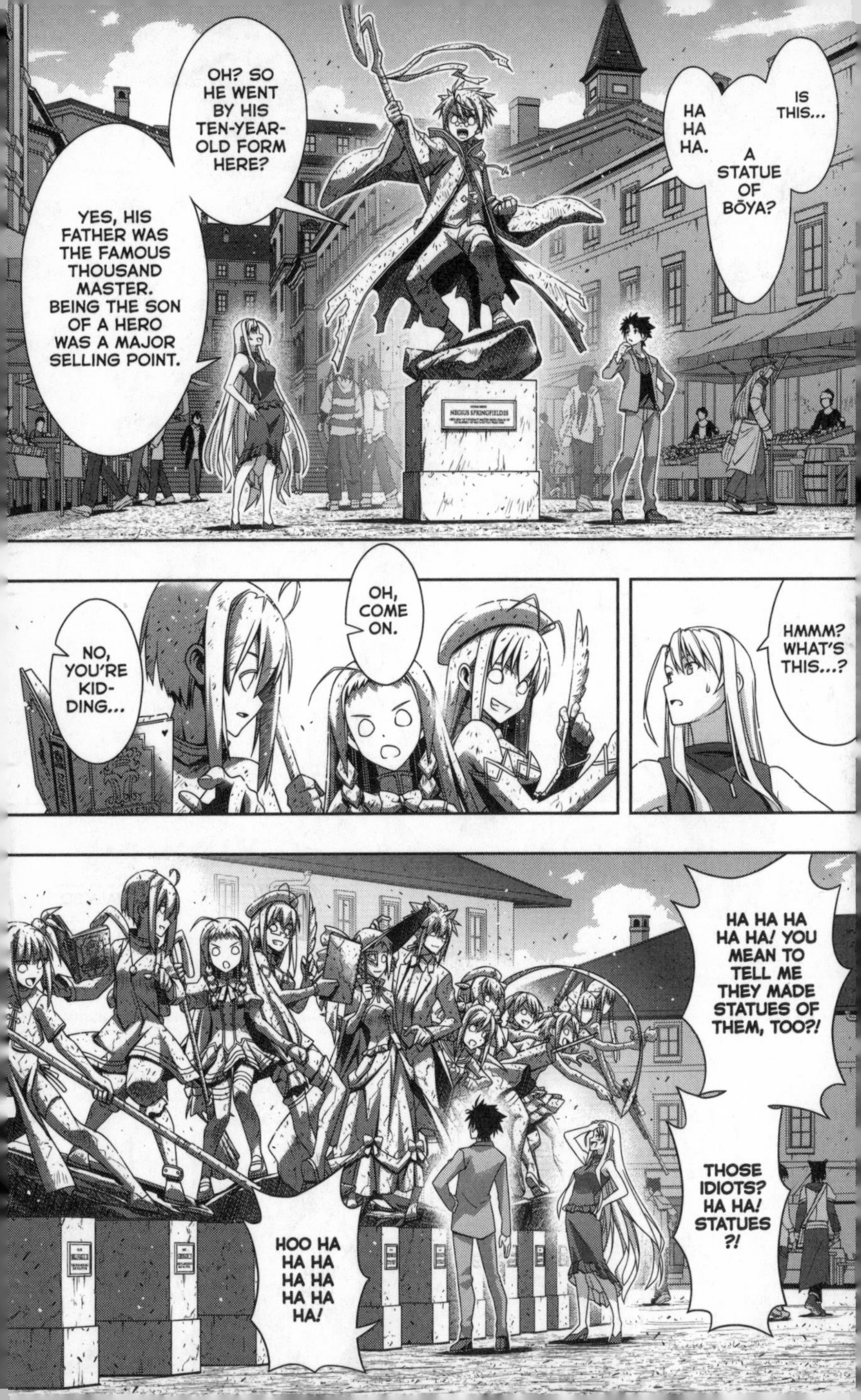
IS THIS... A STATUE OF BŌYA?
HA HA HA.
OH? SO HE WENT BY HIS TEN-YEAR-OLD FORM HERE?
YES, HIS FATHER WAS THE FAMOUS THOUSAND MASTER. BEING THE SON OF A HERO WAS A MAJOR SELLING POINT.
NEGIUS SPRINGFIELDES
HMMM? WHAT'S THIS...?
OH, COME ON.
NO, YOU'RE KID-DING...
HA HA HA HA HA! YOU MEAN TO TELL ME THEY MADE STATUES OF THEM, TOO?!
THOSE IDIOTS? HA HA! STATUES?!
HOO HA HA HA HA HA HA HA HA HA HA!

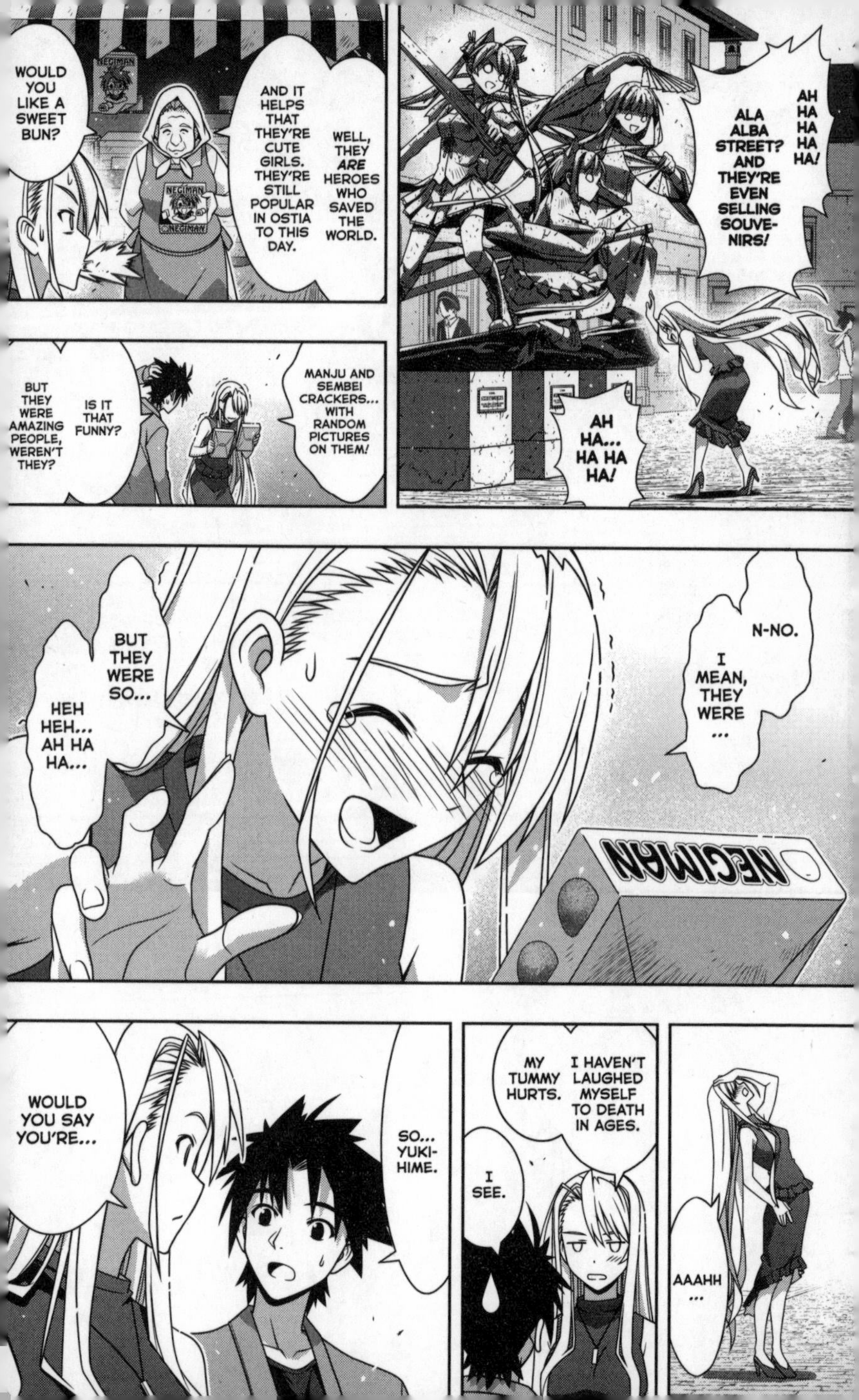
AH HA HA HA HA HA!
ALA ALBA STREET? AND THEY'RE EVEN SELLING SOUVE-NIRS!
AH HA... HA HA HA!
WELL, THEY *ARE* HEROES WHO SAVED THE WORLD.
AND IT HELPS THAT THEY'RE CUTE GIRLS. THEY'RE STILL POPULAR IN OSTIA TO THIS DAY.
NEGIMAN
NEGIMAN
NEGIMAN
WOULD YOU LIKE A SWEET BUN?
MANJU AND SEMBEI CRACKERS... WITH RANDOM PICTURES ON THEM!
IS IT THAT FUNNY?
BUT THEY WERE AMAZING PEOPLE, WEREN'T THEY?
N-NO.
I MEAN, THEY WERE ...
NEGIMAN
BUT THEY WERE SO...
HEH HEH... AH HA HA...
AAAHH ...
I HAVEN'T LAUGHED MYSELF TO DEATH IN AGES.
MY TUMMY HURTS.
I SEE.
SO... YUKI-HIME.
WOULD YOU SAY YOU'RE...

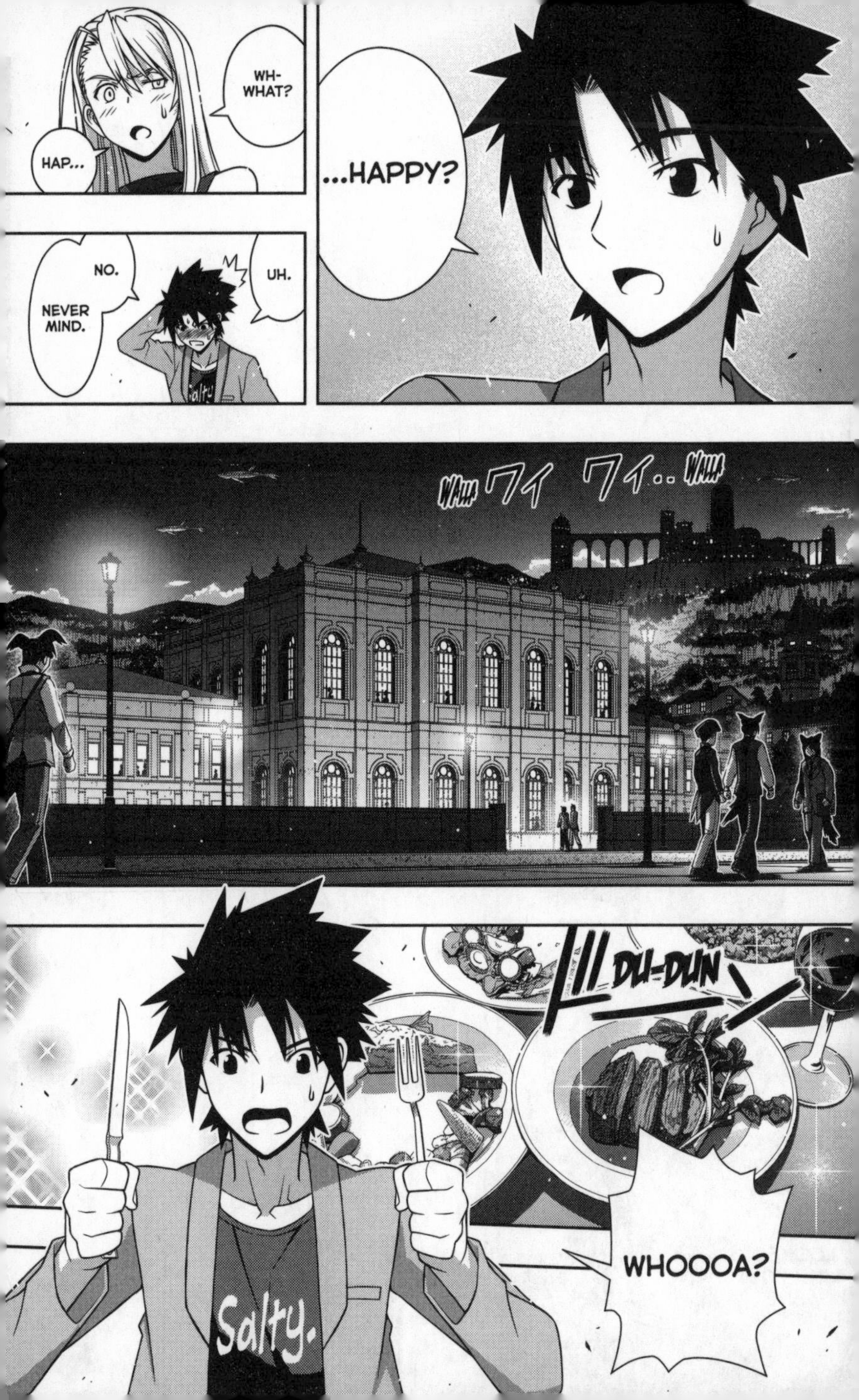
...HAPPY?
WH- WHAT?
HAP...
UH.
NO.
NEVER MIND.
ワイ ワイ..
DU-DUN
WHOOOA?
Salty.

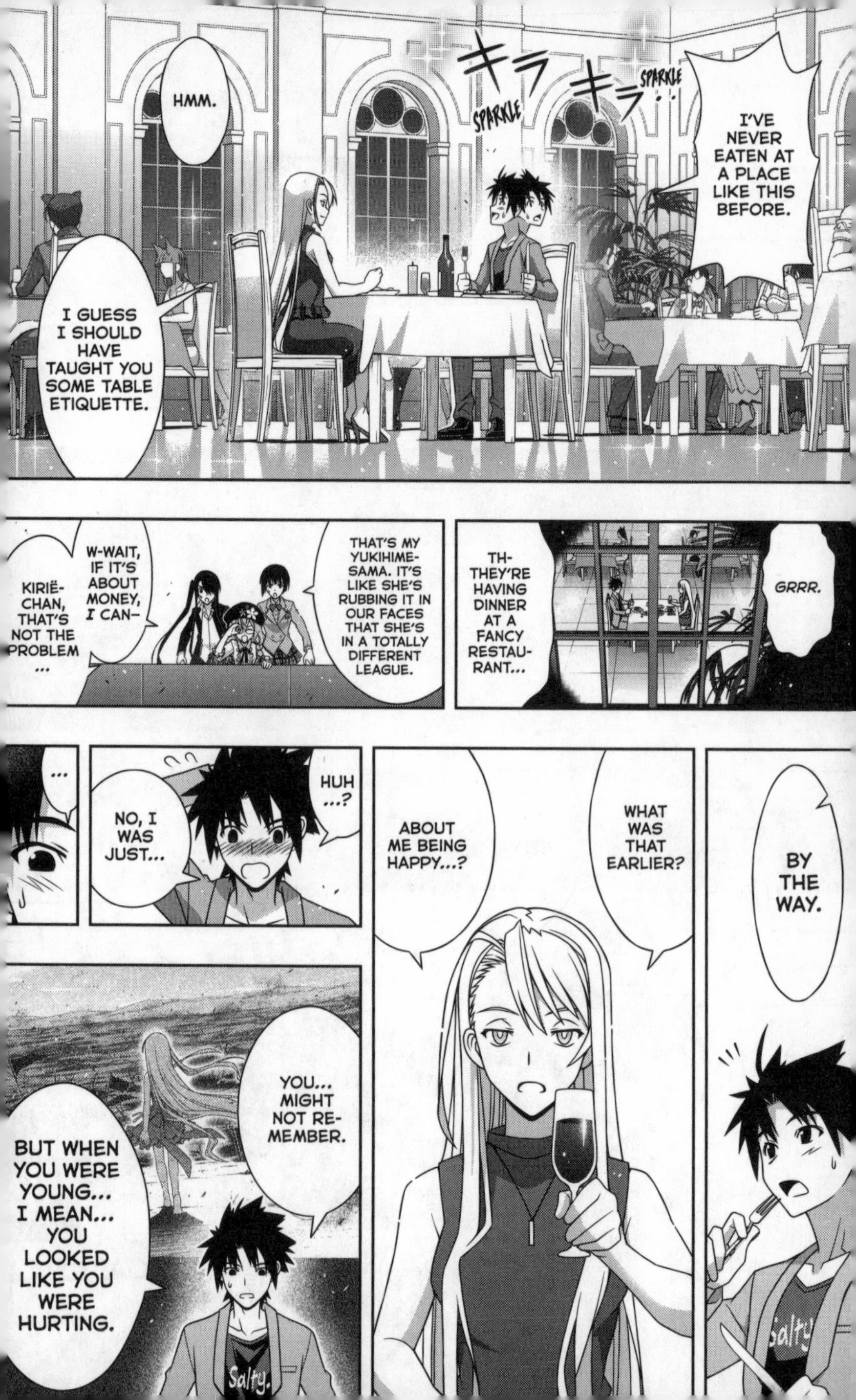
I'VE NEVER EATEN AT A PLACE LIKE THIS BEFORE.
キラ SPARKLE
キラ SPARKLE
HMM.
I GUESS I SHOULD HAVE TAUGHT YOU SOME TABLE ETIQUETTE.
GRRR.
TH-THEY'RE HAVING DINNER AT A FANCY RESTAURANT...
THAT'S MY YUKIHIME-SAMA. IT'S LIKE SHE'S RUBBING IT IN OUR FACES THAT SHE'S IN A TOTALLY DIFFERENT LEAGUE.
W-WAIT, IF IT'S ABOUT MONEY, I CAN–
KIRIË-CHAN, THAT'S NOT THE PROBLEM...
BY THE WAY.
WHAT WAS THAT EARLIER?
ABOUT ME BEING HAPPY...?
HUH...?
NO, I WAS JUST...
...
YOU... MIGHT NOT REMEMBER.
BUT WHEN YOU WERE YOUNG... I MEAN... YOU LOOKED LIKE YOU WERE HURTING.

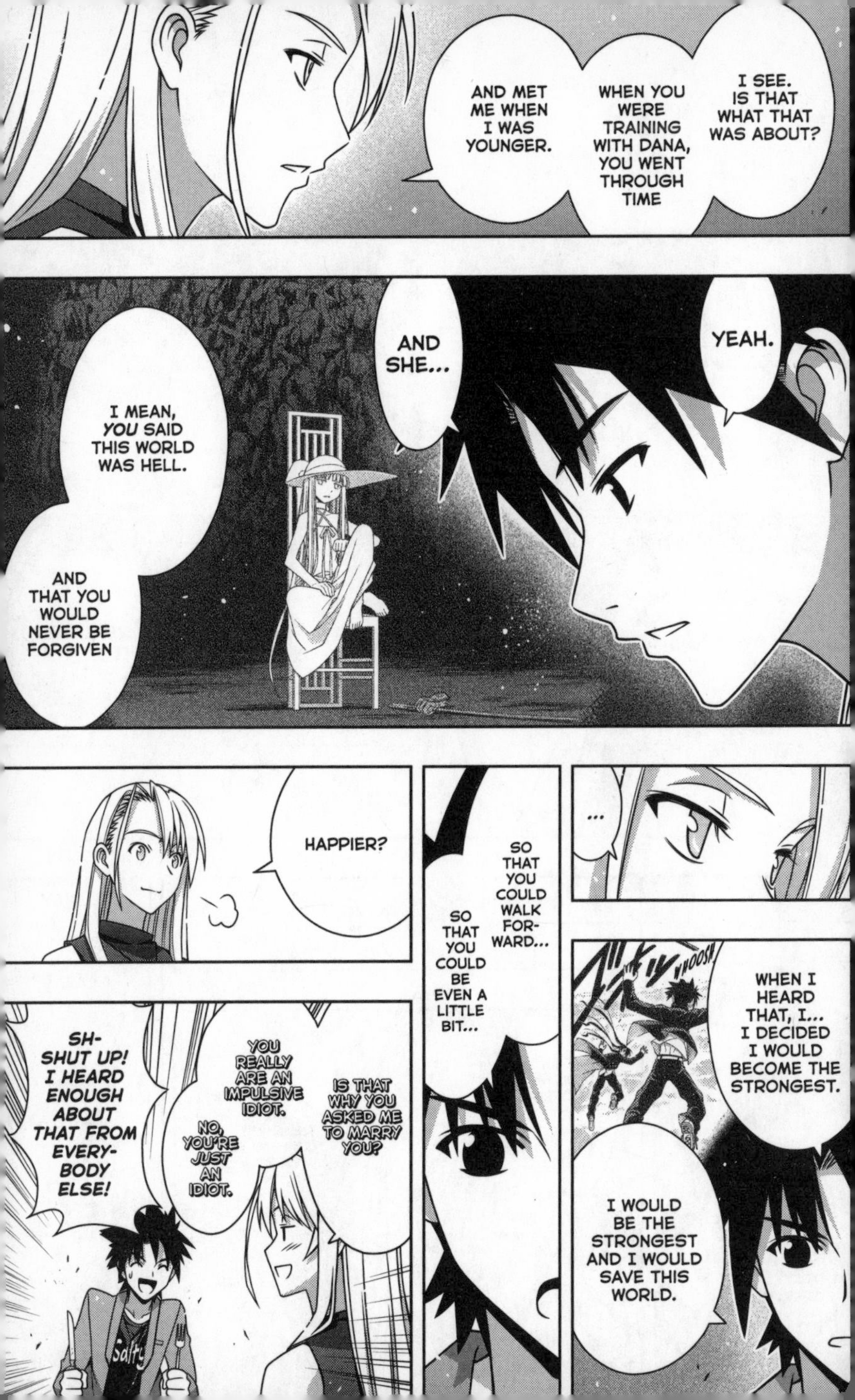

I SEE. IS THAT WHAT THAT WAS ABOUT?
WHEN YOU WERE TRAINING WITH DANA, YOU WENT THROUGH TIME
AND MET ME WHEN I WAS YOUNGER.
YEAH.
AND SHE...
I MEAN, *YOU* SAID THIS WORLD WAS HELL.
AND THAT YOU WOULD NEVER BE FORGIVEN
...
WHOOSH
WHEN I HEARD THAT, I... I DECIDED I WOULD BECOME THE STRONGEST.
I WOULD BE THE STRONGEST AND I WOULD SAVE THIS WORLD.
SO THAT YOU COULD WALK FORWARD...
SO THAT YOU COULD BE EVEN A LITTLE BIT...
HAPPIER?
IS THAT WHY YOU ASKED ME TO MARRY YOU?
YOU REALLY ARE AN IMPULSIVE IDIOT.
NO, YOU'RE JUST AN IDIOT.
SH-SHUT UP! I HEARD ENOUGH ABOUT THAT FROM EVERYBODY ELSE!

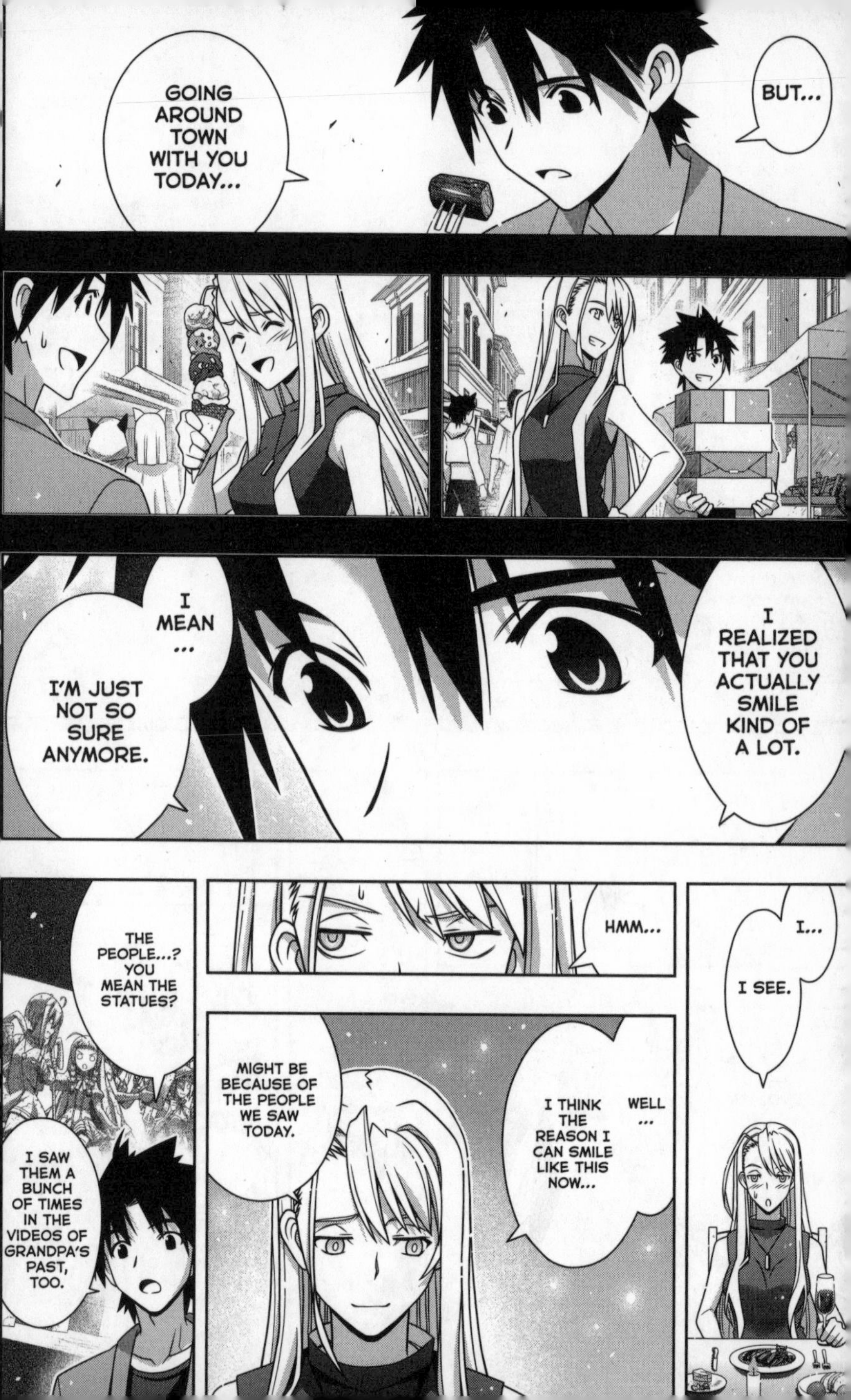
BUT...
GOING AROUND TOWN WITH YOU TODAY...
I REALIZED THAT YOU ACTUALLY SMILE KIND OF A LOT.
I MEAN...
I'M JUST NOT SO SURE ANYMORE.
I...
I SEE.
HMM...
WELL...
I THINK THE REASON I CAN SMILE LIKE THIS NOW...
MIGHT BE BECAUSE OF THE PEOPLE WE SAW TODAY.
THE PEOPLE...? YOU MEAN THE STATUES?
I SAW THEM A BUNCH OF TIMES IN THE VIDEOS OF GRANDPA'S PAST, TOO.

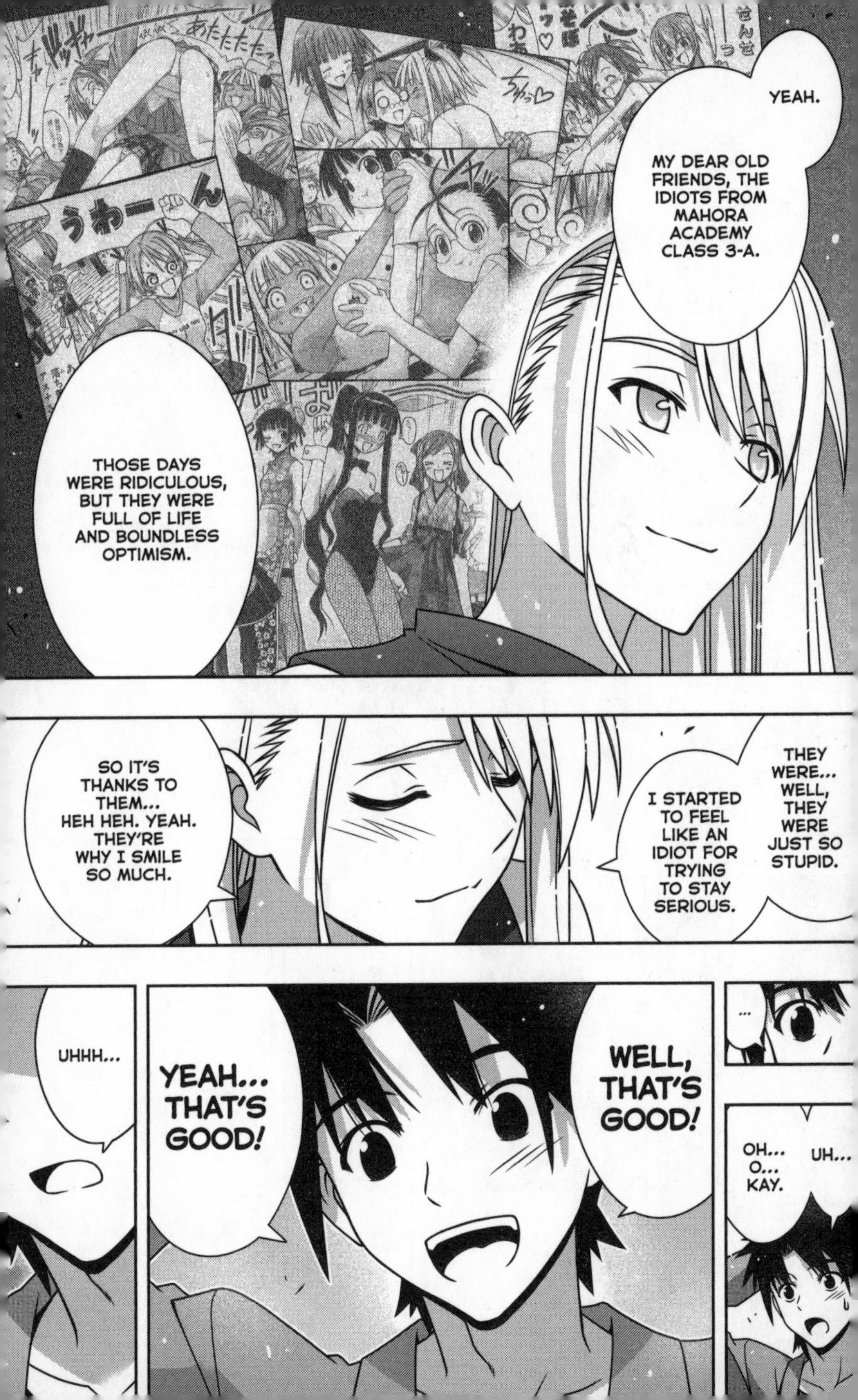
YEAH.
MY DEAR OLD FRIENDS, THE IDIOTS FROM MAHORA ACADEMY CLASS 3-A.
あたたたたっ
うわーーん
THOSE DAYS WERE RIDICULOUS, BUT THEY WERE FULL OF LIFE AND BOUNDLESS OPTIMISM.
THEY WERE... WELL, THEY WERE JUST SO STUPID.
I STARTED TO FEEL LIKE AN IDIOT FOR TRYING TO STAY SERIOUS.
SO IT'S THANKS TO THEM... HEH HEH. YEAH. THEY'RE WHY I SMILE SO MUCH.
...
UH...
OH... O... KAY.
WELL, THAT'S GOOD!
YEAH... THAT'S GOOD!
UHHH...

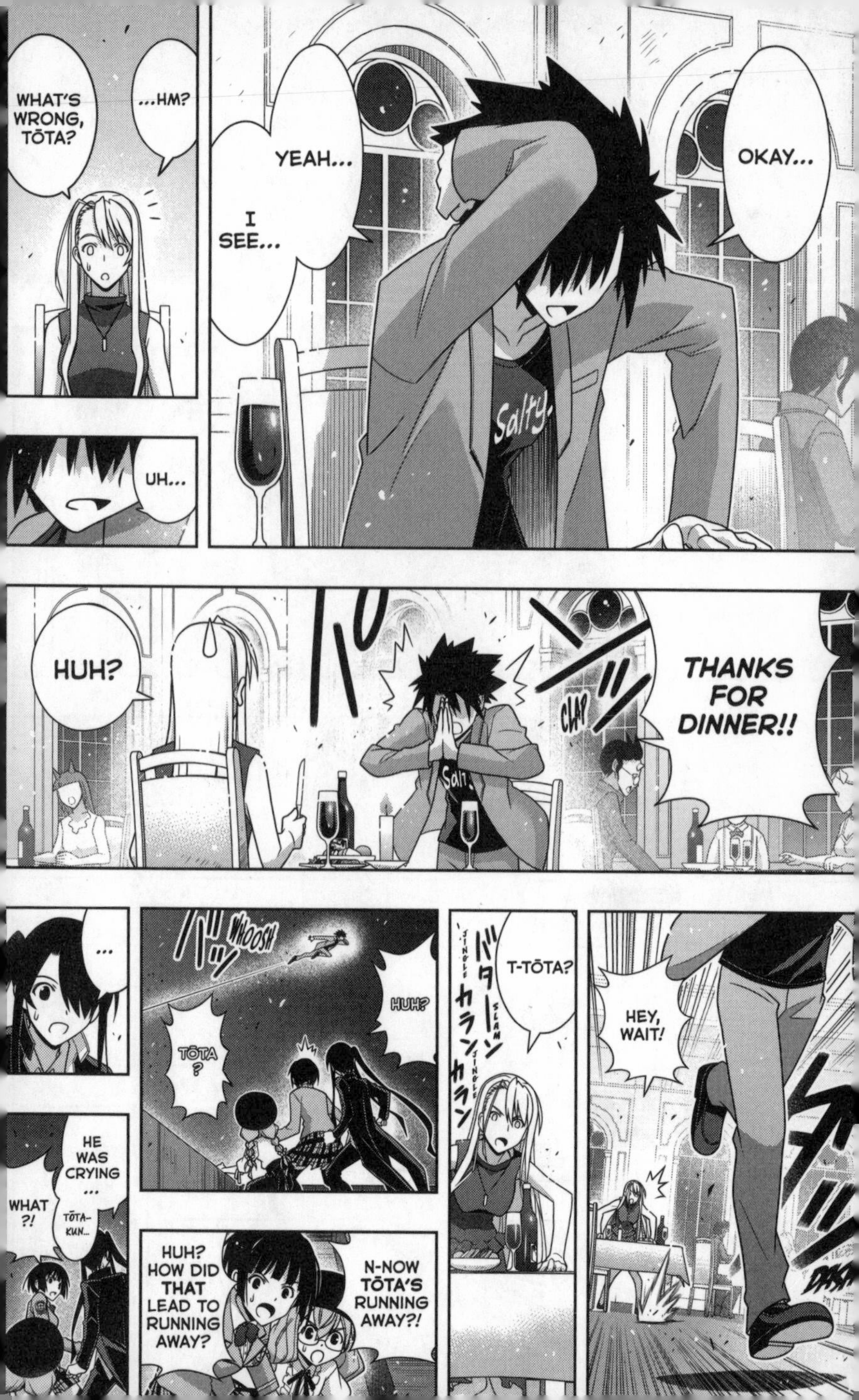
OKAY...
YEAH...
I SEE...
...HM?
WHAT'S WRONG, TŌTA?
UH...
THANKS FOR DINNER!!
CLAP
HUH?
HEY, WAIT!
DASH
T-TŌTA?
バタ―ン SLAM
カラン カラン JINGLE JINGLE
WHOOSH
HUH?
TŌTA?
N-NOW TŌTA'S RUNNING AWAY?!
HUH? HOW DID THAT LEAD TO RUNNING AWAY?
...
HE WAS CRYING...
TŌTA-KUN...
WHAT?!

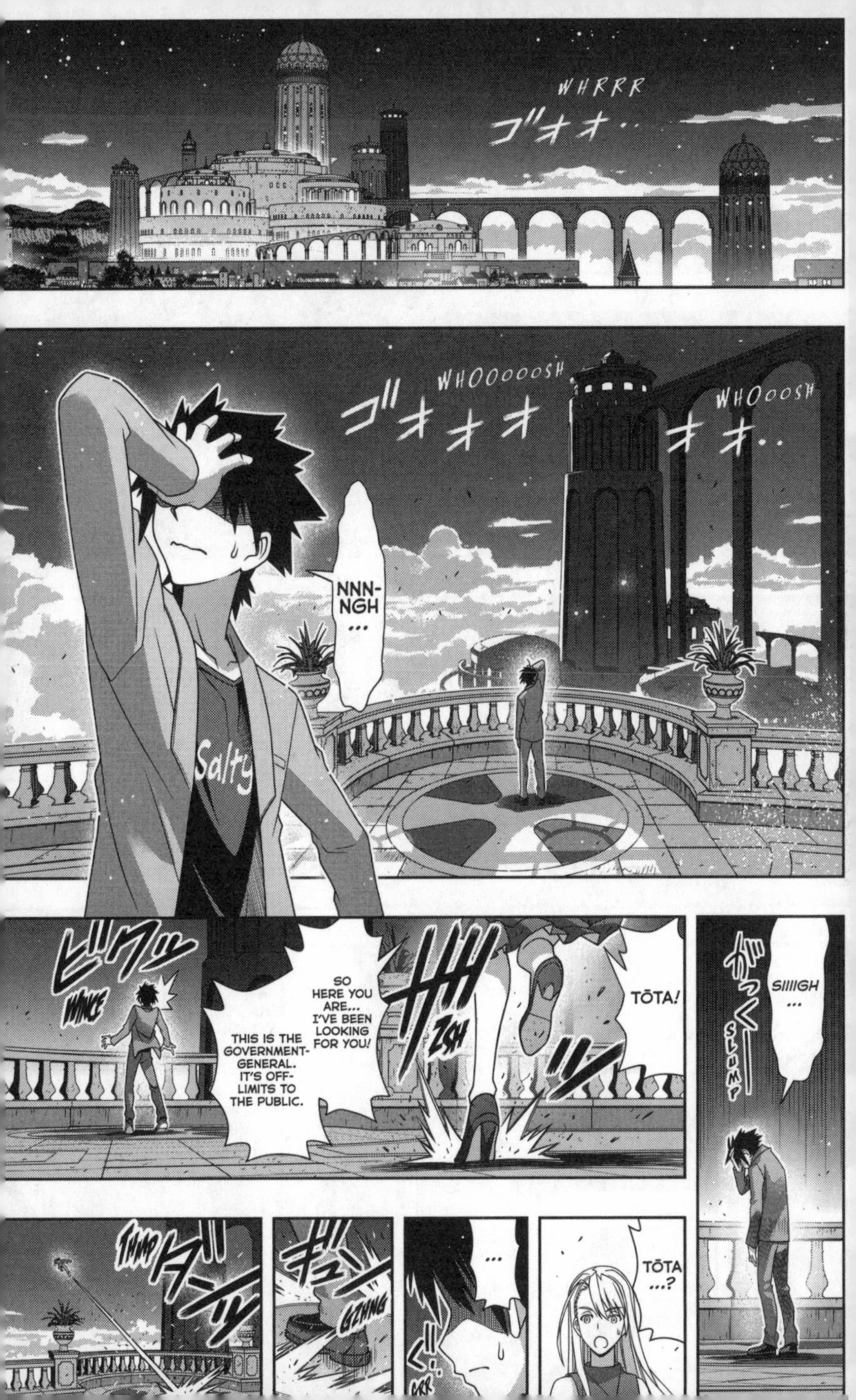
WHRRR
ゴオオ…
WHOOOOOSH
ゴオオオ
WHOOOSH
オオ…
NNN-NGH…
SIIIGH…
SLUMP
TŌTA!
ZSH
SO HERE YOU ARE… I'VE BEEN LOOKING FOR YOU!
THIS IS THE GOVERNMENT-GENERAL. IT'S OFF-LIMITS TO THE PUBLIC.
ビクッ
WINCE
TŌTA…?
…
GRR
GZHNG
THMP

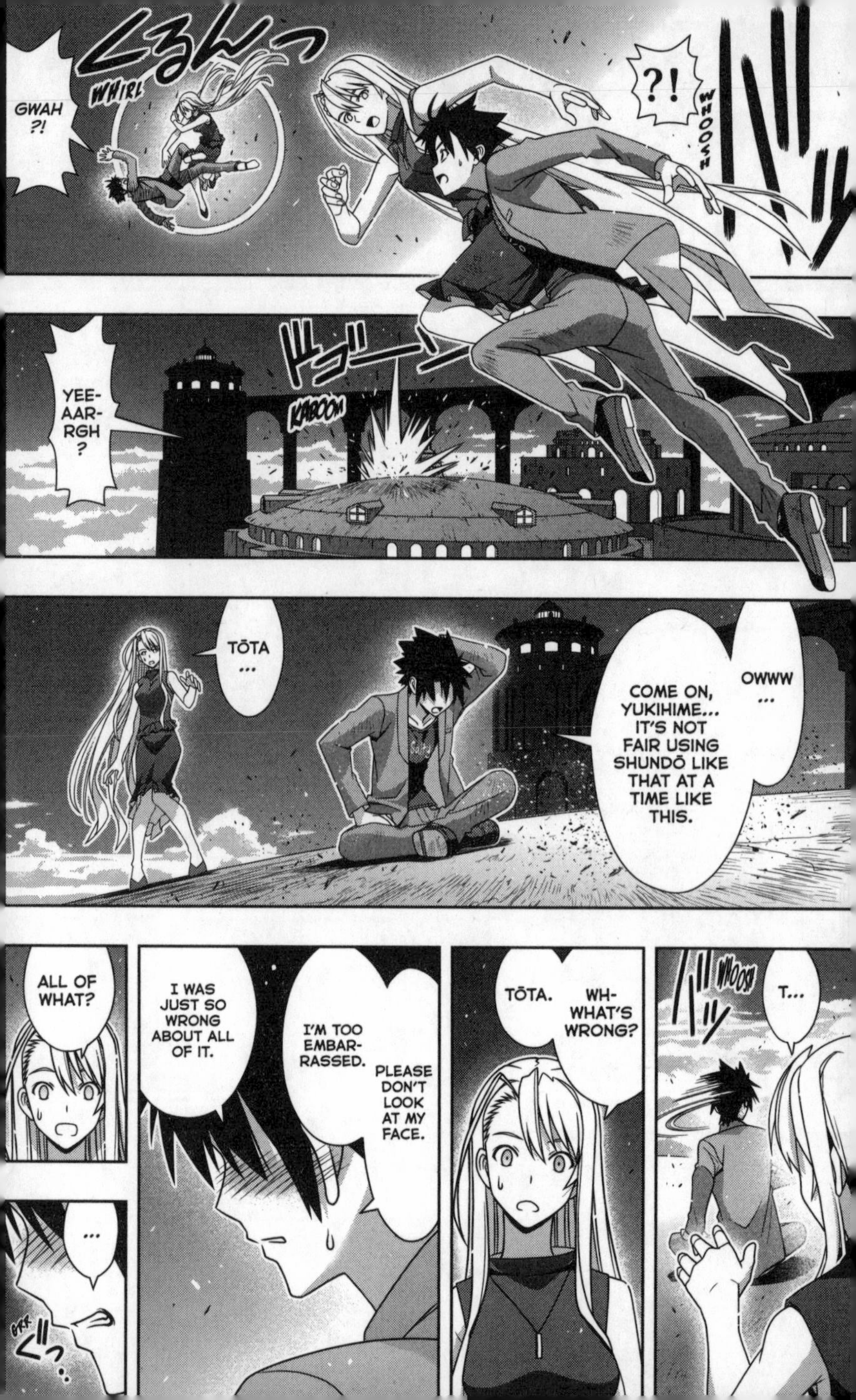
?!
WHOOSH
くるんっ
WHIRL
GWAH ?!
KABOOM
YEE-AARRGH ?
OWWW ...
COME ON, YUKIHIME... IT'S NOT FAIR USING SHUNDŌ LIKE THAT AT A TIME LIKE THIS.
TŌTA ...
T...
WHOOSH
WH-WHAT'S WRONG?
TŌTA.
I'M TOO EMBARRASSED.
PLEASE DON'T LOOK AT MY FACE.
I WAS JUST SO WRONG ABOUT ALL OF IT.
ALL OF WHAT?
...
GRR

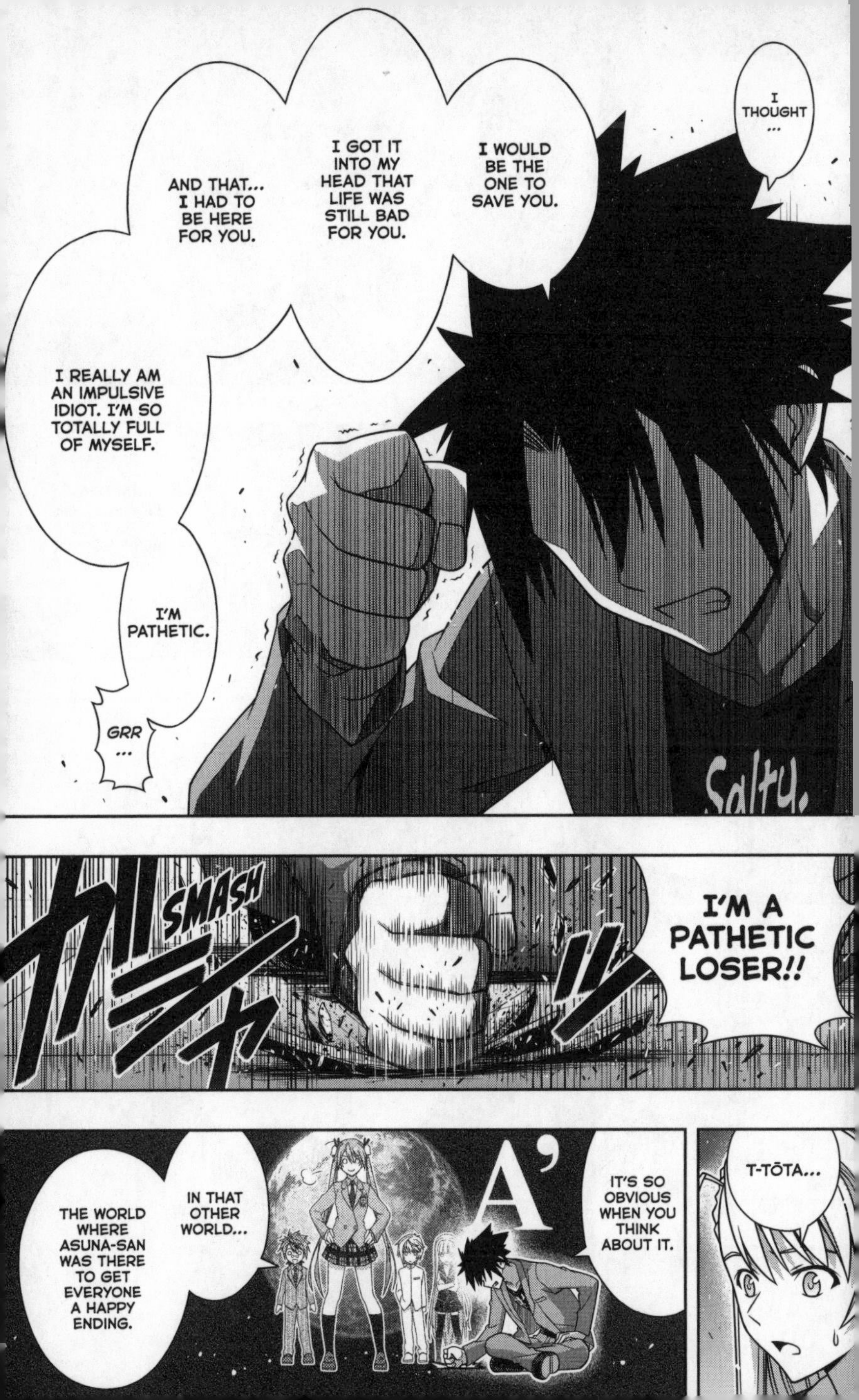
I THOUGHT...
I WOULD BE THE ONE TO SAVE YOU.
I GOT IT INTO MY HEAD THAT LIFE WAS STILL BAD FOR YOU.
AND THAT... I HAD TO BE HERE FOR YOU.
I REALLY AM AN IMPULSIVE IDIOT. I'M SO TOTALLY FULL OF MYSELF.
I'M PATHETIC.
GRR...
Saltu.
I'M A PATHETIC LOSER!!
SMASH
T-TŌTA...
IT'S SO OBVIOUS WHEN YOU THINK ABOUT IT.
A'
IN THAT OTHER WORLD...
THE WORLD WHERE ASUNA-SAN WAS THERE TO GET EVERYONE A HAPPY ENDING.

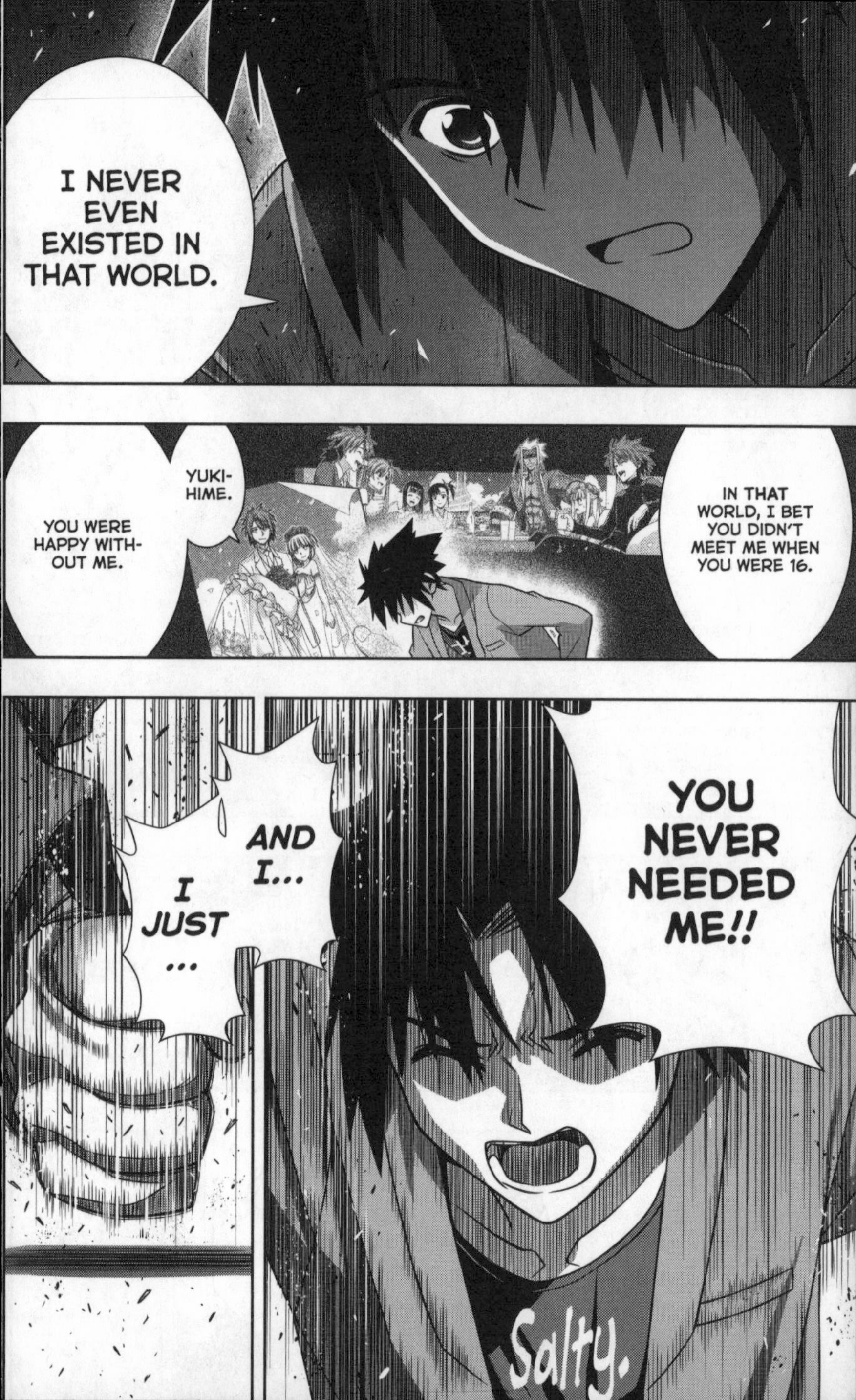
I NEVER EVEN EXISTED IN THAT WORLD.
IN THAT WORLD, I BET YOU DIDN'T MEET ME WHEN YOU WERE 16.
YUKI-HIME.
YOU WERE HAPPY WITH-OUT ME.
YOU NEVER NEEDED ME!!
AND I...
I JUST ...
Salty.

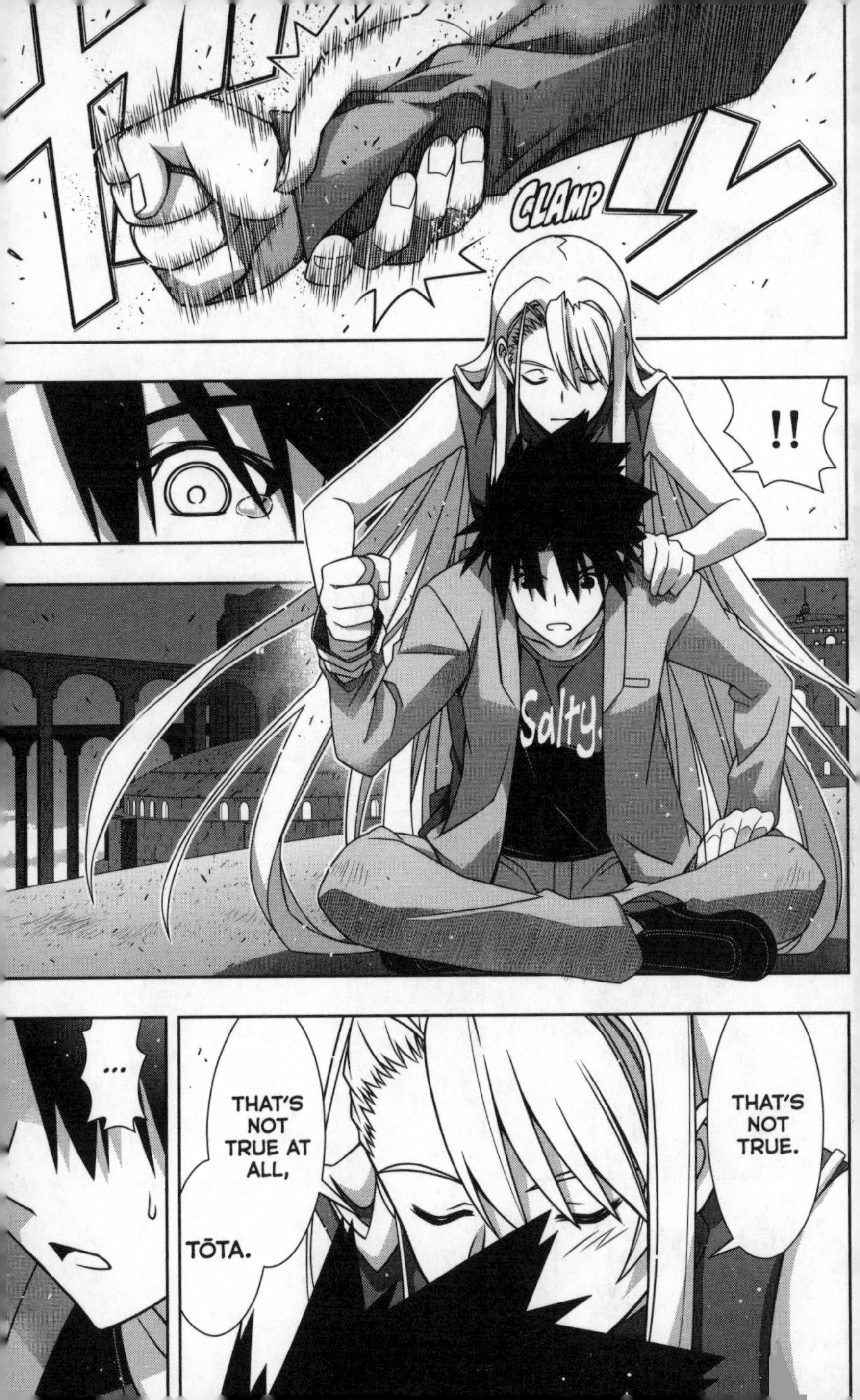
CLAMP
!!
THAT'S NOT TRUE.
THAT'S NOT TRUE AT ALL,
TŌTA.
...

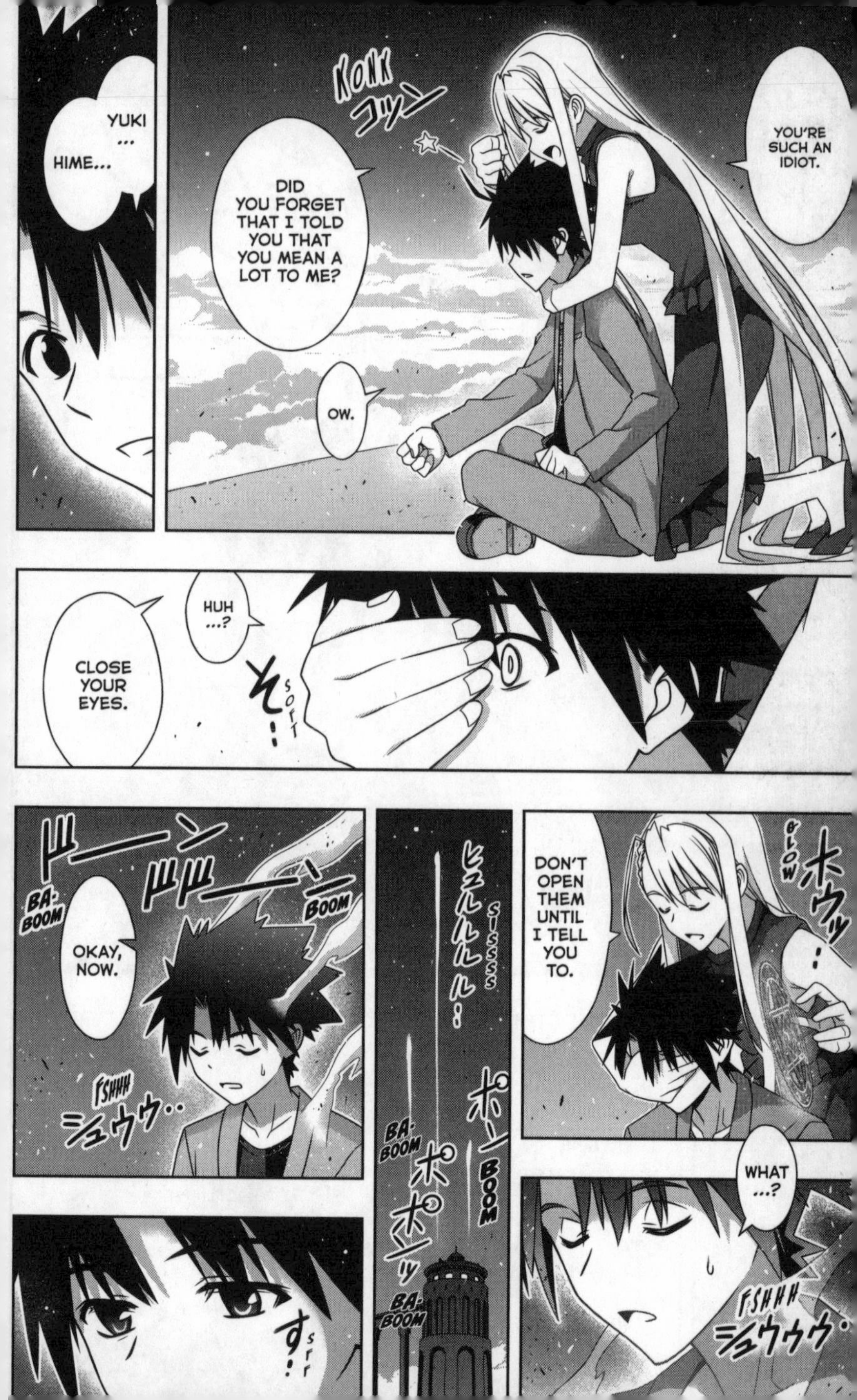
YOU'RE SUCH AN IDIOT.
KONK
コツン
DID YOU FORGET THAT I TOLD YOU THAT YOU MEAN A LOT TO ME?
OW.
YUKI ... HIME...
HUH ...?
CLOSE YOUR EYES.
SOFT
そ…
GLOW
ホウッ…
DON'T OPEN THEM UNTIL I TELL YOU TO.
WHAT ...?
FSHHH
シュウウウ
SISSSS
ヒュルルル…
BOOM
ポーン
BA-BOOM
ボボボンッ
BA-BOOM
BOOM
BA-BOOM
OKAY, NOW.
FSHHH
シュウウ…
SRR
す…

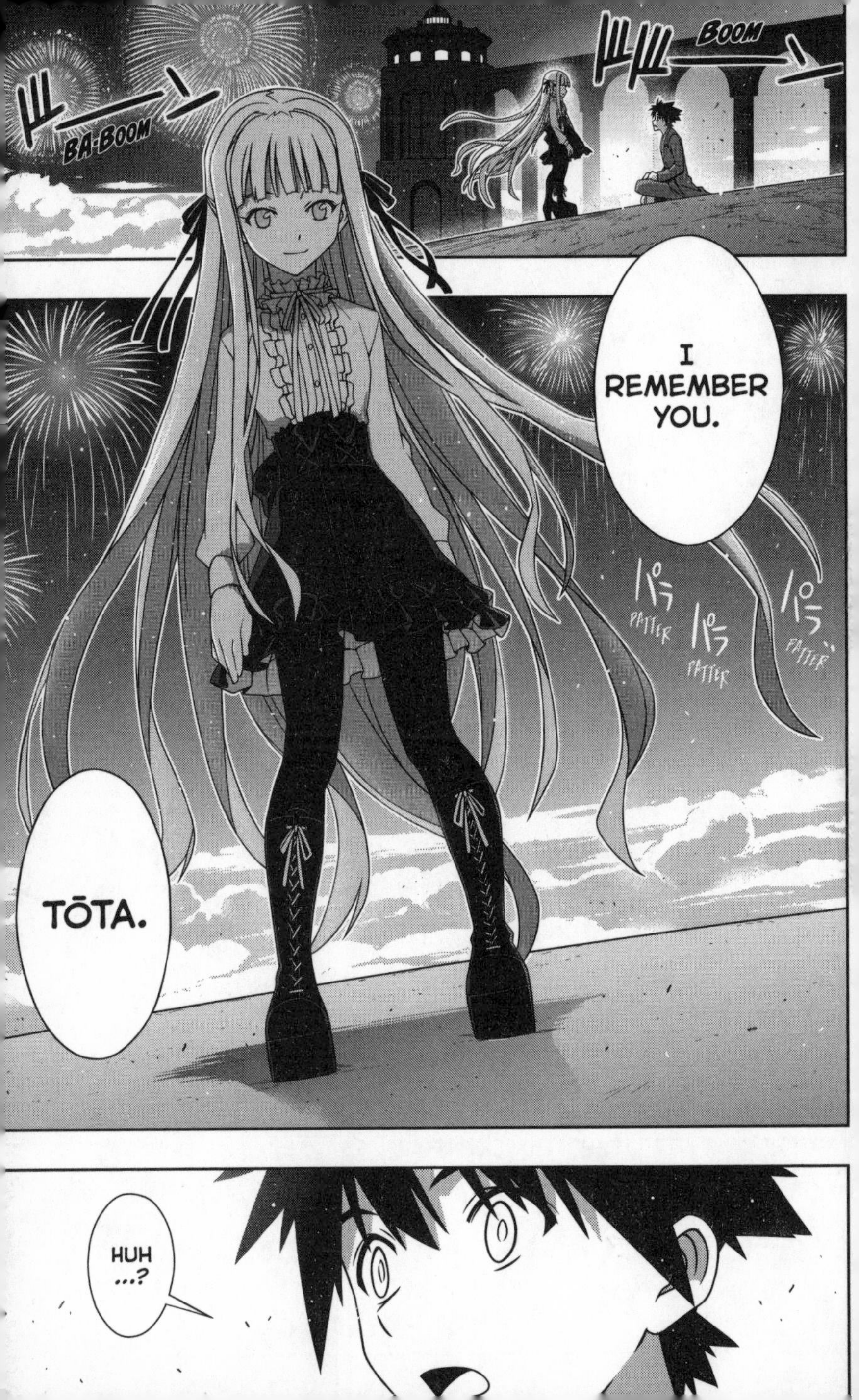
BOOM
BA-BOOM
I REMEMBER YOU.
パラ
PATTER
パラ
PATTER
パラ
PATTER
TŌTA.
HUH ...?

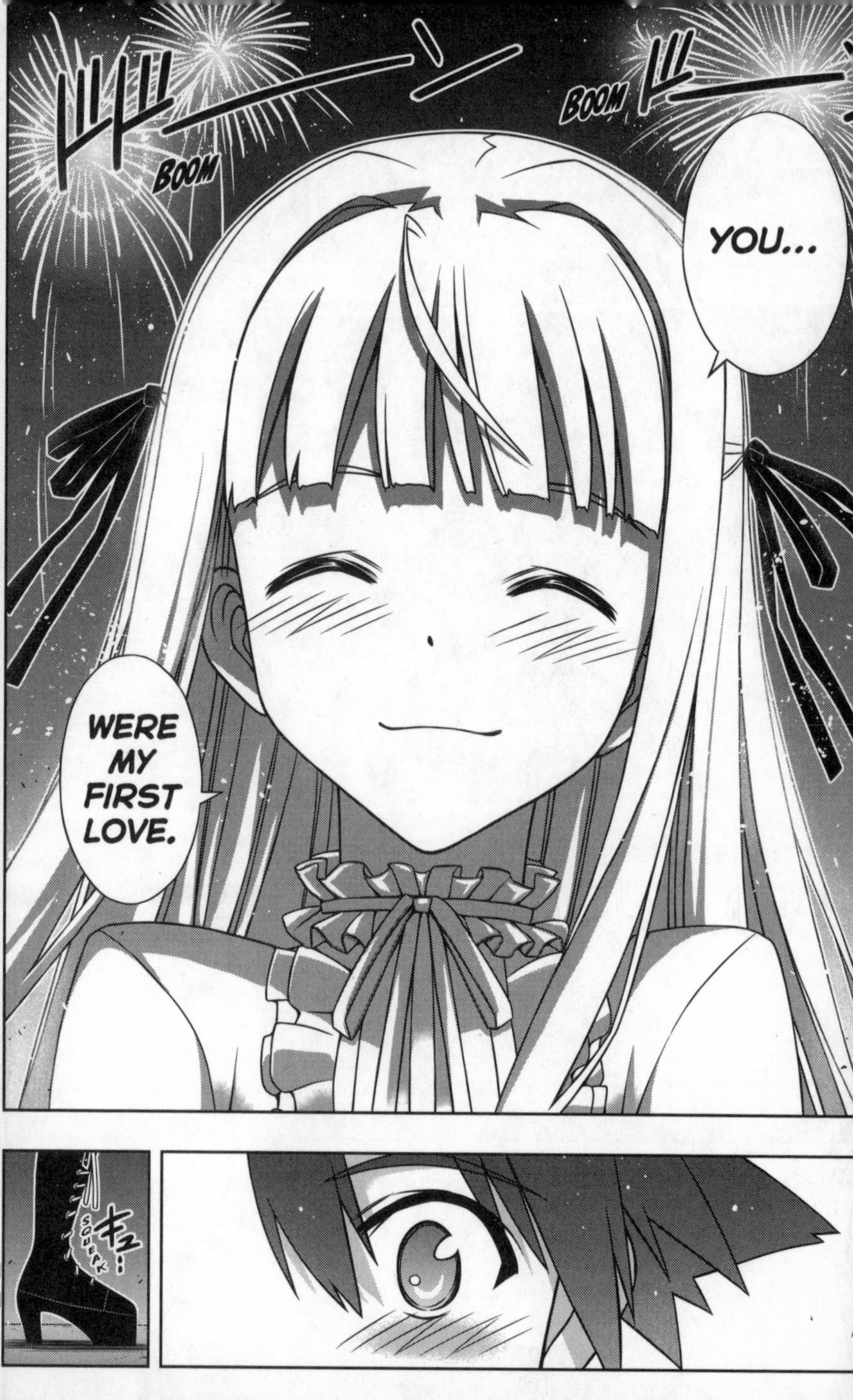
BOOM
BOOM
YOU...
WERE MY FIRST LOVE.
SQUEAK

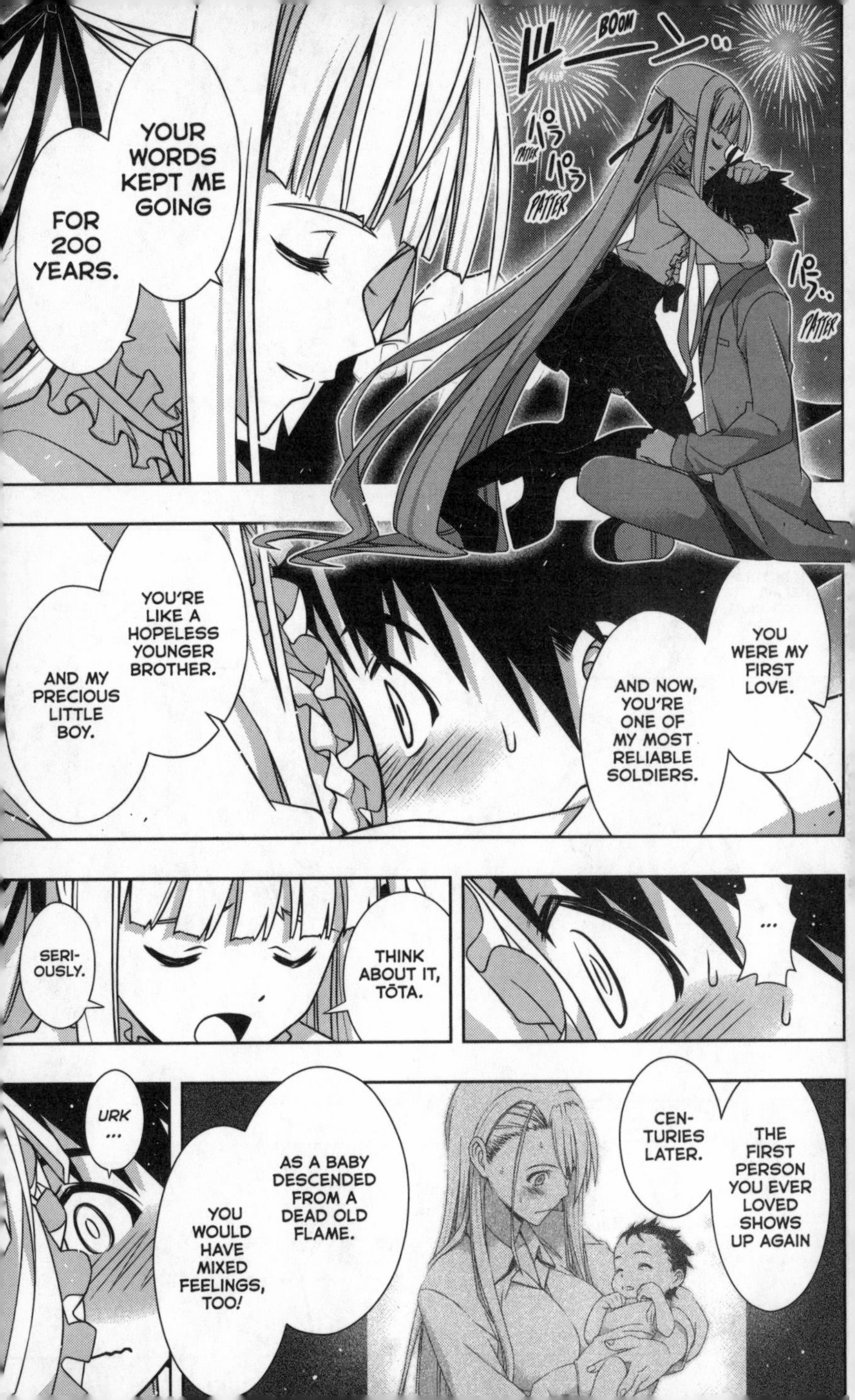
BOOM
PATTER
PATTER
PATTER
YOUR WORDS KEPT ME GOING
FOR 200 YEARS.
YOU WERE MY FIRST LOVE.
AND NOW, YOU'RE ONE OF MY MOST RELIABLE SOLDIERS.
YOU'RE LIKE A HOPELESS YOUNGER BROTHER.
AND MY PRECIOUS LITTLE BOY.
...
THINK ABOUT IT, TŌTA.
SERI-OUSLY.
THE FIRST PERSON YOU EVER LOVED SHOWS UP AGAIN
CEN-TURIES LATER.
AS A BABY DESCENDED FROM A DEAD OLD FLAME.
YOU WOULD HAVE MIXED FEELINGS, TOO!
URK ...

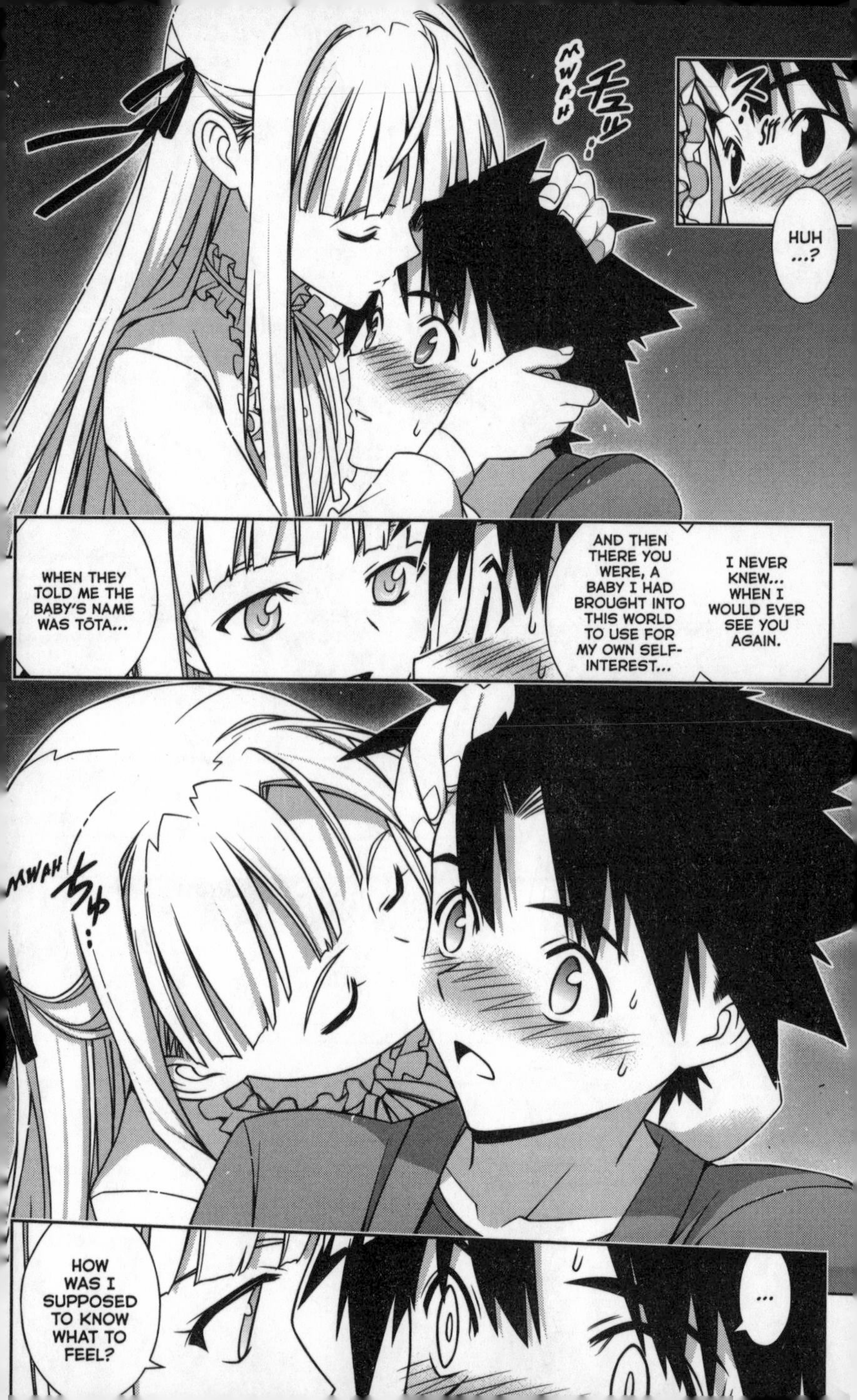
SFFF
HUH ...?
MWAH
I NEVER KNEW... WHEN I WOULD EVER SEE YOU AGAIN.
AND THEN THERE YOU WERE, A BABY I HAD BROUGHT INTO THIS WORLD TO USE FOR MY OWN SELF-INTEREST...
WHEN THEY TOLD ME THE BABY'S NAME WAS TŌTA...
MWAH
...
HOW WAS I SUPPOSED TO KNOW WHAT TO FEEL?

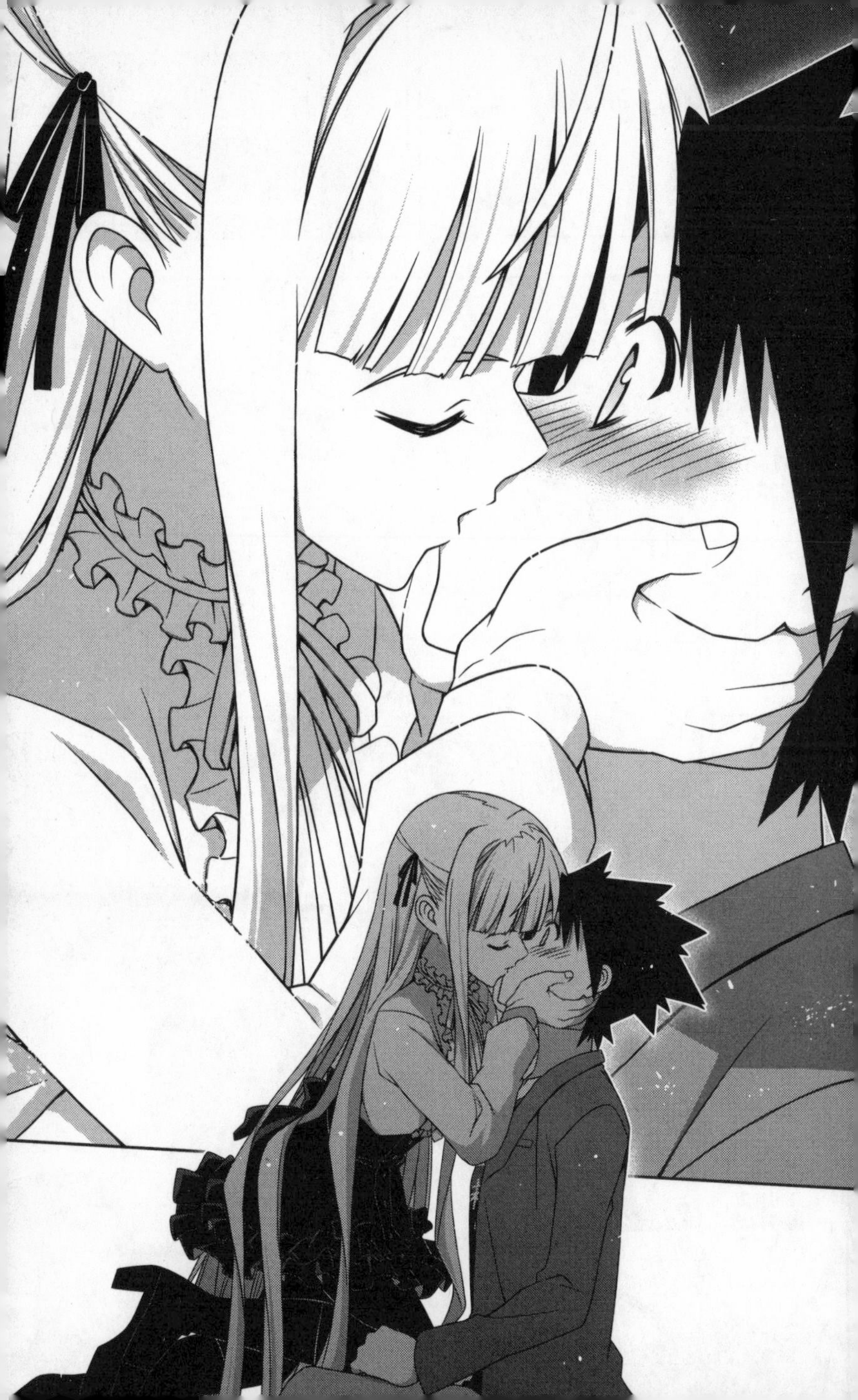

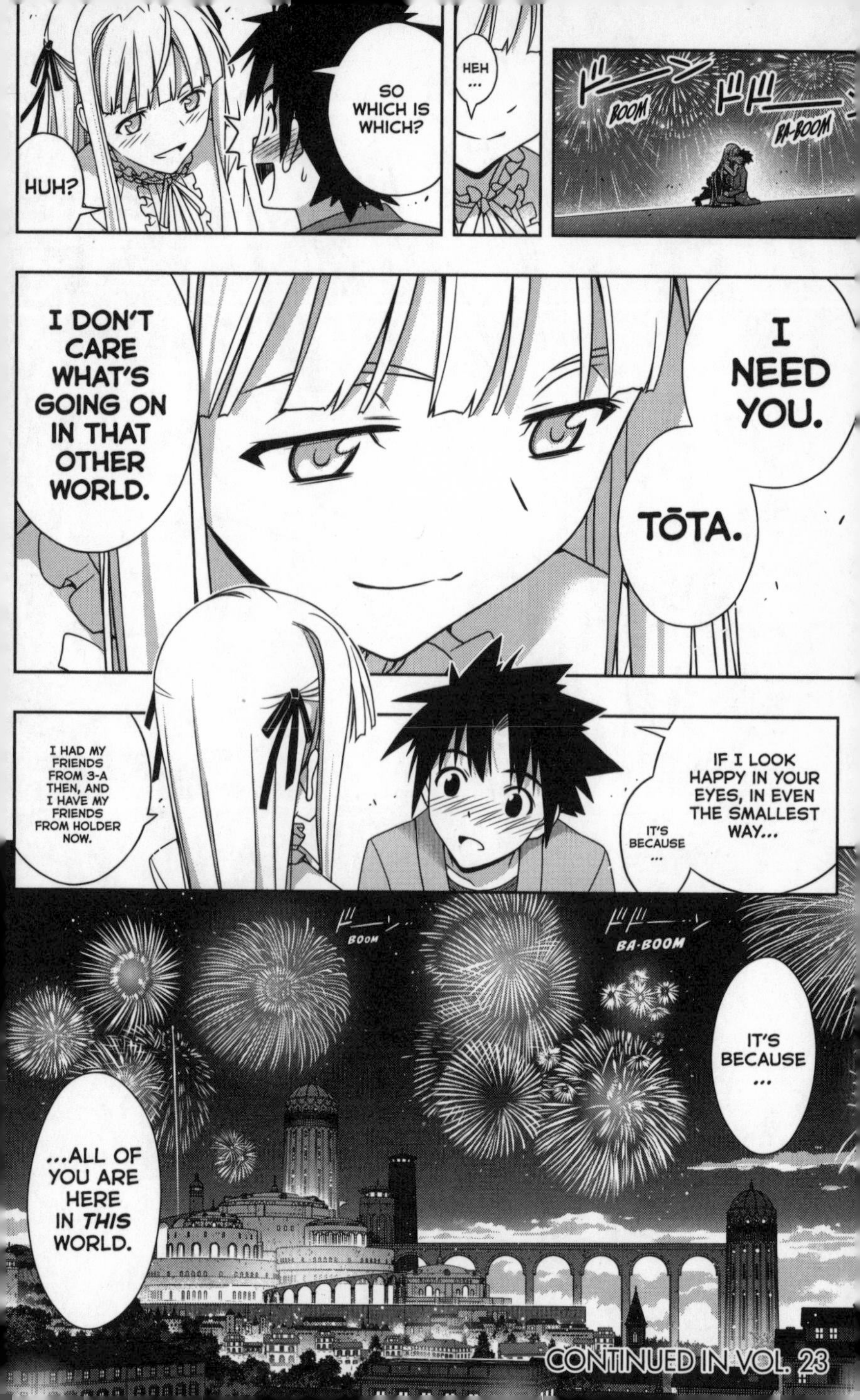
BOOM
BA-BOOM
HEH ...
SO WHICH IS WHICH?
HUH?
I NEED YOU.
TŌTA.
I DON'T CARE WHAT'S GOING ON IN THAT OTHER WORLD.
IF I LOOK HAPPY IN YOUR EYES, IN EVEN THE SMALLEST WAY...
IT'S BECAUSE ...
I HAD MY FRIENDS FROM 3-A THEN, AND I HAVE MY FRIENDS FROM HOLDER NOW.
BA-BOOM
BOOM
IT'S BECAUSE ...
...ALL OF YOU ARE HERE IN *THIS* WORLD.
CONTINUED IN VOL. 23

UQ HOLDER!

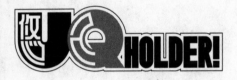

UQ HOLDER!

STAFF

Ken Akamatsu

Takashi Takemoto

Kenichi Nakamura

Keiichi Yamashita

Yuri Sasaki

Madoka Akanuma

Thanks to Ran Ayanaga

Young characters and steampunk setting, like *Howl's Moving Castle* and *Battle Angel Alita*

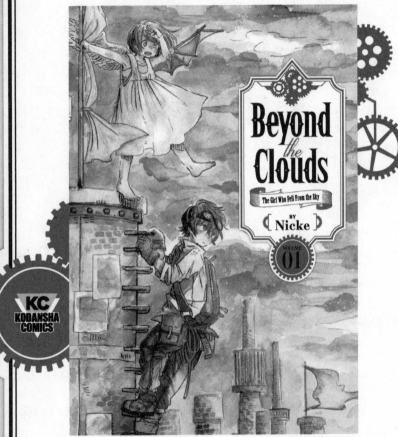

Beyond the Clouds © 2018 Nicke / Ki-oon

A boy with a talent for machines and a mysterious girl whose wings he's fixed will take you beyond the clouds! In the tradition of the high-flying, resonant adventure stories of Studio Ghibli comes a gorgeous tale about the longing of young hearts for adventure and friendship!

The boys are back, in 400-page hardcovers that are as pretty and badass as they are!

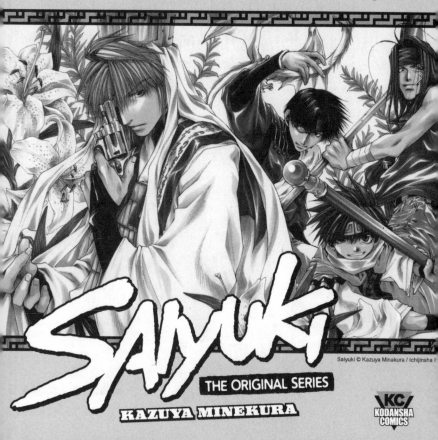

Saiyuki © Kazuya Minakura / Ichijinsha I

SAIYUKI

THE ORIGINAL SERIES

KAZUYA MINEKURA

"AN EDGY COMIC LOOK AT AN ANCIENT CHINESE TALE." —YALSA

Genjo Sanzo is a Buddhist priest in the city of Togenkyo, which is being ravaged by yokai spirits that have fallen out of balance with the natural order. His superiors send him on a journey far to the west to discover why this is happening and how to stop it. His companions are three yokai with human souls. But this is no day trip — the four will encounter many discoveries and horrors on the way.

FEATURES NEW TRANSLATION, COLOR PAGES, AND BEAUTIFUL WRAPAROUND COVER ART!

A SMART, NEW ROMANTIC COMEDY FOR FANS OF *SHORTCAKE CAKE* AND *TERRACE HOUSE*!

A romance manga starring high school girl Meeko, who learns to live on her own in a boarding house whose living room is home to the odd (but handsome) Matsunaga-san. She begins to adjust to her new life away from her parents, but Meeko soon learns that no matter how far away from home she is, she's still a young girl at heart — especially when she finds herself falling for Matsunaga-san.

The adorable new odd-couple cat comedy manga from the creator of the beloved *Chi's Sweet Home*, in full color!

Sue & Tai-chan

Konami Kanata

Sue is an aging housecat who's looking forward to living out her life in peace... but her plans change when the mischievous black tomcat Tai-chan enters the picture! Hey! Sue never signed up to be a catsitter! *Sue & Tai-chan* is the latest from the reigning meow-narch of cute kitty comics, Konami Kanata.

CUTE ANIMALS AND LIFE LESSONS, PERFECT FOR ASPIRING PET VETS OF ALL AGES!

YUZU THE PET VET

KODANSHA COMICS

1

BY **MINGO ITO**

In collaboration with
NIPPON COLUMBIA CO., LTD.

Yuzu the Pet Vet © Mingo Ito / NIPPON COLUMBIA CO., LTD. / Kodansha Ltd.

For an 11-year-old, Yuzu has a lot on her plate. When her mom gets sick and has to be hospitalized, Yuzu goes to live with her uncle who runs the local veterinary clinic. Yuzu's always been scared of animals, but she tries to help out. Through all the tough moments in her life, Yuzu realizes that she can help make things all right with a little help from her animal pals, peers, and kind grown-ups.

Every new patient is a furry friend in the making!

A Kodansha Comics Trade Paperback Original
UQ HOLDER! 22 copyright © 2020 Ken Akamatsu
English translation copyright © 2021 Ken Akamatsu

Published in the United States by Kodansha Comics, an imprint of Kodansha USA Publishing, LLC, New York.

Publication rights for this English edition arranged through Kodansha Ltd., Tokyo.

First published in Japan in 2020 by Kodansha Ltd., Tokyo.

ISBN 978-1-64651-170-9

Printed in the United States of America.

www.kodanshacomics.us

9 8 7 6 5 4 3 2 1
Translation: Alethea Nibley & Athena Nibley
Lettering: James Dashiell
Editing: David Yoo
Kodansha Comics edition cover design by Phil Balsman

Publisher: Kiichiro Sugawara

Director of publishing services: Ben Applegate
Associate director of operations: Stephen Pakula
Publishing services associate managing editor: Madison Salters
Production managers: Emi Lotto, Angela Zurlo